Strategy Representation

An Analysis of Planning Knowledge

Strategy Representation

An Analysis of Planning Knowledge

Andrew S. Gordon
University of Southern California

Psychology Press
Taylor & Francis Group

New York   London

Editor:	Bill Webber
Editorial Assistant:	Kristin Duch
Cover Design:	David Milam
Cover Layout:	Kathryn Houghtaling Lacey
Textbook Production Manager:	Paul Smolenski
Composition:	LEA Book Production

This book was typeset in 10/12pt. Novarese
The heads were typeset in 10.5/13pt. Benguiat Gothic.

First published by **Lawrence Erlbaum Associates, Inc., Publishers**

365 Broadway
Hillsdale, New Jersey 07642

This edition published 2013 by Psychology Press

Psychology Press	Psychology Press
Taylor & Francis Group	Taylor and Francis Group
711 Third Avenue,	27 Church Road
New York, NY 10017	Hove
	East Sussex BN3 2FA

Psychology Press is an imprint of Taylor and Francis, an informa group company

Library of Congress Cataloging-in-Publication Data

Gordon, Andrew S.
     Strategy representation : an analysis of planning knowledge /
     Andrew S. Gordon.
          p.   cm.
     Includes bibliographical references and index.
     ISBN 0-8058-4527-5 (alk. paper)
     ISBN 978-0-415-65202-5 (Paperback)
     1. Mental representation. 2. Planning. 3. Reasoning (Psychology).
     I. Title.
     BF316.6.G67   2003
     153.2—dc22   2003047222
                                                         CIP

Contents

Acknowledgments

This book evolved out of work that I began as a postdoctoral researcher at the IBM TJ Watson Research Center in Hawthorne, New York, and finished as a research scientist at the University of Southern California's Institute for Creative Technologies. I am indebted to John C. Thomas at IBM for his encouragement and support of this project. I would also like to thank the many people who took an interest in this work and offered critical comments, especially Leora Morgenstern, Ernie Davis, Jerry Hobbs, Yusuf Pisan, and Bill Webber. Thanks to Gregg Collins, Larry Birnbaum, Dedre Gentner, and Ken Forbus for giving me some good ideas to work with. Thanks to my parents, Albert and Joanne, my brother Adam, and the rest of my family and friends for keeping the rest of my life relatively strategy-free.

1

Strategies and Cognition

1.1 COGNITIVE MODELING

The field of Cognitive Modeling can probably best be defined by the interest and disposition of the scientists who work in this area. The interest is the mind—the 3-pound universe that emerges as the full richness of human life from a tangled mess of neurons. The disposition, which separates the cognitive modeler from experimental psychologists, neuroscientists, and philosophers, is the belief that the best way to understand something is to try to build it. The goal of Cognitive Modeling is to understand the human mind to such a degree of precision that one could design a computer program that did the same thing. As a result, cognitive modelers tend to be computer scientists as well, and are generally well accepted into a larger computer science field of Artificial Intelligence, whose members share many of the same methods, if not the same values. However, if the computer had never been invented, we might imagine that the cognitive modelers of the world would continue on in some other constructive medium, perhaps designing intricate clockworks using springs and gears rather than algorithms and data structures. But as it stands, the match between Cognitive Modeling and the computer is a convenient one, where mental processes can be specified as algorithms and the knowledge upon which they operate can be encoded in data structures.

In an almost comic manner, cognitive modelers are fascinated with the mundane. It turns out that nearly any behavior in the realm of cognition has a complicated explanation. To model the reasoning of a person deciding what to pack in a suitcase for a weekend trip would require a major research effort. To model the inferences made by a person reading the morning newspaper would require overcoming many outstanding research problems. To build a computer program that would laugh at a funny joke and snarl at a rude one would be monumental, and to build one that could generate a novel joke in response is almost unimaginable. While popular science fiction sometimes exploits our fear of intelligent computer systems that take over the world and dispense with the pesky human race, most cognitive modelers would be impressed with a computer that was as bright as any average toddler. In short, the everyday cognitive life of a person is extraordinarily complex, as will be any satisfying explanations of mental life that we will ever find.

The rest of the scientific world does not generally appreciate a complex explanation. As a result, we're unlikely to see Cognitive Modeling discoveries appearing in the science sections of newspapers or announced at impromptu press conferences. Indeed, it is difficult at first to see why certain Cognitive Modeling discoveries are important at all, and often they seem inanely obvious. If a cognitive modeler were to announce the discovery that people have expectations about what is going to happen next, the response would be anything but excitement, especially from the agency that funded the research. However, it is important to understand that sometimes a discovery like this is very valuable, perhaps if stated in a different manner. If instead the cognitive modeler reports that they have attempted to model a suite of intelligent behaviors, and found it impossible to do so without incorporating a specific knowledge structure to contain the expectations of what is going to happen next, then they have made a potentially significant contribution. Within their own research community, they have provided a suggestion for a knowledge structure that may be useful in modeling other complex intelligent behavior. Extending further into experimental psychological research, they have generated a new hypothesis that can be tested. Validation of such a hypothesis then can be a driver for neuroscience research, which has the unenviable task of explaining how such a construct could exist on the real neural network of the brain. Although there are clearly other reasons why Cognitive Modeling is important, the methodical manner in which it generates testable hypotheses is more advanced than in any other of the cognitive sciences.

One could easily imagine that the hypothesis generation engine of Cognitive Modeling would produce a steady, unending stream of potential mental processes and knowledge structures necessary to model unrelated cognitive phenomenon. Perhaps the greatest discovery of the field of Cognitive Modeling is that this steady, unending stream of possibilities hasn't materialized. Instead, researchers have found an increasing amount of convergence in the mental processes and knowledge structures that they postulate. That is, many researchers have identified certain key ideas in the course of particular modeling projects that are persistent—continually popping up in the models of later researchers who find them perfectly appropriate for seemingly unrelated topics. For example, researchers working in the area of story understanding find that they need a knowledge structure for the expectations that people have about everyday activities, a knowledge structure that is then picked up by different researchers who are working on building models that recognize and generate humorous jokes. In research histories that have been somewhat contiguous, cognitive modelers sometimes find that incredibly complex behaviors can be modeled solely through the composition of mental processes and knowledge structures that have appeared in earlier work. To outsiders it appears that the community has adopted a framework full of idiosyncratic terminology and philosophical biases, while it may be that they have merely collected a particular assortment of ideas that have broad applicability and explanatory power.

More so than the particular models that are developed, it is this collected assortment of ideas that we should be most concerned about. Adopting some of these ideas in new modeling projects saves time at the very least, and at best continues their evolution through success and failure in application. This evolution process is currently a rather tenuous one, however, as practitioners in the field of Cognitive Modeling have rather informal ways of communicating and debating these ideas. Inasmuch as these ideas exist, they are precariously situated in the tacit practices of fragile research communities, often passed from a more advanced graduate student to a beginning one or discussed during coffee breaks among researchers working on wildly different projects. The best of these ideas generally find their ways into publications, making it conceivable that new researchers could continue this work even if they were removed from the communities that originally investigated these ideas. In practice, however, Cognitive Modeling work is inherently cross-disciplinary and applied, resulting in a corpus of research publications where the number of relevant articles is roughly equal to the number of journals, conference proceedings, and books in which they appear. If a budding cognitive modeler were successful in enculturating himself or herself in the tacit practices of these research communities solely by reading past published reports, then they would deserve a doctorate in scientific anthropology on top of any cognitive science work that they accomplished.

Barring major changes in the way that Cognitive Modeling researchers go about communicating their work, few modeling projects will have the necessary scope to be encyclopedic of the assortment of modeling ideas that are floating around at any given moment. One solution is to develop new methodologies that address the problem directly, and to conduct investigations where elaborating the breadth of modeling ideas is the primary purpose. The work that is discussed in this book is an attempt to take this approach, where the breadth of modeling ideas is catalogued in exploring the answer to the question: *What is a strategy?*

1.2   WHAT IS A STRATEGY?

The English language is now full of ambiguous phrases that seem to refer to different modalities of cognitive behavior. Critical reasoning, creative problem solving, and strategic thinking are all phrases that sometimes have specific meanings in particular professions, but more often the three are simply meant to refer to a vague notion of a type of thinking that is different from the mundane, normal mental stupor where most of us like to hang out. Strategic thinking also carries along with it the additional meanings associated with the word *strategy*, a term most often used in warfare and business (e.g., the general's strategy, the corporate strategy). One might surmise that strategic thinking is meant to refer to the special type of reasoning that people in these professions do as part of their work. A quick discussion with a military officer and a corporate executive is enough to cast doubt on this idea, however, as it appears that the types of reasoning done in these two professions have about as much in common as in any two others. Furthermore, the term *strategy* seems appropriate in almost any profession or domain of interest. A physician may have a strategy for caring for alcohol-dependent adolescents. A teacher may have a strategy for motivating students to pursue mathematics outside the classroom. A scientist may have a strategy for ensuring that his or her line of research is well funded in the future.

Regardless of profession or interest, people have particular abilities with regard to strategies that we would like to understand at a cognitive level. We can near-effortlessly recognize a strategy that we've seen before in the behavior of others or in narratives. We can make judgments about the appropriateness of a particular strategy for a given context. We can change our own approach to solving a problem by following a strategy that was suggested to us as advice. We can offer an appropriate strategy as advice to others when they are in situations that have particular characteristics. These behaviors all seem like good examples of strategic thinking, and the set of them can stand in lieu of a more precise (and arbitrary) definition. It is this set of behaviors that we would like to understand to such a great degree that we could design a computer program to do them as well.

In adopting this view of strategic thinking, we are shifting the focus of our attention to the notion of a strategy. For some, it may seem as if we are simply shifting from one ambiguous focus, that of strategic thinking, to another. From a modeling view, however, the shift can be seen as moving our attention from the specification of mental processes to the knowledge that these processes act upon. In so doing, we are making a decision about how we are going to approach the modeling problem, and what sort of methodological tools we'll select from. In some ways, making this kind of decision is analogous to the problem of reverse-engineering a complex software application that uses algorithms along with structured data to perform its calculation. You could learn a lot about the characteristics of the structured data by looking at the algorithm and vice versa, but you would use different techniques based on which of the two you started from.

This book describes a methodology for the analysis of mental representations, where strategies are the subject of attention. By better understanding strategies as a type of represented knowledge structure, we can better understand the sorts of processes involved in strategic thinking and make a judgment as to how this sort of reasoning differs from other sorts of cognitive activity. As is described in the chapters that follow, strategies seem to have a curious dual nature to them, where they can be viewed both as part of the structural commonalities between analogous planning cases and as programmatic patterns to control reasoning processes.

1.3   THE SCALE OF RESEARCH

To continue the comparison between Cognitive Modeling and computer programming, we see that practitioners in both areas are especially concerned with the issue of scale, or magnitude, of the work that they are doing—but in very different ways. For a computer programmer, the concern is for the scalability of the algorithms that they have written, as it is often easy to write something that is computationally intractable as soon as the input data grows to any significant size. For most valuable applications of computer programs, there is never a shortage of input data (e.g., account transactions, polygons to be rendered, and audiovisual samples). In Cognitive Modeling, however, often both the algorithms (mental processes) and the data (knowledge) must be authored. The problem of scalability in Cognitive Modeling isn't that there is too much input data, but that it is often intractable to author enough to build a model that is demonstrably robust under a rich variety of circumstances.

It is at this point that the science of Cognitive Modeling starts to diverge from its close neighbor, Artificial Intelligence. Perhaps more for historical than for philosophical reasons, the Computer Science sub-field of Artificial Intelligence has largely adopted the computer programming view of the scalability problem, placing the research emphasis on the design of algorithms rather than the design of data. From the perspective of a cognitive modeler, the effects of this emphasis are sometimes unfortunate. Artificial Intelligence conferences are held on the topic of knowledge representation where little specific knowledge is actually discussed, where debates seem to center on how one would represent knowledge if such a need were to arise. Journals devoted to Artificial Intelligence are published consisting primarily of new algorithms that make no commitments to the contents of the data on which they operate whatsoever. If a cognitive modeler were to ask what sort of reasoning problems these algorithmic solutions address, the answer seems to be that they provably solve all problems that they are given, correctly and sometimes completely. To the cognitive modeler's ears, this generally means that these solutions address only half of any given reasoning problem, at most.

In looking for a satisfying explanation of strategic thinking, the research described in this book takes the other extreme to the scalability problem by focusing almost exclusively on identifying the knowledge that is used in strategic thinking at the expense of having any computer algorithms to prove the utility of this work. For now, the focus is on strategies themselves—the structured knowledge representations that are used by the mind's suite of mental processes in strategic thinking. By limiting these efforts, at least initially, to the pursuit of representations rather than algorithms, it has been possible to produce a corpus of knowledge representations that is among the largest of its kind.

1.4   PROJECT OVERVIEW

The project that is described in the chapters that follow stem from the belief that the best way to understand strategies is to conduct a large-scale analysis. After deciding on the approach, the bulk of the work that went into this project was distributed across three major phases: strategy collection, strategy representation, and vocabulary control.

In the first phase, strategy collection, the goal is to turn the slippery commonsense notion of a strategy into a large collection of real-world examples. While there may be some value in understanding the idea of strategy in the abstract, the purpose here was to ground our analysis in the realities of everyday commonsense reasoning. What was needed was a list that was in accordance with intuitions about what does and does not count as an example of a strategy. To complicate these matters, the term *strategy* has adopted a number of more technical meanings in various professional communities that are quite different than the sorts of knowledge in the subject of this investigation. An example of the problematic polysemy of the word *strategy* is evident in the domain of business practices, where *strategic planning* or *business strategy* sometimes take the commonsense meaning of the word, but other times refer to the normal planning of business processes that is done by business professionals or to the documents that are the result of this planning.

In this project, collecting strategies took on some of the values of Cognitive Anthropology, where the interest is in the knowledge that is broadly shared across the communities that are engaged in various planning endeavors. A critical idea that aided this process was the notion of a *planning domain*, which borrows meaning from the notion of domain-specific knowledge in the Artificial Intelligence research community. Here, a planning domain is a cluster of numerous human activities that are all related in some specific way. Examples of planning domains include those that are delineated by occupational roles (e.g., the military domain and the business domain), by social roles (e.g., the domain of personal relationships), and by the individual pursuits of people (e.g., the domain of artistic performance). In each of these domains, there exist multitudes of strategies that are culturally shared among the people that engage in these pursuits, but the best approach to collecting these strategies varies according to the degree that these people have made these strategies a specific topic of conversation. In some planning domains, such as the military and politics, the notion of strategy has an enormously long intellectual history, which has resulted in the authoring of manuscripts that are near encyclopedic of strategies in these domains and can be used as source material. In other planning domains, such as the domains of personal relationships and scientific research, the sharing of planning knowledge is much more informal, suggesting the use of directed interviewing as a method for collecting these strategies. Still other domains of human planning are rarely the topic of discussion, debate, or concern, and in these areas, interpretive observation of activity may be the only means to collect the strategies that have become widespread through means other than direct communication. In this project, ten planning domains were chosen for consideration, and all three of these collection methods (analysis of texts, directed interviews, interpretive observations) were employed to collect several hundred strategies for further analysis.

The second phase of this project, strategy representation, consists of authoring descriptions of each of the strategies that were collected, attempting to parallel the structured, symbolic mental representations that participate in human reasoning processes. There are a number of different approaches that could have been chosen to complete this representation task that can roughly be specified by both the degree of formality of the authored representations and the degree to which existing vocabularies are used. In the tradition of Artificial Intelligence knowledge representation research, what are valued are representations that are both formal (typically using either a predicate, modal, or propositional logic) and those that integrate existing vocabularies to minimize the proliferation of extraneous terms. In this current project, these values were relaxed for two main reasons. First, the representations that were authored are not formal representations in the traditional sense of the word—a decision that enabled the *scale* of the project to be much greater. Second, the representations were authored without an attempt to constrain the vocabularies used to those found in previous research—a decision that enabled the *scope* of the project to fall into territory that has received very little attention in the past.

In relaxing these traditional research values, a new type of knowledge description emerged from this work, called *pre-formal representations* for lack of a better term. As discussed in chapter 3, these pre-formal representations substitute natural language (English) for the syntactical structure used in formal representations to bind predicates to arguments, or operators to statements. In addition, all of the concepts that would appear as operators or predicates in formal representations are simply referred to using words or short phrases and set apart from syntactical structure by capitalizing and italicizing each term as it appears. Chapter 3 describes the properties of pre-formal representations in more detail, and chapter 4 contains the full text of each of the 372 pre-formal representations of strategies that were authored in the course of this project.

The third and final phase of this project, vocabulary control, consists of collecting, consolidating, and organizing all of the representational terms that were used in the pre-formal representations. The purpose here was to begin to move from the pre-formal vocabulary that facilitated the magnitude of the representation effort to the more formal representational vocabularies that have traditionally been the product of knowledge representation research in the field of Artificial Intelligence. *Vocabulary control* is a term borrowed from the Library Science community, where special attention must be directed to managing lists of subject keywords (*thesaurus terms*) such that for any given term, there exists only one term in the vocabulary that has the exact same meaning. Likewise, vocabulary control in this project involved reducing all of the variants and synonyms of words and phrases used in the pre-formal representations down to the smallest possible set of distinct concepts.

While a set of fundamental conceptual primitives has long been a pursuit in the field of knowledge representation, the results of this current project are markedly different from these past attempts simply by virtual scale and scope. After consolidating the vocabulary to only those terms that have unique meaning, the controlled vocabulary consists of around one thousand terms. Some of these terms fall into familiar categories found in Artificial Intelligence knowledge representation research, for example, relationships between moments in time, the consequential relationships between events, and the complexities of intention and choice when reasoning about agents. Perhaps the main contribution of this work, however, is to broaden the scope of representation research into areas that have not received enough attention. In this work, this broadening of scope is perhaps most evident in areas concerning the reasoning processes of people, including planning to achieve goals, imagining possible worlds, managing the execution of actions, making decisions in the face of uncertainty, and reasoning about the division between the mind and its embodiment. Chapter 5 lists each member of the set of nearly one thousand concepts that were identified in this project, and serves as an index back to the strategies in which they appeared. Chapter 6 presents an organization of these terms into forty-eight representational areas, and an attempt is made to relate the terms in these categories to the varying amounts of existing knowledge representation research efforts to which they pertain.

1.5 RESEARCH OPPORTUNITIES

As a research community, the field of Cognitive Modeling has a troubling lack of methodologies that it can employ to address new modeling problems. One aim of this book is to add one more methodology to the toolbox. An appropriate name for this methodology might be something like *representational requirements analysis*, which generates representational vocabularies to drive the design of cognitive models. While it is interesting to speculate as to the effectiveness of this approach for knowledge structures other than strategies, it is certain that choosing strategies as a focus has led to results that may have significant impacts on research throughout Cognitive Science. While these opportunities will have to be explored outside the scope of this book, some of them are mentioned below in order to motivate work in these directions.

Among the forty-eight representational areas that serve as categories for the thousand identified concepts (chapter 6) there is a mix of those that have been well studied in knowledge representation research (time, events, states of the world) and those that haven't. These other representational areas largely concern the reasoning processes of people—from their plans, goals, beliefs, expectations, explanations, and preferences to all of the mental events and processes that impact these things. Collectively, they constitute a mental model of the reasoning processes of a person, a model that can be viewed as a framework that people use to understand each other and themselves. While these vocabularies may have a more immediate benefit to the field of Artificial Intelligence knowledge representation (as reviewed in chapter 6), a more ambitious goal is to connect this work to traditional psychological notions of *folk psychology* or *theory of mind*, and to the converging interdisciplinary research efforts in this area.

For the field of Cognitive Modeling, there is an opportunity to capitalize on the scope and breadth of this representation effort to bring together computational models that could not previously be integrated. In identifying forty-eight representational areas that are employed in strategic thinking, this project outlines the daunting scope of the work that will be required to build a computational model of this sort of reasoning. Models of strategic reasoning will include component algorithms for plan construction, plan execution, predication, explanation, counterfactual reasoning, similarity comparisons, memory retrieval, monitoring, and decision making, among others. Fortunately, there are few cognitive capacities referenced in strategy representations that have not received substantial attention within the cognitive sciences, the subject of both empirical investigations and computational modeling efforts.

A viable modeling approach would be to make an *assumption of correspondence* between the sorts of mental representational models of human reasoning that were identified in this project and the actual cognitive processes that are at work in human reasoning. The effect of this assumption is to cause us to view the strategies presented here not only as approximations of a certain class of structured knowledge, but also as programmatic blueprints from which we can derive larger computational models. In examining the representations that are presented in this book in this light, one gets the impression that strategies provide some evidence for the architectural glue that will allow us to tie previously disparate computational models together. It is common to see in any one of these strategies references to multiple, disparate processes such as plan construction, similarity judgments, memory retrieval, control of physical movements, belief revision, decision making, and explanation construction—all components of human reasoning where computational models have been previously constructed. The quality of integrative cognitive architectures of the future could be benchmarked by their capacity to execute formal versions of these strategies—a task that will require the functionality of each of these component computational models.

Regardless of whether this assumption of correspondence leads to better cognitive models, the engineering utility of this approach may still be very high. Certainly one of the most challenging problems across the field of Computer Science is that of human–computer interaction, where it is evident that the power of computation is most constrained by our inability to use it in our daily lives. A persistent dream of human–computer interaction researchers is the development of mixed-initiative problem-solving systems, where computers cooperatively aid in the pursuit of human interests by applying their superior capacity for calculation in appropriate ways. Invariably, the hard part of realizing this dream is getting computers to understand enough about human life to participate in it. Perhaps the greatest opportunity to make progress in this area is to capitalize on the natural human tendency to anthropomorphize computational systems. That is, the mental models that people utilize to understand the reasoning of others are also those used to understand the behavior of computers (as well as animals, cells in the immune system, and whole corporations, among others). By designing computer systems that have explicit representations of their own behavior that are more congruous with those ascribed to them by their users, the disconnect between human expectation and computational reality can be managed in more effective ways. It is simply unreasonable to expect that we will ever be able build knowledge management systems, natural language understanding systems, or cooperative planning systems without addressing the substantial design constraints that human psychology brings to the table.

To state it again, further consideration of many of these opportunities will have to find a different forum than this book, but hopefully the curiosity of the reader has been piqued by bringing them up here. Now our attention turns directly to the ambiguous notion of a planning strategy. Chapter 2 attempts to reduce this ambiguity by capitalizing on the progress made in the field of cognitive modeling on *analogy*, a concept that was previously equally ambiguous.

CHAPTER
2

Strategic Analogies

2.1 THINKING ABOUT PLANNING CASES

> *I once met a heroin addict while waiting for a bus at the Chicago Greyhound bus terminal. He sat down next to me and told me about how hard it was to kick the habit. He had tried countless times, but somehow he always managed to find more heroin as the withdrawal pains became unbearable. Just before we met, he had been kicked out of the last place that he could stay, so he decided that drastic measures were necessary. He used the last bit of heroin that he had on hand, and gathered all of his money to buy a one-way bus ticket to as far away from Chicago as he could afford—Milwaukee. His thought was that he would arrive in Milwaukee broke and desperate, without any means of finding or purchasing more heroin. He expected that the pains of withdrawal would be incredible, and that he would abandon his plan to kick the habit, but hoped that he would have placed himself in an impossible situation—where any of his plans to find more heroin would fail. In effect, he had planned to fail, and hoped to continue to fail until he was no longer addicted. As I left to catch my bus, I wished him luck—hoping that somehow his plan might work.*

FIG. 2.1. The story of a bus station encounter.

Stories like the one in Figure 2.1 seem to serve a number of different functions in our social and psychological lives. They question our own assumptions about the way the world works, challenge the assumptions of others when we use stories to make particular points, and teach us far more about people and the world we live in than we could learn from personal experience alone. The belief that we utilize past stories like these when we are engaged in new problem-solving behavior is the central tenet of the theory of Case-Based Reasoning. While the term is meant to encompass a wide assortment of theoretical approaches, all adopt a metaphorical view of memory as a place in which cases are stored, later to be retrieved, adapted, and applied to current situations that are similar or analogous. This metaphor fits particularly well with the computational metaphors used in Cognitive Modeling, and has generated interest in the development of computational theories of case-based explanation, case-based parsing, and case-based planning.

It is in this last area of Cognitive Modeling, case-based planning, where constructing compelling computational models has been particularly problematic. Theoretically, case-based planning can be viewed as a process of constructing a plan by retrieving a relevant planning case from memory and adapting it so that it solves the planning problem at hand. Among all of the computational systems that have ever been built by cognitive modelers and Artificial Intelligence researchers, there exists no case-based planning system that could incorporate and use the planning case presented in Figure 2.1 to solve a new planning problem. The root of the problem concerns a fundamental question: *What is the computational value of a stored planning case?*

Two reasonable answers to this question have been explored in computational models. First, the value of a stored planning case may be to avoid computing solutions to problems that have already been solved. That is, by storing plans that have already been constructed to meet certain goals, a planning system can reduce the need to search for a solution that they have already found. In this view, memory can be viewed as a sort of cache of previously computed plans, in much the same way that a computer database system may create a cache of responses to frequent queries. This view is in accordance with the design of modern computational planning systems in Artificial Intelligence, where controlling the size of the search space is the paramount concern. The second reasonable answer is that the value of a stored planning case may be in its reuse in planning problems where the effects of the planner's actions are not completely known. When planning systems cannot successfully envision how their actions affect change in the world, they may try to adapt a previously successful plan with the hope that it will be applicable to the new problem. While the problems of uncertainty generally fall outside of the scope of AI planning research, the first attempts to build cognitive models of case-based planning adopted this approach (Hammond, 1989).

While certainly reasonable, both of these potential answers are premised on the belief that the important knowledge contained in stored planning cases are the plans themselves. Whether in caching to reduce search or adapting to handle uncertainty, the computation in these approaches utilizes only the set of ordered (or partially ordered) actions that make up the plan to address the new planning problem. In adopting one or both of these answers, we can begin to define more precisely what we mean when we refer to a stored planning case as a represented structure in a knowledge base. At the very least, we could imagine that a stored planning case consists of some representation of a plan coupled with a description of the sorts of changes in the world that the plan was designed to cause.

As knowledge engineers, we tend to appreciate knowledge representations that are economical, in that they contain only the information that can be manipulated by the cognitive functions that they serve. Accordingly, we may wonder if the plan is the only knowledge with functional utility that is contained in a stored planning case. Another way to ask this question is this: What is the difference between stored plans and stored planning cases? If there is more to a planning case than a plan, then what functional role does this other knowledge play?

Consider the story presented in Figure 2.1. Intuitively, this story appears to be an example of a planning case, in that it concerns the goal-directed actions of a person who has already halfway executed a plan that he created. However, the specific plan that this person devised to achieve his goal—taking the drugs that were available, going to the bus station, buying a bus ticket to an unfamiliar city, and getting on the correct bus—somehow seems to not be the most significant component of this case. In some important way, the plan that was constructed is not nearly as important as the reasoning behind it. What is the problem that this person is trying to solve? Why would a person purposefully give up access to his resources? What did this person imagine would happen as his plan went forward? Most importantly, why would someone set himself up to fail?

The answers to these questions all seem to relate to the particular approach that this person took to address his problem—the way he reasoned about his situation that seems divorced from the concrete specifics of his final plan. In everyday language, the interesting part of this story concerns the strategy that was used. In many respects, the strategy that was used by this individual is a familiar one. For example, much of the same reasoning causes people to give their car keys to bartenders before they begin drinking alcohol. Indeed, many of the answers to the contextual questions are nearly identical in these two analogous cases:

Q: What is the problem that these people are trying to solve?
A: They imagine that they will want to do something in the future that they presently don't want themselves to do, namely taking heroin and driving their car while intoxicated.
Q: Why would they purposefully give up access to their resources?
A: To remove the preconditions, namely access to money and their car keys, which are required to execute the behaviors they are trying to stop.

Q: What did these people imagine would happen as their plans went forward?

A: They imagined that their goals would change, that they would want to take more heroin and drive their cars intoxicated, but they wouldn't be able to acquire heroin in a strange city or their car keys from the bartender.

Q: Why would these people set themselves up to fail?

A: Because they want to stop themselves from achieving unhealthy goals that they cannot prevent themselves from pursuing.

The important thing to note here is that changing the details of the plan—even the characters, the actions, and the goal—could still result in an analogous case. Taking a bus to Milwaukee to quit taking heroin could be analogous to giving car keys to a bartender before beginning to drink alcohol, on the condition that the reasoning that went into creating these plans is similar in some way. It is in noticing that there is a relationship between strategies in planning and the processes of analogical reasoning that we are able us to shed some light on the nature of the knowledge that is wrapped up in these cases. In cognitive science research, our theories of analogical reasoning are far more mature than those that we have for strategic reasoning. In this chapter, it is argued that our theories of analogical reasoning can be used as an investigative tool. By directing this tool toward the abstract notions of planning strategies, we can begin to understand the sorts of knowledge structures that are wrapped up in stored planning cases. After reviewing current theoretical models of analogical reasoning, it will be argued that strategies are part of the relational structure shared by analogous planning cases, and that this relational structure includes representations of the reasoning processes of the people who utilize these strategies.

2.2 THEORIES OF ANALOGICAL REASONING

The subject of analogical reasoning has enjoyed an enormous amount of research attention throughout this history of cognitive science, including theoretical hypotheses, empirical studies, and the development of computational models. In general, the aim of this area of research has been to account for why people would find two cases analogous, how they can draw new inferences by making analogies from cases that are well understood to those that are not, and how human memory enables spontaneous remembering of cases that are analogous to current situations. Among the most resilient theories of analogical reasoning are Structure Mapping Theory (Gentner, 1983) and Multi-Constraint Theory (Holyoak & Thagard, 1989), both of which have led to the development of computational models, some of which use traditional serial algorithms (Falkenhainer, Forbus, & Gentner,

1989), and others of which take a connectionist or neural-network approach (Halford et al., 1994; Hummel & Holyoak, 1997; Kokinov, 1994).

Despite the variety of different modeling assumptions that researchers have adopted, there is incredible agreement among researchers in this area on the sorts of principles that govern the way that analogical reasoning is done. These principles are often referred to as constraints on the possible ways that two cases can correspond to each other, for which two constraints have become widely accepted: the constraint of *one-to-one mapping* and the constraint of *parallel connectivity*. The constraint of one-to-one mapping dictates that each of the entities in one case must correspond to not more than one of the entities in the other case. For example, a bus in one case might correspond to either an airplane or a train in a second, but not both within the same conception of the analogy between the two cases. The constraint of parallel connectivity (also referred to as structural consistency) concerns the set of relations that hold between entities in the representation of a case, dictating that relationships in different cases may be brought into correspondence only if the entities in these relationships can also be brought into correspondence. For example, the ownership of a painting by an art collector in one case may correspond to the ownership of an automobile by its driver in a second, but only if the painting corresponds to the automobile and the art collector corresponds to the driver.

The system of relationships that are brought into correspondence between two analogous cases is referred to as the *shared relational structure*—an interconnected set of relations that can be separated from the specific entities of either of the two cases. In Structure-Mapping Theory and others, it is the breadth and depth of this shared relational structure that determine the relative strength of an analogy among all of the ways that two cases could possibly correspond to each other. When an analogy seems particularly strong or compelling, this can be attributed to the richness of the shared relational structure that exists between the two cases.

One of the perceived strengths of the computational models of analogical reasoning that have been developed is that they make few commitments regarding the representation of cases. Typically, any case that can be represented as a set of first-order predicate logic statements can be translated into the representational conventions used in these computational models. Each of these systems is designed to operate without regard to the details of the formal representational vocabulary that is used to encode cases—as long as there are consistent conventions in the way that any two cases are encoded in memory, these computational models will be able to make analogical comparisons between them. This characteristic underscores the central finding of research on analogy—that analogical reasoning is based on structural similarity of case representations.

The downside of this degree of universality is that the predictive utility of these computational models is severely limited. Given any two cases from real human experience, it is impossible to use these models to predict whether a person would find the cases analogous. To do so requires that we also know how these cases are represented in people's minds. To compensate for this impossibility, these computational models have typically operated on case representations that are, at worst, authored specifically to demonstrate the strength of the model and, at best, authored to address the functional needs of some other reasoning task besides analogy making. True examples of systems of the latter type are almost non-existent, but there is increasing awareness among researchers in the field of analogy that this is the direction in which their models must move (Forbus, 2001). Ultimately, the future of research in analogical reasoning is wrapped up in the details and complexities of how cases are encoded as knowledge representations.

2.3 STRATEGIES ARE SHARED RELATIONAL STRUCTURES

In June of 1941, Germany invaded Ukraine with 3,000,000 troops, threatening to advance eastward into Russia. Soon after, Soviet leader Joseph Stalin announced a scorched-earth policy for Ukraine, ordering that retreating Ukrainians destroy everything that could be of value to the advancing German army, including grains, fuel, and engines that could not be transported east to Russia. In an analogous case, Iraq invaded their oil-rich neighbor Kuwait in August of 1990, leading to the Persian Gulf war. The following January, the United States launched an attack against Iraq, and Saddam Hussein responded by blowing up Kuwaiti oil wells and dumping millions of gallons of oil into the Persian Gulf.

FIG. 2.2. An analogy between WWII and the Persian Gulf War.

Analogies of exactly the sort found in Figure 2.2 have been the subject of a number of experimental studies of analogical reasoning (especially Spellman & Holyoak, 1992) and used to garner support for different theories. In the computational models of analogy that have been constructed in support of these theories, formal representations of cases like this have been authored to demonstrate the operation of the model. Although the computational approach used in a given model determines how these cases are encoded, these representations have some equivalence to a set of first-order predicate calculus statements. It is typical that people, places, and things (e.g., Stalin and Iraq) appear in these representations as entities, while actions, processes, and roles (e.g., destroys and possesses) are encoded as predicates that make up a case's relational structure.

By making these representation decisions, the constraints of analogical reasoning can be applied to determine how these two cases can be in correspondence. The one-to-one correspondence constraint dictates that each of the entities from one case (e.g., Germany, Joseph Stalin, grains) can correspond to, at most, one of the entities in the second (e.g., the United States, Saddam Hussein, oil wells). For example, Kuwait could potentially correspond to the grains, Hitler, Stalin, Germany, Ukraine, or Russia, but not more than one of these entities in any given interpretation of the analogy. Likewise, the constraint of parallel connectivity requires that the sets of relationship correspondences have consistent correspondences between the entities that they concern. For example, because Iraq is an entity in both the relationship of invading and the relationship of destroying, both of these relationships cannot be a part of the same system of analogical correspondences to the WWII case, where Germany did the invading and the Ukraine did the destroying.

It is important to notice the way that representation decisions like these affect the predictions that the computational models will make. In particular, including more or less information in the cases' relational structure can make significant changes in the calculated strength of an analogical correspondence. If we assume representations that are too sparse, we risk predicting that the analogy between this Persian Gulf war case and this WWII case would be highly ambiguous. For example, if Germany is mapped to Iraq, then we have correspondence between the relationship of invading (Germany/Ukraine and Iraq/Kuwait) and the relationship of contained-within (Ukraine/Grains and Kuwait/oil wells). If the Soviet Union is mapped instead to Iraq, then we have a correspondence between the relationship of destroying (Soviet Union/grains and Iraq/oil wells) and that of possession or ownership (Soviet Union/Grains and Iraq/oil wells). If only the relationships of invading, containment, destroying, and possession are included in the relational structure of these cases, then the comparative strength of either analogical interpretation would be the same.

However, the analogy between these two cases is intuitively very strong, lacking the ambiguity that an impoverished representation would predict. The obvious mapping is that Iraq is like the Soviet Union, as their decision to destroy the Kuwaiti oil wells was analogous to when Stalin ordered the destruction of resources in the Ukraine. These cases are two examples of the *exact same strategy*. Instances of this abstract pattern of planning behavior are so prevalent in our culture that we've given the pattern a name, *scorched earth policy*, so that we could refer to it again and again in analogous cases, whether they appear in warfare or in completely different domains such as politics or business. To account for the comparative strength of this interpretation of the analogy over other possibilities, we must assume that the representations of these cases are much richer.

When we consider the abstract similarities that are found in the planning that is done in these two cases, the correspondence between the two cases becomes clear. The agent that is doing the planning in these cases (Stalin/Hussein) has some adversarial relationship with some other agent (Hitler/Bush). This planning agent imagines a likely future where the adversary acquires possession of some resources (grain/oil) that are currently possessed by the planner. They imagine that the adversary will make use of these resources to further the pursuit of their adversarial plan (march on to Russia/control the Middle East). They decide that the best plan is to do something (destroy grain/blow up oil wells) that will cause these resources to be destroyed, or to make it impossible that the adversary could make use of them, and to do so before the adversary gains possession.

While the rich relational correspondence between these two military examples is described using natural language in the preceding paragraph, a corresponding mental representation language would necessarily include structures to refer to the adversarial relationship, the imagination of a likely future, the acquisition of resources, the expenditure of resources in an adversarial plan, the goal of disabling a resource, and the execution deadline. It is this collection of relationships that constitutes the representation of the strategy, and which also makes a significant contribution to judgments of analogical similarity to *every other case* that describes an instance of this sort of strategic behavior.

To clarify, not all of the relational structure shared between analogous planning cases can be thought of as part of a strategy. Certainly there are analogous planning cases that are so not because of any similarity in the strategies of the participating agents. For example, a case where a professional sports team acquires an athlete just before he ore she has an unprecedented season of excellence may be analogous to a corporation that acquires a subsidiary just before it has an unexpected licensing windfall, but the commonalities in these cases may have more to do with unforeseen benefits than strategic planning. In contrast, if we learn that the sports team and the parent corporation both had selected their acquisitions with the belief that past performance records predicted a favorable upturn, we would say that they shared the same strategy—in reference to the portion of the shared relational structure that concerns the planning processes of these agents.

The research opportunity that is evident here concerns the apparent ease that people have in making casual references to large portions of shared relational structure, removing these portions from their context to be considered independently, and assigning to them names like *scorched earth policy* when they are particularly interesting for one reason or another. This ease with strategies enables researchers to collect whole catalogs of naturally occurring analogical mappings, and to argue about how they could be represented on a much larger scale than was possible in previous knowledge representation debates.

2.4 STRATEGIES INCLUDE REASONING PROCESSES

Among computational models of analogy, the most compelling support for structural correspondence theories have used represented cases in the domain of physical systems, where existing representational theories are significantly more mature than in other domains. Notable examples are those that are derived from Qualitative Process Theory (Forbus, 1984), a representational framework that has been used to describe the physics of thermodynamics, fluid dynamics, and solid body motion, among other domain theories. In contrast, the case representations in computational models of analogy that seem the most contrived are those that are more story-like in nature, that is, those involving the intentional behavior of intelligent agents.

A somewhat notorious example of this problem can be seen in the "Karla the hawk" stories that were used in support of the Structure-Mapping Engine (Falkenhainer et al., 1989). The main story concerned the actions of Karla, an old hawk, and her encounter with a hunter who had attempted to shoot Karla with an arrow, but had missed because the hunter's crude arrow lacked the feathers needed to fly straight. Karla knew that the hunter wanted her feathers so she offered some of hers to him, and he gratefully pledged never to shoot at a hawk again. In the dozen propositions that were authored to represent this story, emphasis was placed on describing the actions that were done (e.g., seeing, attacking, offering, obtaining, promising) with only a single, highly ambiguous predicate of *realizing* to refer to the reasoning processes that Karla undertook.

What is lacking from these representations is the richness of planning and reasoning that is ascribed to these characters when we read stories like this—the conceptual glue that allows us to make sense of the story in the first place. Much of this knowledge can be packaged into the form of a single strategy, the one that we guess Karla had in mind when she offered the feathers. Figure 2.3 offers a pre-formal treatment of the representational components of this strategy, where the capitalized and italicized words and phrases come from the set used in our large-scale strategy representation project (as is described in chap. 3). Of course, it is possible to imagine that Karla wasn't thinking strategically at all—often characters in this genre of fable-like stories seem to stumble across some course of action by mere chance, without thinking things through. However, it is difficult to imagine that readers of the story could be as ignorant. Indeed, it is the planning lessons that can be learned from stories of this genre that make them compelling and valuable.

Karla's Strategy:
Turn enemies into friends by improving their capabilities

The planner has an *Adversarial Relationship* with another agent that has had an *Execution failure* of an *Adversarial plan*, with a *Cause of failure* of *Instrument failure*. The planner *Envisions* that this agent will *Attempt the execution* of this *Adversarial plan* in *Future* states against the planner and *Envisions a possibility* that this plan will be *Successfully executed*. The planner has a *Partial plan* to *Reduce the probability* of *Instrument failure* in *Future executions* of the *Adversarial plan* by this other agent that includes *Modifying the instrument* and includes the *Instrumental use of Resources* of the planner. The planner executes a plan to *Make an offer* to the agent where the *Offered action* is that the planner *Transfers possession* of *Resources* that *Enable* the agent to execute the *Partial plan*. The planner then *Adds the expectation* that *If it is the case* that the agent *Accepts the offer*, that the agent will *Terminate his role* in the *Adversarial relationship*, which will cause him to *Abandon plans* that are *Adversarial plans* against the planner. The planner then *Adds a threat* that the *Expectation* is a *False expectation*, and that the agent will execute the *Partial plan* followed by the execution of the *Adversarial plan*.

FIG. 2.3. The strategy of Karla the hawk as a preformal representation.

What should be noticed in Figure 2.3 is that the strategy contains a significant amount of references to mental states of both the planner and the adversary. There is the imagining of future states, of a partial plan not entirely worked out, an expectation of the consequences of an action, and an explicit threat of what might happen if this expectation is wrong. Each of these mental states is critical to the understanding of the story, and we argue that they should be included in the representation of this case to explain analogies to cases where only the strategy is shared.

Just as analogies in physical systems are based on mental models of processes in physical domains, analogies in intentional domains include assertions that only make sense with respect to a mental model of agents and intentional behavior. In arguing for the inclusion of these sorts of assertions in case representations in intentional domains, it is argued that people have a rich model of agents and their reasoning processes.

A great deal of attention has been directed toward developing models of agents and intentional behavior among decision theorists and artificial intelligence logicians, often centered around the notion of Belief, Desire and Intention (BDI) agents. Formalizations of these models (e.g., Cohen & Levesque, 1990) typically strive to maximize the number of simplifying assumptions in order to retain the ability to prove related theorems, but to do so without sacrificing the expressiveness required to compute useful functions. The engineering value of this approach is demonstrated when theories lead to practical applications (see Rao & Georgeff, 1995), but caution must be taken when using this approach for the purpose of cognitive modeling. Certainly there are times where the mental representations that people have may appear to exhibit the qualities of elegance and simplicity, but our aim should be to describe the mental models of people as they are—without simplifying assumptions—if we are to understand and predict how they are manipulated by cognitive processes.

2.5   ANALOGY AS AN INVESTIGATIVE TOOL

> The association of solved problems with those unsolved may throw new light on our difficulties by suggesting new ideas. It is easy to find a superficial analogy which really expresses nothing. But to discover some essential common features, hidden beneath a surface of external differences, to form, on this basis, a new successful theory, is important creative work. (Einstein & Infeld, 1938/1976)

Einstein and Infeld presented this idea to justify making an analogy between a violin string and the wavelike properties of elementary particles. The essential common features that Einstein and Infeld discovered were the concepts of a *standing wave* and a *moving wave*, and the new successful theory that they were forming was that of probability waves in quantum physics. Einstein and Infeld's quote reveals something about the way they approached scientific problem solving, but from a cognitive science perspective, we might also view it as a proposed methodology for forming theories of people's mental models. That is, by analyzing analogous cases—discovering the essential common features that are hidden beneath a surface of external differences—we can form theories of the mental representations that people have that cause these cases to be analogous.

In the idealized version of this methodology, researchers would begin by collecting and cataloging the spontaneous analogies between cases that subjects create in the course of their daily lives. For each analogy, researchers would author their best hypothesis of the contents of the shared relational structure that would account for the analogy. If the size of the analogy catalog is very large, than the representational hypotheses can be aggregated to create larger, more encompassing representational theories whose contents are evidenced by the realities of everyday analogy making. These theories could then be coupled with algorithms for analogical reasoning to form a more complete cognitive model whose predictive utility could be evaluated.

For many reasons, however, this idealized version of the methodology is unrealistic. As researchers, we currently do not have proven methods for collecting spontaneous analogies that occur in the daily lives of people. Even if we did, there is evidence that the majority of these would be based primarily on the similarity of surface features between two cases rather than on the deep relational structure. Furthermore, only portions of the analogies that people make are between planning cases—others will be between cases that describe no goal-directed behavior whatsoever. While many of the problems could be addressed by simply increasing the size of the collection of analogies, at some point the scope of these efforts becomes too great to be completed in the course of reasonably sized research projects. It is partly for these reasons that a researcher would look for an alternative collection of knowledge to drive the analytic process—a type of knowledge that more directly concerned the representational questions at hand.

The arguments that have been made in this chapter suggest that planning strategies serve as an appropriate surrogate for spontaneous planning analogies. Strategies are part of the shared relational structure that causes planning cases to be analogous, and pertain not only to plans of action, but also to the reasoning processes that people use to create plans. If it were possible to understand how strategies are represented in the minds of people, then we could know much about how planning cases are represented in memory, and how people represent the models that they have of their own reasoning and the reasoning of others. In packaging so much representation information into knowledge that is part of the common discussions of everyday human life, strategies offer researchers an accessible window to the answers to some of the most challenging questions of the field of knowledge representation.

Strategies are prevalent throughout our professional, private, and cultural lives, and the relative ease with which strategies can be identified and cataloged gives us the opportunity to turn Einstein and Infeld's intuition into a systematic investigative methodology. The strategies discussed in this chapter—scorched earth policy, enabling your enemies to turn them into allies, and blocking yourself from pursuing an addiction—are three of the hundreds or thousands of strategies that are culturally shared among members of various professional and social communities. Assuming that there is a direct connection between the strategies we talk about and the strategies we think about, then the systematic application of Einstein and Infeld's intuition can begin with a cultural investigation of strategies. The chapter that follows describes a project to systematically implement Einstein and Infeld's intuition using strategies as the subject of analysis.

CHAPTER

3

Representational Requirements

3.1 REPRESENTATION IN MODELS OF PLANNING

One of the hallmarks of Artificial Intelligence planning systems is the general absence of representational commitments. In many ways, this line of research has been successful in achieving its goal of building a *general problem solver* (Newell & Simon, 1963), where this has come to mean an algorithm that searches for a successful solution to a problem (a plan) given any well-specified search space. Over the many years that researchers have developed these algorithms, only a few representational constraints have been needed to advance the technology, notably the introduction a planning operator formalism (Fikes & Nilsson, 1971), a notation for specifying quantified preconditions and context-dependent effects (Pednault, 1989), and a means of describing plans as a hierarchy of tasks (Wilkins, 1988). The strength of this research tradition is that it has enabled comparative evaluations of implemented planning systems, where each is given identical specifications of the search space (McDermott, 2000).

The problematic downside to the representational agnosticism of artificial intelligence planning systems is the gulf that it creates between these technologies and the real humans that would like to use them for everyday problem solving and planning. Highlighted by continuing work on mixed-initiative planning (e.g., Ferguson, 1995), human–computer cooperation will require the development of systems with representational commitments that are more in accordance with people's commonsense understanding of goal-directed behavior. The difficulty in achieving this accord stems from the

23

apparent breadth of our commonsense understanding of intentional action, which includes slippery concepts of commitment, preferences, opportunities, threats, ability, prevention, enablement, failures, constraints, decisions, postponement, interference, and uncertainty, among many others.

The challenge of describing human models of planning has been taken up by researchers in the field of commonsense reasoning, who have produced a body of work under the umbrella label of reasoning about rational action. This research is conducted within the paradigm of formal logic, where the aim is to author statements and axioms that can be employed in deductive inference systems (e.g., Ortiz, 1999a). As an approach for investigating human commonsense reasoning, the key assumption is that formal theories describe our cognitive representations when the provable theorems of these theories match with our natural human inferences (Davis, 1998). Leaving aside potential problems with this assumption, this research approach suffers most in that it scales up very poorly in practice. Consider the amount of research effort required to justify the inclusion of any single commonsense planning concept within a larger theory, perhaps best exemplified in the formal treatment of the concept of *intention* (Cohen & Levesque, 1990). First, it was recognized that there were problems with existing formal theories of planning having to do with intention. Then, researchers authored a new modal logic to enable the expression of a set of axioms that included a handful of new concepts advocated among epistemological philosophers. Finally, it is shown how the inclusion of these new concepts within this new logic enables the proofs of certain theorems that more closely align with our commonsense inferences about planning than did the previous theories.

The significance and impact of this particular work on intention can hardly be understated in light of the enormous attention that it continues to receive. What is in question, however, is whether this work is an appropriate model for how the investigation of representation in commonsense reasoning should proceed. If we imagine that a complete commonsense model of human planning will be on the order of a few dozen concepts and axioms, then this approach is well on its way to success. If, instead, it is on the order of hundreds, thousands, or even millions of such formalizations, then the scope of the endeavor is probably too great for this scientific community to support. As we have had no means of estimating the scale of such a model, the inclination is to pursue alternative research methodologies. Is there a more direct approach to describing the representational components of human commonsense reasoning about planning?

This chapter explores an alternative methodology for the investigation of representation in commonsense models of human planning, one that capitalizes on the curious nature of *strategies*—in the common sense of the word. The notion of strategy takes on paradoxical roles in our intellectual lives. On one hand, strategies are the currency of everyday problem solving—we seem to have an effortless ability to employ and recognize a myriad of strategies in our occupational, recreation, and personal pursuits. On the other hand, individual strategies are uncomfortably abstract, seemingly impenetrable concepts that defy simple attempts at classification or definition. However, to a knowledge engineer, an individual strategy poses a particularly interesting puzzle, one where it is impossible to author a strategy definition without making certain representational commitments about the reasoning processes of the agent executing the strategy.

Consider an example of a strategy used by a budding concert pianist, as he later described it. During one of his early competitive performances his execution of a solo piano piece was derailed by an audience full of distractions, which included audible conversation, chair noises, and even the ringing of a mobile telephone. Determined to avoid this problem in the future, he would purposefully cause distractions to occur during his practice sessions. By setting alarm clocks for odd times, turning on kitchen oven timers, and asking some friends to telephone him during certain hours, he became accustomed to surprise events during his performances, and learned how to ignore them.

It would be difficult to argue that the reasoning done by this pianist was not planning—it is indeed an example of the use of a strategy for learning to ignore distractions during execution. This same strategy might also be useful for surgeons and soldiers, for whom distractions can be deadly. While this strategy may be abstractly defined in such a way that it could be applied across all goal-directed domains, it cannot be done so without carrying along with it the set of modeling assumptions that it entails. Along with the general planning concepts of operators, conditional effects, and preconditions, this strategy has at its core the more subtle planning concepts of *execution failures, distracting events, attention, ability to ignore,* and *practice,* among others. Some existing formal commonsense theories include predicates or other notation that refer to some of these concepts, while other concepts have not yet received formal consideration. What we are arguing for here, however, is that any complete representational theory of commonsense reasoning about planning will include a mechanism for expressing all of them. In analyzing this one strategy and identifying the concepts that must play a role in its definition, we have gathered some weak evidence for the representational requirements of such a theory.

The opportunity here stems from the fact that weak evidence can be aggregated. By systematically analyzing everyday planning strategies on a large scale, and by authoring hundreds of strategy definitions, we can aggregate the evidence provided by each individual strategy to identify the scope and scale of the representation problem and the array of specific planning concepts that must be expressible in a complete, formal representational theory. The remaining sections of this chapter describe a project to pursue this approach, one that is composed of three parts. In the first part of the project, hundreds of strategies were collected from a wide range of different real-world planning domains. In the second part, representations of each of these strategies were authored so as to identify the specific conceptual assumptions that they make about the human planning process. In the third part of this project, all of the concepts used in these representations were extracted from their strategy contexts, and organized into sets of component theories that collectively describe representational elements of our commonsense models of the human planning process.

As a research methodology, the approach that is described in this chapter offers an alternative to the logicians' agenda for the exploration of representation in commonsense reasoning that is not based on the competency of theories to mirror human inferences. As such, the products of this approach have no inferential capacity on their own—the individual concepts that are identified through this methodology outline only the representational elements that would compose axiomatic theories to drive commonsense deductive inference. The specific value of this methodology to logicians whose primary interest is deductive inference is in the lists of representational terms, which suggest specific concepts that should be expressible in future axiomatic theories. While many of the representational areas identified in this project have received a substantial amount of formal attention, few existing formalizations have complete coverage over all of the terms in any given area. Furthermore, there remain several representational areas that have not yet been the subject of formalization efforts. For Artificial Intelligence researchers whose primary concern is not deductive inference (e.g., natural language processing), the opportunity presented by this approach is to treat the problem of commonsense representation as separable from commonsense inference, and to capitalize on progress in the former while the research community makes comparably slower progress on the latter.

3.2 COLLECTING STRATEGIES FROM REAL-WORLD DOMAINS

In selecting an appropriate corpus of strategies to serve as the subject of this analysis, the primary characteristic that is desired is breadth. The ideal collection would span across the widest range of planned human behavior, and capture the commonsense strategies that people use and refer to in all aspects of their lives, from the activities of personal life to those of occupational pursuits. Breadth in the strategy collection helps avoid a pitfall of any analytical approach: the problem of generalizing over a sample that is not representative of the population. Whereas most scientific fields turn to random sampling of a population to avoid this problem, it isn't clear exactly what this would mean in the analysis of strategies. If there already existed an exhaustive catalog of commonsense strategies, perhaps weighted by the frequency that they are referenced across the worlds' cultures, then this list could be sampled to assemble a representative set for analysis. As no such catalog exists, the first part of our efforts was to assemble a collection to use, with the characteristic of breadth as the primary aim.

One factor that greatly aided this collection process is the association between strategies and specific planning domains. While strategies are, in general, applicable across multiple domains, the phrases that people use to refer to strategies often are grounded in specific areas of pursuit. For example, the strategy of employing the spies of your enemy as double agents is easiest to reference in the language of international espionage (as it is done here), but the underlying strategy does not require that governments are the planning agents, that the spies are professionals, or that the information they obtain is political or military in nature. The same strategy may be equally useful in foiling the attempts of a sports team that is attempting to spy on the tactics and plays of their rival as it is in learning about adversarial countries. Yet this strategy seems to find a natural home within the domain of international espionage, presumably because the important actions, people, places, and things of this strategy are all clearly defined, easily referenced, and part of a broader commonsense understanding of this domain. The affinity of strategies to certain domains enables a domain-driven approach to their collection. By selecting first a set of domains, several different techniques can be employed to identify a collection of strategies that are associated with that domain in some way.

A first technique that can be used is to collect strategies that are referenced in existing texts that are nearly encyclopedic of strategies in their respective domains. Examples of these sorts of texts include Sun Tzu's *The Art of War* and Niccolo Machiavelli's *The Prince*, which describe a broad range of strategies in the domains of warfare and governance, respectively. What set these works apart from other non-fiction writing in a domain are three important features. First is the sheer quantity of unique strategies that are discussed; both of these texts, for example, explicitly discuss several dozen strategies. Second is the extremely high ratio of text in these works that focuses on these strategies to that which doesn't. Third is the degree to which the strategies that they contain have pervaded cultures throughout the world over time, such that few of the comments made by their authors strike the contemporary reader as particularly innovative—indeed, the strategies they discuss are now simply commonsense.

A second technique that can be used to collect strategies from a domain is directed interviewing of practitioners in the domain. While it is clear that experts in any given field (e.g., marketing strategists, politicians, musicians) use knowledge that is highly specific to their specialty, they tend to find ways of explaining their expertise to novices that rely more heavily on the commonsense knowledge that is shared between them. When interviewers who are domain novices engage domain experts in a conversation about the strategies that they employ, many experts will choose to base their explanations on the strategies that are naively attributed to their domain. The attentive interviewer can listen specifically for these references (sometimes ignoring the actual explanations) in order to collect the set of associated strategies.

A third technique for collecting strategies is to observe and interpret the planning and problem solving of other people as they are engaged in tasks within a domain. While more scientific observations of behavior strive to objectively gather data about the actual performance of subjects, the intent of interpretive observation is to gather the strategies that are subjectively recognized and reported by the *observers* as they are exposed to the behavior of other people. Interpretive observation of this sort may be most effective when the researcher describing the strategies is also a practitioner within the domain, allowing the researcher to make note of strategic planning behavior within the domain over extended periods of time.

While these three techniques lack many of the qualities that investigative researchers would like to have of their methods, they serve as adequate precursors to the more rigorous and repeatable methods that need to be developed as research in commonsense reasoning progresses. Each of these three techniques was employed to collect the strategies used in this investigation. The domains that were investigated were determined by the availability of the resources necessary to utilize these three techniques, namely access to texts that were encyclopedic of strategies within a domain or access to domain practitioners that could participate in directed interviews or interpretive observation. In all, ten different planning domains were explored. From each of these domains, dozens of strategies were collected, yielding a corpus of strategies consisting of 372 entries. Each strategy entry consisted of a few descriptive sentences and a short title so that it could be easily referenced. The ten domains are described briefly here, along with the number of strategies collected from each one and an example entry:

1.   Animal Behavior (37 strategies). An analysis of an introductory zoology text revealed the strategies that people attribute to animals to explain their behavior in an anthropomorphic manner. Example: *Cowbirds and Cuckoo birds abandon their eggs in the nests of other bird species that will raise the hatchlings along with their own offspring.*

2.   Business (62 strategies). Directed interviews with students of business administration and investment law produced a collection of strategies used in the business areas of marketing, production, and acquisitions. Example: *Companies that compete for repeat business from consumers gain customer loyalty by issuing redeemable points (e.g., frequent flyer miles) with each purchase.*

3.   Counting (20 strategies). Interpretive observation was used to identify the ways that people perform various object counting tasks, where variation is determined by characteristics of the situation. Example: *When counting identical things organized in a circle, people will mark their starting location to avoid over-counting.*

4.   Education (32 strategies). Directed interviews with former primary and secondary school teachers produced a set of strategies that focused on assessment, teaching methods, and techniques for motivating students. Example: *Occasionally delivering an unscheduled "pop quiz" encourages students to study materials in the duration between larger exams.*

5.   Immunology (21 strategies). An analysis of several introductory immunology textbooks produced a set of strategies that anthropomorphically describe the behavior of cells and viruses as goal-directed agents. Example: *One way that cells guard against the spread of viruses is to destroy themselves through programmed cell death when an infection is detected.*

6.   Machiavelli (60 strategies). Niccolo Machiavelli's sixteenth-century text *The Prince* was analyzed to collect a set of strategies to be used by government leaders to obtain and maintain their power. Example: *If established as a lord by the nobility of a territory, a new prince should work to become popular to establish a power base among the citizenry.*

7.   Performance (39 strategies). Directed interviews with concert pianists were used to collect the strategies that musicians use to manage their performance abilities. Example: *To avoid being derailed by distracting events during a performance, musicians will purposefully cause surprising distractions to occur during their practice sessions in order to become accustomed to them.*

8.   Relationships (22 strategies). Interpretive observation of dating couples was used to identify a set of strategies that people use to find, keep, and leave a loving partner. Example: *On a first date, a skeptical person may ask a friend to telephone halfway through to give them a chance to fabricate an emergency that requires them to leave.*

9.   Science (34 strategies). Directed interviews and interpretive observation were used to collect a set of strategies that research scientists use to advance their fields, pursue funding, and garner attention to their work. Example: *To moderate the difficulty of obtaining research funds, many researchers tie their work to some application domain that is backed by wealthy interests, such as the military or pharmaceutical companies.*

10.   Warfare (45 strategies). *The Art of War*, written by Chinese military strategist Sun Tzu around the fifth century BC, was analyzed to collect strategies pertaining to waging war against military adversaries. Example: *By leaving the enemy a means of retreat, the attacking army prevents the threat of extraordinary heroic defenses on the part of a desperate adversary.*

A preliminary investigation of planning behavior in the areas of board games (backgammon) and athletic sports (basketball) indicated that these areas would also be promising sources of strategies, particularly given the abundance of texts that are nearly encyclopedic of tactics for any particular type of game. However, in beginning to collect strategies from these areas it became evident that many of the strategies discussed were geared toward exploiting opportunities that exist within the constraints of the rules of a specific game. While in some cases these strategies were applicable across multiple game genres, strategies for exploiting game rules did not appear to have the same degree of cross-domain applicability as those collected from other domains. As this initial investigation of planning strategies was aimed at identifying representations that would be pervasive across planning tasks, the decision was made to focus attention on the 10 planning domains just listed, and to leave the study of game strategy for future research.

3.3   PRE-FORMAL STRATEGY REPRESENTATIONS

One of the first attempts to explore the computational role of strategies in human planning and problem solving was in the Computer Science dissertation of Gregg Collins at Yale University (1987). In this work, Collins identifies a set of two dozen strategies and describes how each would be applied in the competitive domain of American football. Many of these strategies could be referenced with common phrases (e.g., "hold the fort," "beat them to the punch," and "hedge your bets"). The importance of Collins' work was to recognize that each of these strategies could be defined by identifying its component parts. To decompose each of these strategies, Collins listed a set of statements about the world that would trigger the use of the strategy, along with a set of directives for the planning system.

For example, consider a strategy that Collins labeled "best available resource." The strategy is one that would be applied when a planner is devising a plan for acquiring resources over time, as the coach of a professional sports team would use to select new athletes from all of those that were available. While some sports teams acquire new players that best meet a current need, this strategy argues for selecting the best player available, regardless of whether they would best serve the role that is needed. For example, an American football coach might select an outstanding wide receiver player over a fairly good quarterback, even if it is the role of quarterback that is lacking on the current team roster. Collins offers a decomposition of this strategy as follows:

Best Available Resource:
    Given:
        A cyclical opportunity to acquire a resource.
        Some diversity in the specific roles played by resource items.
        Some way of comparing items across roles.
        A distribution of available resources that matches the distribution of
            needs over time.
        An acquisition plan based on filling roles as they become needed.
    Produce:
        A new acquisition plan in which the best available resource items are
            always selected, regardless of any analysis of immediate needs.

While there may be an interesting debate to be had regarding the inclusion of these particular statements in the definition of this strategy, Collins succeeds in showing that strategies are compositional in nature, where components can be defined using terms that are not specific to any one domain. In describing the strategy in abstract terms, Collins generalizes the definition of this strategy to one that covers a set of planning cases that are all analogous to this one case of selecting athletes for a sports team. As Collins notes, the same approach could be used over time by someone shopping for clothes, where desirable clothes that are on sale are preferred to clothes that fill a need in the collection of clothes that the shopper already possesses. There are few surface-level similarities between the domains of shopping for clothes and sports management, but Collins' definition of this strategy captures the essential common features of these two cases that cause us to recognize them as instances of exactly the same strategy.

As a knowledge structure to serve in computational models of cognition, this definition suffers greatest in its ambiguity. By writing this definition as a collection of English phrases instead of as a formal representation (i.e., logic statements, frame representation, or semantic net), its computational utility is greatly constrained. In its current form, it can be used neither to support the planning process when faced with a resource allocation problem, nor to make inferences about other people that are employing this strategy. To enable the possibility of using this strategy in these types of computation, it must be expressed in a formal manner. That is, it must be expressed in a language containing a set of controlled vocabulary terms (or symbols) coupled with a clearly defined syntax.

The manner in which Collins defined these strategies should not be viewed as an oversight. Indeed, Collins' definitions reflect a problem in the knowledge representation community that persists today. Simply put, no formal language has yet been developed that has a vocabulary that is broad enough to fully represent these strategies. The pursuit of such a language has yielded steady progress, both in the field of Artificial Intelligence planning (e.g., Gil & Blythe, 2000) and in the area of commonsense reasoning about human planning (e.g., Ortiz, 1999a), but these current efforts fall short in their ability to capture many of the subtleties that Collins refers to in the strategies that he defines. In the example given above, some of the problematic concepts include that of distributions of needs and available resources, cyclic opportunities, comparisons of items across roles, and analysis of immediate needs.

While the current lack of a rich formal language prohibits the expression of this strategy in a completely formal manner, two improvements on Collins' representations can be made to move them in the right direction. First, each of the references to specific concepts (such as the problematic list above) can be tagged in the text, marking it as a term that will be part of a complete formal language, or as a concept that must be further defined by those terms that are. Second, each of the English phrases that compose the definition can be written in a manner that reduces the use of these composite terms, favoring references to concepts that are believed to be non-reducible, or perhaps reducible in obvious ways. In applying these improvements to the example strategy above, a concept like *cyclic opportunities* could be tagged as a required part of some future formal language, although it may be more appropriate to change the definition such that it references two component parts of this concept, *opportunities* and *recurring events*.

The effect of these improvements is to produce definitions that are not entirely informal or formal, but somewhere in between. They are perhaps best described as *pre-formal* representations, in that they refer to representational elements that will have to be included in future formal representation languages. The aim of pre-formal representation is to make strong commitments to the inclusion of certain concepts in a representational vocabulary without making strong commitments toward selecting a specific lexical referent (or symbol) or their proper syntactic form. The "pre" in pre-formal is forward-looking to a time when our representation languages contain all of the notations necessary (perhaps as predicates in a first order predicate calculus) to express these definitions in a satisfactory formal manner.

This pre-formal approach, which improves upon Collins' representational forms, was used to represent the strategies described in this chapter. In using a pre-formal approach to create representations of the 372 strategies that were collected, the aim was to author exact definitions of these mental structures with the least amount of ambiguity. As in Collins' strategy definitions, the components of pre-formal representations of strategies generalize the definition to cover the full set of planning cases that are analogous to the one collected from a specific domain. The aim is to describe every planning situation that is an instance of the strategy (regardless of the domain in which it appears), and no others. Unlike the representations of Collins, which group definition phrases into "given" and "produce" categories, the definitions in the current work are each authored as a set of grammatical English sentences in the present tense. The person who is employing the strategy is referred to as "the planner" and others that play roles are "agents." In order to mark certain words or phrases as terms that will need to be part of any future formal language to represent these strategies, they are capitalized and italicized in the text of the pre-formal representation.

Three examples of the 372 pre-formal strategy representations are presented next. Among the entire set of strategy representations, a total of 8,844 words and phrases were tagged as concepts that will need to be expressible in a complete formal vocabulary, an average of 24 concepts for each pre-formal representation.

BUSINESS STRATEGY 59, MACARONI DEFENSE:

Prevent takeover by issuing bonds to be redeemed at high cost if a takeover occurs.
Representation: The planner has a *Leadership* role in an *Organization*, and *Envisions a threat* to goals of the *Organization* that a different agent will execute a plan that includes *Trade* of an *Amount of resources* of the agent for *Portions of ownership* that are a *Majority portion*. The planner executes a plan to *Make an offer* to a different agent where the *Offer requirement* is that the agent *Transfers resources* to the *Organization* of an *Amount of resources*, and the *Offered action* is that the planner will *Schedule* the *Transfer of resources* to the agent of an *Amount of resources* that is greater than in the *Offer requirement*, with the *Offer condition* that *If it is the case* that an *Arbitrary agent* executes the plan, that is the plan in the *Threat*, the *Organization* will *Enable* the agent in the offer to cause the *Organization* to *Reschedule* the *Offer action* with an *Amount of resources* that is greater. The planner then *Schedules a plan* to *Inform* the agent in the *Threat* of this offer after the *Successful execution* of the plan.

MACHIAVELLI STRATEGY 48, FOSTER THEN CRUSH ANIMOSITY TO IMPROVE RENOWN:

"For this reason many consider that a wise prince, when he has the opportunity, ought with craft to foster some animosity against himself, so that, having crushed it, his renown may rise higher."
Representation: The planner has a *Role* in a *Power relationship* over a *Community* and has the goal that a set of agents *Believe* that the planner is the *Best candidate* for this role. There exists an agent that has goals that are in *Goal conflict* with the planner, and that has had a *Planning failure* to achieve their goals with a *Cause* of *Lack of resources* or *Lack of agency*. The planner plans and executes for the goal that the agent *Believes* that there exists an *Opportunity* for this agent to achieve their goals, where no *Opportunity* exists. The planner then *Monitors* the agent for the *Start of execution* of plans to achieve the goals. When this occurs, the planner executes a plan to *Destroy* the agent, with the goal that the first set of agents have *Event knowledge* of the planner's execution.

WARFARE STRATEGY 44, GIVE FALSE INFORMATION TO ENEMY SPIES:

Secretly use enemy spies to send deceptive information to your enemy.
Representation: The planner has an *Adversarial relationship* with another agent. An agent has a *Cooperative relationship* with the agent to execute *Cooperative plans* that include *Informing* the agent of *Information* that involves the planner. The agent has the *False belief* that the planner has a *False belief* that the planner has a *Cooperative relationship* with the agent. The planner *Monitors* planning for *Adversarial plans* that have a *Threat* that the adversary agent will *Successfully execute* a *Counterplan*. In this case, the planner executes a plan to cause the agent to have a *False belief* about the *Adversarial plan*, and then *Enables* the *Cooperative plan* of this agent that includes *Informing*.

3.4   RECURRING STRATEGY PATTERNS

In electing not to use a predetermined strategy frame in these pre-formal representations, such as the "given" and "produce" frame seen in the work of Collins, it was possible to take a somewhat more empirical approach to the determination of such a frame. If there were any inherent structures in strategies, they would possibly appear as recurring patterns in the pre-formal style of representation that was used here. The finding was that, while no single generalization universally characterizes all strategies, there were a number of recurring structural features. In general, a frame was evident that separates a strategy into four components, corresponding to descriptions of a situation, a goal, an envisioned possibility, and a set of planning directives that may lead to the achievement of the goal.

The first two components that are evident in these strategy representations describe a state of the world where the planning agent might consider the application of the strategy. First, there is a description of the situation, which often refers to the types of relationships that the planner has with other people, the state of various plans and processes, and the actions that the planner or other people have already undertaken. Second, within the scope of the situation is a description of the goal of the planner, an apparently inherent structural component that all representations contained. If strategies are viewed as rules in a rule-based planning system, then it is these first two components that serve as the triggering conditions for further consideration of a strategy.

This further consideration is an active reasoning process, which is reflected in a third structural component that appears often, but not always. Here, the planning system determines if the strategy could be applicable to meet its goal by imagining something that isn't already a part of their knowledge—a possible future event, a consequence of an action that hasn't yet been taken that poses a threat or an opportunity, or an imagined world where some specific feature has changed. While it may be simpler to consider these envisioned possibilities as an additional part of a strategy's triggering conditions, they imply an active process of *envisionment* (as in de Kleer & Brown, 1984) as opposed to the more straightforward pattern matching that could be used to recognize an applicable situation and goal.

The strategy representations universally concluded with a set of planning directives that would move the planner closer to the goal. Sometimes these were simply abstract plans in the traditional sense, that is, a partially ordered set of actions whose execution would cause the attainment of the goal. More often, actions were combined with more algorithmic control instructions, such as a directive to adapt an existing plan in a particular way, to begin the process of monitoring for a specific event, or even to modify the planner's own view of what their goal actually is. In many cases, the actual plans to be executed were left completely unspecified, with directives that initiate the planning process itself for a newly added goal, possibly with the addition of certain planning and scheduling preferences or constraints.

In contrast to these four structural components that were generally included in strategy representations, little attempt was made to include a complete causal account of how the execution of a given strategy achieves the planner's goal. That is, the explanation of how a particular strategy works was not generally included in its representation. For example, the business strategy "Macaroni defense" described in the previous section includes a triggering situation, a goal of the planner, and a set of planning directives, but the causal chain that would lead from the execution of the planning directives to the achievement of the goal remains implicit. In the business case, it can be inferred that informing the acquiring company that the target company has outstanding bonds that must be paid in the event of a takeover will cause the acquiring company to abandon the takeover plan, as the target company's value would be undermined. The expectation is that rational planning agents would need to reason through this chain of causality in order to fully evaluate the appropriateness of this strategy for a given planning situation. The convention used in this project was to not account for this sort of causal reasoning in the representations of the strategies themselves, but to suggest that causal explanations of this sort might be generated when applying a strategy to a particular planning problem. Part of the rationale for this decision stems from the central goal in authoring exact strategy definitions, where the component representations describe every planning case that is an instance of a strategy and no others. By not including representations of the causal effects of strategies, the claim is made that this information does not further discriminate between positive and negative examples of strategy instances.

3.5   ORGANIZING REPRESENTATION TERMS

By tagging significant words and phrases in these pre-formal representations (with italics and capitalization), it was possible to extract from this set a list of references to all of the concepts that must be expressible in any complete formal language for strategic planning. To best make use of this list, an effort was made to turn this list into a controlled vocabulary—where a single term represents all of the synonymous occurrences of any given concept in the set of strategy representations. The resulting controlled vocabulary can then be further organized in a manner that best informs the development of a future formal language.

In the 372 representations, there were 8,844 instances where words and phrases were tagged as significant concepts. To develop a controlled vocabulary from this list, three steps were necessary. First, duplicate occurrences of any given lexical usage were removed. Second, a single lexical form was chosen for each set of forms that differed only in their inflection, combining multiple verb tenses or plural and singular forms into one. Third, the remaining forms were organized into groups of synonymous referents, where every member was associated with a single concept, from which one was selected as the controlled term for the concept. Of these three steps, it is this last step that most requires the consideration of the author of the original pre-formal representations. In most cases, the grouping of synonymous terms is an easy one; for example, the notion of a "*Potential motion*" is synonymous to a "*Possible motion.*" However, the decision of whether "*Free time*" is synonymous with an "*Unscheduled duration*" is one that requires a review of how these terms were used in the representation contexts in which they appear.

By controlling the vocabulary in this manner, the initial list of lexical forms was reduced to a vocabulary of 988 unique concepts. To better understand this list, an analysis was performed to determine the frequency in which each term was used within the 372 representations. In ordering the frequencies for each term from most used to least used, it was evident that a small percentage of terms were ubiquitous throughout the 372 representations, but the majority of terms were used only a handful of times. The rate of growth of new terms decreased over the course of the authoring process with the addition of each new representation, but remained positive at the end of this work.

With close to one thousand concepts in the vocabulary, an attempt was made to understand its scope by sorting and organizing this list into groups of associated terms. When the final list was compiled, it was evident that many of the terms referred to concepts that had previously been formalized as part of existing representational theories, or that are related to processes that have been the subject of cognitive modeling efforts in the past. Using these theories and processes to designate different groups, the 988 terms were organized into 48 representational areas, each of which is described briefly in this section.

The intent of presenting this list of representational areas here is to allow us to evaluate the current state of the field of knowledge representation as it relates reasoning about intentional behavior. Many of the first several representational areas in this list have previously received a great deal of attention in the field of commonsense reasoning. These areas, which include representations of time, space, and events, overlap with the breadth of representational areas that have been formalized to build models of qualitative reasoning in physical domains. In contrast, many areas presented here specifically support reasoning about the mental life of people—their goals, plans, and cognitive abilities—which have received comparably little attention as component representational theories. For these areas, this list aims at defining the scope of the research problem at hand as a set of component representational theories that will need to be developed into syntactically formal notations paired with appropriate inference mechanisms.

In reviewing the 48 representational areas that organize the terms used for strategy representation, some generalizations about their scope can be made. The first several areas (listings 1 through 8) are very similar to the sorts of representational theories that have been identified as fundamental to commonsense reasoning about physical systems (e.g., in Hayes, 1985). The second several areas (listings 9 through 22) introduce intentional agents, their plans and goals, and the roles they play in relationships with other agents. This second set is receiving increasingly more formal attention within the commonsense reasoning research community as these classes of representations are seen as critical to certain human–computer interaction technologies. The last half of this list (Items 23 through 48) describe the mental processes of people, including capacities for envisioning states, selecting plans, and mechanisms for executing plans in pursuit of their goals. While these areas have always been the interest of researchers that build computational models of cognitive processes, they have received very little attention as representational theories.

The 48 representational areas are as follows, and are elaborated further in chapter 6:

1.   Time (23 terms): Moments in time, including the current moment, compose durations that have ordering relationships with other moments and durations, and may have indefinite start times or end times. Examples: *Current moment, Immediately before, Variable duration.*

2.   States (18 terms): The world is described in states that change, are partially observable, and where portions of these descriptions define environment contexts. Examples: *Future state, Unchanged state, Persistent state.*

3.   Events (11 terms): Events are interpretations of states changing over time, and may occur multiple times with some frequency, and have temporal relationships with other events. Examples: *Concurrent event, Frequency, Periodic event.*

4.   Space (40 terms): Space is composed of locations in regions with boundary definitions, where locations can define paths through space with directionality and endpoints. Examples: *Boundary definition, Linear path, Direction.*

5.   Physical entities (24 terms): Physical objects and substances, including the physical bodies of agents, are composed of components, can have some state of configuration, and can contain or be attached to other things. Examples: *Substance, Contained thing, Configurable state.*

6.   Values and quantities (21 terms): Qualitative values and their quantifications may be defined by their ranges or in relationship to others, and can describe amounts in the world. Examples: *Variable amount, Unknown quantity, Directly proportional.*

7.   Classes and instances (21 terms): Things in the world are conceptualized as instances of class categories at various levels of abstraction,

with characteristics that are sometimes specified or unknown. Examples: *Class instance, Unknown class, Characteristic change.*

8.   Sets (31 terms): Things in the world can be conceptualized as being members of sets that have certain membership rules, and which may be ordered by applying some ordering principle. Examples: *Arbitrary member, Minority portion, Next in order.*

9.   Agents (22 terms): Agents are intentional things that have certain characteristics and roles, and are distinguished by their relationships to other agents. Examples: *Adversarial agent, Agent role, Unknown agent.*

10.   Agent relationships (18 terms): Relationships between agents are generally distinguished by who does the planning, who does the execution, and whose goals are in pursuit. Examples: *Competitive relationship, Persistent relationship, Symmetric relationship.*

11.   Communities and organizations (10 terms): Sets of agents may be described as organizations and communities, where agents have roles to play determined by the structure of these sets, and where collective processes and goals may exist. Examples: *Organizational goal, Top organizational role, Organizational agency.*

12.   Goals (27 terms): Goals of agents describe world states and events that are desired, and includes both states and events that are external to the planner as well as those that characterize desired internal mental states and processes. Examples: *Auxiliary goal, Knowledge goal, Shared goal.*

13.   Goal themes (6 terms): A potential reason that an agent may have a goal can be based on the role that the agent has in relationships and organizations, or because of a value that they hold. Examples: *Generous theme, Good person theme, Retaliation theme.*

14.   Plans (30 terms): The plans of agents are descriptions of behaviors that are imagined to achieve goals, and can be distinguished by the types of goals that they achieve or by how they are executed, and may be composed of other plans or only partially specified. Examples: *Adversarial plan, Repetitive plan, Shared plan.*

15.   Plan elements (30 terms): Plans are composed of subplans, including branches that are contingent on factors only known at the time of execution. They may have iterative or repetitive components, or include components that are absolutely required for a plan to succeed. Examples: *If–then, Iteration termination condition, Triggered start time.*

16.   Resources (16 terms): Classes of things that are reusable across a broad range of plans are resources, which are described in terms of their amount, and can be managed in a variety of ways. Examples: *Expended resource, Resource class, Transfer resource.*

17.   Abilities (13 terms): Ability is a characteristic of an agent that is predictive of the successfulness of their execution of a plan, and may be qualified at various degrees of skill. Examples: *Ability level, Competent ability, Unknown ability.*

18.   Activities (16 terms): Activities are shared plans and expectations about behavior where agents have roles and where events follow an expected script. Activities are also distinguished by whether they are part of an agent's set of normal behaviors. Examples: *Activity duration, Agent with role, Normal activities.*

19.   Communication acts (23 terms): Some abstract plans deal with transferring information to other agents, and include making and accepting offers, asking and answering questions, requesting permission, persuading and threatening. Examples: *Accept permission request, Offer condition, Threatened action.*

20.   Information acts (12 terms): Some types of beliefs, which may be true or false, can be externalized as information, sometimes encoded into some external physical thing or passed as signals. Examples: *False information, Observed signal, Decode information.*

21.   Agent interaction (21 terms): Many recognizable abstract patterns of events involve the interaction of agents, such as the assignment of ownership over a thing, a defense against an attack, and the execution of offered actions. Examples: *Accept candidate, Assist, Trade.*

22.   Physical interaction (13 terms): Many recognizable abstract patterns of events involve the interaction between agents and physical things, such as configuring a thing into a particular state and the use of something for its designed purpose. Examples: *Configure thing, Copy thing, Instrumental use.*

23.   Managing knowledge (30 terms): The knowledge that agents have is a set of beliefs that may be true or false based on certain justifications, and can be actively assumed true, affirmed, or disregarded entirely. Examples: *Assumption, Justification, Revealed false belief.*

24.   Similarity comparison (16 terms): Agents can reason about the similarity of different things using different similarity metrics, where analogies are similar only at an abstract level. Examples: *Class similarity, Similarity metric, Make analogy.*

25.   Memory retrieval (3 terms): Agents have a memory that they use to store information through a process of memorization, and may use memory aids and cues to facilitate retrieval. Examples: *Memory cue, Memory retrieval, Memorize.*

26.   Emotions (8 terms): Agents may experience a wide range of emotional responses based on their appraisal of situations, which defines their emotional state. Examples: *Anxiety emotion, Pride emotion, Emotion state.*

27.   Explanations (17 terms): Agents generate candidate explanations for causes in the world that are unknown, where preferences for certain classes of explanations are preferred. Examples: *Candidate explanation, Explanation preference, Explanation failure.*

28.   World envisionment (48 terms): Agents have the capacity to imagine states other than the current state, to predict what will happen

next or what has happened in the past, and to determine the feasibility of certain state transitions. Examples: *Causal chain, Envisioned event, Possible envisioned state.*

29.   Execution envisionment (23 terms): One mode of envisionment is that of imagining the execution of a plan for the purpose of predicting possible conflicts, execution failures, side effects, and the likelihood of successful execution. Examples: *Envisioned failure, Side effect, Imagine possible execution.*

30.   Causes of failure (31 terms): In attempting to explain failures of plans and reasoning, agents may employ a number of explanation patterns, such as explaining a scheduling failure by the lack of time, or a planning failure by a lack of resources. Examples: *False triggered monitor, Lack of ability, Successful execution of opposing competitive plan.*

31.   Managing expectations (8 terms): Envisionments about what will happen next constitute expectations, which can be validated or violated based on what actually occurs. Examples: *Expectation violation, Unexpected event, Remove expectation.*

32.   Other agent reasoning (8 terms): Envisionments about the planning and reasoning processes of other agents allow an agent to imagine what he would be thinking about if he were the other agent. Examples: *Guess expectation, Guess goal, Deduce other agent plan.*

33.   Threat detection (15 terms): By monitoring their own envisionments for states that violate goals, an agent can detect threats and track their realization. Examples: *Envisioned threat, Realized threat, Threat condition.*

34.   Goal management (27 terms): Agents actively manage the goals that they have, deciding when to add new goals, commence or suspend the pursuit of goals, modify or specify their goals in some way, or abandon them altogether. Examples: *Currently pursued goal, Goal prioritization, Suspend goal.*

35.   Planning modalities (17 terms): The selection of plans can be done in a variety of different ways, such as adapting old plans to current situations, collaboratively planning with other agents, and counterplanning against the envisioned plans of adversaries. Examples: *Adversarial planning, Auxiliary goal pursuit, Imagined world planning.*

36.   Planning goals (28 terms): The planning process is directed by abstract planning goals of an agent, which include goals of blocking threats, delaying events, enabling an action, preserving a precondition, or satisfying the goals of others. Examples: *Avoid action, Delay duration end, Maximize value.*

37.   Plan construction (30 terms): Agents construct new plans by specializing partial plans, adding and ordering subplans, and resolving planning problems when they arise. Examples: *Candidate plan, Planning failure, Planning preference.*

38.   Plan adaptation (18 terms): Existing plans can be adapted and modified by substituting values or agency, and by adding or removing subplans to achieve goals given the current situation. Examples: *Adaptation cost, Adaptation failure, Substitution adaptation.*

39.   Design (8 terms): One modality of planning is design, where the constructed plan is a description of a thing in the world within certain design constraints, and where the resulting things have a degree of adherence to this design. Examples: *Design adherence, Design failure, Designed use.*

40.   Decisions (38 terms): Agents are faced with choices that may have an effect on their goals, and must decide among options based on some selection criteria or by evaluating the envisioned consequences. Examples: *Best candidate, Decision justification, Preference.*

41.   Scheduling (22 terms): As agents select plans, they must be scheduled so that they are performed before deadlines and abide by other scheduling constraints. Plans may have scheduled start times and durations, or may be pending as the planner waits for the next opportunity for execution. Examples: *Deadline, Pending plan, Scheduling constraint.*

42.   Monitoring (18 terms): Agents monitor both states and events in the world and in their own reasoning processes for certain trigger conditions which may prompt the execution of a triggered action. Examples: *First monitor triggering, Monitoring duration, Monitor envisionment.*

43.   Execution modalities (11 terms): Plans can be executed in a variety of ways, including consecutively along with other plans, in a repetitive manner, and collaboratively along with other agents. Examples: *Concurrent execution, Continuous execution, Periodic execution.*

44.   Execution control (29 terms): A planner actively decides to begin the execution of a plan, and may then decide to suspend or terminate its execution. A suspended plan can later be resumed from the point at which the agent left off. Examples: *Execution delay, Suspend execution, Terminate activity.*

45.   Repetitive execution (16 terms): Some plans and subplans are executed iteratively for some number of times, or repetitively until some termination condition is achieved. Examples: *Current iteration, Iteration completion, Remaining repetition.*

46.   Plan following (30 terms): Agents track the progress of their plans as they execute them in order to recognize when deadlines are missed, preconditions are satisfied, and when they have successfully achieved the goal. Examples: *Achieve precondition, Miss deadline, Successfully executed plan.*

47.   Observation of execution (28 terms): Agents can track the execution of plans by other agents, evaluating the degree to which these executions adhere to performance descriptions known to the observing agent. Examples: *Observed execution, Assessment criteria, Performance encoding.*

48.   Body interaction (15 terms): The physical body of an agent translates intended actions into physical movements, and sometimes behaves in unintended ways. The body modifies the planner's knowledge through perception of the world around it, and by causing a sensation of execution. Examples: *Impaired agency, Nonconscious execution, Attend.*

3.6   THE THEORY OF MIND IN STRATEGY REPRESENTATIONS

One of the most challenging areas of research in the cognitive sciences has concerned the Theory of Mind, in reference to the abilities humans have to perceive and reason about their own mental states and the mental states of other people. Along with the inherent difficulties in investigating behavior that is largely unobservable, researchers in this area are required to be extremely interdisciplinary. Many research fields contribute evidence that influences our understanding of these human abilities, although the methods used to gather this evidence are diverse.

Researchers in developmental psychology largely choose to investigate the Theory of Mind as a set of abilities that emerge progressively in normal child development (Wellman & Lagattuta, 2000). By the last half of their second year, toddlers demonstrate an understanding of the role of intentionality in action, and that other people have subjective experiences. By the age of four and five, children comprehend and use vocabulary to refer to mental states such as thoughts, imaginations, and knowledge. As children advance into grade-school years and adulthood, there is a growing appreciation of people as active constructors and interpreters of knowledge, and awareness that others have ongoing thoughts. There is evidence that Theory of Mind capabilities continue to improve into the later adult years, even while non-social reasoning abilities begin to degrade (Happé, Brownell, & Winner, 1998).

In the research area of abnormal psychology, compelling cases have been made relating illnesses such as autism (Baron-Cohen, 2000) and schizophrenia (Corcoran, 2001) to deficits in Theory of Mind abilities. Neuropathology studies of stroke patients have provided evidence that Theory of Mind mechanisms may be localized in the brain (Happé, Brownell, & Winner, 1999), and ongoing functional neuroimaging studies continue to provide further evidence for localization (Frith & Frith, 2000).

In search of a more process-oriented understanding of Theory of Mind abilities, it is the philosophy community that has made the most contributions, proposing two classes of process theories that have been extensively debated. First, the Theory Theory hypothesizes that Theory of Mind abilities are computed by prediction and explanation mechanisms by employing representation-level knowledge about mental attitudes (Gopnik & Meltzoff, 1997; Nichols & Stich, 2002). The opposing view is that of Simulation Theory (Goldman, 2000), which argues that Theory of Mind abilities are computed by imagining that you are in the place of the other person, then inferring their mental states by monitoring the processing that is done by your own cognitive mechanisms. While some high-level process-oriented cognitive models have been proposed (e.g., Nichols & Stich, 2000), there are many unanswered questions that prohibit the creation of detailed, computational models of Theory of Mind abilities.

Most lacking in our theoretical understanding of Theory of Mind abilities is a description of the specific *contents* of the mental representations that are employed in this reasoning. There is general agreement that these representational elements must include concepts such as *beliefs* and *desires* (e.g., Harris, 1996), and these two concepts in particular have taken a privileged role in the cognitive models that have been proposed. A potential benefit of the focus on these concepts is that this representational area (beliefs, desires, intentionality) is among the very few where established axiomatic theories have been developed in the artificial intelligence community (Cohen & Levesque, 1990). Continued artificial intelligence progress in developing axioms for inference concerning mental states (e.g., Ortiz, 1999b) will greatly support the plausibility of the Theory Theory approach.

However, there is a general sense throughout the fields investigating Theory of Mind abilities that the contents of these representations go far beyond simple notions of beliefs and desires, particularly among developmental psychologists investigating the role that language plays in acquiring mental state concepts. Several studies have been conducted that investigate the linguistic environment of children for the presence of Theory of Mind related terms, where the conceptual scope is much more broadly construed. Dyer, Shatz, and Wellman (2000) best exemplifies the broad conceptual scope of this line of work, which compared the frequency of 455 mental state terms that appear in young children's storybooks. This list included 102 cognitive state terms (e.g., notice, wonder), 152 emotional state terms (e.g., nervous, boring), 84 desire and volition terms (e.g., hope, wish), and 117 moral evaluation and obligation terms (e.g., ought, terrible), where the complete list was compiled from previous language studies.

While these linguistic approaches help to broaden our conception of the scope of representational elements in Theory of Mind reasoning, many of the traditional concerns about the relationship between language and mental representation may apply. Particularly, there is no reason to believe that any full enumeration of mental state terms must parallel the breadth of concepts that are represented and manipulated by reasoning processes. The inherent subjectivity of these concepts may serve to restrict the introduction of new vocabulary in the lexicon as compared with other topics of discourse. Likewise, the remarkable creativity that is evident in human language use may mislead us to believe that there are representational distinctions between concepts that are in fact functionally synonymous. While these linguistic approaches have been persuasive in arguing for a broader scope of

Theory of Mind representations in our cognitive models, a new investigative methodology for concept enumeration would be useful.

The methodology of representational requirements analysis that is presented in this chapter is one that largely avoids the problems of natural language. The subject of this analysis, strategies, has proved to be particularly illustrative of the representational elements of the Theory of Mind, with over half of the component areas dealing specifically with reasoning processes.

There exists no infallible technique for identifying the contents of the mental representations used in reasoning. The approach described here, where our theoretical understanding of analogical reasoning is used as an investigative tool, relies heavily on our analytic abilities in describing the shared relational structure of analogous cases as much as on the validity of the structure-mapping theory itself. While one could rightly question the specific concepts chosen in the course of authoring pre-formal representations of 372 strategies, the scope of these concepts as a whole is difficult to dispute. The evidence provided by terms used in strategy representations suggests that the scope of mental representations that may support Theory of Mind abilities includes concepts for both the mental states of people and of the cognitive processes that they employ.

This evidence of process-oriented mental representations does not by itself provide support for either of the two prominent Theory of Mind theories (Theory Theory and Simulation Theory). However, it does have relevance to how proponents of these theories proceed to produce more detailed, even computational, process models of Theory of Mind abilities.

Proponents of the Theory Theory should view the latter half of these representation areas as a catalog of the component theories that will be necessary to specify a complete folk psychology, in much the same way that artificial intelligence researchers have attempted to define the component theories of naïve physics (Hayes, 1985). If the two endeavors are indeed similar, then terms like those that comprise the representational areas listed here will appear as notations (predicates or otherwise) in formal axiomatic theories that could drive deductive reasoning. Because breadth of component theories for a full folk psychology appears to be at least as rich as those in naïve physics, we would expect that the same methodological problems in specifying these theories would prohibit progress (see Davis, 1998). As folk psychology has received little attention within the artificial intelligence community as compared with naïve physics, few axiomatic theories exist today for the majority of the mental-process representational areas that are listed in this chapter.

While axiomatic theories have not been forthcoming, most of these mental-process representational areas have been extensively studied as cognitive behavior. Cognitive Science and Artificial Intelligence researchers have constructed an enormous number of computational models in support of our theoretical understandings, with one notable exception of Theory of

Mind reasoning itself (representational area 32, Other Agent Reasoning). For proponents of the Simulation Theory it is this set of computational models that will have to be employed in the off-line reasoning that allows a person to perform Theory of Mind tasks. Evidence of mental representations that correspond to these processes could suggest that there is a representational interface to support off-line reasoning. That is, terms like those in each of the representational areas could be viewed as a vocabulary for expressing inputs (e.g., commands and arguments) to these processes as well as their outputs (e.g., inferences). Further agreement within the cognitive modeling community concerning inputs and outputs could potentially promote the development of more modular computational theories, facilitating the integration of models that will be necessary in providing a process account of Simulation Theory, among others.

While the investigation of Theory of Mind representations may affect the theoretical debate only in the long run, its utility in linguistic studies of Theory of Mind language use may be more direct. Specifically, the identification of these representation areas—as well as the specific terms that appear in each—may be valuable in identifying a broader lexicon for use in the analysis of language data. For example, a process-oriented term such as suspend goal (from area 34, Goal Management) is expressible in a wide variety of ways in English, as in "Let's *put it off for now*" or "I'll *come back to it later*" where the direct object in both statements is the suspended goal. Compiling word and phrase lexicons for each of the terms in these representational areas could provide enough coverage over a language to facilitate more automated text analysis approaches, which in turn could greatly scale up the amount of linguistic data that could be analyzed.

3.7 CONCLUSIONS

A common criticism of artificial intelligence research in general is that proposed solutions often do not scale to the degree necessary to address large, real-world problems. In developing formal theories of commonsense knowledge, the problem is compounded by our uncertainty about the scale that would be required. That is, there are few methodologies available to researchers in this area that can be used to define the scope of the problem. Researchers interested in qualitative reasoning about physical systems have, in the past, proposed a number of long-term formalization efforts with only a vague sense of the scope of the work that remains (Hayes, 1985; Davis, 1998). The methodology of large-scale preformal representation that is described here can be seen as a tool to estimate the true scope of required representational theories to support commonsense reasoning.

The application of this methodology as it is described here has defined the scope of the representational requirements for reasoning in intentional domains—reasoning about the situations, plans, goals, and actions of intentional agents. The key to the success of the application of this methodology was the breadth of the subject of analysis, strategies. While other types of knowledge structures, such as narratives and explanations, may cover much of the same representational territory, the relative ease with which strategies could be collected and distinguished from each other greatly facilitated this approach. If this methodology is ever applied to other areas of commonsense reasoning (such as reasoning about physical systems), the first challenge would be to identify an appropriate knowledge structure of equal breadth within the area that also shares these characteristics.

This work has explored the utility of pre-formal representation for large-scale knowledge engineering, where definitions can be quickly authored as a set of tagged natural-language sentences. These pre-formal representations allow a knowledge engineer to make strong commitments concerning the semantic content of a representation without committing to a particular syntactic notation. The primary utility of the use of pre-formal representations in this work was to gather evidence for the concepts that will need to be expressible in future formal languages. However, an additional benefit to using this style of representation was that it enabled an authoring effort that is much larger in scale than typically seen in representation projects. In focusing on scale rather than syntactic formality, an understanding of the breadth of representational requirements was achieved with a tractable amount of knowledge representation effort.

This research has focused primarily on the concepts that must be expressible in future formalizations, but full formal theories of intentional action will also require the inclusion of all of the inference mechanisms that traditionally form the basis of automated commonsense reasoning systems. While many of the representational areas that were identified here have already received some amount of formal attention, there remain many areas that have not. The concepts that are grouped into each of these areas may provide a basis for evaluating the conceptual coverage of any proposed formal language, but the majority of the remaining work will involve authoring sets of axioms for each of these areas to drive the automated reasoning process. Representing strategies on a large scale has identified the scope of the remaining formalization work, providing investigators a roadmap for future commonsense reasoning research.

Strategy Representations

Three hundred and seventy two strategies from ten different planning domains were analyzed and represented in the course of this project. This chapter includes the full representation of each one of these strategies in its original form. Each strategy is described with a short phrase as a title, a sentence (usually an imperative) that describes the strategy as it pertains to the particular planning domain, and a pre-formal representation of the strategy that defines its abstract relational structure. Words and phrases in the representation that are meant to refer to significant planning concepts are capitalized and italicized, and each of these words and phrases is listed in chapter 5 along with a list of all of the strategies in which they appear.

It is certainly a strange thing to see the publication of large amounts of knowledge representation in the context of a scholarly work, but there are a number of reasons why including the full text of these representations is appropriate here. First, because these representations are pre-formal, constructed as a sort of stylized English, they have a level of readability that is much higher than formal representations. Second, they serve as the basis for the representational claims that I have made. By providing the complete evidence for these claims, the hope is to enable the research community to directly dispute these claims by proposing alternatives to the representational choices that I have made. Third, I find that each of these strategies is inherently interesting in a way that no previous represented knowledge has been, and hope that by reading them, you will experience at least part of the excitement that I felt in describing their deep representational structure.

The strategy representations are organized by the planning domains from which they came, which are presented in alphabetical order rather than the order in which they were studied. The original order in which these strategies were authored is as follows: education strategies 1–16, relationship strategies, performance strategies, Machiavelli's strategies, business strategies 1–46, counting strategies, warfare strategies, education strategies 17–32, science strategies, business strategies 47–62, immunology strategies, animal strategies. Examined in their original order, some trends can be observed. First, strategy representations authored early in the project tended to be somewhat shorter in length, where concepts in the strategies seem slightly more compositional than seen in later strategies. Second, later strategies include concepts that have fewer lexical variants than seen earlier, as concepts that are referred to over and over begin to take on a canonical form.

The modified ordering affords the reader a quick means of referencing a particular strategy by the first letter of the strategy's planning domain and the number of the strategy within the domain. For example, the first strategy in the collection (Send disrupting signals, an animal behavior strategy) can be referenced as A1, and the last strategy (Gather survivor stories, a warfare strategy) can be referenced as W45.

4.1 ANIMAL BEHAVIOR (37 STRATEGIES)

The first of the ten planning domains presented in this collection of strategies is animal behavior. Along with the strategies of the human immune system, this planning domain must be viewed as anthropomorphic. That is, we do not imagine that the animals themselves employ the strategies that are presented in this section as part of the process of planning their behavior. Instead, these strategies are ones that are the result of our attempts to make sense of these behaviors, to place them somewhere within our own human conceptual framework of intentionality, decision making, and plan execution.

The strategies that are represented in this section were collected primarily by combing an introductory text on the study of animal behavior (Benyus, 1998). As seen in textbooks describing the immune system, the author has taken extraordinary effort in emphasizing the systemic causes of the behavior that is viewed as strategic (in this case, the processes of evolution), but uses vocabulary to describe these behaviors that strongly imply human-style reasoning. Consider the following paragraph written to describe the first phase of adversarial conflicts between animals.

> The first step is to issue a warning in the form of a threat display. Dominants warn subordinates, "I am your superior"; residents warn intruders, "This property is mine"; and prey animals warn predators, "I am willing to defend myself and my offspring." The threat displays usually show off the animal's weaponry, size, strength, and willingness to back up its claim (even though it usually doesn't have to). Most conflicts end here. A searing glance may be enough to make an animal think twice, turn tail, and run. (Benyus, 1998, p. 73)

Janine Benyus, the author of this book, is certainly an artful wordsmith and educator. However, paragraphs like this one serve to remind us that our language may be somewhat impoverished in its utility to describe behavior of non-human systems. The semantics of phrases such as "issue a warning," "show off," and "willingness to back up its claim" may be impossible to define without a commitment to a model of reasoning that includes considerations of the mental states of others—a model that no self-respecting zoologist would like to attribute to all of the animals that exhibit the kind of behavior that Benyus is referring to.

In contrast to the nine other planning domains described in this chapter, these strategies of animal behavior are perhaps the broadest in their representational scope. Part of the reason for this is surely the breadth of types of goals that these strategies serve, whether it be gather up resources, defend against adversaries, attract partners in relationships, keep an organization working together, or to assist the ones that are cared for. For this reason, they serve as a good introduction to the entire collection, although they were the last of the 372 strategies that were authored in the course of this work.

A1. SEND DISRUPTING SIGNALS

Animal: Some moths produce calls that jam the sonar system of bats.

The planner has an *Adversarial relationship* with another agent, where the other agent is executing an *Adversarial plan* that includes the subgoal of *Achieving a knowledge goal* of the *Location* of the planner and a subplan to achieve this subgoal of *Making a decision* with *Deciding factors* that include *Information* that is *Observed signals* of a specific *Class*. The planner has the goal of *Blocking the execution* of the *Adversarial plan*. The planner executes a *Counterplan* that includes *Imagining a set* of *Signals* in the *Class* that are *Instantiations* of the class, and for which the planner envisions that *If it were the case* that the agent *Observed signals* that were these *Signals*, then the planner would have *False knowledge* of the *Location*. The planner *Monitors* for the execution of the *Adversarial plan*, and *In this event* the planner executes a plan to do *Signal production* of the set.

A2. SCAVENGE FOR FOOD

Animal: Vultures eat the remains of animals that were killed by other predators.

The planner has the goal of *Acquiring resources* that are *Possessed resources* of a different agent, and has a *Partial plan* that includes a *Precondition* that the agent is *Destroyed*. The planner has a *Planning failure* with a cause of *Unsatisfiable precondition*. The agent has an *Adversarial relationship* with other agents, and the planner *Envisions the possibility* that these other agents will execute *Adversarial plans* that include *Destroying* the agent. The planner executes a plan to *Monitor the execution* of plans executed by these other agents for *Adversarial plans* that include *Destroying the agent*, and *In this case* the planner executes a plan to *Wait until the event* that these agents have *Successfully executed* the *Adversarial plan*, and then execute the *Partial plan*.

A3. STORE FOOD AWAY FOR THE WINTER

Animal: Acorn woodpeckers bore small holes in dead trees to store acorns for the winter.

The planner is executing a *Continual plan* that includes the *Expenditure of resources* of a *Quantity* that is equal to the quantity of *Acquired resources* in an *Arbitrary duration*. The planner envisions an *Execution failure* in the subplan to *Acquire resources* with a cause of *Failed search* of the *Resources*. The planner *Replans* the plan that is the *Continual plan* with the

Auxiliary goal of Maximizing a value that is the Quantity of resources that are Acquired resources for an Arbitrary duration in the Continual plan. The planner then Monitors the execution of the subplan for Acquiring resources for the Execution failure, In which case the planner Suspends the continuous subplan and Imagines a duration that is where the End time is the Moment that the planner envisions that If it were the case that the planner executed the subplan, then it would be a Successful execution. The planner then Calculates a value that is the Quantity of Resources where the Calculation elements includes the Duration and the Quantity of Possessed resources of the planner. The planner then Modifies the plan that is the Continual plan with a Value replacement of the Quantity of Expended resources in the original subplan.

A4. HIDE YOUR WASTE TO AVOID DETECTION

Animal: Wild cats bury their feces in a single place to avoid detection by other animals.

The planner is executing a Continual plan that includes the Expenditure of resources, and this subplan has a Side effect of causing the Creation of a thing at a set of Locations. The planner has an Adversarial relationship with a different agent, and has the goal of Blocking the execution of a an Adversarial plan that includes Locating an agent, where the agent is the planner. The planner Adds the threat that If it were the case that the agent achieved a Knowledge goal of the Locations of the Things, then the subplan of Locating the agent will be Successfully executed. The planner Replans the plan that is the Continual plan with the Planning constraint that the Creation of the thing in the Side effect causes the Location of the thing to be a Location that the planner has an Envisioned likelihood that is a Low likelihood that the agent would Achieve the knowledge goal of the Location of the thing.

A5. RE-INGEST WASTE TO EXTRACT MORE NUTRIENTS

Animal: Rabbits and mice re-ingest their feces to extract more from their low-nutrient grass diet.

The planner has a Continual plan that includes Acquiring resources and Expending resources that has a Side effect of causing the Creation of a thing where the Thing is a Compositional thing that includes a Quantity of Resources. In Past planning the planner had a Rejected plan in the set of Candidate plans for Acquiring resources that included the Instrumental use of the set of Things. The planner envisions an Execution failure in the Continual plan in the subplan for Acquiring resources with a cause of Failed search. The planner Modifies the plan that is the Continual plan to Monitor the execution for this *Execution failure*, and in this case, *Substitute the subplan* of *Acquiring resources* for the *Rejected plan*.

A6.   RITUALIZED GROOMING

Animal: Daily preening practices of birds ensure that feathers are well oiled.

The planner is planning a *Continuous plan* and envisions a set of *Possible threats* enabled by a set of *Threat conditions* where the planner *Envisions the possibility* that these conditions are *Caused as Side effects* of the execution of the *Continuous plan*. The planner has set of *Partial plans* to *Prevent* the *Threat conditions*. The planner *Envisions the possibility* that *During the execution of the Continuous plan*, the *Threat conditions* will not be *Observed states* of the planner. The planner executes a plan to *Imagine a set* of *Durations* that are the *Envisioned durations* between the *Threat conditions* and the *Execution failures*, then *Orders the set* with an *Ordering principle* that advances *Durations* that are lesser. The planner then modifies the *Continuous plan* to include a *Periodical subplan* that includes the set of *Partial plans* and where the *Period* is less than the *First in the ordered set* of durations.

A7.   FUMIGATE PARASITES BY BATHING IN DIRT

Animal: Pheasants bathe in dirt to smother and dislodge parasites.

The planner has an *Adversarial relationship* with a set of agents that are executing *Adversarial plans* that have a *Satisfied precondition* that the *Location* of the *Agent* is an *Adjacent location* to the planner. The planner has the goal of *Blocking* the execution of the *Adversarial plan* by these agents. The planner envisions that *If it were the case* that the planner *Transferred locations* to a different *Location*, then the *Adjacent location* of the agents would be an *Unchanged state*. The planner executes a plan to *Find a location* in a *Region*, with the *Search condition* that the planner envisions that *If it were the case* that an agent in the set had a *Location* in the *Region*, then the agent would *Add the goal* to not have a *Location* in the *Region*. The planner then executes a plan to *Transfer locations* to the new *Location*.

A8.   APPLY A MUD PACK

Animal: Wallowing animals, like hippos, bathe in mud to protect their skin against parasites.

The planner has an *Adversarial relationship* with a set of agents that are executing *Adversarial plans* that have a *Satisfied precondition* that the

Location of the *Agent* is an *Adjacent location* to the planner. The planner has the goal of *Blocking* the execution of the *Adversarial plan* by these agents. There is a different *Region* where *Things* have *Locations* in the region that have *Characteristics*, and the planner envisions that *If it were the case* that the planner executed a plan that included the *Transfer of location* where the *Transfer path* included a location that was an *Adjacent location* to a *Thing* in the set, then the *Adjacent location* would be *Persistent* at *Future states* in the *Rest of the execution*. The planner envisions that *If it were the case* that the *Thing* had an *Adjacent location* to the planner, then the execution of the *Adversarial plan* of the agent would fail with a cause of *Blocked transfer of location*. The planner executes a plan to do *Path planning* of a *Transfer path* with the *Planning constraint* that each *Location* that is in the set of *Adjacent locations* of the planner is equal to the *Location* of a *Thing* for a *Moment* in the *Duration of the execution* of the *Transfer of location*.

A9.   DROP YOUR OLD SKIN BEHIND

Animal: Snakes shed their old skin to reveal an underlayer of new and clean cells.

The planner has *Possession* of a *Thing* and envisions an *Execution failure* in *Future plans* that include the *Instrumental use* of the thing with a cause of *Instrument failure* caused by a set of *Changed characteristics* of the thing. The planner envisions that *If it were the case* that the planner did not *Possess* the *Thing*, then the planner would execute an *Unintentional plan* that would cause the planner to *Create a thing* that has a *Class* that is equal to the original thing that would not have the set of *Characteristics* that are the *Changed characteristics*. The planner plans and executes to *Achieve the goal* that the planner does not *Possess* the *Thing*.

A10.   SLEEP WITH ONLY HALF OF YOUR BRAIN

Animal: Dolphins sleep with one eye open to allow half of their brain to shut down.

The planner has a *Cooperative relationship* with a different agent, and is doing *Cooperative planning* and has a *Partial plan* that is the *Cooperative plan*. The planner *Envisions a threat* that a *Required subplan Suspends* the execution of *Monitoring* for a *Duration*, where the *Monitoring* was for an *Event* that has an *Occurrence time* that is a *Moment* in the *Duration*. The planner *Replans the plan* that is the *Cooperative plan* with the *Scheduling constraint* that the *Duration* of the subplan in the *Cooperative plan* of the planner is a *Disjoint duration* of the *Duration* of the subplan in the *Cooperative plan* of the different agent. The planner then causes the different agent to do *Add the scheduling constraint* and *Replan*.

A11. CONTAGIOUS YAWNING AS A SIGNAL

Animal: High-ranking ostriches will start contagious yawning to signal safe sleeping times.

The planner has a *Leadership role* in an *Organization* where agents in the *Organization* execute a *Periodic plan* that includes an *Activity*. The planner envisions that the execution of the *Periodic plan* by these agents will have an *Execution failure* with a cause that the set of *Start times* of the *Periodic plans* are not equal. Agents in the organization are executing an *Unintentional plan* to *Monitor* the *Observed events* for the execution of an *Action* by a different agent, then the agent executes the *Action*. The planner executes a plan to cause the agents in the *Organization* to add an *Planning constraint* against plans that include the *Action*, and to *Monitor for self-execution* of the *Action* by the agent, and *In this event*, execute the *Periodic plan*. The planner then *Periodically schedules* the execution of the *Action*, and *Adds the threat* that *Executed plans* of a subset of agents in the organization are *Unobserved executions* of a different subset of agents.

A12. MEASURE THE THREAT

Animal: Antelope learn the distance required to outrun an attacking wild cat.

The planner is a member of a set of agents that have an *Adversarial relationship* with a different set of agents. Agents in the different set have *Previously executed* an *Adversarial plan*, and a subset of these plans have been *Successful executions*, and the *Rest of the set* has been *Failed executions* with a *Failure cause* of *Successfully executed counterplan* by an agent in the set of the planner. The planner *Envisions a future threat* that an agent in the set of adversaries will *Attempt the execution* of the *Adversarial plan* where the planner is the *Targeted adversary*, and has a *Counterplan* and *Envisionment failure* of the *Envisioned likelihood of success* of this plan. The planner executes a plan to *Imagine a set* two times, where the first is the set of *World state characteristics* that are in the set of *World states* at the *Start time* of the *Previously executed Adversarial plans* that were *Successfully executed*, and the second is that for the *Execution failures*. For each set, the planner *Removes from the set* the set of *World state characteristics* that are in the *Intersecting set* of the two sets. The planner then *Calculates a value* that is the *Envisioned likelihood of success* of the *Counterplan* with *Calculation elements* that include the *Similarity* of the *Envisioned world state characteristics* at the *Start time* of the *Adversarial plan* to the set *Imagined set* for a *Successfully executed Counterplan*, and a second for *Execution failures*.

A13. QUICK TURNS OUTMANEUVER A FASTER OPPONENT

Animal: Rabbits have superfast turning ability to outmaneuver their less agile enemies.

The planner has an *Adversarial relationship* with another agent that has an *Adversarial plan* that includes having a *Location* that is the *Location* of the planner. The planner has a *Counterplan* that includes the *Repetitive subplan* of *Transferring locations* where in *Subsequent repetitions* the *Location* is the location in a *Find a location* subplan. The planner envisions an *Execution failure* of the *Counterplan* with a *Failure cause* that the agent has *Knowledge* of a set of *Destination locations* in the *Counterplan* of the planner, and executes a plan to have one of these *Locations* at the *Moment* that the planner has the *Location*. The planner *Modifies the plan* that is the *Counterplan* to include the *Execution constraint* that the *Direction* between the *Location* in *Subsequent repetitions* is *Dissimilar*.

A14. DASH AND WAIT

Animal: Grouse birds escape predators by flying a short distance into a new hiding space.

The planner has an *Adversarial relationship* with a different agent that is *Executing a plan* that is an *Adversarial plan* where a subplan achieves a *Precondition* that the *Location* of the agent is the *Location* of the planner, and where this subplan includes *Locating an agent* where the agent is the planner. The planner has a *Planning failure* in *Counterplanning* with a cause of an *Unblockable plan* that is the *Locating an agent* subplan of the adversary. The planner *Envisions a duration* between the *Achievement of the precondition* in the *Adversarial plan* and the *Completion of execution* of the *Transferring location* to the *Location* of the planner. The planner *Modifies the plan* that is the *Counterplan* to be a *Repetitive plan*, where in each *Repetition* the planner *Finds a location* and *Transfers location* with the condition that the agent does not have *Knowledge* of the *Location* of the planner, and adds a *Scheduling constraint* that the *Start time* of the *Repetition* is the *Achievement of the precondition* and the *Deadline of execution* is the end of the *Duration*. The planner then *Adds the expectation* that the adversary will *Re-*

petitively execute the *Adversarial plan* for a *Quantity of repetitions*, and then *Terminate the execution*.

A15.   STAY CLOSE TO THE FORT

Animal: Prairie dogs stay close to their burrows to guard against a quick bird attack.

The planner has an *Adversarial relationship* with a set of agents that have an *Adversarial plan* that includes *Transferring locations* to the *Location* of the planner to *Achieve a precondition* of having the *Location* of the planner. The planner has a *Counterplan* that has the *Precondition* that the planner has a *Location* that is in a *Region*, where the planner has a *Planning failure* in *Other agent planning* for an *Arbitrary member of the set* of adversaries to *Achieve the precondition* that the agent has a *Location* in the *Region*. The planner has *Envisioned future plans* that include having a *Location* that is not in the *Region* for a *Duration*, and *Envisions a threat* that an agent in the set of adversaries will *Attempt the execution* of the *Adversarial plan* in this *Duration*, and that this would be a *Successful execution*, and where there is a *Duration* between the *Moment* that the planner *Observes the execution* of the *Adversarial plan* and the *End time* of the *Transferring locations* by the agent. The planner executes a plan to *Imagine a region* where *Locations* in the region have a *Condition* that the planner has an *Envisioned likelihood of success* of a *Transfer of locations* between the *Location* in the *Region* and an *Arbitrary location in the region* of the *Counterplan* with an *Execution constraint* that the *Execution duration* is less than the *Duration* in the *Threat*. The planner then adds the *Planning constraint* against *Future plans* that include *Locations* that are not in the *Imagined region*.

A16.   PLAY DEAD

Animal: A sparrow in the jaws a domestic cat will go limp to cause the cat to lay it down.

The planner has an *Adversarial relationship* with a different agent that has an *Adversarial plan* that includes a *Subgoal* of *Permanently blocking* the *Agency* of the planner. The agent has *Partially executed* the plan, and the planner envisions in *Future states* the subgoal will be an *Achieved subgoal*. The planner plans and executes to achieve the goal that the agent has the *False belief* that the *Subgoal* is an *Achieved subgoal* with a *Deadline* of the *Envisioned end time* of the *Subplan*, where the plan includes the *Suppression of actions* by the planner. The planner then does *Counterplanning* of the *Adversarial plan* with the *Planning constraint* that the *Termination of the execution* of the *Suppression of actions* plan *Immediately precedes* the *Start time* of the *Counterplan*.

A17. SHOW A STARTLING DISPLAY

Animal: A frilled lizard pops open an umbrella of skin around its jaws to scare off predators.

The planner has an *Adversarial relationship* with another agent, and envisions that the agent will *Successfully execute* an *Attack* on the planner in *Future events*. The planner envisions that *If it were the case* that the agent *Believed* that it had *False beliefs* of the *Execution abilities* of the planner, then the agent would *Replan*. The planner executes a plan to *Generate subplans* for an *Unknown goal* with the *Planning constraint* that the *Duration* of the subplan is less than the *Duration* between the *Current time* and the *Envisioned start time* of the execution of the *Attack* by the agent, and that the execution of the subplan is an *Observed execution* by the agent. The planner then *Iterates* through the set of subplans, and for each does *Other agent reasoning* with the goal of *Explaining the cause* of the execution of the subplan by the planner, and *In the condition* that there is an *Explanation failure*, the planner *Terminates the iteration*, and executes the subplan.

A18. HAVE FEATURES OF THE PREDATOR OR OF YOUR PREDATOR

Animal: Butterflies have spots that look like owl eyes to scare off predators.

The planner has an *Adversarial relationship* with another agent, and the other agent has an *Adversarial relationship* with a third agent. The third agent has an *Adversarial plan* against the other agent that includes an *Attack* on the agent, and the other agent has a *Counterplan* that includes *Monitoring* the *Observation of states* for the third agent, and *In this event* executing a plan that includes *Transfer locations*. This agent has an *Adversarial plan* with the planner that includes an *Attack* on planner with a *Precondition* that the *Location* of the planner is the *Location* of the agent. The planner has the goal of *Blocking the execution* of this plan. The planner executes a plan to *Achieve a knowledge goal* of the set of *Observable characteristics* of the third agent, then *Maximizes a value* that is the *Quantity* of *Observable characteristics* of the planner that are equal to those in the set. The planner then *Adds the expectation* that the *If it is the case* that the second agent *Attempts the execution* of the *Adversarial plan*, then there will be an *Execution failure* with a cause of a *Triggered monitoring* that is in the *Counterplan* of the other agent that is a *Falsely triggered monitoring* with a cause of *Similarity of characteristics* of the agent and the third agent.

A19.   PRETEND TO HAVE THE WEAPONS OF A PREDATOR

Animal: Wild and domestic cats spit and hiss like snakes when threatened.

The planner has an *Adversarial relationship* with another agent, and the other agent has an *Adversarial relationship* with a third agent. The third agent has an *Adversarial plan* against the other agent that includes the *Instrumental use* of a *Thing* in an *Attack* on the agent where the *Thing* is not in the set of *Observed states* of the other agent. This agent has an *Adversarial plan* with the planner that includes an *Attack* on the planner with a *Precondition* that the *Location* of the planner is the *Location* of the agent. The planner has the goal of *Blocking the execution* of this plan. The planner envisions that *If it were the case* that the other agent envisioned that the planner had an *Execution ability* of the *Adversarial plan* of the third agent, then this other agent will have an *Envisioned failure* of their *Adversarial plan* on the planner. The planner *Imagines a world* state where the planner had *Possession* of the *Thing* in the *Adversarial plan* of the third agent, and does *Imagined world planning* in this world state of a *Partial plan* to execute an *Attack* on the other agent with the *Planning constraints* that the plan includes the *Instrumental use* of the *Thing* and that the execution of the partial plan is an *Observable execution*. The planner then *Monitors* the execution of plans by the other agent for execution of the *Adversarial plan*, *In which case* the planner executes the *Partial plan*. The planner *Adds the expectation* that the *Adversarial plan* of the other agent will fail with a *Failure cause* of *Terminated execution* with a cause of *Envisioned failure*.

A20.   SACRIFICE PART OF YOURSELF TO ESCAPE

Animal: Some lizards will drop their tails and flee before a predator attacks the rest of them.

The planner has a *Physical body* that is *Composed thing*, and a *Partial plan* to cause one *Component of the thing* that is the body to be a *Detached component*. The planner has an *Adversarial relationship* with another agent, and has the goal to *Block the execution* of an *Adversarial plan* of this agent that includes *Iterating* over the set of *Components of the thing*. The planner has a *Planning failure* of a *Counterplan* that includes *Transferring locations* with a *Failure cause* of a *Missed deadline* by a *Duration*. The planner envisions that the *Duration* of the *Iteration* for the *Component of the thing* that is in the *Partial plan* is a *Greater duration* than the one in the *Failure cause*. The planner *Modifies the plan* that is the *Counterplan* by *Adding a subplan* at the *Start time* of the *Counterplan* that is the *Partial plan*.

A21. REDUCE INDIVIDUAL RISK BY JOINING A GROUP

Animal: Frigatebirds nest in colonies, where their eggs are less likely targets of predators.

The planner is a member of a set of agents that have an *Adversarial relationship* with a different agent. The different agent has an *Adversarial plan* that includes *Locating an agent* that is a member of the set of agents of the planner. The planner has a *Planning failure* of a *Counterplan* to this *Adversarial plan*. The planner envisions that *If it were the case* that *During the execution* of the *Adversarial plan*, the agent had *Knowledge* of the *Location* of a subset of agents in the set of the planner, then the agent would *Select from the set* with a *Selection criteria* of *Random choice*. The planner executes a plan to *Maximize a value* that is the *Quantity* of agents in the set that have *Locations* that are *Adjacent locations* to the *Location* of the planner.

A22. PARTNER WHEN MONITORING IS FULL TIME

Animal: Most birds partner with their mate so one can guard eggs while the second gathers food.

The planner is a member of a set of agents that are executing *Normal plans* that include *Acquiring resources* and *Expending resources* of an *Amount of resources* to *Achieve preservation goals*. The planner has a different goal, and has a *Planning failure* of a *Partial plan* that includes *Monitoring a thing* with a *Failure cause* of *Conflicting plans* between the *Partial plan* and the *Normal plans*. The planner envisions that there exists other agents in the set that have the different goal and that have the *Planning failure*. The planner then executes a plan to *Locate an agent* that has the different goal, then causes the agent to have a *Cooperative relationship* with the planner where the *Cooperative plan* of one agent includes the execution of the *Partial plan* and the *Cooperative plan* of the other agent is a *Modified plan* of the *Normal plans* with the *Plan modification* of *Replacing a quantity* that is the *Amount of resources* with an *Amount of resources* that is multiplied by two, and the *Additional subplan modification* of a subplan that includes *Transferring resources* equal to the *Amount of resources* to the other agent.

A23. SEARCH IN LARGE GROUPS THAT WILL SHARE FINDINGS

Animal: Birds flock together so that individual birds can profit from the findings of others.

The planner is a member of a set of agents that are executing *Normal plans* that include *Locating a thing* that is an *Instance of a class*. The planner envisions that the *Locations* of *Instances of the class* are *Spatially clustered*, and that *If it were the case* that the planner *Successfully executed* the *Locating a thing* subplan, then this would *Enable the execution* of the subplan for a different *Instance of the class*. The planner envisions that these *Normal plans* will have an *Execution failure* in this subplan with a *Failure cause* of an *Exorbitant search space*. The planner executes a plan to *Maximize a value* that is the *Quantity* of agents that have a *Cooperative relationship* with the planner, where the *Cooperative plan* includes the *Monitoring* for the *Successful execution* of the subplan, *In which case* the agent *Informs* the other agents of the *Location* of the *Thing*.

A24. MARK YOUR TERRITORY

Animal: Territorial animals leave scent markings to avoid unnecessary defensive actions.

The planner has a *Competitive relationship* with a set of agents, and has a *Competitive plan* that includes the *Monitoring of execution* of plans of the other agents for *Locations of execution* that are *Locations* in a *Region*, and *In this case* the execution of an *Attack* on the agent. A *Threat* exists that the execution of the *Attack* will be a *Failed execution* with a cause of a *Successfully executed counterplan*. The planner envisions that *If it were the case* that agents in the set had *Knowledge* of the *Competitive plan* of the planner, then a subset of the agents would add a *Planning preference* against plans that had a *Location of execution* in the *Region*. The planner executes a *Repetitive plan* to *Encode information* that is the *Competitive plan* of the planner and *Transfer locations* of the *Encoding of information* to a *Location* that is in the *Region*, where the *Location* is *Selected from the set* with a *Selection criteria* of *Random choice*.

A25. AVOID AGGRESSION BY BEHAVING PREDICTABLY

Animal: Subordinate pack animals avoid domination by behaving in a predictable manner.

The planner has a *Control relationship* under a different agent. The planner *Envisions the possibility* that *Future plans* will *Violate goals* of the different agent that are *Unknown goals* to the planner, and that this will cause the planner to execute an *Adversarial plan* against the planner. The planner has the goal of *Blocking the execution* of this *Adversarial plan*. The planner plans and executes to *Achieve the knowledge goal* of the set of *Expected normal plans* that the agent has of the planner, then adds a *Planning preference* against plans that are not in this set.

A26. KICK THE DOG

Animal: Subordinate pack animals divert aggression against dominate members to other outlets.

> The planner is in a *Control relationship* under a different agent. The planner has the goal of executing an *Attack* on the different agent, and has had a *Planning failure* to achieve this goal with a cause of *Bad consequences* in that the planner envisions that this execution will cause the agent to execute an *Adversarial plan* against the planner that violates *Preservation goals*. The planner has a *Control failure* in *Abandoning the goal*, and envisions that the planner will execute the attack in *Future states*. The planner executes a plan to *Modify the goal* so that the agent to be attacked is an *Unspecified agent*. The planner then executes a plan to *Locate an agent* that is not the agent in the *Control relationship*, and executes an *Attack* on this agent to *Achieve the goal*.

A27. ESTABLISH A DOMINANCE HIERARCHY

Animal: Chickens establish linear pecking order to avoid fighting.

> The planner has a *Leadership role* in an *Organization* of agents that have a *Competitive relationship* with each other, where the *Competitive goal* is to *Maximize a value* that is the *Quantity* of agents in the organization that are under the agent in a *Control relationship*. Agents in the organization have *Competitive plans* to *Achieve the goal* that include *Repetitively executing* a plan to execute *Adversarial plans* against different agents in the organization, where in each *Repetition* the subgoal is to cause a *Control relationship* over the agent in the *Repetition*. The planner envisions that the execution of these *Competitive plans* will *Disable the execution* of *Cooperative plans* to achieve *Organizational goals*. The planner executes a plan to *Order the set* of agents in the *Organization*, with an *Ordering principle* that advances agents where the planner envisions that have a greater *Envisioned likelihood of successful execution* of the *Competitive plan* against an *Arbitrary member of the set*. The planner then *Informs* the agents in the set of the *Ordered set*, and causes the agents to have a *Planning constraint* against the execution of *Competitive plan* against agents that are not the *Next most advanced in the ordered set*. The planner then *Monitors* for the execution of the *Competitive plan*, and *In this event If it is the case* that the plan is *Successfully executed*, the planner *Reorders the ordered set* to advance the agent executing the plan to the *Next most advanced in the ordered set* and the agent that was the target of the *Attack* to be the *Next least advanced in the ordered set*, then *Informs* agents in the *Organization* of the new *Ordered set*.

A28.   SHOW YOUR WEAPONS

Animal: Avoid conflicts with rivals by demonstrating your willingness and ability to fight.

> The planner is a member of a set of agents that have *Competitive relationships* with each other, and have *Competitive plans* that include executing an *Attack* on other agents in the set that include the *Instrumental use* of a *Thing* that is *Possessed* by the agent, and the goal of *Minimizing a value* that is the *Quantity* of agents that *Attempt the execution* of the *Competitive plan* on the agent. The planner has a *High envisioned likelihood* that *If it were the case* that agents from a subset of these agents *Attempted the execution* of the *Competitive plan*, then the execution would have an *Execution failure* with a cause of *Successful opposing competitive plan* that is executed by the planner. The planner envisions that *If it were the case* that the agents had *Knowledge* of the *Execution ability* of the planner of the *Competitive plan*, then the agents would *Make a planning decision* against the execution of the *Competitive plan*. The planner executes a plan to *Monitor the envisionment* of the planner for *Future states* where an agent from this subset *Attempts the execution* of the *Competitive plan*, and *In this event* the planner *Schedules* a plan to *Inform* the agent of the *Execution ability* of the planner of the *Competitive plan* with a *Deadline* of the *Envisioned moment* that is the *Start time* of the execution.

A29.   RITUALIZED FIGHT

Animal: Avoid serious damage by having a ritualized play fight to reveal who is stronger.

> The planner has a *Competitive relationship* with another agent, and each have *Competitive plans* that are *Opposing competitive plans* that include executing an *Attack* on the other agent. The planner has an *Envisionment failure* in envisioning the *Envisioned likelihood of success* of the *Adversarial plan* with a cause of *Unknown execution ability* of the *Opposing adversarial plan* by the other agent. A *Threat* to *Preservation goals* exists that *In the case that* the *Competitive plan* is *Successfully executed* by the other agent. The planner envisions that the other agent has an equal *Envisionment failure*. The planner executes a plan to *Make an offer* to the competitive agent where the *Offered action* is that the planner will *Modify the plan* that is the *Competitive plan* by adding the *Planning constraint* against subplans of the *Competitive plan* that *Violate goals* that are *Preservation goals* of the other agent, and then will execute the modified *Competitive plan*. The *Offer condition* is that the other agent *Modify the plan* that is the *Competitive plan* of the other agent with the same *Planning constraint*, and then execute the *Competitive plan*. In the case that the *Making an offer* is *Successfully executed*, the planner executes the *Offered action*, and

Achieves the knowledge goal of the *Envisioned likelihood of success* as a *High envisioned likelihood In the case that* the modified *Competitive plan* is *Successfully executed*, and *In the other case*, a *Low envisioned likelihood*.

A30. PLAY HARD TO GET

Animal: Female peacocks ignore potential mates to force them to display quality traits.

The planner is executing a subplan of *Locating an agent* that has the goal of having a *Cooperative relationship* with the planner with the *Condition* that the agent has an *Execution ability* of a *Cooperative plan*. The planner has *Located an agent* that is a *Candidate agent*, and the planner has an *Execution failure* to achieve the subgoal with a *Failure cause* of an *Unsatisfied knowledge goal* that is the *Condition*. The planner envisions that *If it were the case* that the agent had a *Low envisioned likelihood* that the agent will be the agent in the *Locating an agent* subplan of the planner, then this will cause the agent to plan and execute plans, and these plans will be *Observed executions* by the planner that will *Enable an envisionment* of the *Execution ability* of the agent of the *Cooperative plan*. The planner executes a plan to *Resume the execution* of the *Locating an agent subplan*, and to *Monitor the execution* of plans by the *Candidate agent*, and *In this event If it is the case* that the execution *Enables the envisionment*, then the planner *Makes a planning decision* whether the *Condition* is a *Satisfied condition*.

A31. ABANDON YOUR CHILDREN TO OTHERS

Animal: Cowbirds drop off their eggs in the nests of more responsible parents.

The planner has an *Assistive relationship* with another agent, where the *Assistive plan* is a *Continual plan* that *Satisfies goals* that are *Preservation goals* of the other agent. The planner has a *Planning failure* of a different goal with the *Failure cause* of *Conflicting plans* in that it *Requires* the *Termination of the plan* that is the *Assistive plan*, which will cause the *Violation of goals* that are *Preservation goals* of the other agent. A different agent has an *Assistive relationship* with a set of other agents and is executing *Assistive plans* at an *Execution location*. The planner envisions that *If it were the case* that this agent envisioned the *Violation of goals* that were *Preservation goals* of the agent in the *Assistive relationship* with the planner, then the agent would *Begin a relationship* that was an *Assistive relationship* with the agent. The planner executes a plan to cause the agent to have a *Location* that is the *Execution location*, and then *to Transfer locations* to a different location, *Terminate the relationship* that is the *Assistive relationship*, and add the

Planning constraint against plans where the planner envisions that the *Location* of the planner is equal to the *Location* of the agent in the old *Assistive relationship* or the agent that was executing *Assistive plans* at the *Execution location*, and *Add the expectation* that this agent executed a plan to *Begin the relationship* that is the *Assistive relationship*.

A32. SHELTER YOUR CHILDREN INSIDE OF YOU

Animal: Kangaroos return inside of their mothers after they are born to be protected.

The planner has an *Assistive relationship* with another agent, and the other agent has an *Adversarial relationship* with a third agent that has an *Adversarial plan* with a *Precondition* that the *Location* of the agent is equal to the location of the agent in the *Assistive relationship*. The *Assistive plan* of the planner includes execution of a *Counterplan* to the *Adversarial plan* that requires the *Location* of the planner be the *Location* of the adversarial agent. The planner has a *Planning failure* for a different goal with a *Failure cause* of an *Enabled threat* in that the plan *Requires* the *Transfer of location* with a *Origin location* that is the *Location* of the agent in the *Assistive relationship*, which *Enables the execution* of the *Adversarial plan* by the third agent. The planner *Modifies the plan* with the *Addition of a subplan* to cause the agent in the *Assistive relationship* to have a *Location* that is in the *Region* that is equal to the *Physical volume* of the agent.

A33. PRODUCE ENORMOUS QUANTITIES OF OFFSPRING

Animal: Frogs deposit staggering numbers of eggs to improve chances that a few will survive.

The planner has a plan that includes *Creating an agent* that is an *Instance of a class* and has the goal that the *Future plans* of this agent are *Successfully executed*. The planner envisions an *Execution failure* in this plan with a cause of a *High envisioned likelihood* of *Events* that will cause the agent to be *Destroyed* before the *Envisioned moment* of the *End time* of the execution of the *Future plans* by the agent. The planner envisions that *If it were the case* that a set of agents existed that were *Instances of a class*, then the *Combined envisioned likelihood* that the *Events* will cause every member of the set of agents to be *Destroyed* is a *Lesser likelihood*. The planner *Modifies the plan* to have a *Repetitive subplan* that is the subplan that includes *Creating an agent*, with a *Repetition termination condition* that the *Quantity* of *Repetitions* is greater than an *Unknown quantity*. The planner then *Monitors* for the *Execution failure*, and *In this case Explains the failure* as *Insufficient quantity* that is the *Unknown quantity*.

A34. MAKE A DISTRACTION

Animal: A male ostrich will cause a distraction while remaining family escapes a predator.

> The planner has an *Assistive relationship* with another agent, where both of the agents have an *Adversarial relationship* with a third agent. The third agent has an *Adversarial plan* that includes executing an *Attack*, with a *Precondition* that the *Execution location* of the plan is the *Location* of the target of the *Attack*. The planner *Envisions a threat* that the third agent will execute the *Adversarial plan* on the agent in the *Assistive relationship*. The assisted agent has a *Counterplan* that includes *Transferring locations* to a *Destination location* that is an *Unknown location* to the third agent. The planner envisions that *If it were the case* that the assisted agent executes the *Counterplan*, then it will be a *Failed execution* with a cause that the *Transfer of location* will be an *Observed execution* to the third agent, which will cause the agent to *Achieve the knowledge goal* of the *Destination location*. The planner does *Adversarial planning* of an *Adversarial plan* to *Violate preservation goals* of the third agent, with the *Planning preference* for plans that have *Counterplans* that *Require* that the agent *Attend* to *Execution* of the plan by the planner. The planner then *Monitors the plans* of the third agent for the execution of the *Adversarial plan* with the assisted agent as the target, and *In this event* the planner *Suspends the execution* of *Currently executed plans*, and executes the *Partial plan* that is the *Adversarial plan*.

A35. CARAVAN IN A LINE

Animal: Young shrews bite the tail ahead of them, allowing the mother to relocate.

> The planner has an *Assistive relationship* with a set of agents. The planner has the goal that the planner and the set of agents *Transfer locations* to a *Destination location*. The planner has a plan for *Transferring locations*, and envisions that *If it were the case* that an agent in the set *Attempted the execution* of the plan then there would be an *Execution failure* with a cause of *Poor execution ability*. The planner envisions that *If it were the case* that an agent in the set is *Physically attached* to a *Thing* that is *Transferring locations*, then in *Future states* the *Destination location* of the *Transferring locations* will be the *Location* of the agent. The planner executes a plan *Select from the set* two agents with a *Selection criteria* of *Random choice*, and to cause the *Remaining set* of agents to execute a plan to cause agents to be *Physically attached* to exactly two other agents in the set. Then the planner causes the first *Selected member* to execute a plan to be *Physically attached* to exactly one agent in the set, and the second *Selected member* to be *Physically attached* to exactly one agent in the set and to the planner.

The planner then *Monitors* for the *Successful execution* of the plans of the agents, then *Transfers location* to the *Destination location*.

A36. COMMUNAL DAY CARE

Animal: Penguins allow others to care for their offspring while they search for food.

The planner has a *Leadership role* in an *Organization* of agents that have *Assistive relationships* with a second set of agents, where the *Assistive plan* includes *Monitoring the execution* of plans by the assisted agents for executions for which they *Envision the possibility* that the execution will cause the *Violation of preservation goals* of these agents. Agents in the organization have *Planning failures* for other goals with a *Cause of failure* of *Conflicting plans* in that it *Requires* the *Termination of the plan* that is the *Assistive plan*. The planner executes a plan to cause the agents to *Modify the plan* that is the *Assistive plan* to *Substitute* the *Monitoring of the execution* of an agent for the *Monitoring* of the execution of a set of agents, then do *Planning* of a subplan to *Achieve the goal* that a different agent in the *Organization* of the planner *Begin the execution* of the *Assistive plan* with a target of the assisted agent of the agent, then do *Collaborative scheduling* of *Future plans* with the *Scheduling constraint* that *At all times* is the *Quantity* of agents in the *Organization* of the planner executing the *Assistive plan* be greater than one.

A37. PRETEND TO BE INJURED

Animal: Some birds lure predators from discovering nests by pretending to be injured.

The planner has an *Assistive relationship* with a second agent, and the two have an *Adversarial relationship* with a third agent. The third agent has an *Adversarial plan* that includes *Locating an agent*, and executing an *Attack* on the agent, where the *Execution location* is the *Location* of the agent. The planner has a *Counterplan* that includes *Transferring locations* with the *Scheduling constraint* that the *Start time* of the *Counterplan* be before the *Start time* of the *Attack*. The assisted agent does not have a *Counterplan*, and the planner envisions that *If it is the case* that the third agent executes the *Adversarial plan* and the agent in the *Locating an agent* subplan is the assisted agent, then the *Adversarial plan* of the agent will be *Successfully executed*. The planner has the goal of *Blocking the execution* of the *Adversarial plan* where the target is the assisted agent. The planner envisions that *If it were the case* that the third agent *Observed the execution* of the planner that was a *Failed execution* with a *Failure cause* of *Impaired agency* of the planner, then the third agent would *Add the expectation* that if the planner *Attempted the execution* of the *Counterplan*, then it would be a *Failed execution* with a cause of *Impaired agency* of the planner, and then execute the *Adversarial plan* where the planner is the *Located agent*. The planner executes a plan to *Monitor envisionment* for *Future states* where the third agent *Achieves the knowledge goal* of the *Location* of the assisted agent, and *In this case* executes a plan to *Transfer locations* to a *Location* where the *Direction* from the third agent to the assisted agent is an *Opposing direction* of the *Direction* from the third agent to the new *Location*, and where the planner envisions that *If it is the case* that the planner had the *Location*, then it would be an *Observed state* by the third agent. The planner then adds an *Execution constraint* against a subset of *Potential motions* of the *Physical body* of the planner, and *Attempts to execute* the *Counterplan*, and *Adds the expectation* that the *Counterplan* will be a *Failed execution* with a *Failure cause* of *Overconstrained execution*. *During the execution*, the planner *Monitors* the execution of the third agent for the *Start of execution* of the *Adversarial plan*, *In which case* the planner *Schedules* the execution of a plan to *Remove the execution constraint* and execute the *Counterplan* with a *Deadline* of the *Start time* of the *Attack*.

4.2 BUSINESS (62 STRATEGIES)

The second planning domain in this collection of strategies is of the business world. In many ways, the world of corporations and their consumers is often seen as an anthropomorphic domain as well, where companies are treated as individuals with goals, intentions, and plans of their own. In these representations, however, an attempt was made to describe companies as organizations of people who held these goals, intentions, and plans—some of which were their own and others of which are attributed to the organization as a whole. The effect of this representational choice was to highlight some of the characteristics that we attribute to organizations in general, including the structure of the professional relationships that hold between people, the organizational processes that are shared plans, and organizational agency that has a higher degree of ambiguity than conceptions of the agency of specific people.

The business strategies that are represented in this section could be divided roughly into three sections. The first set of strategies are those that generally address the management of the business process of a company, with a particular focus on reducing costs and improving quality for companies that produce some product. Many of these strategies were popularized by the writings of W. Edwards Demming, who was instrumental in rebuilding Japanese industry after the Second World War. These include approaches to quality management such as learning the expected variation of a production process to avoid over- or under-reacting to production failures, and empowering all workers with the ability to stop production when they judge it is appropriate. Mixed with these visionary strategies are the ones that corporations have used to survive in times economic hardship, such as moving production across national borders to take advantage of weaker labor regulations, or retaining only the employees that incur the least cost to the corporation in salary or benefits.

The second set of strategies addresses marketing goals, where corporations are competing for the attention and money of a consumer population. The breadth of creative marketing strategies seems to become most apparent in highly competitive, fast-paced market sectors where traditional marketing approaches may simply not be applicable. Accordingly, most of the strategies in this second set have been explored by software and computer hardware corporations over the last several years. When Apple Computer aggressively supported local user groups in the 1980s, they were nurturing a sense of loyalty among their niche consumers, an approach that certainly contributed to their survival as a computer manufacturer. When Netscape gave away their flagship product, an Internet web browser, at no cost to the consumer, they established a large user base that could sustain them as the Internet transitioned from a consumer curiosity to a legitimate marketplace. When Microsoft supported third-party developers of software products that worked only on their operating systems, they were able to turn any successful marketing done by these companies into immediate sales of their own.

The third set of strategies in this set are those that involve corporate mergers and acquisitions, and are perhaps among the best examples of strategies that have acquired persistent lexical referents, if only among stockbrokers and financial analysts. Here terms like *greenmail, hostile takeover, white knight, golden parachute, crown jewels, macaroni defense,* and *people pill* all refer to recurring patterns of behavior when the ownership or control of a corporation is at stake.

B1. MAKE YOUR SUPPLIERS DEPENDENT ON YOU

Business: Lower costs of materials by becoming a significant buyer for supplier.

> The planner is executing a *Continuous plan* that includes *Making a work product* and which *Expends resources*. The plan includes *Acquiring resources* through *Trade* with one of a set of other agents, each of whom do *Trade* with a set of agents that include the planner. The planner and the agents do *Trade* that includes *Negotiation* of the *Cost* of the *Resources* of the agent. The planner has the goal that this *Cost* is lower. The planner executes a plan to achieve the goal that the *Amount of resources* in the *Trade* is increased, and that the agent has the *Expectation* that the *Continuous plan* will *Continue indefinitely*. The planner then *Monitors* the *Executed plans* of the agent for plans that have *Preconditions* that the planner execute the *Continuous plan*. In this case, the planner plans and executes to cause the agent to *Envision the possibility* that the *Continuous plan* could *Terminate*. The planner then does *Negotiation* of the *Cost* of the *Resources* with the goal of having the *Cost* be lower.

B2. MAXIMIZE PRODUCTION TO AMORTIZE COSTS

Business: Run your factories around the clock to reduce per-unit costs.

> The planner is executing a *Continuous plan* that includes *Making a work product*. The plan includes *Expending resources* to *Enable* multiple *Making a work product* subplans, in addition to *Expending resources* in each *Making a work product* subplan. Each *Work product* has a *Quantity* that is the number of *Work products* made in an *Arbitrary duration* divided by the *Resources expended* in the duration. The planner has the goal that this cost is lower. The planner executes a plan to *Adapt* the *Continuous plan* to *Repetitively Make the work product* with the goal of *Maximizing* the *Number of repetitions* with the *Planning constraint* that the *Resources expended* to *Enable* the repetitions does not change.

B3.   HAVE BROAD PRODUCT SCOPE TO ENSURE PRODUCTION OPTIONS

Business: Manufacture many products to take advantage of supplier opportunities.

The planner is planning a *Continuous plan* to achieve a *Continuous goal* of *Acquiring resources* of a specific *Resource type*, and has a partial plan that includes *Making work products*, which itself includes *Expending resources* of a set of different *Resource types*. The partial plan includes *Acquiring these resources* by *Trade* with one of a set of other agents. The planner *Adds a subgoal* that the *Work products* be a *Diverse set*, where the *Similarity measure* is based on the *Resources expended* to produce the product in the *Making a work product* activity. The planner *Adds to the partial plan* the *Monitoring* of the *Trade* activities for *Opportunities* to *Acquire resources* at a low *Cost*. *In this event*, the planner *Takes the opportunity*, and *Adapts* the *Continuous plan* to *Make work products* in the set that use the *Resource*.

B4.   LEVERAGE THE DEMAND OF SOME PRODUCTS TO PRODUCE OTHERS

Business: Use other revenue to support production of something that lacks current demand.

The planner is *Successfully executing* a *Continuous plan* that includes the *Making of work products* and *Trade* of these *Work products* for *Resources*. The planner has the goal that the *Work product* that is produced be of a different type, and has an *Adapted plan*, but envisions an *Execution failure* in the *Adapted plan* caused by *Insufficient resources*, an *Additive effect* of *Negotiation* during *Trade* with a low *Cost*. The planner executes a plan to *Adapt* the *Continuous plan* so that the *Making of work products* includes both the previous and goal *Work product* at a specific *Proportion*. The value of the *Proportion* is set to be that of the *Limit of failure* in a *Quantitative envisionment* of *Trade* in the *Continuous plan*. The planner then *Monitors* the activity of *Negotiation* during *Trade* for changes in the *Cost*, and *Adapts* the *Proportion* based on a new *Quantitative envisionment*.

B5.   MOVE PRODUCTION TO WHERE THE LABOR IS CHEAPEST

Business: Move the factories to parts of the world with low costs of living.

The planner is executing a *Continuous plan* to achieve a goal of *Acquiring resources* that includes the *Employment* of agents to *Make a work product* in a specific *Location*, which requires *Payment* of resources. The planner has the goal that the *Amount* of the *Payment* be lower. The *Making of a work product* activity done by these agents requires a set of *Performance skills*. The location is in a *Populated region* that is *Populated* by agents that have this skill set. A set of other *Populated regions* exist that are also *Populated* by agents that have this skill set, and where the planner *Envisions* that the *Payment* in the *Employment* of these agents to do the same *Make a work product* is lower. The planner executes a plan to do *Plan adaptation* of the *Continuous plan* where the *Location* is in the *Populated region* with the lowest expected payment. The planner executes a plan to *Terminate the execution* of the previous *Continuous plan*, which includes *Terminating* the *Employment* of the agents. The planner then plans to achieve the *Startup preconditions* of the new *Continuous plan*, which includes the *Employment* of agents in the new region.

B6. MOVE PRODUCTION TO WHERE GOVERNMENT IS MOST FACILITATING

Business: Take advantage of tax incentives offered by municipalities or countries.

The planner is executing a *Continuous plan* to achieve a goal of *Acquiring resources* that includes *Making a work product* in a particular *Location*. The planner is a member of a *Community* that has an *Inclusion definition* that is based on *Location*. The *Community* has a set of *Execution rules*, and the planner plans with the goal of *Following these execution rules*. A subset of these rules *Require* the planner to *Expend resources* by *Transferring resources* to the *Community*. Other *Communities* exist that have different *Execution rules* that *Require* the planner to *Expend resources* of a lesser *Amount*. The planner executes a plan to do *Plan adaptation* of the *Continuous plan* where the *Location* is in the *Region* with a lower *Amount*. The planner executes a plan to *Terminate the execution* of the previous *Continuous plan*. The planner then plans to achieve the *Startup preconditions* of the new *Continuous plan* and *Begin its execution*.

B7. FAVOR RETAINING CHEAPER EMPLOYEES

Business: Lay off employees who have expensive benefit plans.

The planner is executing a *Continuous plan* to achieve a goal of *Acquiring resources* that includes the *Employment* of a set of agents. The planner *Expends resources* on the *Employees*, which may include their *Payment*, that equal a certain *Amount*. The planner has the goal of *Terminating* the *Employment* of a subset of the agents, and is doing planning that includes *Imagining a set*, which is the set of agents with *Employment* to be *Termi-*

nated. The planner adds a *Planning preference* to favor *Employees* where the *Amount* is high.

B8. REDUCE EMPLOYEE TURNOVER

Business: Retain highly skilled employees with special skills to reduce training costs.

The planner is executing a *Continuous plan* with the goal *Acquiring resources* that includes the *Employment* of a set of agents, where the *Employed work* requires *Performance ability*. The *Continuous plan* includes activities where agents that do not have the *Performance ability Learn the ability*. These activities require that the planner *Expend resources* or they are *Substituted* for the *Continuous plan Subplan* where the agent does the *Employed work*. The planner has the goal that the *Amount* of *Expended resources* for these activities is smaller or that the *Amount* of *Employed work* is greater over an *Arbitrary duration*. The planner plans and executes to cause the agents to have the goal that the *Employee role* is *Persistent*, and *Monitors* the *Executed plans* of agents for those that have *Inferred goals* to *Terminate* the *Employment* in an *Envisioned future state*. In these cases, the planner executes a plan to *Persuade* the agent to *Abandon the goal*.

B9. HIRE TEMPORARY EMPLOYEES

Business: Use temporary employees when labor needs are expected to fluctuate.

The planner is executing a *Continuous plan* for the goal of *Acquiring resources* that includes the *Employment* of agents for the execution of *Employed work*. The execution of the *Continuous plan* has *Added a subgoal* of executing an *Amount* of *Employed work* over a *Duration* that is greater than the amount that the planner envisions can be executed by the agent during this time. The planner envisions that after the *Duration* the amount of *Employed work* is *Unpredictable*. The planner has a plan for increasing the number of agents that have the *Employee role*. The planner envisions that the execution of this plan *Causes a threat* to the *Continuous plan* which is a *Realized threat* if the *Amount* of *Employed work* after the *Duration* is lower. The planner executes a plan to *Adapt the subplan* so that the *Candidates for the role* of *Employee* in the *Employment* have the *Expectation* that the employment will be *Terminated* if the *Amount* of *Employed work* is lower after the *Duration*.

B10.   JUST-IN-TIME MANUFACTURING

Business: Reduce costs of storage by having supplies delivered just in time.

The planner is planning a *Continuous plan*, and has a *Partial plan* that includes *Making a work product* at a specific *Location*, where this activity includes *Expending resources*. The plan includes the *Acquisition of these resources* from another agent, and the planner is *Scheduling* a *Periodic event* which is the *Transfer of possession* of these *Resources* to the *Location*. The planner envisions that there is a *Periodic duration* with a *Start time* of when the *Resources Change location* to the *Location* and with an *End time* of when the *Expending resources* occurs. The planner *Schedules* the *Periodic event* with the *Minimum value* for the *Duration*, and *Adds a threat* that there will be a *Plan failure* if the agent does not execute the *Transfer of possession* of the *Resources* to the *Location* at or before the *Start time*, with a cause of *Lack of resources*.

B11.   AVOID QUEUES IN THE ASSEMBLY LINE

Business: Streamline the assembly process so that each step produces at the same rate.

The planner is planning a *Continuous plan*, and has a *Partial plan* that includes the *Employment* of multiple agents, where the *Employed work* is the *Cooperative execution* of *Making a work product*. *Making a work product* is a *Compositional activity*, and the *Cooperative execution* is of the *Consecutive execution* type, where each execution is a *Subactivity*. The planner is doing the *Subdivision* of the activity. The planner *Adds a planning preference* to favor a set of *Subdivisions* where the *Duration* of all of the subdivisions is equal.

B12.   WARN YOUR SUPPLIERS

Business: Provide information to suppliers so they can anticipate production needs.

The planner is executing a *Continuous plan* that includes *Making a work product* at a *Location*, which itself includes *Expending resources*. The *Continuous plan* includes *Acquiring these resources* by *Transfer of possession* from another agent to the *Location*. In the planner's *Envisionment of the plan* there is the *Possibility* that the *Amount* of *Expended resources* for *Making a work product* over a *Duration* is greater than the *Amount* that is the *Expected amount* for the other agent in *Future durations* of the same size. The planner *Adds a threat* to the *Continuous plan* in the event that the other agent does not *Transfer possession* of *Resources*, caused by *Lack of preparedness*. The planner executes a plan to execute a *Concurrent continuous plan* to *Inform* the agent of the *Range* of *Amounts* of *Expended resources* in the planner's *Envisionment*.

B13.   LEARN THE EXPECTED VARIATION

Business: Study statistical variations to make decisions about changes to equipment.

> The planner is *Generating an explanation* for an *Execution failure* in a *Subplan* of a *Continuous plan* that included the *Instrumental use* of a *Physical object*. A *Candidate explanation* exists, which is that *Instrument failure* was the cause of the failure. The planner executes a plan to *Add an explanation candidate* of *Instrument variance*. The planner plans and executes to achieve the *Knowledge goal* of the *Envisioned likelihood* of an *Execution failure* in a *Plan* equal to the *Subplan* including the *Instrumental use* of a *Physical object* over an *Arbitrary duration*, with the *Envisionment constraint* against *Execution failures* involving *Agency* or *Instrument failure*. The planner then *Monitors* the execution of the *Continuous plan* for *Execution failures* that include the *Instrumental use* of the *Physical object* that have *Candidate explanations* of *Instrument failure*, in which case the planner *Calculates* the *Frequency* of *Execution failures* over a *Duration* with a *Start time* of the first *Execution failure* and end time of the latest one. After multiple *Monitoring occurrences*, the planner *Iterates* over the set of *Pending explanations* of *Execution failure*, and *On the condition that* the *Frequency* is greater than the *Envisioned likelihood*, *Selects* an *Explanation* for each that is the *Instrument failure* explanation, and the *Instrument variance* otherwise.

B14.   EMPOWER THE LINE WORKERS

Business: Allow assembly-line workers to stop processes when something goes wrong.

> The planner is executing a *Continuous plan* that includes the *Employment* of a set of agents where the *Employed work* is *Cooperative execution* of *Subactivities* of *Making a work product*. The *Cooperative execution* is of the type *Consecutive execution*, where each agent *Repetitively executes* the *Subactivity* that includes a *Work product* that is different in each *Repetition*, and where the agents are *Executing simultaneously*. The planner envisions

that an *Execution failure* of any *Subactivity* will cause the *Work product* of that activity to have *Properties* that are different from the *Properties* that are the *Preconditions* of a later *Subplan* of the *Continuous plan*. The planner *Envisions the possibility* that there are *Execution failures*, the agent executing the *Subplan* would believe that there was an *Execution failure*. The planner executes a plan to *Inform* the agents that the planner has the *Goal* that the agents execute the subplans while *Monitoring* for *Execution failures*, and *In this event* the agent should execute a plan to *Suspend the execution* of the *Continuous plan* and *Inform* the planner of the *Execution failure*.

B15. LISTEN TO EXPERIENCED WORKERS

Business: Capitalize on workers' experience in design and implementation decisions.

The planner is *Adapting* a *Continuous plan* that the planner had been executing that includes the *Employment* of a set of agents where the *Employed work* is *Making a work product*. The planner executes a plan to *Order* the set of agents, with an *Ordering principle* that advances agents with greater *Duration* of the *Employment*. The planner then *Imagines a set* which is a *Highest subset* of the agents in the ordered set. The planner then plans and executes to cause the agents in this subset to do *Collaborative planning* with the planner to *Adapt* the *Continuous plan*.

B16. MINIMIZE MANUFACTURED PRODUCT PARTS

Business: Design products with fewer parts to reduce defective product costs.

The planner is planning a *Continuous plan* and has a *Partial plan* that includes *Making a work product* where the *Work product* is *Compositional*. In the planner's envisionment, there is an *Envisioned likelihood* with a *High likelihood* value that *Any one in the set* of *Making a work product* activities will have an *Execution failure* where the cause is that a *Component* does not *Exist as designed*. The planner has the goal that this likelihood value is lower. The planner executes a plan to *Design* a new *Work product* by *Adapting the design* of the previous product with the *Design goal* of *Minimizing a value* where the value is the number of *Components* in the product. *On the condition that* this plan is *Successfully executed*, the planner *Adapts* the *Partial plan* by *Substituting* the new *Work product* for the previous one.

B17. DESIGN FOR DISTRIBUTION

Business: Design products to facilitate their easy packaging and distribution.

The planner is planning a *Continuous plan* and has a *Partial plan* that includes the *Making of a work product* in a *Location* followed by *Trade* of the *Work product* for *Resources* in a second *Location*. The planner has a *Subplan* for *Transferring the location* of the *Work product* to the second location. The subplan includes *Expending resources* to cause an effect which *Prevents* the *Destruction* of the *Work product* during the subplan. The planner has the goal that the *Amount of Expended resources* is lower. The planner executes a plan to *Design* a new *Work product* by *Adapting the design* of the previous product with the *Design goal* of *Minimizing a value* where the value is the *Amount* of *Resources expended* in the subplan for *Transferring the location*. On the condition that this plan is *Successfully executed*, the planner *Adapts* the *Partial plan* by *Substituting* the new *Work product* for the previous one.

B18. PROMOTE INTERNAL COMMUNICATION

Business: Foster communication across job responsibilities to avoid wasted work.

The planner is executing a *Continuous plan* that includes *Employment* of a set of agents where the *Employed work* is a *Component of the activity* of *Making a work product*. The agents each make *Execution decisions* based on *Envisionments of the past* and future *Envisionments* that include the *Employed work* of other agents. The planner envisions the *Possibility* that the *Envisionments* are *Wrong envisionments*, and that this causes *Execution decisions* that *Prevent a goal* of the planner to *Maximize a value* or *Minimize a value* in the *Execution* of the *Continuous plan*. The planner executes a plan to cause the agents to *Periodically execute* a plan to *Inform* the other agents of the their *Envisionments*.

B19. SELECT THE BEST SUPPLIERS

Business: Select the best suppliers to have the highest quality products.

The planner is planning and has a *Partial plan* that includes *Making a work product* followed by *Trade* with a set of agents of the *Work product*. The *Work product* is *Compositional*, and the planner has a *Partial subplan* to *Acquire objects* which are the *Subcomponents* of the *Work product* by *Trade* with an agent in a set of agents. An additional set of other agents have *Plans* that include *Making a work product* followed by *Trade*, where the *Work product* is *Similar*. The planner envisions that agents in *Trade* activity with the planner that follows the *Making of a work product* will *Make a planning decision* that includes *Selecting from a choice set* where the *Choice set* is the set of *Work products* in the plans of the planner and the other agents. The *Selection criteria* of the agents includes a *Comparison of characteristics* of the *Work product*. A *Threat* to the *Trade* subplan exists *In the event that* the agents' *Selected member of the set* is not the *Work product* of the planner. The planner executes a plan to *Order the set* of agents in the *Acquire objects* subplan where the *Ordering criteria* advances members based on *Other agent planning* where the other agents are the agents in the *Trade activity* and the *Planning* is *Comparison of characteristics*. The planner then *Specifies the subplan* to *Acquire objects* so that the agent in this subplan is the *First in the ordering*. Then the planner *Informs* the agents in the *Trade* activity of this *Executed plan*.

B20. CREATE A DEMAND WITH ADVERTISING

Business: Devote significant resources to advertising to develop product image.

The planner has the goal of *Acquiring resources* and has a plan that includes *Trade* of a set of *Work products* or *Work services* with an *Unspecified set of agents* that have the resource. The plan *Requires* the execution of plans by the agents in the set. A *Threat* to the plan exists *In the case that* the *Quantity* of agents that have the goal of executing these plans is less than an *Amount*. The planner executes a plan to *Identify a set of agents* where the goal of executing the plans is a *Compatible goal* to the agents' current set of goals. The planner then *Designs information* with the *Design criteria* that an *Envisionment* of executing an *Inform* action of the *Information* to *Any one in the set* of agents causes the agent to have the goal of executing the plan. The planner then executes a plan to *Inform* agents in the set of the *Information*.

B21. TARGET A NICHE GROUP OF BUYERS

Business: Target a niche market group so that you are their best choice.

The planner is planning to achieve the goal of *Acquiring resources* and has a *Partial plan* that includes *Making a work product* followed by *Trade* of the *Work product* for *Resources* with a set of agents. The planner envisions that a set of other agents will execute plans that include *Making a work product* followed by *Trade* with the same set, where the *Work products* are *Similar* to the *Work product* in the plan of the planner. The set is a *Diverse set*, with a *Similarity metric* based on a *Comparison* of goals. The planner envisions that this set of agents will *Make a planning decision* that includes *Selecting a choice* from the set of *Work products* of the planner and the other agents. A *Threat* exists that the *Quantity* of agents that *Select a choice* which is the *Work product* of the planner will be lower than some *Value*. The planner executes a plan to *Identify a subset of the agents* whose *Quantity* is greater than the *Value* and that is a *Similar set* based on the same *Similarity metric*. The planner then *Designs* the *Work product* with the *Design goal* of *Satisfying the goals* of the agents in the similar set. The planner then *Informs* the similar set of the execution of this plan.

B22. DIFFERENTIATE WITH CUSTOMER SERVICE

Business: Differentiate your product by providing great customer service.

The planner is planning to achieve the goal of *Acquiring resources* and has a *Partial plan* that includes *Making a work product* followed by *Trade* of the *Work product* for *Resources* with a set of agents. The planner envisions that a set of other agents will execute plans that include *Making a work product* followed by *Trade* with the same set, where the *Work products* are *Similar* to the *Work product* in the plan of the planner. The planner envisions that this set of agents will *Make a planning decision* that includes *Selecting a choice* from the set of agents that includes the planner, the *Selected choice* will be the agent with a *Work product* with which the agent does *Trade*. A *Threat* exists that the *Quantity* of agents that *Select a choice* which is the planner will be lower than some *Value*. The planner executes a plan to *Imagine a set* that is all of the *Subplans* that include *Activities* with *Activity roles* where the planner and the agents both *Have a role*. The planner then *Imagines a set* that is all of the *Analogous sets* where the role that the planner had is had by each one of the different agents that have *Work products*. The planner then *Replans* the *Subplans* that include the planner with the goal that the *Envisioned execution Satisfies execution goals* of the other agent at an *Amount* greater than the *Analogous subplans*. The planner then *Informs* the agents of this plan.

B23. CONFORM TO INDUSTRY STANDARDS

Business: Establish your company as the one that follows industry standards.

The planner has a *Competitive relationship* with a set of agents where the *Competitive goal* is that a different set of agents execute a plan that includes *Selecting a choice* that is a *Work product* of the planner and the *Choice set* is the set of all *Work products*. This different set of agents has plans that include the *Instrumental use* of the *Work product* which is the *Selected choice*. A *Precondition* of the *Instrumental use* is *Compatibility of features* between the *Work product* and other *Designed physical objects* that are in the *Possession* of these agents. The *Compatibility of features* include *Characteristics* that are *Specified classes*. The planner has a *Partial plan* that includes *Designing* an object that is the *Work product* and *Making the work product*. The planner adds a *Design constraint* to the *Design* subplan that the object have *Characteristics* that are the *Specified classes* where the planner envisions that the *Precondition* of *Compatibility of features* will be a *Satisfied precondition*. The planner then *Informs* these other agents that a *Threat* to their *Instrumental use* subplan exists if the *Precondition* can not be a *Satisfied precondition*, and then *Informs* these agents of the *Design constraint*.

B24.   BECOME THE STANDARD ESTABLISHER

Business: Work to be the company that establishes standards for the industry.

The planner has a *Competitive relationship* with a set of agents where the *Competitive goal* is that a different set of agents execute a plan that includes *Selecting a choice* that is a *Work product* of the planner *Work product* and the *Choice set* is the set of all *Work products*. This different set of agents has plans that include the *Instrumental use* of the *Work product* which is the *Selected choice*. The *Instrumental use* of *Work products* in the set have a *Precondition* of *Compatibility of features* between the *Work product* and other *Designed physical objects*. The planner has a *Partial plan* that includes the *Design* of an object which is the *Work product* and the *Making of the work product*. The planner executes a plan to achieve the goal that the *Precondition* of *Compatibility of features* is a *Satisfied precondition* when *Characteristics* of the *Work product* are *Specified classes*, where the plan includes the *Specification of a class* activity where the planner *Has a role* which is the *Actor*. The planner then *Designs* the object with the *Design constraint* that the *Work product* have the *Characteristics* that are the *Specified classes*. The planner then *Informs* these other agents that a *Threat* to their *Instrumental use* subplan exists, caused by an *Unsatisfied precondition*, caused by *Compatibility failure* of *Compatibility of features*, and then *Informs* these agents of the *Design constraint*.

B25.   SUPPORT USER GROUPS

Business: Improve customer loyalty by supporting user groups of your products.

The planner has a *Competitive relationship* with a set of agents where the *Competitive goal* is that a different set of agents execute a plan that includes *Selecting a choice* that is a *Work product* of the planner, the result of the planner's *Continual plan* that includes *Making a work product*, and the

Choice set is the set of all agent's *Work products*. This different set of agents have plans that include the *Instrumental use* of the *Work product*, and the planner envisions that *Threats* to this use exist that can be *Avoided* with *Information*. The planner executes a plan to achieve the goal that agents in this set are in a *Joined community* where the *Common element* is that an agent has plans that include the *Instrumental use* of the *Work product*. The planner then executes a plan to *Have a role* in a *Cooperative relationship* with the agents that are members of the *Community*, with the *Cooperative expectation* that agents in the community will *Select the choice* which is the planner's *Work product In the case that Future plans* include *Selecting a choice* where the *Choice set* includes *Work products* of the planner.

B26. ISSUE REDEEMABLE POINTS

Business: Give customers frequent flyer miles or purchase credits.

The planner has a *Competitive relationship* with a set of agents where the *Competitive goal* is that a different set of agents execute a plan that includes *Selecting a choice* that is a *Work product* of the planner, the result of the planner's *Continual plan* that includes *Making a work product*, and the *Choice set* is the set of all agent's *Work products*. The planner envisions that agents that *Select the choice* that is the planner's *Work product* will later execute plans that include *Selecting a choice* from a choice set that includes a different *Work product* of the planner. The planner adapts the *Continuous plan* to *Make an offer* to each agent that executes a plan that includes *Selecting a choice* which is the *Work product* of the planner where the *Offer* is to *Transfer possession* of a *Work product* or to execute a *Work service* for the agent *On the condition* that the agent *Select the choice* which is the *Work product* of the planner in the execution of future plans that include *Selecting a choice* that includes the *Work product of the planner*.

B27. HAVE PERIODIC UPGRADES

Business: Offer new feature upgrades to customers who have bought your product.

The planner is planning a *Continuous plan* that includes *Making a work product* followed by *Trade* with a set of agents for the goal of *Acquiring resources*. The planner envisions that the agents will execute plans that include the *Instrumental use* of the *Work product* to achieve a set of goals, and that this *Instrumental use* includes a set of *Designed uses* that are *Partial plans*. The planner has a plan that includes *Changing an object* that is the *Work product* that would cause the *Quantity* of *Designed uses* in the set to increase, which would *Enable* the execution of plans by the agents that would *Achieve goals* of the agents. The planner executes a plan to *Periodically schedule* the execution of a plan that includes *Making an offer* to the set of agents that have executed the *Trade* activity with the planner for the *Work product*, where *Offering* is that the planner will execute a plan that includes the *Partial plan* of *Changing the object* that is the *Work product* in the *Trade*, *On the condition that* the agents *Transfer resources* to the planner. After the execution of the *Periodic plan*, the planner *Adds the goal* that the planner has a new *Partial plan* that includes *Changing an object* which is the new *Work product* that would cause the *Quantity* of *Designed uses* in its set to increase, with a *Deadline* of the *Moment* of the *Next scheduled period plan*.

B28. SUPPORT THIRD-PARTY DEVELOPERS

Business: Support third-party product developers that work with your product only.

The planner has a *Competitive relationship* with a set of agents where the *Competitive goal* is that a different set of agents execute a plan that includes *Selecting a choice* that is a *Work product* of the planner, the result of the planner's *Continual plan* that includes *Making a work product*, and the *Choice set* is the set of all agent's *Work products*. Another set of agents have plans that include *Trade* with the same agents that make the selection where the trade is of a *Work product* with a *Design* that is the result of *Designing* by these agents. This *Work product Enables* the execution of plans that include the *Instrumental use* of a member of the set of *Work products* that includes the planner's product. The planner executes a plan to cause agents in this other set to do *Designing* of the *Work product* with the *Design constraint* that their *Work product Enables* the execution of plans that include the *Instrumental use* of the *Work product* of the planner, and does not *Enable* the execution of plans that include *Work products* in the *Remaining set*. The planner then *Informs* the agents that are *Selecting a choice* of the *Design*.

B29. ENCOURAGE SPECIFIC CUSTOMER NEEDS

Business: Develop a customer need for which your products are the only solution.

The planner has a *Competitive relationship* with a set of agents where the *Competitive goal* is that a different set of agents execute a plan that includes *Selecting a choice* that is a *Work product* of the planner, the result of the planner's *Continual plan* that includes *Making a work product*, and the

Choice set is the set of all agents' *Work products*. The planner envisions that this different set of agents will execute plans that include the *Instrumental use* of a work product that is the *Selected choice*. The planner executes a plan to *Iterate* through the *Choice set*, and for each do *Envisionment* of execution of plans that include its *Instrumental use* with the *Envisionment goal* of *Identifying the goals* which is a set that the agents have. The planner then *Imagines a set* which is the *Disjoints* of the goals for the planner's *Work product* and the *Conjunction* of all remaining sets. In the case that the *Disjoint set* is non-empty, then the planner executes a plan to cause these agents to do *Prioritization of goals* where goals in the *Disjoint set* have a *Higher priority* than the other goals.

B30.   GIVE AWAY YOUR PRODUCTS

Business: Give away your products for free to establish a large customer base.

The planner has the goal of *Acquiring resources* and has a *Partial plan* that includes *Trade* of two *Work products* to two different sets of agents. The first set of agents are *Executing plans* that include the *Instrumental use* of a *Work product* from a set of products that includes one of the products of the planner. The second set of agents are *Executing plans* that include *Selecting a choice* where the *Choice set* is a set of *Work products* that include the second product of the planner. The *Selection criteria* includes the *Quantity* of *Executed plans* where the *Agency* is that of agents in the first set, and where the *Work product* in this execution is one that has *Characteristics* that are *Compatible characteristics* with the *Characteristics* of the *Selected choice*. The planner *Modifies the partial plan* so that *Transfer of possession* is *Substituted* for *Trade* with the first set of agents, and to *Increase the amount* which is the *Amount of resources* in the *Trade offer* with the second set of agents by the *Amount of resources* in the first *Trade offer*.

B31.   SELL AS PART OF A BUNDLE

Business: Sell your product to a company that will bundle it with their own.

The planner has the goal of *Acquiring resources* and has a *Partial plan* that includes *Trade* of a *Work product* for *Resources*. A set of agents have plans that include the *Instrumental use* of a set of *Work products* that include *Instances of a class* where the *Class* is that of the *Work product* of the planner. The other products in the set are the *Work products* of a different set of agents. The planner executes a plan to have a *Cooperative relationship* with these other agents, with a *Cooperative plan* that these other agents execute a *Trade* with the agents doing instrumental use of a set including the *Work product* of the planner and of the cooperating agent, and where the *Cooperating agent Transfers resources* to the planner, and the planner *Transfers possession* of the *Work product* to the agent.

B32. SELL WITH SWEEPSTAKES

Business: Give incentive for buying your product with contests or sweepstakes.

The planner has a *Competitive relationship* with a set of agents where the *Competitive goal* is that a different set of agents execute a plan that includes *Selecting a choice* that is a *Work product* of the planner, the result of the planner's *Continual plan* that includes *Making a work product*, and the *Choice set* is the set of all agents' *Work products*. This different set of agents have goals that are *Satisfied* by the *Expenditure of resources* of an *Amount* that is greater than the amount that is the *Expected amount* of *Expended resources* in *Normal plans* to achieve goals for these agents. The planner has an *Amount of resources* that is greater than this amount. The planner *Modifies* the *Continual plan* with the goal that the *Execution* of the *Trade activity* causes the agent to become a *Candidate* in an *Agent selection* where the *Selection criteria* is *Random chance* and where the *Selected agent* is the receiving agent of a *Transfer of possession* activity by the planner of an *Amount of resources* that is equal to the amount in the expenditure. The planner then *Informs* the agents of this plan modification.

B33. MARKET WITH AN UNRELATED BUSINESS

Business: Partner on sales campaigns with an unrelated business to gain new markets.

The planner has the goal to *Acquire resources* and has a *Partial plan* that includes *Trade* of a *Work product* for *Resources*, where the *Work product* is the result of *Making a work product* executed by the planner. The planner is planning to *Achieve a precondition* of this plan that some *Unspecified agent Accepts a role* in the *Trade*, where the agent has *Resources* and has the goal of *Possessing* the *Work product*. There exists other agents that are *Successfully executing Continuous plans* that include *Making a work product* and *Trade* of the *Work product* for the goal of *Acquiring resources*, where the *Work product* is *Dissimilar* to the one of the planner. The planner plans and executes to achieve the goal that the planner has a *Cooperative relationship* with the agents with the other *Work product*, where the *Cooperative plan* is that the other agents *Make a trade offer* to the agents that they trade with, where the agent in the *Trade* is the planner and the *Trade offer* is the *Work product* of the planner.

B34. PARTNER WITH COMPLEMENTARY BUSINESSES

Business: Create agreements so that complementary businesses sell your product with theirs.

> The planner has the goal of *Acquiring resources* and has a *Partial continuous plan* that includes *Trade* with *Unspecified agents* of a *Work product*. The planner *Imagines an agent* which is the agent in the *Trade* that has a plan that includes the *Instrumental use* of an *Instance of a class* of *Work product* for which the product of the planner is also a *Class instance*, and this is the cause of the subgoal to do *Trade* with the planner. The plan also includes *Preconditions* that are met by *Expending resources* in *Trade* with a set of agents other than the planner. The planner executes a plan to *Locate agents* that are executing *Continuous plans* that include *Trade* with a set of agents where the *Trade offer* is not an *Instance of the class*. The planner then plans to achieve the goal of having a *Cooperative relationship* with agents in this set where the *Cooperative plan* is that these agents execute a *Subplan* after executing the *Trade* activity in their *Continuous plan*, where the *Subplan* is to *Make a trade offer* that is the *Work product* of the planner, and *In the case that* the other agent *Accepts a role* in the *Trade*, the *Trade* is executed by the planner.

B35. INCREASE THE MARKET SIZE

Business: Work to grow the entire market so that your fixed market share increases.

> The planner has a *Competitive relationship* with a set of agents where the *Competitive goal* is that a different set of agents execute a plan that includes *Selecting a choice* that is a *Work product* of the planner, the result of the planner's *Continual plan* that includes *Making a work product*, and the *Choice set* is the set of all agents' *Work products*. A *Proportion* of the set of agents doing the selection have a *Selected choice* of the *Work product* of the planner, and this *Proportion* is *Constant across the continuous execution*. The planner envisions that *If it were the case* that the *Quantity* of agents in the set were greater, the *Proportion* would be the same. The planner *Adds the goal* that the number of agents in the set is greater.

B36. TURN YOUR BUYERS INTO SELLERS

Business: Work to have the buyers of your products market them to others.

> The planner has the goal of *Acquiring resources* and has a *Partial plan* that includes the *Making of a work product* followed by *Trade* with a set of agents of the *Work product* for *Resources*. The set of agents is an *Unspecified set*,

and the *Quantity* of unspecified agents in the set is greater than the *Number of iterations* that the planner can execute a *Subplan* that includes *Locating an agent* which is an agent that has the goal of *Having a role* in the *Trade* activity. The planner *Adds to the partial plan* such that the *Trade* activity includes *Instilling a goal* in the other agent that they *Locate an agent* that has the goal of *Having a role* in the *Trade* activity.

B37. SELL PRODUCTS THAT REQUIRE MULTIPLE BUYERS

Business: Sell products that are to be used with other people who have bought the product.

The planner is planning a *Continuous plan* that includes the *Making of a work product* followed by *Trade* of the *Work product* with a set of agents for *Resources*. The planner *Imagines an agent* that is an agent in the *Trade* that has the goal of *Possessing* the *Work product* as a *Precondition* for its *Instrumental use* in plans of the agent. The planner does *Designing* of the *Work product* with the *Design goal* that the *Designed use* is one of *Instrumental use* in a *Cooperative plan*, where *Cooperating agents* execute these plans with different instances of the *Work product*, and where planning that includes *Substituting* one of the *Work products* of the planner for another *Work product* will cause the *Plan execution to fail* with a *Cause of failure* being *Incompatibility of characteristics* between the two *Work products*.

B38. FACILITATE THE FINANCES OF BUYING

Business: Provide financing and leasing plans to expand possible customer base.

The planner is executing a *Continuous plan* that includes *Trade* of a *Work product* for *Resources* to an *Unspecified set of agents*. The planner has the *Expectation* that the *Quantity* of agents that have the goal of *Having a role* in the *Trade* is greater than the *Quantity of agents* that *Begin the execution* of this *Subplan*. The planner *Imagines an agent* that is the agent in the *Trade* that has the goal of *Possessing* the *Work product*. The planner envisions that *If it were the case* that the *Amount of resources* that were *Possessed* by the imagined agent *Varied over time* and the *Upper bound of the variation* was less than the *Amount of resources* of the *Trade offer*, that the agent would *Fail to plan* to execute the *Trade*. The planner *Modifies* the *Continuous plan* so that the *Trade offer* includes the *Offer option* that the *Transfer of resources* to the planner is executed by a *Subplan* that includes the *Iterative execution* of *Transfer of resources* of an *Amount of resources* that is less than the *Upper bound of the variation*.

B39. GIVE COUPONS

Business: Publish coupons to give customers a reason to switch their product choices.

The planner is in a *Competitive relationship* with a set of other agents, each executing a *Continuous plan* that includes *Trade* with a different set of agents of a *Work product* for *Resources*. The *Competitive goal* is that this different set of agents execute plans that include *Making a selection* where the *Selection options* are the *Work products* of the planner and the other agents, where the *Selected choice* is the *Work product* of the *Advancing competitor*. The planner envisions that *Any specific agent in the set Repeatedly executes* the plan, with equal *Selected choices* during each *Repetition*, where the *Selection criteria* in each *Repetition* is that of a *Previously selected choice*. The planner executes a plan to *Repetitively execute* a plan to *Encode information* and to *Transfer possession* of the encoding to agents who execute the selection. The planner then *Modifies* the *Trade activity* so that the *Trade offer* includes the *Offer option* that the *Amount of resources* in the *Transfer of resources* is less *In the condition that* the agent *Transfer possession* of the encoding to the planner.

B40. HONOR COMPETITOR COUPONS

Business: Honor competitor coupons to keep your customers from switching.

The planner has a *Competitive relationship* with a set of agents, each of whom are executing *Continuous plans* that include *Trade* of a *Work product* for *Resources* with a different set of agents. The *Competitive goal* is that this different set of agents execute plans that include *Selecting a choice* where the *Choice set* is the set of *Work products* of the planner and the *Competing agents* and where the *Selected choice* is the *Work product* of the *Advancing competitor*. A subset of these agents *Repetitively execute* plans that include *Selecting a choice* with the *Choice criteria* of the *Previous selected choice*, which is the *Work product* of the planner. A subset of the *Competitive agents* have the goal that the *Previously selected choice* of this subset of agents be equal to their own *Work products*, and are executing plans that include the *Trade offer* with an *Offer option* that *In the case of* a *Condition*, the *Amount of resources* transferred to the *Competing agent* is less than in another *Offer option*. The planner executes a *Counterplan* to *Modify the plan* that are their own *Trade* subplan to include the *Offer option* that in the *Condition*, the *Amount of resources* in the *Transfer of resources* is equal to the *Amount of resources* in the *Offer option* of the competitor.

B41.   DELAY STANDARDS DECISIONS

Business: Delay standards decisions to reduce the ability of competitors to design and plan.

> The planner has a *Competitive relationship* with a set of agents, each of whom are executing plans that include the *Design* of a *Work product*, followed by the *Making of the work product* and *Trade* with a set of agents. The *Competitive goal* is that a different set of agents execute *Selecting a choice* where the *Choice set* is the *Work products* of the competing agents, and where the *Selected choice* is that of the *Advancing* competitor. The *Competing agents* have a *Cooperative plan* that includes the *Cooperative specification* of *Characteristics* of the set of *Work products*, the existence of which is a *Precondition* for the *Designing* of the *Work product*. The planner envisions that the result of the *Cooperative specification* will be equal to a *Specification of characteristics* that the planner has done that is currently *Unknown* to the other *Competing agents*. The planner executes a plan to *Design* the *Work product* with their own *Specification of characteristics*, and *Delays* the execution of the *Cooperative specification*, with an *End of delay time* that is a *Moment* where the *Preconditions* for the *Trade* are *Satisfied preconditions*.

B42.   PRICE BELOW COSTS TO KILL COMPETITION

Business: Drop prices below production costs to drive others out of business.

> The planner has a *Competitive relationship* with another agent, and both are executing *Continuous plans* that include *Trade* of a *Work product* for *Resources* with a different set of agents. The *Competitive goal* is that this different set of agents will execute plans that include *Selecting a choice* from a *Choice set* of the *Work products* of the *Competing agents* where the *Selected choice* is that of the *Advancing* competitor, followed by *Trade* with the *Advancing* competitor of the *Work product* for *Resources*. The planner envisions that *Any unspecified agent* in the set that does the selection will do *Selecting a choice* with the *Selection criteria* of *Minimizing a value* that is the *Amount of resources* that are *Expended resources* in the *Trade*. The planner has an *Amount of resources* that is greater than that of the *Competing agent*, and the plans of both agents include *Expending resources* of an *Amount of resources* that is *Directly proportional* to the *Amount of resources* that are *Acquired resources* from the *Trade*, where the *Proportions* are *Similar* for both *Competing agents*. The planner executes a plan to *Calculate a value* that is the *Amount of resources* that are *Expended resources* in the *Continuous plan* divided by the *Quantity* of executed *Trades* in the plan for an *Arbitrary duration*. Then the planner *Suspends the execution* of

the *Continuous plan* for a *Duration*, and executes a *Modified plan* where the *Trade offer* includes the *Transfer of resources* from agents that is less than the calculated value. The planner then *Adds the expectation* that the amount of *Resources* of the planner and of the *Competing agent* will be *Decreasing*, and that the *Competing agent* will envision an *Execution failure* with a cause of *Lack of resources*, causing them to *Terminate the execution* of their *Continuous plan*. The planner then *Monitors* for this *Termination of the execution*, and *If this occurs*, the planner *Resumes the execution* of the *Continuous plan*.

B43.   ATTRACT PARTNERS WITH INFORMATION

Business: Entice partner companies by offering advanced product information.

The planner is executing a *Continuous plan* that includes the *Design* of a *Work product*, followed by the *Making of the work product* and *Trade* with a different set of agents. The planner has the goal that another agent do *Cooperative planning* with the planner, where the other agent executes plans that include the *Work product* of the planner, and does not have the goal of doing *Cooperative planning* with the planner. The planner executes a plan to *Make an offer* to the other agent where the *Commitment* of the planner would be to *Periodically execute* a plan to *Inform* the other agent of the *Design* of *Work products* before *Trade* activities that include the products. *Commitment* of the other agent would be to do *Cooperative planning* with the planner.

B44.   LOOK FOR COMPETITOR STRATEGIES THAT CAN BACKFIRE

Business: Encourage behavior that causes competitor promotions to backfire.

The planner is in a *Competitive relationship* with another agent where both are executing *Continuous plans*, and where the *Competitive goal* is that a different set of agents execute specific plans. The competing agent *Executes occasionally* a *Modification of the plan* where the *Reason* for the agency is to *Instantiate a strategy*. The planner *Monitors* for the *Modification of the plan* by the other agent, and *If this occurs*, the planner does *Plan recognition* on the execution of the agent. The planner then does *Expectation deduction* for *Expectations* of the *Agency* of member of the different set. For each *Expectation*, the planner envisions for *If it were the case* that there was an *Expectation violation*. The planner then *Imagines a set* which is the set of *Expectation violations* that both cause an *Execution failure* for the other agent, and *Satisfy the goals* of the planner. The planner then *Iterates* through this set, and *Adds the goal* that the agents in the different set execute plans that are these *Expectation violations*.

B45.   HIRE CONSULTANTS FOR BEST PRACTICES

Business: Use experienced consultants to learn the best practices of the industry.

The planner is in a *Competitive relationship* with a set of other agents, all of whom are executing *Continual plans* that are the result of planning by the agent of the execution and a set of *Plan modifications*. The *Plan modifications* of the plans of the *Competing agents* are the result of *Collaborative planning* where the *Collaborating agent* for each *Competitor* is the same agent. The planner executes a plan to achieve the goal that the *Collaborating agent* do *Collaborative planning* with the planner to *Modify the plan* that is the *Continual plan* of the planner, with the *Planning preference* that favors *Substitution of Subplans* in the plan for those of *Analogous subplans* in the plans of the *Competitive agents* that *Achieve subgoals* at a *Greater degree of goal achievement*.

B46.   BE EXPLICIT IN YOUR STRATEGIES

Business: Make your business strategies explicit to avoid clobbering competing goals.

The planner is executing a *Continuous plan* that is an *Instantiation of a strategy*, and which includes the *Employment* of multiple agents, a subset of which have *Employed work* that includes *Planning*. The planner envisions a *Possible future state* where the *Continuous plan* has an *Execution failure* with a cause of *Subplan execution clobbers subgoal* where the *Subplan* and *Subgoal* are the results of planning by different agents in the *Employment*. The planner executes a plan to *Inform* the agents of the *Strategy*. The planner then *Monitors* the planning of these agents for *Competing subgoals*, and *If this occurs*, the planner executes a plan to cause the agents to do *Collaborative planning* for the two subgoals.

B47.   ESTABLISH ANTITRUST LAWS

Business: Encourage healthy competition by regulating anti-competitive practices.

The planner has a *Leadership role* over a set of agents that have a *Competitive relationship* with each other, and are doing *Competitive planning* and executing *Competitive plans* to achieve the *Competitive goal*. The planner has goals that are achieved by the *Continual execution* of *Competitive plans* by the set of agents. The planner *Envisions a threat* to this goal that the set of *Competitive plans* executed by these agents include plans that *Block the execution* of *Competitive plans* by other agents in the set. The planner executes a plan to cause the agents in the set to have *Execution rules* that *Prevent the execution* of plans that *Block the execution* of *Competitive plans* by other agents in the set.

B48.   STOCK BUYBACK

Business: Increase the value of a company's stock by buying and canceling a portion.

> The planner has a *Leadership role* in an *Organization* that is *Owned* by a set of agents, where these agents have a *Reusable plan* for *Trading ownership* of their *Portion of ownership* for an *Amount of resources*. The planner has the goal of *Maximizing the value* that is the *Amount of resources*. The planner envisions that *If it were the case* that the *Quantity* of the set of *Portions of ownership* were less, then the *Amount of resources* would be greater. The planner executes a plan to cause the *Organization* to execute a plan that includes *Trading ownership* of *Portions of ownership* of agents in this set for *Resources* that are *Possessed* by the organization. The planner then plans and executes to *Cancel ownership* of the *Portions of ownership* of the *Organization*.

B49.   GREENMAIL

Business: A potential corporate raider forces stock buyback from fearful executives.

> The planner has the goal of *Acquiring resources* and has *Possessed resources* of a certain *Amount of resources*. An *Organization* has *Possessed resources* that are equal or greater than this *Amount of resources*. The *Organization* is *Owned* by a set of agents, and agents with *Leadership roles* in the organization do *Planning* with the *Execution constraint* of *Following execution rules* that include *Managed rules* of agents in the first set. The planner executes a plan to *Acquire ownership* of a *Quantity* of *Portions of ownership* of the organization from agents in the first set. The planner then *Informs* agents in the second set of a *Threat* that the planner will execute a plan to *Acquire ownership* of a *Quantity* of *Portions of ownership* that is greater than the first *Quantity*, which will *Enable* the planner to *Manage rules* that are those in the *Execution constraint*, and that the planner will cause *Execution rules* that will cause *Planning failures* for the agents with a cause of *Constraining execution rules*. The *Threat* has a *Threat condition* that *Prevents the threat* if the *Organization* executes a plan that includes *Trading* of the *Portions of ownership* of the planner for the *Amount of resources* of the *Organization*.

B50. LEVERAGED BUYOUT

Business: Purchase a corporation by using its assets to secure the necessary capital.

The planner has the goal of *Owning* an *Organization* that *Possesses resources* of an *Amount of resources*. A set of agents *Own* the organization, and the planner has a *Partial plan* to *Trade* the *Portions of ownership* of agents in this set for an *Amount of resources* that is greater than the *Amount of resources* of the planner. A different agent has an *Amount of resources* that is equal to or greater than the amount in the *Partial plan*. The planner executes a plan to *Make an offer* to this agent with an *Offer requirement* that the agent *Transfer resources* to the planner of the *Amount of resources*, and an *Offered action* that the planner will *Execute the partial plan*, *Schedule* the *Transfer of resources* of the *Amount of resources* or greater to the agent from the *Organization*.

B51. LIQUIDATION

Business: Merge and consume the assets and debts of a company to end its existence.

The planner has a *Leadership role* in an *Organization*, and has the goal to *Destroy* a different *Organization* that has *Possessed resources* and that has *Scheduled the execution* of *Subplans* that include other agents to achieve goals of *Fulfilling an agreement*. The planner executes a plan to cause the *Organization* of the planner to *Acquire ownership* of the different *Organization*, and then *Permanently block* the *Agency of the organization*, *Transfer the resources* of the organization to that of the planner, and then *Adapts the plans* the *Scheduled plans* of the different organization with an *Adaptation* of *Change of agency* of the organization of the planner for the different organization, and then *Schedules the execution* of these plans by the *Organization* of the planner.

B52. INITIAL PUBLIC OFFERING

Business: Finance growth in a private company by offering a portion up for public investment.

The planner has a *Leadership role* in an *Organization* that the planner *Owns*, and has a plan to achieve goals of the *Organization* that have an *Unmet precondition* of the *Possession of resources* of an *Amount of resources*. The planner envisions that *If it were the case* that the planner *Made an offer* with a different set of agents to *Trade* a *Portion of ownership* of the organization for an *Amount of resources*, then the set would *Accept the offer*. The planner *Calculates a quantity* of *Portions of ownership* with the *Amount of resources* in the envisionment and the *Amount of resources* in the goal, then executes a plan to *Make the offer* to the different set of agents.

B53.   HOSTILE TAKEOVER

Business: Control an adversarial company by buying a majority of its stock.

The planner has the goal that agents in an *Organization* execute plans that achieve goals of the planner. Agents in the organization do *Planning* with the *Planning constraint* of *Following execution rules* that are *Managed rules* of a set of agents that *Own* the *Organization*. The planner executes a plan to *Make an offer* to this set to *Trade* a *Portion of ownership* of the organization for an *Amount of resources* of the planner. *In the case that* the set of agents *Agree to the offer* and execute the *Trade*, the planner then *Modifies the rules* that are the execution rules to *Constrain the planning* of the agents in the *Organization* to cause the agents to execute the plans in the goal.

B54.   WHITE KNIGHT

Business: Counter a hostile takeover by asking a friendly third party to acquire stock.

The planner has an *Adversarial relationship* with another agent, and has the goal of *Blocking the execution* of an *Adversarial plan* of the agent to *Own* an *Organization* in which the planner has a *Leadership role*, which includes the *Making an offer* of *Trade* with a set of agents that have *Portions of ownership* of the *Organization* for an *Amount of resources* of the adversary. The *Amount of resources* is greater than the *Amount of resources* of the *Organization*. The planner executes a plan to *Locate an agent* that has an *Amount of resources* that is equal to the *Amount of resources* in the *Adversarial plan*, and then plans and executes to *Achieve the goal* that the planner has a *Cooperative relationship* with this other agent, with a *Cooperative plan* that includes the *Making an offer* of *Trade* with the set of agents with *Portions of ownership* for the *Amount of resources*, and then *Adding a planning constraint* to *Refuse an offer* that includes *Trade* of the *Portions of ownership* with for a *Constraint duration*.

B55. EMPLOYEE STOCK PURCHASE PLAN

Business: Influence employee performance by having them become shareholders.

> The planner has a *Leadership role* in an *Organization* and has the goal that agents in the *Organization* have a *Planning preference* for plans that *Achieve goals* that are *Organizational goals*. A set of agents have *Portions of ownership* of the *Organization*, and the planner has a *Partial plan* for *Trade* of the *Portions of ownership* for an *Amount of resources* of the *Organization*. The planner executes a plan to cause the *Organization* to execute the *Partial plan* to have the *Portions of ownership*, and then *Makes an offer* to agents in the organization of *Trade* of the *Portions of ownership* for an *Amount of resources* that is equal or greater than that in the *Partial plan*.

B56. GOLDEN PARACHUTE

Business: Get an employee contract that protects your benefits in the face of hostile takeovers.

> The planner has the goal of having a *Leadership role* in an *Organization*, and the *Organization* has executed plans that include *Making an offer* to the planner that the planner will *Have the role* and the *Organization* will execute a *Periodic plan* that includes *Transferring resources* to the planner from the organization. Agents in the organization do *Planning* with the *Planning constraint* of *Following execution rules* that are *Managed* by a set of agents that *Own* the organization. The planner *Envisions the possibility* that a different agent will execute plans that include *Trade* of the *Portions of ownership* of the organization to this agent, and that this agent will *Modify rules* that cause agents in the organization to *Terminate the execution* of the *Periodic plan*. The planner executes a plan to *Reject the offer*, and *Informs* the *Organization* that *If it were the case* that the *Making an offer* included that agents in the organization *Added a planning constraint* that *Blocked* the *Termination of execution* of the *Periodic plan*, then the planner will *Accept the offer*.

B57. INSIDER TRADING

Business: Illegally purchase or sell stock based on knowledge that is not yet public.

> The planner is a member of a set of agents that have a *Reusable plan* to *Trade* the *Portions of ownership* of an *Organization* for an *Amount of resources* that is a *Variable amount*. Agents in the *Organization* do *Planning*

that includes *Making planning decisions* that are *Influencing factors* for the *Quantity* of the *Variable amount*, and have a *Planning constraint against* the execution of a plans that include *Trade* in the *Reusable plan* before *Informing* the set of agents of the *Planning decision*. The planner has the goal of *Maximizing a value* that is the *Amount of resources* of the planner. The planner executes a plan to *Monitor* for *Planning decisions* of the *Organization* that are *Influencing factors* that have not been included in *Executed plans* to *Inform* the set of agents. The planner then *Suspends the planning constraint*, and executes the *Reusable plan* that includes the *Trade*.

B58.   SELL OFF THE CROWN JEWELS

Business: Prevent a hostile takeover by selling off the assets that are most desirable.

The planner has a *Leadership role* in an *Organization*, and *Envisions a threat* to goals of the *Organization* that a different agent will execute a plan that includes *Trade* of an *Amount of resources* of the agent for *Portions of ownership* that are a *Majority portion* to cause the *Satisfaction of a precondition* to have a *Leadership role* in the organization, followed by the execution of plans that include *Resources* of the organization of a specific *Type class*. The planner executes a plan to cause the *Organization* to *Trade* their *Resources* of the *Type class* in the *Envisionment* for *Resources* of a different *Type class* that are *Resources* that are *Possessed* by a third agent.

B59.   MACARONI DEFENSE

Business: Prevent takeover by issuing bonds to be redeemed at high cost if a takeover occurs.

The planner has a *Leadership role* in an *Organization*, and *Envisions a threat* to goals of the *Organization* that a different agent will execute a plan that includes *Trade* of an *Amount of resources* of the agent for *Portions of ownership* that are a *Majority portion*. The planner executes a plan to *Make an offer* to a different agent where the *Offer requirement* is that the agent *Transfers resources* to the *Organization* of an *Amount of resources*, and the *Offered action* is that the planner will *Schedule* the *Transfer of resources* to the agent of an *Amount of resources* that is greater than in the *Offer requirement*, with the *Offer condition* that *If it is the case* that an *Arbitrary agent* executes the plan that is the plan in the *Threat*, the *Organization* will *Enable* the agent in the offer to cause the *Organization* to *Reschedule* the *Offer action* with an *Amount of resources* that is greater. The planner then *Schedules a plan* to *Inform* the agent in the *Threat* of this offer after the *Successful execution* of the plan.

B60. PEOPLE PILL

Business: Prevent takeover by promising that the entire management team would resign.

The planner is a member of a set of agents that have *Leadership roles* in an *Organization*, and *Envisions a threat* to goals of the *Organization* that a different agent will execute a plan to achieve a subgoal of having a *Leadership role* over this set of agents, then cause the agents to cause the *Organization* to execute plans that *Achieve goals* of this agent. The planner envisions that *If it were the case* that a different set of agents had the *Leadership roles* in the *Organization*, then the plan of the agent would have an *Execution failure* with a cause of *Lack of ability*. The planner executes a plan to cause the agents in the set of the planner to *Inform* the agent in the *Threat* of a *Conditional plan* that they have to *Terminate the role* that is the *Leadership role* with the *Trigger condition* that the agent executes the plan to achieve the subgoal of having a *Leadership role*.

B61. PAC-MAN DEFENSE

Business: Prevent a takeover from a company by taking it over.

The planner has a *Leadership role* in an *Organization* that has an *Adversarial relationship* with a second *Organization*, that is *Owned* by a set of agents. The planner *Envisions a threat* to *Organizational goals* of the organization that the second *Organization* will execute a plan to achieve the subgoal of *Owning* the organization of the planner, and that this will *Enable* the second *Organization* to have a *Leadership role* over the *Organization* of the planner. The planner envisions that *If it were the case* that the set of agents that own the second organization executed a plan of *Blocking the execution* of the plan of the *Organization*, then this would be *Successfully executed*. The planner executes a plan to cause the agents that own the second organization to *Trade* a *Portion of ownership* of the organization that is a *Majority portion* to the *Organization* of the planner for an *Amount of resources* that are *Resources* of the organization of the planner.

B62. PUMP AND DUMP

Business: Illegally purchasing stock to be sold off after hyping its value to a large audience.

The planner is a member of a set of agents that have a *Reusable plan* that includes *Trade* of resources of the agent for *Portions of ownership* of an *Organization* from other agents in the set. The planner has the goal of *Maximizing a quantity* that is the *Amount of resources* of the planner. The planner envisions that *If it were the case* that a *Quantity* of agents in the set of members executed this *Reusable plan* that the *Amount of resources* in the *Trade* would *Increase*. The planner executes the reusable plan, and then cause agents in the set to do *Collaborative planning* with the planner, with the *Planning constraint* that the plans of the agents include execution of the *Reusable plan* by agents in the set. The planner then *Periodically schedules* the *Making of an offer* of *Trade* of the *Portions of ownership* of the planner for an *Amount of resources* of agents in the set that is greater than the *Amount of resources* in the plan.

4.3 COUNTING (20 STRATEGIES)

Perhaps the most unique among the ten strategic planning domains examined was that of object counting. The ability to count objects in the world is something that we all learn as children. As adults, we almost never think about the counting process itself. However, there is a large range of human behavior that all falls under the umbrella of object counting—and the type of behavior that a person will perform in service of a counting task seems highly dependent on certain characteristics of the counting situation. Consider the way that you might count how many coins were placed in the palm of your hand. If there are only a few, you might spread them so that they do not overlap, and then focus visually on each coin as you spoke (perhaps silently) its cardinal value. If there were somewhat more coins in your hand, you might employ the pointer finger of your other hand to help you keep track of the coin on which you are focusing. If there are several more, you may choose a different approach entirely, perhaps to use your thumb and index and middle fingers to move each coin, one at a time, from the hand that has the coins to your empty hand or onto a table in front of you. You'd use a different approach again if the objects were stationary, such as the number of computers in a large computer lab, or if they could not all be seen from your location, such as the number of computers on one floor of an office building. Your approach changes again if the things to be counted are moving all the time, such as when counting the number of employees that are currently in an office building, or the number of cattle that are within the bounds of a grazing range.

As counting tasks become less local and more complex, it feels more comfortable to talk about them as counting strategies. That is, it is reasonable to say that one might have a counting strategy for determining the number of employees that are currently in an office building. However, from a conceptual or principle-based perspective, the similarity between low-level perceptual-motor counting tasks (e.g., counting coins in your hand) and high-level, strategic counting tasks is very high. Indeed, at some level of abstraction, the algorithm for performing the count successfully may be the same regardless of whether it is a perceptual-motor task or a more conscious problem-solving task. The question that arises is whether these abstract, more conceptual procedures play a functional role in the perceptual-motor, often non-conscious behavior of people engaged in simple, local counting tasks.

The domain of object counting has been a persistent area of interest in developmental psychology research for many decades—a research history that has been successful without focusing its attention on strategic knowledge. The most supported view of object counting behavior (in children) is that counting skills are based on a set of principles which govern what is permissible and required in the successful execution of a counting task (Gelman

& Gallistel, 1978; Gelman & Meck, 1983; Shipley & Shepperson, 1990). Greeno, Riley, and Gelman (1984) made the strongest connection between these principles and planning behavior, arguing that implicit knowledge of these principles is encoded in various competencies that are used to derive a plan given a particular counting situation. In this model, features of the setting and current goal are paired with schema-based knowledge of the actions (or planning operators) that a person can execute, and a counting plan is generated through means-ends-analysis, guided by heuristics for planning. These researchers made a point of not arguing for this particular method of plan derivation—only for the content of the knowledge that is attributed to people and to the structures that are implied by that knowledge.

In describing the abstract patterns of human counting behavior, the counting strategy representations offered in this section offer an alternative view of the content of this knowledge and the structures that are implied by it. Rather than viewing counting plans as compositions of action schemas, we can instead view them as instantiations of one of the various counting strategies that people have for use in any given counting task. The process of coming up with an appropriate plan for a particular counting situation would involve selecting an appropriate counting strategy, and then binding the abstractions that are represented in the strategy to the particular elements in the situation. Successful development of counting skills in children could alternatively be viewed as including the acquisition of a catalog of counting strategies (each of which is based on counting principles) and the ability to apply them in the right situations.

This section offers representations of twenty counting strategies that describe a broad range of human counting behavior, both for low-level perceptual tasks as well as for higher-level strategic counting behavior.

C1. FOLLOW THE LAYOUT

Counting: Use the layout of things as a path for counting.

> The planner has the *Knowledge goal* of the *Quantity* of members in a set of *Physical objects*. The set of *Locations* have a *Perceivable shape* that is a *Path* with two *Endpoints*. The planner executes a plan to *Select from the set* of *Endpoints* using the *Selection criteria* of *Random choice*, and then *Repetitively executes* a plan to *Attend* to a *Physical object* and *Imagine a number*. In the *First repetition* the *Physical object* is the one at the *Endpoint* that was the selected choice, and the number is 1. In *Subsequent repetitions* the *Physical object* is the *Nearest object* on the *Path* that is *More near* the other *Endpoint*, and the *Number* is the addition of 1 to the number in the *Previous repetition*. The *Stop condition of the repetition* is when the *Physical object* is at the other *Endpoint*. The planner then *Achieves the knowledge goal* with the *Quantity* being equal to the number in the *Last repetition*.

C2. MARK THE START LOCATION

Counting: Use a marker in a circular path to prevent counting in closed loops.

The planner has the *Knowledge goal* of the *Quantity* of members in a set of *Physical objects*. The set of *Locations* of these objects have a *Perceivable shape* that is a *Closed loop*. The planner executes a plan to *Select from the set* of *Physical objects* using the *Selection criteria* of *Random choice*. The planner then plans and executes a plan to *Enable* the planner to *Recognize* the *Physical object* as a *Specific member* of the set of *Physical objects*. The planner then *Imagines a set* which is the two *Path directions* that exist at the *Location* of the *Selected choice*, and *Selects from this set* a *Path direction* using a *Selection criteria* of *Random choice*. The planner then *Repetitively executes* a plan to *Attend* to a *Physical object* and *Imagine a number*. In the *First repetition* the *Physical object* is the *Selected choice*, and the number is 1. In *Subsequent repetitions* the *Physical object* is the *Nearest object* on the *Path* to the object in the *Previous repetition* and in the *Path direction* that was the *Selected choice*, and the *Number* is the addition of 1 to the number in the *Previous repetition*. The *Stop condition of the repetition* is when the *Physical object* is the *Specific member* of the set. The planner then *Achieves the knowledge goal* with the *Quantity* being equal to the number in the *Last repetition*.

C3. COVER THE SPACE

Counting: Use a path that covers the whole space regardless of the layout.

The planner has the *Knowledge goal* of the *Quantity* of members in a set of *Physical objects*. The set of *Locations* of these objects are each *Contained in an area* and there exists a *Path* with two *Endpoints* that includes all *Possible locations* in the *Area*. The planner *Selects from the set* which are the *Endpoints* with the *Selection criteria* of *Random choice*, and then *Repetitively executes* a plan to *Attend* to a *Location* on the *Path* where in the *First repetition* the *Location* is the *Selected choice* and where in *Successive repetitions* the locations are those that are *Nearer locations* to the *Not selected choice*. During the execution of this plan the planner *Monitors* for the *Perception* of the *Physical objects* in the *Location* of the *Attending action*, at which time the planner *Imagines a number*. In the case that this is the *First triggering in monitoring*, the number is 1, and otherwise the number is the addition of 1 to the previously *Imagined number*. The *Termination of repetition condition* is that the *Location* of the *Attending* action is the not-selected *Endpoint*, at which time the planner *Achieves the knowledge goal* with the *Quantity* being equal to the *Imagined number* of the *Last triggering in monitoring*.

C4. MARK YOUR CURRENT LOCATION

Counting: Use a marker as a pointer to keep from losing your place in a count.

The planner is executing a plan to achieve the *Knowledge goal* of the *Quantity* of members in a set of *Physical objects*, where the plan includes the *Repetitive execution* of a *Subplan* that includes a *Location* on a *Path*. The planner envisions an *Execution failure* with a *Cause of failure* being due to a *Lack of certainty* with regard to the *Location* on the *Path*. The planner modifies the *Subplan* to include *Changing locations* of a *Physical object* to a *Location* that has a specific *Spatial relationship* to the *Location* in the *Path* and to plan a *Subplan* to *Invert the relationship* to achieve the *Knowledge goal* of the *Location* on the *Path*. The planner then *Monitors* the execution of the *Repetitive plan* for *Lack of certainty*, and *In this case*, the planner *Suspends* the repetitive plan, executes the *Subplan*, *Affirms the certainty* of the *Location*, and *Resumes* the *Repetitive plan*.

C5. FORCE INTO A LINE

Counting: Move things to be counted toward an axis so they form a line.

The planner has a *Knowledge goal* of the *Quantity* of member in a set of *Physical objects*. The set of *Locations* of these objects are in an area and do not have a *Spatial organization*. The planner executes a plan to *Identify a location* that is a *Linear path*, such that the planner has a *Subplan* to *Transfer the location* of *Physical objects* to a *Location* that is *On the path*. The planner then executes the *Subplan*. The planner then *Selects from the set* of two *Path directions* using a *Selection criteria* of *Random choice*, then *Identifies the object* in the set for which no different object has a *Location* that is *On the path* and *In the direction* from the *Identified object* that is the *Path direction*. The planner then executes a *Repetitive plan*, where in each *Repetition*, the planner *Attends* to a *Physical object* and *Imagines a number*. In the *First repetition* the object is the *Identified object* and the number is 1. In *Subsequent repetitions* the object is the object that is *Closest to* the object in the *Previous repetition* and *In the direction* from this object that is not the *Selected choice* that is the *Path direction*, and the number is the addition of 1 to the *Imagined number* in the *Previous repetition*. The *End of repetition* condition is that no object exists with a *Location* that is in the *Path direction* of the object in the *Previous repetition*. The planner then *Achieves the knowledge goal* that is the *Imagined number* in the *Last repetition*.

C6. KNOW YOUR CAPACITY

Counting: Use a space that has a fixed capacity and count remaining spaces.

The planner has the *Knowledge goal* of the *Quantity* of *Physical objects* in a set. The *Possible locations* is a set of a specific *Quantity*. There is a *Physical constraint* that the *Physical location* of two objects cannot be equal. The planner executes a plan to *Imagine a set* that is the disjunction of the set of *Possible locations* from the set of *Locations* of the *Physical objects*. The planner then achieves the *Knowledge goal* that is the subtraction of the *Quantity* of members in this set from the *Quantity* of members in the set of *Possible locations*.

C7. TRANSFER BETWEEN SPACES

Counting: Collect all of the things to be counted in a space, then move them to another.

The planner has the *Knowledge goal* of the *Quantity* of *Physical objects* in a set. There exists a set of two *Disjoint regions*, where every object has a *Location* that is *Contained within the region* that is a member of the set. The planner has a *Subplan* to *Transfer the location* of a specific object that is *Contained within a region* of the set to a different *Location* that is *Contained within the other region*. The planner executes a plan to achieve the goal that all of the objects in the set have a *Location* that is *Contained within the region* that is the *Start location* in the *Transfer of location* subplan. The planner then *Repetitively* executes a subplan where the planner executes the *Transfer of location* subplan and *Imagines a number*. In the *First repetition*, the number is 1, and in *Subsequent repetitions* the number is the addition of 1 to the *Imagined number* in the *Previous iteration*. The *Termination of repetition condition* is that the planner has an *Execution failure* of the subplan with a cause of *Unfound object in start location*. The planner then *Achieves* the *Knowledge goal* that is the *Imagined number* in the *Last repetition*.

C8. TRANSFER INTO A CONTAINER

Counting: Count things as you move them into an empty container.

The planner has the *Knowledge goal* of the *Quantity* of members in a set of *Physical objects*. The *Locations* of the *Physical objects* are *Contained within a region*. The planner has possession of a *Physical container* where the *Contents* of the container is a set of *Physical objects* that does not include members of the set of unknown quantity. The planner has a subplan to *Transfer the location* of the physical objects of unknown quantity from the

Region to a *Location* such that they are members of the set of *Contents* of the container. The planner then *Repetitively executes* a subplan where the planner executes the *Transfer of location* subplan and *Imagines a number*. In the *First repetition*, the number is 1, and in *Subsequent repetitions* the number is the addition of 1 to the *Imagined number* in the *Previous iteration*. The *Termination of repetition condition* is that the planner has an *Execution failure* of the subplan with a cause of *Unfound object in start location*. The planner then *Achieves* the *Knowledge goal* that is the *Imagined number* in the *Last repetition*.

C9. FORCE THROUGH A BOTTLENECK

Counting: Use a bottleneck to force objects to be sequential.

The planner has the *Knowledge goal* of the *Quantity* of members of a set of *Physical objects*. The planner has a subplan for *Transferring the location* of the set that includes a *Path*. The planner executes a plan to cause a *Physical constraint* to exist for the *Path* such that the *Transfer of location* of objects is *Serial* and not *Parallel*. The planner executes the subplan, while *Monitoring* for the event that an object *Moves past a point* in the *Path*. In this event, the planner *Imagines a number*. In the *First triggering of the monitoring*, this number is 1. In *Subsequent triggering of the monitoring*, the *Imagined number* is the addition of 1 to the *Imagined number* in the *Previous triggering of the monitoring*. At the *Completion of execution* of the subplan, the planner *Achieves the knowledge goal* that is the *Imagined number* of the *Last triggering of the monitoring*.

C10. MARK THOSE THAT ARE COUNTED

Counting: Apply a new mark to objects that have been counted.

The planner has the *Knowledge goal* of the *Quantity* of members of a set of *Physical objects*. The planner has a subplan where a member of this set *Has a role*, the execution of which causes a specific *Characteristic* to be added to the set of *Perceptible characteristics* of the object. No member of the set of *Physical objects* has this *Perceptible* characteristic. The planner executes a plan to execute a *Repetitive plan* where in each *Repetition*, the planner *Locates an object* that is a member of the set and that does not have the *Perceptible characteristic*. The planner then executes the subplan on this object, and *Imagines a number*. In the *First repetition*, the *Imagined number* is 1. In *Subsequent repetitions*, the *Imagined number* is the addition of 1 to the *Imagined number* of the *Previous repetition*. The *Termination of repetition condition* is that the planner has an *Execution failure* in the

STRATEGY REPRESENTATIONS 103

subplan for *Locating an object* with a cause of *No remaining objects*. The planner then *Achieves the knowledge goal* that is the *Imagined number* of the *Last repetition*.

C11. KNOW YOUR CLUSTER SIZE

Counting: Add up the number of members in clusters of things.

The planner has the *Knowledge goal* of the *Quantity* of members in a set of *Physical objects*. The set is *Compositional*, where *Components* of the set of are subsets where each subset is of equal *Quantity*. The planner plans and executes to *Achieve the knowledge goal* of the *Quantity* of subsets in the set, and *Achieves the knowledge goal* of the *Quantity* of members in the original set as the multiplication of the two *Quantities*.

C12. FLIP THE STATE OF THOSE THAT ARE COUNTED

Counting: Change a selectable state of things to be counted from one to another.

The planner has the *Knowledge goal* of the *Quantity* of members in a set of *Physical objects*. The objects have a *Configuration* with a set of *Configurable states*. The planner has a subplan to *Change the configuration* of a member of the set of objects to a *Configuration* that no member of the set currently has. The planner executes a plan to execute a *Repetitive plan* where in each *Repetition*, the planner *Locates an object* that is a member of the set and that does not have the *Configuration*. The planner then executes the subplan on this object, and *Imagines a number*. In the *First repetition*, the *Imagined number* is 1. In *Subsequent repetitions*, the *Imagined number* is the addition of 1 to the *Imagined number* of the *Previous repetition*. The *Termination of repetition* condition is that the planner has an *Execution failure* in the subplan for *Locating an object* with a cause of *No remaining objects*. The planner then *Achieves the knowledge goal* that is the *Imagined number* of the *Last repetition*.

C13. HAVE PEOPLE TAKE A NUMBER

Counting: Count agents by requiring them to take a number.

The planner has the *Knowledge goal* of the *Quantity* of agents in a set. The agents each *Have a role* in a plan that is the result of planning by the planner. The planner has a subplan for *Achieving the knowledge goal* of whether or not all agents have executed the plan. The planner *Identifies a subplan* of the plan where every agent in the set has *Agency*. The planner then *Modifies the subplan* by *Adding a precondition* that the execution of the subplan is preceded by an *Inform* action by the planner to the agent. The planner schedules to *Monitor* for *Requests* to execute the *Inform* action, and *In this event*, the planner executes an *Inform* action. In the *First triggering of the monitoring*, the *Information* is the number 1. In *Subsequent triggering of the monitoring*, the *Information* is the addition of 1 to the *Information* in the *Previous triggering of the monitoring*. The planner then *Schedules a repetitive plan* to execute the subplan for *Achieving the knowledge goal*, and *In the case* that all of the agents have executed the plan, the planner *Terminates monitoring* and *Terminates the repetitive plan*, and achieves the knowledge goal that is the *Information* in the *Last triggering of the monitoring*, or the number 0 *In the case that No triggering of the monitoring occurred*.

C14. HAVE PEOPLE FORM A LINE

Counting: Count agents by requiring them to line up.

The planner has the *Knowledge goal* of the *Quantity* of agents in a set. The planner executes a plan to *Select a choice* from the set with a *Selection criteria* of *Random choice*. Then the planner *Persuades* the other agents to plan and execute to achieve the goal that they have a *Spatial relationship* with another agent in the set that is either the *Selected choice* or an agent that has *Successfully achieved* this goal, and where they are the only agent to have this *Spatial relationship* with the other agent. The planner then *Monitors* for the case that all of the agents have successfully executed this plan. The planner then executes a *Repetitive plan* to *Locate an agent* and *Imagine a number*. In the *First repetition*, the agent is the *Selected agent* and the number is 1. In *Subsequent repetitions*, the agent is the agent that has the *Spatial relationship* with the agent in the *Previous repetition* and the number is the addition of 1 to the *Imagined number* of the *Previous repetition*. The *Termination of repetition condition* is that the planner has an *Execution failure* of a *Repetition* with a cause of *Failure to locate* an agent with the *Spatial relationship*. The planner then *Achieves the knowledge goal* that is the *Imagined number* of the *Last repetition*.

C15. COUNT WHAT IS GIVEN TO EACH PERSON

Counting: Count agents by counting what remains of something distributed to each.

The planner has the *Knowledge goal* of the *Quantity* of agents in a set, where the *Range of possible quantities* has an *Upper bound*. The planner plans and executes to *Locate a set* of *Physical objects* with a specific *Quantity* that is greater than or equal to the *Upper bound*. The planner then executes a plan to *Persuade* the agents in the set to execute a plan to *Remove from the set* one *Physical object*. The planner then *Monitors for the state* that every agent in the set has executed the plan, and plans and executes to *Achieve the knowledge goal* of the *Quantity* of *Physical objects* that are still in the set. The planner then *Achieves the knowledge goal* of the *Quantity* of the set of agents as the subtraction of the original *Quantity* of the set of objects with the current *Quantity*.

C16. INSTRUMENT A PROCESS

Counting: Count agents by instrumenting a process that will be done one time by each.

The planner has the *Knowledge goal* of the *Quantity* of executions of a specific plan by a set of agents during a *Duration*, where the plan has an *Execution environment*. The planner plans and executes to *Modify the world state* to the *Execution environment* a *Device* that has a *Configuration* that *Encodes information*, where the *Deadline of the execution* of this plan is the *Start time* of the *Duration*. The planner *Configures* the *Device* to *Encode the information* that is the number 0. The planner then *Modifies the Execution environment* so that the execution of the specific plan will cause a *Change in the configuration*, where the *Encoded information* is the addition of 1 to the previous *Encoded information*. The planner schedules at the *End time* of the *Duration* to *Decode information* from the *Configuration* of the *Device*, and *Achieves the knowledge goal* that is this *Information*.

C17. DIVIDE THE TOTAL BY THE INDIVIDUAL

Counting: Count uniform things by dividing their total weight by their individual weight.

The planner has the *Knowledge goal* of the *Quantity* of *Physical objects* in a set, where members of the set have *Physical characteristics* that are equal. The planner has a *Subplan* to *Make a measurement* of a *Physical characteristic* of a set of *Physical objects*. The planner executes the subplan two times. First, the planner executes the subplan on the set of *Physical objects*. Second, the planner executes the subset on a single object that is a member of the set. The planner then *Achieves the knowledge goal* that is the division of the first *Measurement* by the second *Measurement*.

C18.   APPLY SUCCESSIVE FILTERS

Counting: Count categories of things by successive application of filters.

The planner has the *Knowledge goal* of the *Quantity* of *Physical objects* in a set. The planner has a subplan to *Remove from the set* an *Arbitrary subset* of a specific *Quantity* of *Physical objects*. The planner executes a *Repetitive plan* where in each *Repetition*, the planner executes the subplan and *Imagines a number*. In the *First repetition*, the *Imagined number* is 1 and in *Subsequent repetitions* the *Imagined number* is the addition of 1 to the *Imagined number* of the *Previous repetition*. The *Termination of repetition condition* is the *Execution failure* of the subplan with a *Cause of failure* that the *Quantity* of objects in the set is not equal to the specific *Quantity* specified in the subplan. The planner then executes a plan to *Achieve the knowledge goal* of the *Quantity* of *Physical objects* in the set. Then the planner *Achieves the knowledge goal* of the *Quantity* of *Physical objects* in the original set as the addition of the achieved knowledge goal to the multiplication of the *Imagined number* of the *Last repetition* and the *Quantity* in the subplan.

C19.   COUNT IN A RHYTHM

Counting: Use a fixed rhythm to limit possible over- or under-counting.

The planner is executing a *Repetitive plan* and envisions *Execution failures* with the *Cause of failure* being *Uncoordinated execution*. The planner envisions that the set of *Duration* of the *Repetitions* not be equal, and that these *Durations* will have an *Upper bound*. The planner modifies the *Repetitive plan* so that the *Start time* of the *Subsequent repetition* is equal to the addition of a *Duration* to the *Start time* of the current *Repetition*, where the *Duration* is equal to the *Upper bound*.

C20.   NOD YOUR HEAD

Counting: Control eye movements by nodding your head opposite to the visual path.

The planner has an *Execution failure* of a plan that includes *Perception* with a *Cause of failure* of *Nonconscious behavior conflicting with planned behavior*. The planner *Modifies* the plan to include *Concurrent execution* of a plan that causes the planner to have a *Perceptual behavior constraint* that *Blocks* the *Execution of nonconscious perceptual behavior*.

4.4 EDUCATION (32 STRATEGIES)

The fourth of the ten planning domains presented here is that of the field of education, broadly defined to include the classroom activities of educational institutions as well as the informal approaches that people will use to teach or train others.

The first 16 of the 32 education strategies were the very first of the strategy representations that were authored in this study, and are markedly shorter, with a rougher style, than seen in later representation work. They were collected using a directed interview method, where the interviewees included former schoolteachers and administrators. Perhaps reflecting the realities of current educational practice, the strategies appear to be reactionary to the traditions and methods of didactic teaching, with emphasis on test taking and peer competition, all from the perspective of the student operating in this environment. Within this framework, the goals achieved by strategies concern garnering more than your share of teacher attention, cheating and lying to get ahead, and managing your way through exams when you are unprepared.

Much later in the course of this project, after representing the strategies of several other domains, the strategies of education were revisited—this time from the opposite perspective. Instead of looking at the way that students pursue their goals, the methods of teachers, administrators, and academic theorists were considered, collected through my own research interactions with members of these groups over the last several years. In contrast to the goals met by student strategies, the goals of the second set of 16 strategies all concern advancement of knowledge or ability in others. The concerns of these strategies are of selection of teaching methods, approaches to assessment, and ways of motivating students to pursue an area of study. Compared to the first 16, these strategies are markedly longer and have a representation style that is more consistent with that of other planning domains.

Notably missing from this collection are tutoring strategies that teachers employ during one-on-one interaction with their students. The notion of a tutoring strategy has continued to receive attention over the last few decades of educational research. Fueled by studies indicating that tutored students show dramatic improvements in scholastic achievement, many researchers have attempted to mirror this type of interaction in computer software-based tutoring systems, where tutoring strategies are often implicitly (but sometimes explicitly) represented. Educational technologists continue to debate the merits of different strategic approaches, but the best work on cataloging and describing tutoring strategies generalizes over the observed behaviors of human tutors as they interact with their students (Lepper, Woolverton, Mumme, & Gurtner, 1993).

E1.   INTERRUPT INFORMATION FLOW

Education: Interrupt a lecture when something is unclear to avoid being lost in the future.

A group of agents are engaged in a *One-to-many information delivery activity* where the many agents, including the planner, are engaged in *Information processing*. The planner has an *Information processing failure* and envisions that this will cause future *Information processing failures*. The planner executes a plan of *Interruption of activity* followed by an *Activity request* to the one agent to do a *One-to-one information delivery activity* with the planner followed by a *Resumption of interrupted activity*.

E2.   TAKE NOTES

Education: Taking notes of testable information helps you study for future exams.

A planner is engaged in *Information processing* and envisions a future state where the planner will be the subject of an *Assessment of knowledge* and that the *Degree of information decay* will cause the planner to do poorly on this assessment. The planner executes a plan of *Categorizing information* on the result of the *Information processing*, into two categories, based on the envisionment of the *Assessment of knowledge*. One category of information is *Disregarded*. The other category of information is used in doing an *External encoding of information*. The planner then schedules a *Decoding of external information* to happen before the *Assessment of knowledge* such that the *Degree of information decay* is low when the assessment occurs.

E3.   REQUEST INDIVIDUAL ATTENTION

Education: Ask an instructor to give you special attention over others.

A group of agents are engaged in a *One-to-many transfer of expertise activity*, where the many agents includes the planner. The planner envisions that the *Scheduled activity duration* will not be enough to raise the *Level of expertise* of the planner to that of the transferring agent. The planner makes a plan to make an *Activity request* that the transferring agent *Reschedule* so that a *One-to-one transfer of expertise activity* is in the place of some or all of the *One-to-many transfer of expertise activity*.

E4.   COPY THE WORK OF OTHERS

Education: Copy the work of your peers and claim that it is your own.

An agent makes an *Activity request* to the planner to *Make a work product* which will be used in a future *Assessment of work product* activity. The planner executes a plan to *Accept a request* to do the activity *Make a work product*, but does not do this activity. The planner then *Gains possession* of a thing which is the result of some other agent's execution of *Making a work product*, done in response to an equivalent *Activity request*. The planner *Duplicates* this thing, and *Informs* the assessing agent that the thing is the result of their own execution of *Making a work product*.

E5.   POSTPONE ANSWERS UNTIL KNOWN

Education: Turn in your assignments after you are told what the correct answers are.

An agent makes an *Activity request* to the planner and a group of other agents to *Make a work product* which will be used in a future *Assessment of work product activity*. This agent also informs the planner and the other agents that there is a *Deadline for submission* for the product of this activity. The planner executes a plan where the planner makes a *Permission request* to *Submit after the deadline*. On the agent's *Acceptance of a permission request*, the planner waits until after the *Deadline for submission*, *Observes* the *Assessment of work product activity* of the other agents and their things, and *Learns* the *Assessment criteria*. Then the planner performs the *Make a work product activity*, using the learned *Assessment criteria*. Finally, the planner does the *Submit after deadline activity*.

E6.   INVOKE SYMPATHY BEFORE ASSESSMENT

Education: Bias an assessment in your favor by making a teacher feel sorry for you.

The planner envisions that they will be the subject of a future *Assessment*, and that they will do poorly. The planner executes a plan to *Inform* the agent of the assessment that the planner has *Impaired abilities* caused by *Mental anxiety* caused by events *Outside the current context*. These events are *Narrated* to the agent with the goal of *Invoking emotions* which are *Sympathetic* to the planner.

E7.   TRIAL AND ERROR

Education: Learn how to do something by exploring the scope of possibilities.

The planner has the goal of *Learning a skill*, and the skill is a *Fallible* and includes the execution of a set of *Decisions*. The planner executes a *Repetitive plan* terminated at the *Successful execution of the skill*. In each *Iteration*, the planner *Enumerates possible decisions* of the skill, and *Randomly selects* a *Decision series* that has not been chosen in a *Previous iteration*. The planner then *Attempts skill execution* using the selected *Decision series*. If a *Successful execution of the skill* occurs, then the selected *Decision series* is *Memorized* for future use.

E8.   FABRICATE RESULTS

Education: Avoid doing investigations by fabricating reasonable results.

An agent has the goal that the planner *Gather data* by *Executing a procedure*. The planner has the goal of *Avoiding* this execution. The planner executes the following plan. For each *Datum* in the *Data set*, the planner *Guesses* a *Possible data value* which would be the result of *Executing a procedure*. The planner *Informs* the agent that the *Guesses* are actually the *Data set* obtained by *Gathering data*.

E9.   POSTPONE WORK UNTIL DEADLINE

Education: Schedule work at the last possible time to increase your focus and intensity.

A planner has the goal of *Submitting before a deadline* and must *Schedule* the action of *Making a work product*. The planner knows the *Total duration* of this work necessary for the work to be completed, and envisions that *Low intensity effort* or *Distractions* will cause the work not to be of *Satisfactory quality* or will increase the *Total duration* or that the *Deadline* may be changed or the *Goal* will become an *Abandoned goal*. The planner schedules the *Making a work product activity* so that only this activity can be done between the *Start time* and the *End time*. During the work activity, *Execution problems* are *Resolved* by *Increasing intensity*, and *Distracting goals* are *Postponed* or *Left unsatisfied*.

E10. GET TUTORING

Education: When having trouble doing work, get a tutor to teach you how to do it.

> An agent has the goal that the planner *Make a work product* with the goal that the planner will *Practice a skill*. The planner executes the following. First, the planner *Locates an agent* who has an *Expertise in the skill* that is necessary to *Make a work product*. Second, the planner creates a plan to cause the expert to have the goal that the planner *Improves a skill*. The expert and the planner schedule and execute a *One-to-one transfer of expertise* which includes *Guided execution* which produces the thing which satisfies the first agent's goal.

E11. DELEGATE ASSIGNED WORK

Education: To get out of assigned work, get someone else to do it for you.

> An agent has the goal that the planner *Make a work product* with the goal that this *Execution* will cause the achievement of an *Educational goal*. The planner has the goal of *Avoiding* this work. The planner executes a plan to cause it to be that a third agent has the goal of *Making a work product* and *Transferring possession* of the result to the planner. The planner then *Waits* until the third agent *Achieves the goals*, then *Informs* the first agent that they have *Achieved the goals* of the first agent, by producing the thing which is the product of *Making a work product* activity.

E12. LEARN TESTABLE MATERIALS FIRST

Education: On the way to gaining an expertise, start by learning what is going to be on the test.

> A planner envisions that an *Assessment of knowledge* will be given to them in the future. This assessment will have an *Assessment coverage* that is a subset of a *Field of knowledge*. The planner has the goal of *Having expertise* in this field, which includes a varied set of *Abilities*. The agent envisions that the amount of time before the *Assessment of knowledge* is less than the time required to schedule *Learning activities* for each of the *Abilities* involved in *Having expertise*. The planner executes a plan of *Ordering ideas* on the *Abilities* based on the envisionment of the *Assessment of knowledge*. The *Envisioned likelihood* that an *Ability* will be an *Assessment criteria* in the *Assessment of knowledge* determines the ordering. The planner schedules *Learning activities* for the *Abilities* in this order, until *The schedule is full*.

E13. TAKE A PRACTICE EXAM

Education: In order to improve your test-taking abilities, take a practice exam.

A planner envisions that an *Assessment of knowledge* will be given to them in the future. The planner is having an *Envisionment problem* that the *Assessment result* cannot be *Predicted with high probability*. This problem may be causing a *Feeling of anxiety*. Alternatively, the planner may believe that they have *Poor ability* in doing an *Assessment of knowledge* which will cause a *Poor assessment result*. The planner executes a plan to cause a different *Assessment of knowledge* that includes *Similar events* to those in the envisioned assessment, and *Schedules* this plan before the real event.

E14. ANSWER EASY QUESTIONS FIRST

Education: When taking a test under time pressure, answer the easy questions first.

A planner is doing an *Assessment of ability* that includes a *Question set* of *Assessment questions*. The planner executes a plan to *Iterate over* the *Question set*. In each *Iteration*, the planner does an *Ability prediction* for each *Assessment question* which results in a *Degree of confidence*. At the *Termination of iteration* the planner *Orders the subtasks* where the *Ordering metric* is the *Degree of confidence* and the subtasks are the *Assessment of ability* subtasks for the *Assessment questions*.

E15. GUESS WHEN FACING DEADLINES

Education: If you run out of time when taking tests, randomly guess at remaining questions.

A planner is doing an *Assessment of knowledge* that has a *Completion deadline* and that includes a *Question set* of *Assessment questions*. The planner envisions that when the *Completion deadline* arrives, one or more subtasks of the *Assessment of ability* for the *Assessment questions* will be not be achieved. The planner executes a plan to *Iterate over* the *Assessment questions* of these subtasks. For each question, the planner *Randomly guesses* a *Possible answer*, and uses the result to complete the subtask.

E16.   BE A TEACHER'S PET

Education: Bias the assessments you receive by being your teacher's favorite student.

> A group of agents are engaged in a *One-to-many transfer of expertise*, where the many agents include the planner. The planner envisions that they will be the subject of a future *Assessment of expertise* given by the one agent. The planner envisions that the *Assessment result* that they will receive is less than the *Perfect assessment result*. The planner executes a plan with the goal of *Invoking emotions* that are *Liking emotions* where the object is the planner or *Pride emotions* where the indirect object of the one agent is the planner.

E17.   SINK OR SWIM

Education: Throw someone in a pool in order to force them to learn to swim.

> The planner has the goal that a different agent have an *Execution ability* for a *Skill*. The planner envisions that *If it were the case* that the agent *Attempted the execution* of the *Skill*, that during the *Duration of execution* the *Execution ability* of the agent would increase to *Competent ability* before a *Deadline* at which time there would be an *Execution failure* with a cause of *Incompetency of ability*. The agent is executing a plan to *Avoid the execution* of the *Skill* with a cause that an *Envisioned threat* exists that an *Execution failure* of the skill will *Violate goals* that are *Preservation goals* of the agent. The planner executes a plan to *Modify the world state* such that the planner envisions that *Preservation goals* of the agent will be *Violated goals* at some future state, and that *Blocking the goal violation Requires* the *Successful execution* of the *Skill*. The planner *Adds the expectation* that the agent will *Terminate the execution* of the plan to *Avoid the execution*, and will *Attempt the execution* of the *Skill*.

E18.   LEARN BY DOING

Education: Learn a skill by repetitively trying and failing.

> The planner has the goal of having an *Execution ability* for a *Skill*. The planner envisions that *If it were the case* that the planner *Attempted the execution* of the *Skill*, there would be an *Execution failure* with a cause of *Incompetent ability*, and that this *Execution failure* would not *Violate goals* of the planner. The planner executes a plan to execute a *Repetitive plan* that includes the *Attempted execution* of the *Skill*, and the *Adding of the*

expectation that there will be an *Execution failure* and that the *Execution ability* for the *Skill* will increase in *Subsequent repetitions*. *During the execution* of the *Repetitive plan*, the planner *Monitors* for *Execution decisions* during the *Attempted execution*, and *Adds the explanation preference* for *Explanations of execution failure* that include the *Execution decisions* made during the *Repetition*.

E19.   LEARN BY SIMULATED DOING

Education: Learn a skill with high failure costs by trying and failing in a simulated environment.

The planner has the goal that a different agent have an *Execution ability* for a *Skill*. The planner envisions that *If it were the case* that the agent executed a *Repetitive plan* that included the *Attempted execution* of the *Skill*, that there would be *Execution failures* caused by *Incompetent ability* for a *Quantity of Execution repetitions*, followed by *Successful executions* of the skill. The planner envisions that an *Execution failure* of the agent would cause changes in the *Execution environment* that result in *Violation of goals* of the planner. The planner executes a plan to *Modify the world state* such that there exists a new *Execution environment* where *Characteristics of the environment* are *Similar* to the *Environment characteristics* of the other *Execution environment*, where the planner envisions the execution of the *Repetitive plan* by the agent will cause *Successful execution* after a *Quantity of repetitions*, and where the planner envisions that an *Execution failure* of the agent *Attempting the execution* of the *Skill* in the new *Execution environment* will not *Violate goals* of the planner. The planner then plans and executes to *Achieve the goal* that the agent executes the *Repetitive plan* in the new *Execution environment*, and *Monitors* for *Successful execution* of the *Skill*. The planner *Monitors for planning* that includes the execution of the skill by the agent in a different *Execution environment*, in which case the planner *Adds the threat* of an *Execution failure* with a cause of *Incompetent ability*, itself caused by the *Disjunctive set* of the two sets of *Characteristics of the environments*.

E20.   SKILL APPRENTICESHIP

Education: Become an apprentice to a skilled master to learn their skill.

The planner has the goal of having an *Execution ability* for a *Skill*. A different agent has an *Execution ability* for this skill, where the *Level of ability* of this agent is a *High ability*. The *Normal plans* of this agent include the execution of this skill and *Subplans* for which the planner has an *Execution ability*. The planner executes a plan to achieve the goal that the agent has the goal that the planner has an *Execution ability* for the skill and executes a plan to *Modify the plans* which are the *Normal plans* of the agent so that they are *Cooperatively executed* by the planner and the agent, with the *Planning preference* that favors plans where the planner executes subplans in the execution of the *Skill*. The planner then *Schedules* to *Periodically execute* a plan to achieve the goal that the agent *Modify the plans* which are the *Normal plans* with the *Planning preference* where the set of *Subplans* is greater. The planner *Adds the expectation* that after some *Quantity* of *Periodic executions*, all of the *Subplans* of the *Skill* will be in the set, at which time the planner will *Terminate the execution* of the plan.

E21.   LECTURE AND TEST

Education: Teach something to a group by lecturing and then testing their comprehension.

The planner has the goal that a set of agents *Achieve a knowledge goal* of *Information* that is *Known* by the planner. The planner has a *Partial plan* that includes *Informing* and *Explaining* the *Information* to an agent with *Execution decisions* that are made with *Information* that is the result of *Communication* with the agent, and has a *Planning failure* in *Iteratively executing* the plan over the set of agents with a cause of *Lack of time*. The planner *Modifies the partial plan* so that the *Informing* and *Explaining* is done to the set of agents rather than a single agent. The planner *Modifies the partial plan* to include subplans during the execution to achieve a set of *Knowledge goals* where each is the *Information* for the *Execution decisions* in the original partial plan for each of the agents in the set. The planner *Schedules the subplans* during the *Partial plan* before the planner envisions *that Execution decisions* using the *Information* are made.

E22.   INDEPENDENT STUDY

Education: Study on your own when your interests are too specialized.

The planner is a member of a set of agents, and has scheduled a *Shared plan* for *Achieving goals* that are *Knowledge goals* that include *Collaboratively executing* a plan with a subset of the set that has *Knowledge goals* of *Information* that are equal, and where the execution of the *Shared plans* satisfies a *Precondition* that is a *Requirement* to *Achieve a goal* not a *Knowledge goal*, and is a goal of every agent in the set. The planner has the *Knowledge goal* of *Information* that is not equal to the *Knowledge goals* of other agents in the set, and has a different plan for *Achieving the knowledge goal*, and has a *Scheduling failure* for the different plan with a cause of *Lack of time*. The planner executes a plan to achieve the goal that the execution of the different plan also satisfies the *Precondition* that is the *Requirement*, and *Removes from the schedule* the *Shared plan* for achieving the other *Knowledge goal*.

E23. LIBERAL ARTS CURRICULUM

Education: Liberal arts curriculums aim to have graduates who are well rounded.

The planner has the goal that a set of agents *Achieve knowledge goals* that are *Unspecified goals* that *Enable the execution* of plans that *Achieve goals* that are *Envisioned future goals* of these agents. The planner has a *Planning failure* caused by an *Envisionment failure* of the *Knowledge preconditions* of the plans that these agents will execute to achieve these goals. The planner *Specifies the goals* to be a set of *Knowledge goals* that are the *Top several in a set* of an *Ordered set* of *Knowledge goals* that *Satisfy preconditions* that *are Knowledge preconditions* for *Envisioned possible plans* of the agents, with an *Ordering principle* that advances those that satisfy *Knowledge preconditions* in a greater number of plans.

E24. PERFORMANCE EXAM

Education: Assess the abilities of people by testing them in real environments.

The planner has the *Knowledge goal* of knowing the *Execution ability* of a *Skill* for an agent that has *Executed a plan* to achieve the goal of having this *Execution ability*. The execution of the *Skill* is an *Observable execution*. The planner envisions that *If it were the case* that the agent had an *Execution failure* in executing the *Skill* then there is a set of *Possible causes* that includes *Lack of ability*. The planner plans a *Partial plan* to cause the agent to *Execute the skill* where the planner *Observes the execution*. The planner then *Iterates* over the set of *Possible causes* that are not *Lack of ability* and for each *Adds to the partial plan* a *Subplan* to *Block the cause* of the *Execution failure* in an *Unknown execution environment*. The planner then executes the plan, and *If it is the case* that the plan is *Successfully executed*, then the planner *Achieves the knowledge goal* of the *Execution ability*.

E25. SELF-GRADING

Education: Ask students what grades they think they should get to avoid bad estimations.

> The planner has the *Knowledge goal* of knowing the *Execution ability* of a *Skill* for an agent that has *Executed a plan* to achieve the goal of having this *Execution* ability. The planner has a plan for achieving this goal that includes the *Execution of the skill* by the *Agency* of the agent, but a *Threat* exists that the achievement of the *Knowledge goal* will cause *False knowledge* with a cause that the *Observed execution* of the *Skill* caused an *Inaccurate induction*. The agent has *Knowledge* of the *Execution ability* of the agent, and the planner envisions that *If it were the case* that the plan *Requested information* that was this *Knowledge*, then the *Envisioned likelihood* that the agent would *Inform* the planner of *Information* that is not *False information* is a *High envisioned likelihood*. The planner *Modifies the plan* to include *Requesting information* of the *Knowledge* of the *Execution ability* of the agent, and *Adds a threat* that the *Information* is *False information*.

E26. EVERYONE PASSES

Education: Eliminate competitive behavior and pandering by passing everyone.

> The planner is planning a plan to achieve the goal that a set of agents have an *Execution ability* for a *Skill* and has a *Partial plan* to *Maximize the value* that is the *Quantity* of agents in the set that have this *Execution ability* that includes the *Execution of a Shared plan* by all of the agents. Agents in the set have the goal of having the *Execution ability* for the skill, and the *Auxiliary goal* that the planner *Informs* other agents that their *Execution ability* is a *Greater ability* than other agents in the set. The planner *Envisions the possibility* that *During the execution* of the plan, the agents will do *Competitive planning* and will execute plans to achieve *Competitive goals* that will cause the *Quantity* of agents in the set that have the *Execution ability* to be lower than a *Possible envisioned maximized value*. The planner executes a plan to *Inform* the agents in the set that in *Future states*, *If it were the case* that the planner *Informs* agents of the *Execution ability* of the agents, the planner will *Inform* the agents that the *Execution ability* is equal to that of the other agents in the set.

E27. STUDY A FIELD THROUGH ITS HISTORY

Education: Read about the discoveries in the history of a field to understand current theories.

The planner has the goal of achieving a set of *Knowledge goals* where the *Knowledge* is *Shared knowledge* of *Domain experts* in a *Domain of interest*. In *Previous world states*, the *Shared knowledge* of the set of *Domain experts* in the same *Domain of interest* was not equal to the current *Shared knowledge*. The planner executes a plan to *Imagine a set* of *Shared knowledge* in these *Previous states*, and then *Orders the set* with an *Ordering principle* that advances *Shared knowledge* at *Earlier past world states*. The planner then executes a plan to *Iterate through the set* of *Shared knowledge*, and for each *Achieve a knowledge goal* of the *Explanation* for why the *Shared knowledge In the current iteration* is different from the *Shared knowledge* that is the *Next in the ordered set*.

E28. POP QUIZ

Education: Ensure that students are doing their work with the threat of a pop quiz.

The planner has the goal that an agent achieve a set of *Knowledge goals* and has a *Plan* with a *Plan duration* that includes the *Agency* of the agent to execute *Subplans* that are not *Observed executions* by the planner. The planner *Envisions a threat* to the plan in that the agent does not execute the *Subplan* with a cause that it is not a *Subplan* of a goal of the agent, and the planner *Envisions the possibility* that the *Successful execution of the plan* would not achieve the goal. The planner *Modifies the plan* by *Scheduling* a set of *Subplans* at *Start times* that are *Randomly selected* from *Moments* in the *Duration*. In each subplan the planner *Requests the execution* of a plan by the agent such that the *Successful execution* of the plan *Requires* that the agent *Executed the subplan* in the goal that were *Subplans previously scheduled*, and where a *Failed execution* will cause a *Violation of a goal* of the agent. The planner adds a *Planning constraint* against plans that cause the agent to have *Knowledge* of the *Scheduled start time* of these subplans.

E29.   ENHANCE A PHYSICAL SKILL WITH A MENTAL MODEL

Education: Understand the physics of a physical skill to scaffold the learning process.

> The planner has the goal of having an *Execution ability* for a *Skill* that includes *Subconscious execution* of a plan with *Execution decisions* that *Modify characteristics* that are *Characteristics* of the *Execution environment* that cause a *World state* that is the goal achieved by *Executing the skill*. The planner has a plan for achieving this goal that includes *Iteratively executing* a plan that includes an *Attempted execution* of the skill. The planner *Modifies the plan* to include a *Preceding subplan* to achieve the *Knowledge goal* of having *Causal chain* of how the *Characteristics* of the *Execution environment* cause the *World state* and how different *Characteristics* of the *Execution environment* cause different *World states*.

E30.   PAIR STUDENTS FOR COLLABORATION

Education: Have students work together when collaboration aids understanding.

> The planner has the goal that a set of agents achieve a *Knowledge goal* and has a plan that includes the execution of a *Partial plan* with the *Agency* of the set of agents, with an *Envisioned likelihood of success* that is not a *Definite likelihood* with a cause that a subset of the agents will have an *Execution failure* of the partial plan with a cause of *Lack of understanding*. The planner envisions that *If it were the case* that the *Partial plan* was *Collaboratively executed* by the agent and *One of a set* of agents that includes a subset of the other agents in the set, then the *Envisioned likelihood of successful execution* of the *Partial plan* would be greater. The planner executes a plan to *Divide the set* of agents into two sets where the *Quantity* of agents in the set is equal, and then *Iterate* through the set that is the first set and *Select from the set* that is the second set with a *Selection criteria* of *Random choice*. In each *Iteration*, the planner *Imagines a set* that includes the agent of the iteration and the randomly selected agent. The planner then *Modifies the plan* such that the *Partial plan* is *Collaboratively executed* by agents that are members of the imagined sets.

E31. FIELD TRIP

Education: Ground theory in reality with an excursion to where knowledge is applicable.

The planner has the goal of achieving a set of *Knowledge goals* in a *Knowledge domain* and is executing a plan to achieve these goals that includes the *Agency* of other agents to *Inform* the planner of *Information* or *Parsing encoded information* by the planner. The planner is *Making a planning decision* whether to *Abandon the knowledge goals* with a *Decision justification* of an *Envisionment failure* of how the *Achievement of the knowledge goals Enables plans* that *Achieve goals* that are other goals of the planner. The planner *Suspends the planning decision* and executes a plan to *Locate an agent* that is *Executing plans* that are *Possible future plans* of the agent that have *Knowledge preconditions* that are met by the *Knowledge* in the *Knowledge goals*. The planner then *Observes the execution* of these plans, then *Resumes the planning decision*.

E32. NATIONAL STANDARDS

Education: Encourage professional learning by teachers by installing common teaching goals.

The planner has a *Leadership role* over a set of agents, where each agent has the goal that a different set of agents achieves a different set of *Knowledge goals*. Each agent in the first set of agents has a plan for *Achieving their goal*, all of which include the *Execution of a skill*. The planner envisions that a subset of these agents will have an *Execution failure* in the *Execution of the skill* with a cause of *Lack of ability*, which will cause subsets of the different sets of agents to *Fail to achieve the goals* that are the *Knowledge goals*. The planner envisions that *If it were the case* that the *Knowledge goals* were equal for two agents in the first set, this would *Enable the execution* of *Collaborative planning* for these two agents. The planner plans and executes a plan to achieve the goal that the *Knowledge goals* that are in the goals of each of the agents in the first set are equal, and that these agents do *Collaborative planning* to achieve these goals with other agents in the set.

4.5 **IMMUNOLOGY** (21 STRATEGIES)

The fifth set of strategies presented here is in the domain of cellular immunology, and like the strategies of animal behavior presented earlier, they are anthropomorphic in nature. The processes of cellular biology that comprise the body's immune system involve a complex system of interactions between cells that has the effect of reducing the body's susceptibility to bacteria and viruses that would otherwise interfere with normal biological functions. Any deep understanding of immunology is rooted in the chemistry of cells, but for those of us who would prefer more shallow explanations, the immune system is an irresistible target for anthropomorphic reasoning.

In the anthropomorphic world of immunology, the body is seen as a sort of territory populated by cells of many sorts. Red and white blood cells travel the highways of arteries and back roads of capillaries servicing the more stationary population of tissue cells. The nearly impenetrable boundary of this territory is the skin, but materials and supplies must be brought inside into the respiratory and digestive organs to be traded and processed before they can be distributed. When defenses are weak, or the opposing force is strong, the territory can be invaded by the archenemies of the cells: bacteria and viruses. Once inside the territory, these adversaries hunt down cells that are susceptible to their attacks, sometimes simply destroying them and other times taking over their will, forcing them to assist them in multiplying so that more cells can be attacked. To defend themselves, the cells sometimes kill themselves rather than aid their adversaries when they feel they are losing control of their actions, or they frantically send signals to other cells to warn them of an invasion before knocking themselves out cold. Certain cells patrol the territory, looking for signs of an invasion, ready to kill fellow cells that show signs of assisting the enemy, kill the enemy outright if possible, or call for help when things get out of hand. In the most complex display of defensive teamwork, a special operations force is sometimes sent out to gather intelligence data on the enemy, which is reported back to a team of engineers that will design, manufacture, and distribute throughout the territory a killing device that exploits the enemy's unique and hidden weaknesses.

The 21 immunology strategies presented here are those that become evident when trying to explain the biological processes of the immune response from within this anthropomorphic vision. In some cases, these strategies may push the analogical framework in ways that are novel, but in most cases the strategies that are presented here are based on the way these processes are described in several introductory immunology textbooks. Each process was then recast as a strategy, largely by borrowing from the intentional vocabulary that is used in a process's description. Pedagogically, the use of highly intentional vocabulary may provide a sort of anthropomorphic scaffolding for novice students, allowing them to draw correct inferences about these complex processes by relating them to human intentions. Presumably, these expectations and inferences are later replaced with stronger systemic theories as these novices delve further into the mechanics of the domain.

11. HAVE MECHANICAL BARRIERS TO ANTIGENS

Immunology: Skin, gastrointestinal tract lining, and lung epithelium block antigens from tissues.

> The planner has a *Leadership role* in an *Organization* where agents in the organization have *Locations* that are in a *Region* that has a *Boundary definition* that is a *Relative boundary* that includes the *Location* of the agents. A set of agents exist that have an *Adversarial relationship* with agents in the *Organization*, and that have *Locations* that are not in the *Region*. The planner envisions that *If it were the case* that an agent in the set had a *Location* that was in the *Region*, that this *Enables* an *Adversarial plan* of the agent. The planner executes a plan to do *Design of a thing* with the *Design goal* that *If it is the case* that the thing is at a *Location* that is on the *Boundary* of the *Region*, then a plan executed by a member of the set of adversaries that includes *Changing locations* with a *Transfer path* that includes the *Location* on the *Boundary* will have an *Execution failure* with a *Failure cause* of *Blocked transfer path*. The planner executes a *Repetitive plan* to *Make the thing* and *Transfer location* of the thing to a *Location* that is on the *Boundary* and that is not currently the *Location* of a thing in a *Previous repetition*, with a *Repetition termination condition* that the *Transfer location* subplan has an *Execution failure* with a cause of *Unsatisfied condition*.

12. SECRETED TOXINS PREVENT ANTIGENS

Immunology: Acid in stomach destroys antigens before they can enter other tissues.

> The planner has a *Leadership role* in an *Organization* where agents in the organization have *Locations* that are in a *Region*. A set of agents exist that have an *Adversarial relationship* with agents in the *Organization*, and that have an *Adversarial plan* with a *Precondition* that the agent has a *Location* in the *Region*. The planner has a plan that includes *Making a thing*, and envisions that *If it were the case* that the *Thing* had an *Adjacent location* to an agent in the set of adversaries, then it would *Block the execution* of the *Adversarial plan* by the agent. The planner executes a *Repetitive plan* that includes *Making of the thing* and the *Transfer of locations* of the thing to a *Location* that the planner *Selects from a set* of *Locations* in the *Region* with the *Selection criteria* of *Random choice*.

I3.   NATURAL KILLER LYMPHOCYTES

Immunology: NK cells kill infected cells by recognizing abnormal cell surface features.

> The planner has a *Leadership role in an Organization*. The planner *Envisions the possibility* that agents in the *Organization* have an *Adversarial relationship* with other agents in the organization, and has the goal that these agents are *Destroyed*. The planner executes a plan to cause a subset of agents in the *Organization* to execute *Normal plans* that include the execution of a plan to achieve the goal of having an *Acquaintance* with every agent in the organization, and to *Monitor* for *Expectation violations* of the *Observed execution* of an agent. In this event, the agent in the subset executes a plan to *Destroy* the agent in the *Expectation violation*.

I4.   CELL-MEDIATED IMMUNITY

Immunology: Processed antigens cause sensitized T cells to bind to other antigen-displaying cells.

> The planner has a *Leadership role* in an *Organization* of agents and has the *Knowledge goal* of the set of agents in the organization that have an *Adversarial relationship* with other agents in the organization. The planner has an *Acquaintance* with an agent in the *Organization* that is a member of the set of *Adversaries*, and this agent has a set of *Characteristics*. The planner executes a plan to achieve the *Knowledge goal* of the set of *Characteristics* of agents in the *Organization* that are not a member of the set of *Adversaries*. The planner then *Imagines a set* of agents that includes only the agent in the *Acquaintance*. The planner then executes a plan to cause a subset of the *Organization* to execute a *Repetitive plan* of *Locating an agent* in the *Organization* that has *Characteristics* that are equal to one in the disjoint set of the two sets of characteristics, followed by *Informing* the planner of the agent. The planner then *Monitors* for *Informing* by members of the subset for a *Monitoring duration*, and *In this event*, adds to the imagined set the agent in the *Information*. At the *End time* of the *Duration*, the planner achieves the *Knowledge goal* with the *Imagined set*.

I5.   INFLAMMATION RESPONSE

Immunology: Triggered T cells excrete lymphokines to attract other cells to wall off antigens.

> The planner is in an *Organization* and has *Partially executed* a plan in an *Execution location* that is in a *Region*, where the plan includes *Locating an agent* in the organization that has an *Adversarial relationship* with the other

agents in the organization, with a *Remaining plan* that includes *Destroying the agent*. The planner envisions an *Execution failure* in the *Remaining plan* with a cause of *Successful counterplan* by the agent, where the *Counterplan* includes *Transfer of location* of the agent. The planner *Suspends the execution* of the *Remaining plan*, and executes a plan to achieve the goal that other agents in the *Region Transfer locations* to *Locations* that are *Adjacent locations* to the agent. The planner then *Adds the expectation* that the *Execution of the counterplan* will be a *Failed execution* with a cause of *Blocked transfer* path in the *Transfer of location*. The planner then *Resumes the execution* of the plan.

---

16. CYOTOXIC RESPONSE

Immunology: Triggered CD8+ cells destroy cells before they release replicated viruses.

The planner is an agent in an *Organization* and has the goal that agents in the organization do not have an *Adversarial relationship* with other agents in the organization. A set of agents in the organization have an *Adversarial relationship* with the other agents in the organization, and are executing an *Adversarial plan*, which includes having a *Control relationship* over an agent in the *Organization*, then causing the agent to execute a *Repetitive plan* to *Create an agent* where the created agents have an *Adversarial relationship* with the other agents in the *Organization*, and where the *Termination of repetition condition* is the *Destruction* of the agent executing the repetitive plan, which *Enables the execution* of the *Adversarial plan* by the created agents. The planner plans and executes to *Achieve the goal* of having an *Execution ability* to *Make a decision* that an arbitrary agent in the *Organization* is the subject of a *Control relationship* by a member of the set of *Adversarial agents*. The planner then executes a *Repetitive plan* to *Locate an agent* that is the subject of the *Control relationship*, and *Destroy* the agent with a *Deadline* for the *Completion of execution* of this action that is the *Termination of repetition condition*.

---

17. HUMORAL IMMUNITY

Immunology: B cells bind to antigen then start the production of antibody-producing plasma.

The planner has a *Leadership role* in an *Organization*, where agents in the organization have *Locations* that are in a *Region*. A set of agents exist that have an *Adversarial relationship* with agents in the *Organization* and that have *Locations* that are in the *Region*. The planner has the goal to *Permanently block* the execution of *Adversarial plans* by these agents. The set of *Characteristics* of the agents in the adversarial set are equal and are *Unknown* to the planner, and a subset of these *Characteristics* are a disjoint subset of the characteristics of the agents and of the agents in the *Organization*. The planner executes a plan to cause two subsets of the *Organization* to execute plans. The first subset executes a plan that includes *Achieving a knowledge goal* of the unknown subset of characteristics, and then *Informing* the second subset of this knowledge. The second subset executes a plan to *Wait for the event* of the *Informing* by the first set, then do *Designing a thing* with the *Design goal* that if the *Thing* has a *Location* that is an *Adjacent location* to an agent that has the *Characteristics* in the knowledge, then the *Thing* will *Prevent* the *Agency* of the agent. At the *Completion of execution* of the plan of the second subset, the planner executes a plan to cause a third subset of agents in the *Organization* to execute a *Repetitive plan* for a *Duration* to *Make a thing* that is the *Designed thing*, and to *Transfer location* of the thing to a *Location* that is in the *Region*.

---

18. FILTER BLOOD IN SPLEEN

Immunology: Identified antigens are filtered from blood in the spleen.

The planner has a *Leadership role* in an *Organization* where agents in the organization have *Locations* that are in a *Region*. A set of agents have an *Adversarial relationship* with the *Organization*, and have *Locations* that are in the *Region*. The planner has the goal of *Destroying* agents in this set. The planner has a *Partial plan* for *Making a decision* that an agent is a member of the set, and a *Partial plan* for *Destroying* an agent. The planner envisions that every agent in the *Region* will have a specific *Location* at different *Moments* in a *Duration*. The planner *Schedules the execution* of a *Repetitive plan* with an *Execution location* of the specific *Location*, where the plan includes the execution of the *Partial plan* to *Make a decision* if the agent at the *Location* is a member of the set of adversarial agents, and *If it is the case*, then the planner executes the *Partial plan* to *Destroy* the agent, where the *Start time* of the plan is the *Start time* of the *Duration*, and the *Repetition termination condition* is that the *Current time* is greater than the *End time* of the *Duration*.

---

19. PROGRAMMED CELL DEATH

Immunology: Cells destroy themselves after detecting that they have been infected by a virus.

The planner is a member of an *Organization* of agents, and has the goal of *Achieving goals* that are goals of the *Organization*. An agent with an *Adversarial relationship* with the *Organization* is executing an *Adversarial plan*, and has *Successfully executed* a *Partial plan* that includes having a *Control relationship* over the planner. The planner envisions that the *Remaining plan* of the agent will include the *Agency* of the planner in the *Execution* of a *Repetitive plan* to *Create an agent* that has an *Adversarial relationship* with the *Organization*, with a *Termination of repetition condition* of the *Destruction* of the planner, which will *Enable the execution* of *Adversarial plans* by the created agents. The planner executes a plan to *Terminate the execution* of all plans, and to cause the *Destruction* of the planner.

110. INTERFERON RESPONSE

Immunology: Virus-infected cells secrete interferon to warn others and shut down cell processes.

The planner is a member of an *Organization* of agents, and has the goal of *Achieving goals* that are goals of the *Organization*. An agent with an *Adversarial relationship* with the *Organization* is executing an *Adversarial plan*, and has *Successfully executed* a *Partial plan* that includes having a *Control relationship* over the planner. The planner envisions that the *Remaining plan* of the agent will include the *Agency* of the planner in the *Execution* of a *Repetitive plan* to *Create an agent* that has an *Adversarial relationship* with the *Organization*, with a *Termination of repetition condition* of the *Destruction* of the planner, which will *Enable the execution* of *Adversarial plans* by the created agents on agents that have *Adjacent locations* to the planner. The planner has a *Partial plan* that includes *Making a thing* that is a *Designed thing* with the *Design goal* of *Blocking the execution* of plans by the agent that executes the *Making of the thing*, and *Informs* agents that have an *Adjacent location* to this agent of the execution of the *Partial plan*. The planner *Terminates the execution* of *Currently executing plans*, and executes the *Partial plan*.

111. ATTACK IMMUNE SYSTEM WITH TOXINS

Immunology: Antigens survive by releasing toxins to the cells of the immune response.

The planner has an *Adversarial relationship* with an *Organization* of agents that have *Locations* in a *Region*, and has a *Partial plan* that is an *Adversarial plan* with an *Execution location* in the *Region*. The planner *Envisions a threat* to the *Partial plan* with a cause of the execution of a *Counterplan* by a subset of the *Organization* with an *Execution location* that is equal to the *Execution location* of the planner. The planner has a subplan that includes *Making a thing*, and envisions that *If it were the case* that the *Thing* had an *Adjacent location* to an agent in the subset, that it would *Block the execu-*

tion of the *Counterplan* by the agent. The planner *Modifies the plan* to include a *Repetitive subplan* before the execution of the *Adversarial plan* and in the *Execution location* to *Make the thing*, with a *Repetition termination condition* that a *Quantity* of the thing has the *Execution location*. The planner then *Adds the expectation* that the *Counterplan* will have an *Execution failure* with a cause that includes the *Thing*, and then executes the *Adversarial plan*.

---

112. FORM A BARRIER TO DEFENSIVE AGENTS

Immunology: Antigens survive by forming a protective coating against immune response cells.

The planner has an *Adversarial relationship* with an *Organization* of agents that have *Locations* in a *Region*, and has a *Partial plan* that is an *Adversarial plan* with an *Execution location* in the *Region*. The planner *Envisions a threat* to the *Partial plan* with a cause of the execution of a *Counterplan* by a subset of the *Organization* that includes a *Precondition* that agents in the subset have the *Location* that is the *Location of execution* of the *Adversarial plan* of the planner. The planner executes a plan to *Design a thing* with the *Design goal* that *If it is the case* that an agent in the subset *Attempts the execution* of a *Transfer of location* with a *Transfer path* that includes the *Location* of the thing, then there will be an *Execution failure* with a cause of *Blocked transfer path*. The planner then *Adds to the partial plan* that is the *Adversarial plan* a subplan with a *Precondition* that the planner has the *Execution location* to *Imagine a set* that is the *Possible transfer paths* in the *Transfer of location* of the subset of the organization in the *Counterplan*. The planner then *Iterates* through this set, and for each, *Makes the thing* that is the *Designed thing* and *Transfers the location* of this thing to a *Location* that is on the *Possible transfer path*, with a *Deadline* of the *Start time* of the execution by agents in the subset of the subplan of *Transferring location* to the *Execution location* of the *Adversarial plan*.

---

113. LOCALIZE IN INACCESSIBLE SITES

Immunology: Antigens survive in sites that are inaccessible to immune response cells.

The planner has an *Adversarial relationship* with an *Organization* of agents that have *Locations* in a *Region*, and has a *Partial plan* that is an *Adversarial plan* with an *Execution location* in the *Region*. The planner *Envisions a threat* to the *Partial plan* with a cause of the execution of a *Counterplan* by a subset of the *Organization* that includes a *Precondition* of *Physical contact* with the planner. The planner executes a plan to *Imagine a set* of all *Loca-*

tions in the *Region* that the planner envisions a *Successful execution* of the *Adversarial plan If it were the case* that the *Execution location* of the *Adversarial plan* was the *Location*, and there were no agents in the *Location*. The planner then *Orders the set* with an *Ordering criteria* that advances *Locations* where the planner has an *Envisioned likelihood of success* that is lesser for the execution of a plan by an *Arbitrary member* of the subset to *Achieve the goal* of have a *Location* that is equal to the location in the set. The planner then *Specifies the partial plan* so that the *Execution location* is the *First in the ordered set* of locations.

114. RESIDE WITHIN HOST CELLS

Immunology: Antigens resist detection by taking residence in host cells.

The planner has an *Adversarial relationship* with an *Organization* of agents that have *Locations* in a *Region*, and has a *Partial plan* that is an *Adversarial plan* with a *Precondition* that the *Execution location* be in the *Region*. The planner *Envisions a threat* to the *Partial plan* with a cause of the execution of a *Counterplan* by a subset of the organization that includes *Locating an agent* where the agent is the planner. The planner envisions that *If it were the case* that the *Execution location* of the *Partial plan* was in a *Region* that is equal to the *Physical volume* of an agent in the *Organization*, then the *Locating an agent* would be a *Failed execution* and the execution of the *Partial plan* would be a *Successful execution*. The planner *Adds to the partial plan* a subplan that includes *Locating an agent* that is an agent in the *Organization*, followed by *Transferring locations* to a *Location* that is in the *Region* that is equal to the *Physical volume* of the agent, and then executes the *Remaining plan*.

115. INCORPORATE THE IDENTITY OF THE HOST

Immunology: Antigens resist detection by incorporating the DNA of the host.

The planner has an *Adversarial relationship* with an *Organization* of agents that have *Locations* in a *Region*, and has a *Partial plan* that is an *Adversarial plan* with a *Precondition* that the *Execution location* be in the *Region*. The planner *Envisions a threat* to the *Partial plan* with a cause of the execution of a *Counterplan* by a subset of the organization that includes *Locating an agent* where the agent has *Characteristics* that are *Characteristics* of the planner and not *Characteristics* of agents in the *Organization*. The planner envisions that *If it were the case* that the planner had a subset of the *Characteristics* of agents in the organization, then the *Locating an agent* plan of the subset of agents would have an *Execution failure* with a cause of *Unfound condition*. The planner *Adds to the partial plan* a subplan to *Modify characteristics* of the planner to be equal to the subset of *Characteristics* of the agents in the organization.

---

116.   MOLECULAR MIMICRY

Immunology: Part of virus protein resembles host proteins that are attacked by immune response.

The planner has an *Adversarial relationship* with an *Organization* of agents, and has an *Adversarial plan*, and envisions an *Execution failure* of the plan with a cause of a *Successful counterplan* executed by a subset of agents in the organization that includes *Achieving a knowledge goal* of the *Characteristics* of the planner, *Locating an agent* that has a subset of these *Characteristics*, and *Destroying* this agent. The planner executes a plan to cause agents in the subset to have a *False achievement of a knowledge goal* with *Characteristics* that are characteristics of a different subset of agents in the *Organization*. The planner then *Adds the expectation* that the subset of agents will *Locate agents* that are in this different subset, and execute the *Destroy* plan with the *False belief* that these agents have an *Adversarial relationship* with the organization.

---

117.   WILD TYPE ADENOVIRUS

Immunology: A virus antigen starts replication and blocks programmed cell death.

The planner has an *Adversarial relationship* with an *Organization* of agents, and has an *Adversarial plan* that includes having a *Control relationship* over an agent in the *Organization*, followed by causing the agent to execute a *Repetitive plan* to *Create an agent* that has an *Adversarial relationship* with the *Organization*. The planner envisions an *Execution failure* of the plan with a cause of a *Successful counterplan* executed by the agent after the planner has the *Control relationship* that includes *Making a thing* that *Blocks the agency* of the agent. The planner executes a plan to *Design a thing* with the *Design goal* that *If it is the case* that the thing is *Located* at the *Execution location* of the *Counterplan*, then the *Thing Blocks the execution* of the *Making of a thing* by the agent. The planner then *Modifies the plan* that is the *Adversarial* plan to include the *Making of the thing* that is the *Designed thing* at the envisioned location of execution of the *Counterplan* before the execution of the *Adversarial plan*.

118.   DISABLE THE IMMUNE RESPONSE

Immunology: HIV infects T cells through CD4 marker and depletes these immune cells.

The planner has an *Adversarial relationship* with an *Organization* of agents, and has an *Adversarial plan* to *Destroy* a subset of agents in the organization that includes a *Repetitive subplan* of *Locating an agent* in the subset and *Destroying* the agent. The planner envisions an *Execution failure* of the *Adversarial plan* with a cause of a *Successful counterplan* by a different subset of agents in the organization that includes *Achieving a knowledge goal* of *Characteristics* of the planner and *Locating the agent* that has the *Characteristics*, followed by *Destroying* the agent, which is the planner. The planner *Adapts the plan* that is the *Adversarial plan* with an *Adaptation* that is a *Replacement adaptation* of the subset of the agents in the original plan for the subset of agents that are executing the *Counterplan*.

119.   GENE THERAPY

Immunology: Viruses are modified to include genetic material to replace defective material.

The planner has a *Cooperative relationship* with an *Organization*, where the *Cooperative goal* is to cause agents in the *Organization* that have an *Adversarial relationship* with other agents in the organization to have *Cooperative relationships* with these other agents where the *Cooperative plan* is the execution of a set of *Normal activities*. A set of agents that are not in the *Organization* have an *Adversarial relationship* with the *Organization*, and have an *Adversarial plan* that includes having a *Control relationship* over an agent in the *Organization*, followed by causing the agent to execute a *Repetitive plan* to *Create an agent* that has an *Adversarial relationship* with the *Organization*. The planner executes a plan to *Locate an agent* that is in the set of adversaries not in the organization, and then cause the agent to have a *Cooperative relationship* with the planner. The planner then does *Cooperative planning* with the agent that includes to *Modify the plan* that is the *Adversarial plan* by *Replacing the subplan* of causing the *Repetitive plan* with a subplan of executing the *Normal activities*. The planner then causes the agent to execute the *Cooperative plan*.

I20.   IMMUNIZATION THROUGH VACCINATION

Immunology: Harmless variants of antigens are introduced in order to provoke immune response.

The planner has a *Cooperative relationship* with an *Organization* where agents in the organization have *Locations* in a *Region*. A different set of agents have an *Adversarial relationship* with the organization and have an *Adversarial plan* that includes *Transferring location* to a *Location* in the *Region*, having a *Control relationship* over an agent in the *Organization*, and then causing the agent to execute a *Repetitive plan* to *Create an agent* that has an *Adversarial relationship* with the *Organization*. Agents in the organization have a *Counterplan* that includes *Locating an agent* that has an *Adversarial relationship* with the agents in the organization, *Achieving a knowledge goal* of the *Characteristics* of this agent, *Designing a thing* where the *Design goal* is that the *Thing Blocks the agency* of the agent, and *Making the thing*. The planner *Envisions a threat* to the plan that the *Duration* of the *Counterplan* is greater than the *Duration* of the *Adversarial plan*. The planner executes a plan to *Locate an agent* that is in the set of adversaries, and cause the agent to have a *Cooperative relationship* with the planner. The planner then does *Cooperative planning* with the agent to *Modify the plan* that is the *Adversarial plan* by *Removing subplans* that cause the agent in the *Organization* to execute the *Repetitive plan*. The planner then *Enables* the agent to execute the *Modified plan* in a *Location* in the *Region*, and *Adds the expectation* that agents in the *Organization* will execute the *Counterplan*. The planner then *Monitors the execution* of agents in the *Organization* for the *Successful execution* of the *Counterplan*, then *Adds the expectation* that *If it were the case* that a different agent in the set of adversaries *Attempted the execution* of the original *Adversarial plan*, then the *Duration* of the *Counterplan* subplan of *Designing a thing* would be a lesser *Duration*.

I21.   INJECTION OF GAMMA GLOBULINS

Immunology: Antibody-rich blood serum is injected into patients who lack their own antibodies.

The planner has a *Cooperative relationship* with an *Organization*. A set of agents have an *Adversarial relationship* with the *Organization*, and are executing an *Adversarial plan* that includes having a *Control relationship* over an agent in the organization, then causing the agent to execute a *Repetitive plan* to *Create an agent* that has an *Adversarial relationship* with the organization, and then *Enable the execution* by these adversarial agents of the *Adversarial plan*. A different *Organization* also has an *Adversarial relationship* with this set of adversarial agents. In *Past events*, these agents have *Attempted the execution* of this *Adversarial plan*, and had an *Execution fail-*

ure with a cause of a *Successful counterplan* by agents in the *Organization* that includes *Achieving a knowledge goal* of the *Characteristics* of this agent, *Designing a thing* where the *Design goal* is that the *Thing Blocks the agency* of the agent, and *Making the thing*. The planner envisions that *If it were the case* that the agents in the first organization *Attempted the execution* of the *Counterplan*, that it would be a *Failed execution* with a cause of *Lack of ability*. The planner executes a plan to have a *Cooperative relationship* with the second organization, and then does *Cooperative planning* with agents in the *Organization* with the *Cooperative goal* being the *Transfer of location* of the *Things* in the *Making of the thing* to the *Location of execution* of the *Adversarial plan* by the set of adversaries.

4.6 MACHIAVELLI   (60 STRATEGIES)

The beginning of the sixteenth century found the Italian city-state of Florence in a period of great change. In 1512 the Medici family, with the aid of Spanish forces, recaptured political control of Florence from reformists, among them the writer and diplomat Niccolo Machiavelli (1469–1527). Subsequently tortured and exiled from political life, Machiavelli was to spend the majority of his remaining years writing with the intent of gaining the favor of the Medici family, ultimately with success. In December of 1513 he first reports the completion of his most famous work, known to English readers as *The Prince* (Machiavelli, 1995). In this infamous work that stands among the most important in political philosophy, Machiavelli offers practical, strategic advice for the heads of monarchies. When it was published five years after his death, *The Prince* began a long career in the spotlight of controversy that has had great impact on modern political thought. Originally, condemnation of the work was probably motivated more by political agendas than by objections to its content, but *The Prince* (and its author) ultimately became commonly associated with any government whose actions are seen as self-serving, autocratic, or immoral.

This section contains 60 strategies collected by analyzing Machiavelli's classic text, which may be considered to be nearly encyclopedic of culturally shared strategies in the planning domain of monarchy rule and dictatorship. While some of the strategies still strike the contemporary reader as immoral (e.g., strategy 41, Favor cruelty to mercifulness), the majority of the strategies that are offered in the work are more practical in nature, and sometimes even benevolent. Machiavelli explores a broad range of topics including the acquisition of power from both the nobility and through popular means, managing relationships with neighboring lands, military defenses and campaigns, foreign expansion, public perception, economic development, and selection of servants and advisors. These 60 representations are presented along with English excerpts from W. K. Marriott's translation of the work (Project Gutenberg, 1998) in lieu of paraphrased summaries. The ordering of the strategies is both as it is in the text and as they were represented.

M1.   EXTINGUISH THE FAMILY OF THE FORMER LORD

Machiavelli: "He who has annexed [dominions that are of the same country and language], if he wishes to hold them, has only to bear in mind two considerations: the one, that the family of their former lord is extinguished;"

> The planner has achieved a goal to have a *Role* in a *Power relationship* over a *Community* and has the goal that this role be *Permanent*. Agents in the *Community Believe* that the *Role* is a *Successional* role based on a *Rela-*

tionship type between the *Role player* and the *Successor*. In the past, an agent had this *Role*, and there are a set of agents that each have a role in the *Relationship type* with this previous agent. The planner is not a member of this set. The planner executes a plan to *Iterate* over the set of agents, and for each, *Prevent all possibilities* that the agent could have the *Role* in the *Power relationship*.

M2.   CHANGE NO LAWS OR TAXES

Machiavelli: "He who has annexed [dominions that are of the same country and language], if he wishes to hold them, has only to bear in mind two considerations: … the other, that neither their laws nor their taxes are altered, so that in a very short time they will become entirely one body with the old principality."

The planner has achieved a goal to have a *Role* in a *Power relationship* over a *Community* and has the goal that this role be *Permanent*. Agents in the *Community* do *Planning* with the goal of *Following execution rules*, where a subset of the *Rules* are *Explicit rules* that are *Known* by all members of the *Community*, and which are *Maintained* by a set of agents that includes the planner. The planner adds a *Planning constraint* that the set of *Explicit rules* remains constant, and executes a plan to *Prevent* other agents in the set from *Executing* plans that changes the rules.

M3.   TAKE RESIDENCE IN NEW LAND

Machiavelli: "But when states are acquired in a country differing in language, customs, or laws, there are difficulties, and good fortune and great energy are needed to hold them, and one of the greatest and most real helps would be that he who has acquired them should go and reside there."

The planner has achieved a goal to have a *Role* in a *Power relationship* over a *Community*. The planner has the goal that this role be *Permanent*, but *Threats* to this goal exist and *Future threats* are *Expected*. The planner's *Normal activities* occur in a *Location* that is equal to the *Location* of *Activities* that are performed by a different *Community*. The planner executes a plan to *Modify normal activities* so that their *Location* is that of the *Activities* performed by the *Community* in the power relationship.

M4. SEND COLONIALS TO NEW LANDS

Machiavelli: "The other and better course is to send colonies to one or two places, which may be as keys to that state, for it [is] necessary either to do this or else to keep there a great number of cavalry and infantry."

The planner has achieved a goal to have a *Role* in a *Power relationship* over a *Community*. The planner has the goal that this role be *Permanent*, but *Threats* exist that involve the *Agency* of members of the *Community*. The planner's *Normal activities* occur in a *Location* that is equal to the *Location* of *Activities* that are performed by a second *Community* that is also in a *Power relationship* with the planner. The planner executes a plan to *Select a subset* of members from both the first and second *Community*. The planner causes the first subset to change the *Location* of their *Normal activities*, and causes the second to do *Normal activities* in the previous location of the first. The planner *Acquires possession* of the *Possessions* of the members of the first, and *Gives possessions* of these things to the second. The planner has the expectation that the first subset will have the goal of *Retaliation*, and *Counterplans* by *Reducing agency*.

M5. AVOID MAINTAINING ARMED FORCES

Machiavelli: "But in maintaining armed men there in place of colonies one spends much more, having to consume on the garrison all income from the state, so that the acquisition becomes a loss."

The planner has achieved a goal to have a *Role* in a *Power relationship* over a *Community*. The planner has the goal that this role be *Permanent*, but *Threats* exist that involve the *Agency* of members of the *Community*. The planner has a *Role* in a *Power relationship* over a second *Community*, which has *Resources* or *Generates resources*. The planner is *Planning* to *Block* these threats. The planner *Favors against Blocks* that involve agents from the second community *Executing Persistent plans* that *Expend the resources* of the second community.

M6. BECOME DEFENDER OF NEIGHBORS

Machiavelli: "Again, the prince who holds a country differing in the above respects ought to make himself the head and defender of his powerful neighbors, ..."

The planner has a *Role* in a *Power relationship* over a *Community*, and has the goal that this role be *Permanent*. There is a set of communities that are *Adjacent*, such that if they were *Adversaries*, they would be *Threats* to the planner's goal. A subset of these communities are not adversaries. The planner plans and executes to achieve the goal that for each community in this subset, either the planner has a *Power relationship* over the community or the planner's community has a *Protective relationship* over the other community, such that the *Adversaries* of the other community are not *Threats* to the goals of the community.

M7.   WEAKEN POWERFUL NEIGHBORS

Machiavelli: "Again, the prince who holds a country differing in the above respects ought to … weaken the more powerful amongst [his neighbors] …]."

The planner has a *Role* in a *Power relationship* over a *Community*, and has the goal that this role be *Permanent*. There is a set of communities that are *Adjacent* who are not *Adversaries*, such that if they were *Adversaries*, they would be *Threats* to the planner's goal. The planner executes a plan to *Order* these communities with the *Ordering rule* based on the planner's *Judgment* of the *Envisioned likelihood* that the community would *Achieve* an *Unspecified goal*. The planner then plans and executes to achieve the goal that for the *First few in the order*, this *Envisioned likelihood* is lower.

M8.   PREVENT FOREIGN FOOTHOLDS

Machiavelli: "Again, the prince who holds a country differing in the above respects ought to … taking care that no foreigner as powerful as himself shall, by any accident, get a footing [amongst neighbors]; for it will always happen that such a one will be introduced by those who are discontented, either through excess of ambition or through fear, as one has seen already."

The planner has a *Role* in a *Power relationship* over a *Community*, and has the goal that this role be *Permanent*. *Adjacent* communities exists where the *Envisioned likelihood* that the community could *Achieve* an *Unspecified goal* is less than for the planner's community. Other communities that are not *Adjacent* exist as well, which have equal or greater *Envisioned likelihood* that the community would *Achieve* an *Unspecified goal* than the planner's community. The planner *Assigns as a threat* the *State* in which the *Adjacent* communities are in a *Cooperative relationship* with these powerful communities, and plans to *Prevent* the *Adjacent* community from having the goal of having a *Cooperative relationship* of this sort.

M9.   SUPPORT WEAK NEIGHBORS

Machiavelli: "So that in respect to these subject states he has not to take
any trouble to gain them over to himself, for the whole of them quickly rally
to the state which he has acquired there.... And he who does not properly
manage this business will soon lose what he has acquired, and whilst he
does hold it he will have endless difficulties and troubles."

> The planner has a *Role* in a *Power relationship* over a *Community*, and has
> the goal that this role be *Permanent*. Several *Adjacent* communities exist
> as well that are not *Adversaries*. The planner executes a plan to *Order* these
> communities with the *Ordering rule* based on the *Judgment* of the *Envi-
> sioned likelihood* that the community would *Achieve* an *Unspecified goal*.
> The planner then plans to form an *Assistive relationship* with the *Last few in
> the order*, where the planner is the assisting agent. During *Assistive plan-
> ning*, the planner *Assigns as a threat* the states where the planner judges
> that the assisted community has a greater *Envisioned likelihood*.

M10.   CONQUER BY USING DISCONTENTED MEMBERS

Machiavelli: "... One can easily enter there by gaining over some baron of
the kingdom, for one always finds malcontents and such as desire a
change. Such men, for the reasons given, can open the way into the state
and render the victory easy."

> The planner has the goal of having a *Role* in a *Power relationship* over a
> community. The community includes *Components* that have roles in a
> *Power relationship* under a set of other agents. The planner executes a plan
> to *Locate an agent* that is both a member of this set of agents and who has
> *Blocked goals* where the *Causal agent* of the *Block* is an agent that has the
> *Role* in the *Power relationship* in the whole community. The planner then
> plans and executes to achieve a goal to have a *Cooperative relationship*
> with this agent.

M11.   DISMANTLE LANDS WITH TRADITION OF SELF-RULE

Machiavelli: "But in republics there is more vitality, greater hatred, and
more desire for vengeance, which will never permit them to allow the
memory of their former liberty to rest; so that the safest way is to destroy
them or to reside there."

> The planner has achieved a goal of having a *Role* in a *Power relationship*
> over a community, and has the goal that this role be *Permanent*. Before this
> goal was achieved, the community did not have a *Role* in a *Power relation-
> ship*, and did planning with the goal of *Following execution rules*, a subset

of which were *Explicit rules* that were *Known* to and *Managed* by members of the community. The planner *Abandons the goal* and executes to achieve the goal that the community is *Destroyed*, and the planner has *Possession* of the *Resources* of the former community.

M12. BACK IDEOLOGICAL REVOLUTIONS WITH FORCE

Machiavelli: "Hence it is that all armed prophets have conquered, and the unarmed ones have been destroyed."

The planner has the goal of having a *Role* in a *Power relationship* over a *Community*, and is executing a plan to achieve this goal that includes *Persuading* members of the community to have the goal that the planner has this role. The planner envisions that other agents will have the goal to *Prevent* the planner from achieving the goal, but that these plans will *Fail* because the set of persuaded agents will execute plans to *Prevent* these other agents from *Preventing* the planner. The planner executes a plan to *Enable an action* for the persuaded set that would *Threaten preservation goals* of the other agents, and to achieve the goal that the persuaded set *Make a planning decision* to *Threaten* the other agents to *Prevent* them from *Preventing* the planner.

M13. ESTABLISH STABLE POWER BASE IN FAVOR OF POPULARITY

Machiavelli: "Besides the reasons mentioned, the nature of the people is variable, and whilst it is easy to persuade them, it is difficult to fix them in that persuasion. And this it is necessary to take such measures that, when they believe no longer, it may be possible to make them believe by force."

The planner has achieved the goal of having a *Role* in a *Power relationship* over a *Community* by *Executing a plan* that included *Persuading* agents in the community to have the goal that the planner has this role. The planner adds an *Expected future state* to their *Envisionments* that these agents will *Abandon this goal* and *Adopt the goal* that the planner not have this role. The planner executes a plan to *Enable an action* that *Violates Preservation goals* of members of the *Community*, including the persuaded agents, and to make the *Preconditions* of the action *Persistent*.

M14.   ABOLISH OLD ARMIES FOR NEW ONES

Machiavelli: "This man abolished the old soldiery, organized the new, ...; and as he had his own soldiers and allies, on such foundations he was able to build any edifice: thus, whilst he had endured much trouble in acquiring, he had but little in keeping."

The planner has achieved the goal of having a *Role* in a *Power relationship* over a *Community*, a role that a different agent had previously, and has the goal that this role be *Permanent*. An *Organization* exists that has a *Power relationship* under the agent who has the *Role* that the planner has, and previously this was the other agent. The planner envisions that *Future goal pursuit* will *Require* the *Agency* of this *Organization*, and that *If it were the case* that the *Power relationship* between the planner and the *Organization Terminated*, the planner's goals would be *Violated*. The planner executes a plan *Destroy* the *Organization*, then plans and executes for the goal that there exists a second *Organization* of the same *Class* type as the first, with equal *Properties*, that has a *Power relationship* under the planner.

M15.   ABOLISH OLD ALLIANCES FOR NEW ONES

Machiavelli: "This man ... gave up old alliances, made new ones; and as he had his own soldiers and allies, on such foundations he was able to build any edifice: thus, whilst he had endured much trouble in acquiring, he had but little in keeping."

The planner has achieved the goal of having a *Role* in a *Power relationship* over a *Community*, a role that a different agent had previously, and has the goal that this role be *Permanent*. The *Community* is in a *Cooperative relationship* with a set of other *Communities*. The planner envisions that *Blocks* to *Threats* to the planner's goal *Requires* the *Agency* of *Communities* that have a *Cooperative relationship* with the planner's community. The planner executes a plan to *Terminate* the *Relationships* with the cooperating communities, and to achieve the goal that the *Community* has a role in *Cooperative relationships* with a disjoint set of communities.

M16.   PARTNER WITH FORCES THAT CAN BLOCK YOUR ENEMIES

Machiavelli: "Alexander ... decided to act in four ways.... Secondly, by winning to himself all the gentlemen of Rome, so as to be able to curb the Pope with their aid, as has been observed."

The planner has a *Role* in a *Power relationship* over a *Community* and has the goal that this role be *Permanent*. A *Threat* to this goal exists that includes the *Execution of plans* of another agent, for which the planner currently has no *Block*. There exists a third agent or a set of agents that can *Execute plans* that would *Prevent* this *Execution* of the agent. The planner executes a plan to have a *Role* in a *Cooperative relationship* with these third agents, and to achieve the goal that if the agent has the goal of executing the plan, these third agents will *Prevent* it.

M17. SCHEDULE ALL BLOWS TO CITIZENS AT ONCE

Machiavelli: "Hence it is to be remarked that, in seizing a state, the usurper ought to examine closely into all those injuries which it is necessary for him to inflict, and to do them all at one stroke so as not to have to repeat them daily; and thus by not unsettling men he will be able to reassure them, and win them to himself by benefits."

The planner has achieved a goal to have a *Role* in a *Power relationship* over a *Community*, and has *Plans* to achieve the goal that this role be *Permanent*. A subset of these plans are *Adversarial* to agents in the *Community*, in that they include actions that *Violate the goals* of these agents. The planner *Schedules the execution* of these plans so that the adversarial actions are executed *Simultaneously* or *Consecutively*, but not *Periodically*.

M18. AVOID OPPRESSING THE PEOPLE

Machiavelli: "Therefore, one who becomes a prince through the favor of the people ought to keep them friendly, and this he can easily do seeing they only ask not to be oppressed by him."

The planner has achieved the goal of having a *Role* in a *Power relationship* over a *Community* by *Executing plans* that included a *Precondition* that the agents in the *Community* had the goal that the planner has this role. The planner has the goal that this role be *Permanent*. The planner *Adds a persistent goal* to *Avoid* a state where the agents have the *Expectation* that their plans will fail, and that the *Cause of the failure* is the planner.

M19. SECURE POPULARITY AFTER BEING ESTABLISHED BY NOBLES

Machiavelli: "But one who, in opposition to the people, becomes a prince by the favor of the nobles, ought, above everything, to seek to win the people over to himself, and this he may easily do if he takes them under his protection."

The planner has achieved the goal of having a *Role* in a *Power relationship* over a *Community* by *Executing plans*. These plans included a *Precondition* that a set of other agents had the goal that the planner has this role. The planner has the goal that this role be *Permanent*. *Threats* to the *Preservation goals* of the agents exist, or there are *Expected future threats*. The planner *Adds the goal* that the agents in the *Community* have the goal that the role the planner has be *Permanent*. The planner executes a plan to *Block* these *Threats*.

M20.   MAKE YOURSELF NEEDED BY YOUR PEOPLE

Machiavelli: "Therefore a wise prince ought to adopt such a course that his citizens will always in every sort and kind of circumstances have need of the state and of him, and then he will always find them faithful."

The planner has a *Power relationship* over a *Community*, and has the goal that this *Role* be *Permanent*. The agents in the community do *Normal goal pursuit* by *Planning* and *Executing plans*. The planner has the *Top position* in an *Organization* that has a *Cooperative relationship* the *Community*. *Plans* to achieve a subset of the *Normal goals* of the agents in the community *Require* the *Agency* of the planner, or the *Agency* of agents in the *Organization*. The planner plans and executes to achieve the goal that this subset is equal to the whole set of the *Normal goals* of the agents in the community. For each *Normal goal* that is not a member of the subset, the planner creates a *Planning option* to either *Add the goal* that the agents *Abandon the goal*, or *Add the goal* that *Plans* to achieve the goal *Require* the *Agency* of agents in the *Organization* or of the planner.

M21.   FORTIFY YOUR TOWNS BUT NOT THE COUNTRYSIDE

Machiavelli: "In the second case one can say nothing except to encourage such princes to provision and fortify their towns, and not on any account to defend the country."

The planner has a *Power relationship* over a *Community*, and has the goal that this *Role* be *Permanent*. The planner envisions a *Possible future threat* to this goal on the *Condition* that an *Adversary* of the planner *Executes* an *Attack* on the *Community*. The *Community* has a *Boundary definition* that defines a *Region*, and this region is *Composed of Subregions*. The planner has a *Partial plan* for *Preventing* the success of an *Attack* of an *Adversary* for any one of these *Subregions*, that includes the *Defense* of the *Subregion*, and *Envisions* that a plan to *Iterate* this *Subplan* over the *Subregions* will result in a *Plan failure* due to *Insufficient resources*. The planner executes a plan to *Order* the subregions with an *Ordering principle* based on a

Cost-benefit analysis, where the *Costs* are the envisioned *Expended resources* to *Defend* the subregion, and the *Benefits* are *Quantifications of the value* of the *Resources* in the subregion, where the *Perspective of value* is that of the agents in the *Community*.

M22. BUILD PROTECTING WALLS AND DITCHES

Machiavelli: "The cities of Germany are absolutely free … because they are fortified in such a way that every one thinks the taking of them by assault would be tedious and difficult, seeing that they have proper ditches and walls, …."

The planner has the goal of *Preventing* an *Attack* executed by any *Adversary* where the target of the attack is a *Region*. The planner envisions that *Adversaries* will have *True information* about the *Defenses* that the *Region* has. The planner executes a plan to create a *Defense* that includes one or more *Obstacles* to exist at the *Boundary* of the *Region* that will cause *Execution problems* for any agent executing an *Attack* that include the *Expenditure of resources* that are *Limited* and *Instrumental* in multiple *Subplans* of the *Attack*.

M23. ESTABLISH SUFFICIENT ARTILLERY

Machiavelli: "The cities of Germany are absolutely free … because they are fortified in such a way that every one thinks the taking of them by assault would be tedious and difficult, seeing that …, they have sufficient artillery, …."

The planner has the goal of *Preventing* an *Attack* executed by any *Adversary* where the *Target* of the attack is a *Region*. The planner envisions that *Adversaries* will have *True information* about the *Defenses* that the *Region* has. The planner executes a plan to have a *Defense* that includes the *Potential agency* of a set of agents in a *Control relationship* under the planner, where the agents have *Skills* and *Resources* that *Threaten* the *Preservation goals* of one or more agents executing an *Attack* and their *Quantity* is such that the planner envisions that an *Attack* plan would fail.

M24.   STOCKPILE FOOD AND WAR SUPPLIES

Machiavelli:"The cities of Germany are absolutely free ... because they are fortified in such a way that every one thinks the taking of them by assault would be tedious and difficult, seeing that ... they always keep in public depots enough for one year's eating, drinking and firing."

> The planner has a *Role* in a *Power relationship* with a *Community*, and has the goal that this role be *Permanent*. A *Potential future threat* to this goal exists that involves the *Execution* of an *Attack* by an *Adversary*. The planner has a *Defense* for this *Attack* that *Suspends* its execution, and envisions that this *Defense* will be *Successfully executed* for a *Duration*, during which time the *Community* will *Expend* resources at a *Faster* rate than they *Acquire resources* of the type that are *Instrumental* to *Preservation goals* and to the execution of the *Defense*. The *Lack of resources* will cause agents in the community to *Add goals* that are in *Goal opposition* to the planner's goal, which will cause the *Defense* to *Fail*. During the *Duration*, the *Adversary* will *Expend resources* at a *Faster rate* than they can *Acquire resources*, and the planner envisions that an *Adversary* will have *Resources to Expend* resources at this rate for a second *Duration*. The planner executes a plan to *Acquire resources* and *Maintain resources* of the type that are *Instrumental* to *Preservation goals* of agents in the *Community* and to the execution of the *Defense* to a *Quantity* such that the *Envisionment* of the *Duration* of the *Defense* is greater than the second *Duration*.

M25.   GIVE USEFUL WORK TO THE COMMUNITY

Machiavelli: "And beyond this, to keep the people quiet and without loss to the state, they always have the means of giving work to the community in those labors that are the life and strength of the city, and on the pursuit of which the people are supported; ..."

> The planner has a *Role* in a *Power relationship* over a *Community*, and has the goal that this role be *Permanent*. The *Normal goal pursuit* of the agents in the *Community* includes *Compensated work* where the agents in the community have the *Worker* role. A subset of agents in the community have the goal of having this role, but *Plans* to achieve this goal have been *Failed plans* with a *Cause* of *Lack of opportunity*. The planner executes a plan to have the *Employer* role in a set of *Compensated work* activities, and where the members of the subset of agents have the *Worker* role. The work activity will include *Making a work product* that is *Instrumental* to the goals of the set of agents in the community or the planner, or *Doing a work service* that *Satisfies preconditions* of plans that are the planner's or are included in the *Normal goal pursuit* of the set of agents in the community.

M26. HOLD AWE-INSPIRING MILITARY EXERCISES

Machiavelli: "… they also hold military exercises in repute, and moreover have many ordinances to uphold them."

The planner has the *Top role* in an *Organization* whose *Agency* is included in *Plans* of *Defense* of a *Community*. The planner has the goal that an *Adversary* make a *Planning decision* to not *Attack* the *Community*. The *Adversary* has *True information* about the *Activities* of agents in the *Community*. The planner executes a plan to cause the agents in the *Organization* to do an *Activity* that includes the *Execution of skills* and which is *Observed* by the agents in the community, where the *Skills* are those that are included in the *Plans* of *Defense*, and where the planner envisions that the *Observation* will cause the community agents to *Believe* that the organizational agents have an *Execution ability* for the *Skills* that has a *High* proficiency.

M27. GIVE HOPE THAT SIEGES WILL BE BRIEF

Machiavelli: "And whoever should reply: If the people have property outside the city, and see it burnt, they will not remain patient, and the long siege and self-interest will make them forget their prince; to this I answer that a powerful and courageous prince will overcome all such difficulties by giving at one time hope to his subjects that the evil will be not for long, …"

The planner has a *Role* in a *Power relationship* over a *Community*, and has the goal that this role be *Permanent*. The planner has an *Adversary* that is *Executing* an *Attack* on the community, which has been *Suspended* because of a *Defense* which includes a *Blockade* that *Separates* the adversary from the community, and has a *Side-effect* of *Preventing* plans to *Acquire resources* by the *Community*, of the type that are *Expended* to maintain *Preservation goals* of the agents in the *Community*. The planner plans and executes to achieve the goal that the agents in the community have the *Expectation* that the *Adversary* will *Abandon the execution* of the *Attack* in the future, that the agents will be able to execute plans to *Acquire resources*, and that this will occur before *Preservation goals* of the agents are *Violated goals*.

M28.   CAUSE FEAR OF THE CRUELTY OF A SIEGING ENEMY

Machiavelli: "And whoever should reply: If the people have property outside the city, and see it burnt, they will not remain patient, and the long siege and self-interest will make them forget their prince; to this I answer that a powerful and courageous prince will overcome all such difficulties by giving at one time … fear of the cruelty of the enemy."

> The planner has a *Role* in a *Power relationship* over a *Community*, and has the goal that this role be *Permanent*. The planner has an *Adversary* that is *Executing* an *Attack* on the community, which has been *Suspended* because of a *Defense* which includes a *Blockade* that *Separates* the adversary from the community, and has a *Side-effect* of *Preventing* plans to *Acquire resources* by the *Community*, of the type that are *Expended* to maintain *Preservation goals* of the agents in the *Community*. The planner executes a plan to *Invoke an emotion* in the agents of the community, which is a *Fear emotion* where the *Feared possible future event* is that the *Adversary* will have the planner's *Role* in the *Power relationship* over the community, and will execute plans that *Violate goals* of the agents, and where the *Theme role* that causes the goals for these plans is that of an *Evil agent*.

M29.   USE YOUR OWN ARMIES RATHER THAN MERCENARIES

Machiavelli: "In conclusion, in mercenaries dastardy is most dangerous; in auxiliaries, valor. The wise prince, therefore, has always avoided these arms and turned to his own; and has been willing rather to lose with them than to conquer with others, not deeming that a real victory which is gained with the arms of others."

> The planner has a *Role* in a *Power relationship* over a *Community*. The planner has an *Envisioned future goal* of *Executing* an *Attack* on an *Adversary*, and has a *Partial plan* of attack that involves the *Skilled agency* of an *Organization* for which the planner has the *Top role*. A *Planning option* exists for *Satisfying this precondition* where the planner has the role of *Employer* in a *Compensated work* activity and where the *Employee* role is held by an *Organization* of agents that are not agents in the *Community*. The planner adds a *Planning constraint* that the agents in the *Organization* are agents in the *Community*.

M30.   STUDY ONLY THE ART OF WAR

Machiavelli: "A prince ought to have no other aim or thought, nor select anything else for his study, than war and its rules and discipline; for this is the sole art that belongs to him who rules, and it is of such force that it not only upholds those who are born princes, but it often enables men to rise from a private station to that rank."

> The planner has a *Role* in a *Power relationship* over a *Community*, and has the goal that this role be *Permanent*. During the *Normal goal pursuit* of the planner, *Free time* exists for *Auxiliary goal pursuit*. The planner adds an *Auxiliary goal* of *Learning a field* where the *Field subject* is *Adversarial planning and execution*, and adds a *Planning constraint* that no other *Learning a field* goals are *Pursued*.

M31.   KEEP ARMIES ORGANIZED

Machiavelli: "As regards action, he ought above all things to keep his men well organized ...."

> The planner has the *Top role* in an *Organization* that has an *Organizational structure*. The *Skilled agency* of agents in the organization is *Required* in a *Partial plan* that the planner has to *Execute an attack* to achieve a goal or an *Envisioned future goal*. The planner *Schedules* a *Periodic plan* of *Ordering* the set of set of all *Instances of the class of Organizational structures*, with an *Ordering principle* of the *Envisioned likelihood* that the planner could *Execute* the *Partial plan In the case that* the *Organizational structure* of the organization was the *Instance*. On the condition that the *First ordered* structure does not equal the current *Organizational structure*, the planner executes a plan to *Reorganize* the organization with the first ordered structure.

M32.   KEEP ARMIES DRILLED

Machiavelli: "As regards action, he ought above all things to keep his men well ... and drilled, ..."

> The planner has the *Top role* in an *Organization*. The *Skilled agency* of agents in the organization is *Required* in a *Partial plan* that the planner has to *Execute an attack* to achieve a goal or an *Envisioned future goal*. The planner envisions that the *Execution ability* for the *Skills* of the agents will be of *Poor ability On the condition that* they do not *Execute these skills* for a *Duration* of time. The planner plans and executes to achieve the goal that the agents in the *Organization Schedule* to *Execute the skills Periodically* where the *Duration of the period* is less than the *Duration* of poor ability.

M33. LEARN THE GEOGRAPHY OF YOUR COUNTRY

Machiavelli: "As regards action, he ought above all things ..., to follow incessantly the chase, by which he accustoms his body to hardships, and learns something of the nature of localities, and gets to find out how the mountains rise, how the valleys open out, how the plains lie, and to understand the nature of rivers and marshes, and in all this to take the greatest care. Which knowledge is useful in two ways. Firstly, he learns to know his country, and is better able to undertake its defense; ...."

> The planner has a *Role* in a *Power relationship* over a *Community*. The *Normal activities* of the agents in the community *Take place* in a *Region* that is *Composed* of *Subregions* that have different sets of *Physical characteristics*. The planner envisions a *Possible future* that an *Adversary* will *Execute* an *Attack* on the *Community* which includes the *Agency* of the *Adversary* that *Takes place* in the *Region*. The planner executes a plan to *Schedule Periodically Activities* that *Take place* in the set of *Subregions* of the *Region*, and adds an *Auxiliary goal* that is a *Knowledge goal* of the *Physical characteristics* of these *Subregions*.

M34. LEARN HOW TO LEARN THE GEOGRAPHY OF OTHER COUNTRIES

Machiavelli: "... afterwards, by means of the knowledge and observation of that locality, he understands with ease any other which it may be necessary for him to study hereafter; because the hills, valleys, and plains, and rivers and marshes that are, for instance, in Tuscany, have a certain resemblance to those of other countries, so that with a knowledge of the aspect of one country one can easily arrive at a knowledge of others."

> The planner has a *Role* in a *Power relationship* over a *Community*. The *Normal activities* of the agents in the community *Take place* in a *Region* that is *Composed* of *Subregions* that have different sets of *Physical characteristics*. The planner envisions a *Possible future goal* to *Execute* an *Attack* on an *Adversary* that will include *Activities* that *Take place* in a *Region* that is other than the first *Region*. The planner envisions that this second *Region* will have a *Similar* set of *Physical characteristics* as one of the *Subregions*. The planner executes a plan to *Schedule Periodically Activities* that *Take place* in the set of *Subregions* of the *Region*, and adds an *Auxiliary goal* that is a *Knowledge goal* of the *Physical characteristics* of these *Subregions*.

M35. STUDY THE HISTORY OF PAST RULERS

Machiavelli: "But to exercise the intellect the prince should read histories, and study there the actions of illustrious men, to see how they have borne themselves in war, to examine the causes of their victories and defeat, so as to avoid the latter and imitate the former; ..."

> The planner has *Role* in a *Power relationship* over a *Community* and has the goal that this role be *Permanent*. There exists a set of *Encodings* of *Events* that include an agent that had a role in a *Power relationship* over a *Community* that is *Similar* to the first *Community*. The planner executes a plan to *Decode* the set of *Encodings*. For each agent, the planner *Makes an analogy* between the events and *Past events* and *Envisioned events* with an *Analogical mapping* between the agent and the planner. The planner then *Replans* for their goals with a *Planning preference* to *Select from competing plans* that are the result of *Analogical planning* that included the *Analogies*.

M36. PERMIT YOURSELF TO BE MEAN ONCE YOU ARE ESTABLISHED

Machiavelli: "Therefore, a prince, not being able to exercise this virtue of liberality in such a way that it is recognized, except to his cost, if he is wise he ought not to fear the reputation of being mean, for in time he will come to be more considered than if liberal, seeing that with his economy his revenues are enough, that he can defend himself against all attacks, and is able to engage in enterprises without burdening his people; ..."

> The planner has achieved the goal of having a *Role* in a *Power relationship* over a *Community* and has the goal that this role be *Permanent*. The planner has *Successfully blocked* past *Threats* to this goal, and no current *Threats* exist. The planner is planning to achieve another goal, and a *Planning problem* exists that the planner envisions a *Side effect* that *Violates* an *Auxiliary goal* that agents in the *Community Believe* that the planner has a *Role theme* of being an *Evil person*. The planner *Suspends the auxiliary goal* and *Replans*, executes the plan, and then *Resumes the auxiliary goal*.

M37.   FAVOR BEING LIBERAL TO BEING MEAN BEFORE YOU ARE ESTABLISHED

Machiavelli:"Either you are a prince in fact, or in a way to become one. In the first case this liberality is dangerous, in the second it is very necessary to be considered liberal; ..."

The planner has the goal of having a *Role* in a *Power relationship* over a *Community*, and is *Executing a plan* to achieve this goal. The planner *Adds a goal* that the agents in the *Community Believe* that the planner has a *Role theme* of being *Generous person*. The planner adds an *Envisionment requirement* of the *Beliefs* of the agents in the community that have a *Relationship* with the planner. The planner adds a *Planning constraint* that this goal cannot be *Violated*. Finally, the planner *Replans* to achieve this goal, and *On the condition that* the new plan is different from the old plan, the planner *Terminates the execution* of the old plan, and executes the new one.

M38.   BE CONSERVATIVE WITH THE WEALTH OF YOUR PEOPLE

Machiavelli: "Either a prince spends that which is his own or his subjects' or else that of others. In the first case he ought to be sparing, ..."

The planner has a *Role* in a *Power relationship* over a *Community* and has the goal that this role be *Permanent*. The planner has *Acquired resources* as a result of the *Agency* of the agents in the *Community*, or by a *Transfer of possession* between these agents and the planner. The planner is doing *Planning* and has a *Partial plan* that includes these *Resources*. The planner adds a *Planning preference* to *Avoid the action* of *Expending these resources*, and *In the case that* this *Preference is negated* the planner makes a *Planning decision* to *Select a range value* which is the *Minimum value* for any *Range* in the plan of the *Amount of resources* that are *Expended*.

M39.   BE LIBERAL WITH THE WEALTH OBTAINED FROM OTHER LANDS

Machiavelli: "Either a prince spends that which is his own or his subjects' or else that of others. ..., in the second [case] he ought not to neglect any opportunity for liberality."

The planner has a *Role* in a *Power relationship* over a *Community* and has the goal that this role be *Permanent*. The planner has *Successfully executed* an *Attack* on a different community, which has *Enabled* the *Acquisition of resources* which were the *Resources* that were previously *Possessed* by agents in this second *Community*. The planner *Adds a goal* to *Execute plans* which include *Expending resources* and which *Satisfy goals* of the agents in the first *Community*.

M40.   SUPPORT ARMIES BY PILLAGE, SACK, AND EXTORTION

Machiavelli: "And to the prince who goes forth with his army, supporting it by pillage, sack, and extortion, handling that which belongs to others, this liberality is necessary, otherwise he would not be followed by soldiers."

> The planner has the *Top role* in an *Organization* whose *Agency* is included in a set of plans that the planner has to *Execute Attacks* on a set of *Communities*. The planner envisions that these plans will include *Expending resources*, and that the *Successful execution* of an *Attack* will *Enable* the *Acquisition of resources* which were the *Resources* that were previously *Possessed* by agents in each *Community*. The planner envisions that the *Amount of resources* acquired will be greater than the amount expended, resulting in an *Amount of resources* which is the difference. The planner *Modifies the plans* to include the *Execution of subplans* which include *Expending resources* equal to this amount and which *Satisfy goals* of the agents in the *Organization*.

M41.   FAVOR CRUELTY TO MERCIFULNESS

Machiavelli: "Therefore a prince, so long as he keeps his subjects united and loyal, ought not to mind the reproach of cruelty; because with a few examples he will be more merciful than those who, through too much mercy, allow disorders to arise, from which follow murders or robberies; for these are wont to injure the whole people, whilst those executions which originate with a prince offend the individual only."

> The planner has a *Role* in a *Power relationship* over a *Community* and has the goal that this role be *Permanent*. An agent in the *Community* has *Executed plans* that *Violate goals* of the planner. The planner envisions that the *Future goal pursuit* of other agents in the *Community* includes *Planning* that includes *Risk benefit analysis*, where benefits are the results of *Executed plans* that *Violate goals* of the planner, and risks include *Executed plans* of the planner. The planner *Adds the goal* of *Executing plans* that *Violate goals* of the one agent, which includes *Events* which are *Perceived* by other agents in the *Community*, and which *Violate the expectations* which are the *Expected risks* of the other agents in that a greater number of *Goals are violated*.

M42.   FAVOR BEING FEARED TO BEING LOVED

Machiavelli: "Upon this a question arises: whether it be better to be loved than feared or feared than loved? It may be answered that one should wish to be both, but, because it is difficult to unite them in one person, is much safer to be feared than loved, when of the two, either must be dispensed with."

The planner has a *Role* in a *Power relationship* over a *Community* and has the goal that this role be *Permanent*. The planner is *Planning*, and a *Planning decision* exists with two different *Envisionments*. In the first envisionment, the *Execution of the plan* causes the agents in the *Community* to *Invoke an emotion* which is a *Fear emotion* where the *Feared event* is the *Execution of plans* by the planner. In the second envisionment, the *Execution of the plan* causes the agents in the *Community* to *Invoke an emotion* which is a *Love emotion* where the subject is the planner. The planner adds a *Planning preference* to *Make a planning decision* of the first choice.

M43.   UPHOLD THE APPEARANCE OF GOOD QUALITIES WHILE ACTING OTHERWISE

Machiavelli: "Therefore it is unnecessary for a prince to have all of the good qualities I have enumerated, but it is very necessary to appear to have them. And I shall dare say this also, that to have them and always to observe them is injurious, and that to appear to have them is useful; ..."

The planner has a *Role* in a *Power relationship* over a *Community* and has the goal that this role be *Permanent*. Agents in the *Community* do *Planning* with the goal of *Following execution rules*, a subset of which are those *Caused* by a *Role theme* of *Being a good person*. The planner adds a *Planning constraint* against plans that *Cause* the agents to *Believe* that the planner does *Planning* with the goal of *Following execution rules* which include this subset. The planner *Self-monitors* for the goal of *Following execution rules* which include this subset, *In which case* the planner *Removes the execution rules* and *Replans*.

M44.   APPEAR RELIGIOUS

Machiavelli: "There is nothing more necessary to appear to have than [the quality of being religious], inasmuch as men judge generally more by the eye than by the hand, because it belongs to every body to see you, to few to come in touch with you."

The planner has a *Role* in a *Power relationship* over a *Community* and has the goal that this role is *Permanent*. Agents in the community have a set of *Beliefs* that are *Common beliefs*, *Instructed beliefs*, and *Explanatory be-*

liefs, and which cause the agents to have a *Role theme* of *Following beliefs*. The planner plans and executes to achieve the goal that the agents in the community *Believe* that the planner has the *Role theme* of *Following beliefs* that are these beliefs, and that the *Justification* for the *Executed plans* of the planner are these *Beliefs*.

M45. USE AN ARBITER TO MANAGE CONFLICT BETWEEN PEOPLE AND NOBILITY

Machiavelli: "... therefore, to take away the reproach which he would be liable to from the nobles for favoring the people, and from the people for favoring the nobles, he set up an arbiter, who should be one who could beat down the great and favor the lesser without reproach to the king."

> The planner has a *Role* in a *Power relationship* over a *Community* that is *Compositional* and has the goal that this role be *Permanent*. Two *Components* of the community consist of agents that have an *Adversarial relationship* with each other, and have a set of *Conflicting goals*, where *Goal resolution Requires* that the planner *Make a decision*. The planner envisions that *Making the decision* will *Create a threat* to the permanence goal, in that the agents in one of the *Components* will have an *Adversarial relationship* with the planner. The planner *Employs an agent* that is not a member of either component to *Perform a service* for the *Community* which includes *Communicating* with agents in components, followed by *Making a decision*. The planner *Informs* the agents in the components that the *Decision* of the agent will be equal to the *Decision* of the planner. The planner then *Makes a decision* which is the same as the employed agent.

M46. ARM CONQUERED PEOPLE THAT ARE UNARMED TO BUILD LOYAL ARMIES

Machiavelli: "There never was a new prince who has disarmed his subjects; rather when he has found them disarmed he has always armed them, because, by arming them, those arms become yours, those men who were distrusted become faithful, and those who were faithful are kept so, and your subjects become your adherents."

> The planner has achieved a goal of having a *Role* in a *Power relationship* over a *Community* and has the goal that this role be *Permanent*. The planner *Envisions future goals* of *Executing an attack* or *Executing a defense*, and has *Partial plans* for these goals that includes the *Agency* of an *Organization*, where this *Agency Requires* the *Instrumental use* of *Physical ob-*

jects. The *Community* is *Compositional*, and before the planner achieved the goal, agents in a *Component* did not have *Possession* of the *Physical objects* that are *Instrumental* to *Executing an attack* or *Executing a defense*. The planner adds the goal that the *Organization* includes the agents from the *Component*.

M47. DISARM A NEW TERRITORY WHEN ADDING TO AN EXISTING LAND

Machiavelli: "But when a prince acquires a new state, which he adds as a province to his old one, then it is necessary to disarm the men of that state, except those who have been his adherents in acquiring it; and these again, with time and opportunity, should be rendered soft and effeminate; as matters should be managed in such a way that all the armed men in the state shall be your own soldiers who in your old state were living near you."

The planner has a *Role* in a *Power relationship* over a *Community*, and has achieved a goal of having a *Power relationship* over a second *Community*. Agents in the second *Community* have *Possession* of *Physical objects* which are *Instrumental* to *Partial plans* for *Executing an attack* or *Executing a defense*. The planner executes a plan to *Take possession* of these *Physical objects* from the agents in the second community.

M48. FOSTER THEN CRUSH ANIMOSITY TO IMPROVE RENOWN

Machiavelli: "For this reason many consider that a wise prince, when he has the opportunity, ought with craft to foster some animosity against himself, so that, having crushed it, his renown may rise higher."

The planner has a *Role* in a *Power relationship* over a *Community* and has the goal that a set of agents *Believe* that the planner is the *Best candidate* for this role. There exists an agent that has goals that are in *Goal conflict* with the planner, and that has had a *Planning failure* to achieve their goals with a *Cause* of *Lack of resources* or *Lack of agency*. The planner plans and executes for the goal that the agent *Believes* that there exists an *Opportunity* for this agent to achieve their goals, where no *Opportunity* exists. The planner then *Monitors* the agent for the *Start of execution* of plans to achieve the goals. When this occurs, the planner executes a plan to *Destroy* the agent, with the goal that the first set of agents have *Event knowledge* of the planner's execution.

M49. LOOK FOR LOYALTY IN GROUPS DISTRUSTED AT THE BEGINNING OF YOUR RULE

Machiavelli: "Princes, especially new ones, have found more fidelity and assistance in those men who in the beginning of their rule were distrusted than among those who in the beginning were trusted."

The planner has achieved a goal of having a *Role* in a *Power relationship* over a *Community* and has had this role for a certain *Duration*. The planner has the goal of *Locating an agent* who is an agent in the *Community*, and who the planner envisions will *Make planning decisions* that *Satisfy* the planner's goals rather than *Violate* the planner's goals with a *High envisioned likelihood*. The planner executes a plan to do *Past state envisionment* where the *Time* is the *Start time* of the *Duration*, and the role is the planner. The planner *Imagines a set* of agents who the planner envisions will *Make planning decisions* that *Violate* the planner's goals rather than *Satisfy* them with a greater *Envisioned likelihood*. The planner then makes a *Planning preference* to *Select candidates* from this set.

M50. BUILD FORTRESSES WHEN YOU FEAR YOUR PEOPLE MORE THAN FOREIGN POWERS

Machiavelli: "... the prince who has more to fear from the people than from foreigners ought to build fortresses, but he who has more to fear from foreigners than from the people ought to leave them alone."

The planner has a *Role* in a *Power relationship* over a *Community* and has the goal that this role be *Permanent*. There exists, or the planner envisions a *Possible world* where there exists, a *Place* where *In the case* that the planner is *Located* at this place, the *Executed attacks* of agents not *Located* at this place against the planner will have an *Execution failure*. The planner executes a plan to *Order* the set of *Threats* to the planner's goal with the *Ordering principle* favoring *Threats* that have a greater *Likelihood of realization*. *In the case that* the *Highest ranked* member of the set is a threat that involves the *Agency* of members of the *Community*, then the planner *Adds the goal* that the *Place* exists, *In the case that* it does not. Otherwise, the planner *Adds the goal* that the *Place* does not exist.

M51. ACKNOWLEDGE EXTRAORDINARY THINGS DONE BY CITIZENS

Machiavelli: "Again, it much assists a prince to set unusual examples in internal affairs, similar to those which are related of Messer Bernabo da Milano, who, when he had the opportunity, by any one in civil life doing some extraordinary thing, either good or bad, would take some method of rewarding or punishing him, which would be much spoken about."

The planner has a *Role* in a *Power relationship* over a *Community* and has the goal that this role be *Permanent*. The planner executes a plan to *Monitor* the *Executed plans* of agents in the *Community* for those that are *Expectation violations* of the *Expectations* that include the *Normal activities* of agents in the *Community*. When this occurs, the planner does *Plan assessment* to determine whether the plan *Progresses* or *Regresses* the planner's goals. If the plan progresses the planner's goals, then the planner plans and executes to *Satisfy* the agent's goals, and otherwise executes plans to *Violate* the agent's goals, and executes a plan to achieve the goal that the other agents in the community have *Event knowledge* of this execution.

M52. DECLARE FAVOR TO ONE PARTY WHEN TWO ARE WARRING

Machiavelli: "A prince is also respected when he is either a true friend or a downright enemy, that to say, when, without any reservation, he declares himself in favor of one party against the other; which course will always be more advantageous than standing neutral; ..."

Two agents who are not the planner are in an *Adversarial relationship* and are *Executing plans* to achieve *Conflicting goals*. The planner does not have an *Adversarial relationship* or *Cooperative relationship* with either agent, and the set goals of the planner do not intersect with the set of *Conflicting goals*. The planner *Chooses from the set* of agents one agent with a *Choice criteria* of *Random choice*, and *Informs* the agents that the planner has the goal that the chosen agent's goals are *Satisfied* and the other agent's goals are *Violated*.

M53. REMOVE BARRIERS TO THE FINANCIAL SUCCESS OF YOUR CITIZENS

Machiavelli: "At the same time he should encourage his citizens to practice their callings peaceably, both in commerce and agriculture, and in every other following, so that the one should not be deterred from improving his possessions for fear lest they be taken away from him or another from opening up trade for fear of taxes; but the prince ought to offer rewards to whoever wishes to do these things and designs in any way to honor his city or state."

The planner has a *Role* in a *Power relationship* over a *Community* and has the goal that this role be *Permanent*. The agents in the *Community* do *Planning* with the goal of *Following execution rules*, a subset of which are *Explicit rules* that are *Managed by the planner*. The agents have goals of *Acquiring wealth* or that the *Perceived value* of *Physical objects* that they *Possess* is greater. The agents have *Partial plans* to achieve these goals and envision that these plans will *Fail* because of an *Envisioned undesirable subsequent state* that the execution of the plan will be followed by the *Taking possession* of the *Physical object* or the *Acquisition of the wealth* by the planner. The planner executes a plan to *Add a planning constraint* against plans that involve the *Taking possessing* or *Acquisition of wealth* of agents in the community where the *Possession* or *Wealth* is the result of the execution of these *Partial plans* by the agents. The planner than executes a plan to *Inform* the agents of this *Planning constraint*.

M54. ENTERTAIN THE PEOPLE WITH SEASON FESTIVALS

Machiavelli: "Further, he ought to entertain the people with festivals and spectacles at convenient seasons of the year; ..."

The planner has a *Role* in a *Power relationship* over a *Community* and has the goal that this role be *Permanent*. The *Physical environment* has *Physical states* that are *State changes* because of *Causes* that are *Periodic*. The agents in the community have a set of goals that are not *Satisfied* by the *Normal activities* that they execute. The planner has a *Partial plan* to *Satisfy other agent goals* where the goals are this set of goals and the agents are agents in the community. This *Partial plan* includes *Activities* that include an *Activity role* of a *Community*, and *Requires* the *Expenditure of resources* by the planner. The planner *Imagines a set* of *Moments in a period* where the period is equal to *Period* of the *Causes*. The planner then *Orders the set* with the *Ordering principle* that advances *Moments* that result in lesser *Amount of resources* in an *Envisionment* of the *Execution of the partial plan* where the *Start time* is the *Moment*. The planner then *Periodically schedules* the *Activity* with a *Start time* that is the *Moment* that is the *First in the order* of the set.

M55.   SUPPORT COMMERCIAL GUILDS AND SOCIETIES

Machiavelli: "… and as every city is divided into guilds or into societies, he ought to hold such bodies in esteem, and associate with them sometimes, …"

> The planner has a *Role* in a *Power relationship* over a *Community* and has the goal that this role be *Permanent*. A set of agents in the community have achieved the goal to have a *Role* in an *Organization* by *Executing plans* that had a *Precondition* that the *Normal activities* of the agent included *Making a work product* or *Providing a work service*. The *Organization* includes a set of *Organizational processes* that are *Executed plans* of agents in the organization. The planner *Adds the goal* that agents in the community *Believe* that the *Execution of these plans Satisfies* goals of the planner. The planner *Periodically schedules* to do *Collaborative planning* with agents having the *Top role* in the organization that result in plans that include both the *Organization* and the planner.

M56.   MAINTAIN THE MAJESTY OF THE RANK

Machiavelli: "[The prince should] show himself an example of courtesy and liberality; nevertheless, always maintaining the majesty of his rank, for this he must never consent to abate in anything."

> The planner has a *Role* in a *Power relationship* over a *Community* and has the goal that this role be *Permanent*. Agents in the community have *Expectations* about the *Executed plans* of the *Agent that has this role* that do not overlap with the set of *Expectations* about the *Executed plans* of other agents in the community. The planner adds a *Planning constraint* against plans that include activities that are *Expectation violations* of the *Expectations* of the *Agent that has the role* and not *Expectation violations* of the *Expectations* of the other agents. The planner adds a *Planning preference* for plans that include activities that are in the non-overlapping set.

M57.   CHOOSE SERVANTS WHO THINK ONLY OF THEIR MASTER

Machiavelli: "But to enable a prince to form an opinion of his servant there is one test which never fails; when you see the servant thinking more of his own interest than of yours, and seeking inwardly his own profit in everything, such a man will never make a good servant, nor will you ever be able to trust him; …"

> The planner has the *Role* of *Employer* in an *Employment relationship* with an agent that has the *Employee* role, where the *Work* includes the *Execution of plans* that are the result of *Planning* done by the planner. The planner

has the goals that the plans are *Successfully executed*, and that *In the case that* there existed an *Opportunity* to *Satisfy goals* of the agent by *Executing plans* that *Violated* the planner's goals, the agent would *Make a planning decision Not to execute* these plans. The planner executes a plan to *Monitor* the *Actions* of the agent for those that have a *Goal justification* that involves either the planner's or the agent's goals, in which case the planner *Increments a counter*, one of two counters for the planner and the agent. After a *Duration*, the planner *Compares counters* to determine which of the two is greater. In the case that the agent's counter is greater, the planner adds the *Expectation* that there will be *Execution failures* in the plans, and that *In the case that* there existed an *Opportunity* to *Satisfy goals* of the agent by *Executing plans* that *Violated* the planner's goals, the agent would *Make a planning decision* to *Execute these plans*.

M58. ALLOW FREE SPEECH AND ADVICE ONLY FROM SELECTED WISE PEOPLE

Machiavelli: "Therefore a wise prince ought to hold a third course by choosing the wise men in his state, and giving to them only the liberty of speaking the truth to him, and then only of those things of which he inquires, and of none others; but he ought to question them upon everything, and listen to their opinions, and afterwards form his own conclusions."

The planner has a *Role* in a *Power relationship* over a *Community* and has the goal that this role be *Permanent*. The agents in the community do *Planning* with the goal of *Following execution rules*, a subset of which are *Explicit rules* that are *Managed* by the planner. The planner executes a plan to *Locate agents* in the community where the planner has an *Envisioned likelihood* that *Planning done* by the agents will be *Successful planning*, and the *Cause* will be the *Event knowledge* of the agents, and their *World models* that are *Highly predictive*. The planner *Adds a rule* to the *Explicit rules* that are the *Execution rules* of the agents in the *Community* that *Prohibits Informing* the planner of the results of *Other person planning* for the planner for agents who are not the *Located agents*, and *Prohibits* the *Located agents* from *Informing* the planner of the results of *Other person planning* for the planner *Except on the condition that* the planner makes this *Request*. Then the planner *Self-monitors* for *Planning* that includes *Uncertainty*, in which case the planner *Requests* that the *Located agents* do *Other person planning* for the agent and *Inform* the planner of the results.

M59.   IGNORE UNSOLICITED ADVICE AND STICK TO YOUR PLANS

Machiavelli: "... outside of [advisors], he should listen to no one, pursue the thing resolved on, and be steadfast in his resolutions. He who does otherwise is either overthrown by flatterers, or is so often changed by varying opinions that he falls into contempt."

> The planner has a *Role* in a *Power relationship* over a *Community* and has the goal that this role be *Permanent*. The planner has completed *Planning* to achieve a goal and has *Scheduled* to execute a plan or subplan in the future. The planner executes a plan to *Monitor* for the execution of other agents for an *Inform* plan by an agent that the planner did not *Request* the action of *Informing*, where the information is the results of *Other agent planning* done by the agent for the planner. The planner executes a plan to *Forget the information*, and adds a *Planning constraint* against *Replanning* or *Rescheduling* involving the plan or subplan.

M60.   BE ADVENTUROUS RATHER THAN CAUTIOUS TO CONTROL FORTUNE

Machiavelli: "For my part I consider that it is better to be adventurous than cautious, because fortune is a woman, and if you wish to keep her under it is necessary to beat and ill-use her; and it is seen that she allows herself to be mastered by the adventurous rather than by those who go to work more coldly. She is, therefore, always, woman-like, a lover of young men, because they are less cautious, more violent, and with more audacity command her."

> The planner envisions that *Future plan execution* will have *Execution failures* where the *Cause* is *Randomness*, with an *Envisioned likelihood of failure* at some *Likelihood*. The planner has the goal that this *Likelihood* is a *Lesser likelihood* than it is. The planner adds a *Planning preference* for *Goal pursuit* of goals with an *Envisioned likelihood of achievement* that is a *Low likelihood*, and a *Planning preference* for plans for goals that are *Threatened goals* over those that are not.

4.7 **PERFORMANCE** (39 STRATEGIES)

The seventh planning domain concentrates on the strategies of artistic performance, where artistic compositions are interpreted and executed by skilled performers. While the full breadth of this domain includes theater performance, dance performance, and the improvisational arts, the focus here is strictly on solo musical performances by instrumentalists. The 39 performance strategies presented here were collected through directed interviews with near-professional pianists, including those judged as top amateurs in national competition. Strategies 1 through 7 aid in becoming more familiar with a new performance piece. Strategies 8 through 15 focus specifically on the challenge of memorizing a piece so that it can be performed without the aid of notation. Strategies 16 though 25 describe approaches to overcoming problems that come up on the way to performance proficiency. Strategies 26 though 39 focus on the final delivery of a performance to an audience, where anxiety, the environment, the instruments, and even the audience can be a source of performance problems.

It is perhaps in the strategies of performance that one can see the strongest evidence for a dualism between body and mind in our commonsense theories of psychology. That is, there seems to be a real difference between how we think about the conscious execution of plans and the non-conscious execution of a performance. We imagine that this non-conscious capacity for the execution of performance mysteriously improves if we take a break from practice and concentrate on something else for a while (Strategy 6). It is intimately tied with the senses and the conscious control of the body, as we imagine that paying attention to the sensations of performance execution aids in the memorization of a piece (Strategy 12). This non-conscious execution is at its best when it feels natural and fluid, and any sensations of awkwardness should be regarded as potential problems (Strategy 18). Where conscious attention to performance aids in the learning of pieces, the more proficient performer will loosen the ties between attention and execution, striving to achieve the ability to continue performances in the face of distractions (Strategy 27). Even when attention can be managed, anxiety and nervousness can erode away your proficiency, and a strategic performer will learn to think about something else before they perform (Strategy 31).

This collection is limited to the strategies of the performance of artistic pieces, and has only hinted at the richness of our commonsense understanding of non-conscious execution. A more complete investigation of this sort of mind-body dualism could explore other types of musical performance, especially improvisational music, and other sorts of performance arts including dance and theatrical performance. Conceptually, these domains have much in common with athletic performance, where an athlete's skills are rarely explainable but still strategically managed and developed in very conscious ways.

P1. PLAN FOR FAILURES IN REPERTOIRE

Performance: Attempt pieces that are challenging, knowing that some will fail.

The planner envisions a future *Scheduling* of *Executing a performance* where the specific *Performance* is not yet known by the planner. The planner envisions a *Likely future* that the *Performance* will be one of a known set. The planner has the goal that when the *Scheduling* occurs, the planner has an *Ability* to *Execute a performance* for this set of *Performances*. The planner executes a plan to *Iterate* over the set of *Performances*, and for each, *Plan* and *Execute* with the goal of *Learning* the *Ability* to *Execute a performance* of the specific *Performance*. During *Execution*, the planner *Monitors* for *Replanning* to pursue the *Learning* goal that includes *Envisionments* where the *Achievement of the goal* is *Unlikely*. When these events occur, the planner *Cancels the goal* of *Learning* the *Performance*, removes the *Performance* from the original goal set, and continues the *Iteration*.

P2. LEARN THE SMALLEST UNITS FIRST

Performance: Start learning a piece by first identifying all of the notes.

The planner has the goal of *Learning* the *Ability* to *Execute a performance*. The planner *Possesses* a *Description of the performance*, which is *Compositional* and is an *Ordered set of actions*. The planner executes a plan to *Parse* to the *Description*. As each *Ordered set of actions* is *Parsed*, the planner *Executes the action*. During this execution, the planner *Monitors* for *Execution failures* in the *Action*, which trigger the planner to *Execute the action* again. The planner *Iterates* over the entire *Parsing plan* until it is *Executed* without *Execution failures*.

P3. LEARN FIRST AT A SLOW SPEED

Performance: Learn a piece by playing it very slowly until the notes are learned.

The planner has the goal of *Learning* the *Ability* to *Execute a performance*. The *Performance* is *Compositional* and is an *Ordered set of actions*, each of which has an *Expected action duration* in the *Execution of the performance*, which is within the range of *Possible action durations* for the actions, each of which is a multiplicative of a *Performance tempo*. The planner executes a plan to *Specify a performance* that is exactly the same as the old performance with the exception that the *Performance tempo* is a smaller value. The planner *Executes the performance*, and *Monitors* for *Execution failures*, *Terminating the execution* if there are several. After the *Ex-*

ecution, the planner *Repeats this plan*, increasing the *Performance tempo* if no *Execution failures* occur during *Execution*, and decreasing it if the *Execution* was *Terminated* before *Execution completion*. The *Repetition terminates* when the *Performance tempo* reaches the original value, or the *Plan fails* when this value does not increase after many repetitions.

P4.   DECOMPOSE A PERFORMANCE FOR PRACTICE

Performance: Divide a piece into parts, and work on parts individually.

The planner has the goal of *Learning* the *Ability* to *Execute a performance*. The *Performance* is *Compositional*. The planner executes a plan to *Iterate* over the set of *Performance components*, and for each, *Specify a performance* that is equal to the *Performance component*. The planner then *Iterates* over the set of *Performances*, and *Executes a performance* for each, *Monitoring* for *Execution failures*. When *Execution failures* do not occur during the *Execution*, the *Performance* is removed from the set. The planner then *Repeats* the *Iteration* over the remaining sets, and the *Repetition terminates* when the set is empty.

P5.   SHIFT LEARNING AFTER ACHIEVING BASIC ABILITY

Performance: After you've learned to play a piece badly, change the way you improve.

The planner is has the goal of *Improving an ability* to *Execute a performance* and is engaged in *Planning* to achieve this goal. The *Partial plan* contains a *Repetition* with an *Indefinite repetition termination*. The planner *Schedules* to *Periodically Envision* the planner as a subject of an *Evaluation of execution*, where the execution is of the *Performance*. When the planner envisions that the *Execution of the performance* would result in an *Execution failure*, the *Repetition continues*, but when this *Envisionment* results in a *Successful execution*, the planner *Terminates the repetition*, and begins the *Execution* of a *Subplan* in the *Plan*.

P6.   DO SOMETHING ELSE FOR A WHILE

Performance: After you've achieved basic ability on a piece, take a break from its practice.

The planner has the goal of *Improving an ability* to *Execute a performance* and is engaged in *Planning* to achieve this goal. The planner *Periodically schedules* to *Envision* the planner as a subject of *Evaluation of execution*, where the execution is of the *Performance*. *If it is the case* that the *Envisionment* changes from resulting in an *Execution failure* to resulting in a *Successful execution*, the planner *Suspends the execution* of the *Improving an ability* plan for a period of time, and *Executes Pending plans* that do not include the *Execution of the performance*. After the period of time, the planner *Resumes execution of the plan*. The planner *Expects* that the *Ability* to *Execute the performance* will be greater at the *Resumption time* than at the *Suspension time*, and will *Attribute expectation failures* to the *Duration* of the *Suspension time*.

P7. IMPROVE WITH PRACTICE CYCLES

Performance: Learn musical pieces by cycling through the same type of practice many times.

> The planner has the goal of *Improving an ability* to *Execute a performance* and is *Planning* to achieve this goal, and has one or more *Partial plans* for achieving this goal. The planner executes a plan to *Select a Partial plan* to *Repeat* several times, and adds an *Expectation* that the *Ability* of the planner to *Execute the performance* will be greater at each *Repetition*, and will *Attribute expectation failures* to an incorrect *Selection* of the *Partial plan*.

P8. BEGIN MEMORIZATION AFTER ACHIEVING BASIC ABILITY

Performance: Begin memorizing a musical performance after you can play the sheet music.

> The planner has the goal of having the *Ability* to *Execute a performance*. The planner has a *Description of the performance*, and has a *Partial plan* to *Learn the ability* to *Execute the performance* that includes the *Description*. The planner envisions that after the *Execution* of the *Partial plan*, the planner will be able to *Execute the performance* with the *Instrumental use* of the *Description of the performance*. The planner executes a plan to *Add a subgoal* after the *Partial plan* to *Memorize* the *Description* of the performance.

P9. EMPLOY MULTIPLE MEMORIZATION TECHNIQUES

Performance: Memorize a musical performance in lots of ways, even if one is the best.

> The planner has the goal of *Memorizing* a *Description of a performance* and is *Executing a plan* to achieve this goal. The planner has selected a set of *Memory cues* during this execution. The planner executes a plan to *Evalu-*

ate the set of *Memory cues* to determine their *Class similarity*. If the *Evaluation result* is that the *Class similarity* is high, the planner *Monitors* for the *Selection* of *Memory cues* in the execution, where the planner *Selects* those that have a low *Class similarity* to the existing set.

P10. MEMORIZE LOCAL AND GLOBAL STRUCTURE

Performance: When trying to memorize a piece, identify the structure of the piece.

The planner has an *Execution ability* for a *Performance* with the *Instrumental use* of a *Performance description*. The planner has the goal of an *Execution ability* for a *Performance* without the *Instrumental use* of the *Performance description*. The *Performance* is *Compositional* and its *Components* are themselves *Compositional*. The planner executes a plan to achieve the goal of *Analyzing* the *Performance description* to *Know* a set of new *Performance descriptions* at different *Levels of composition*. The planner then plans and executes for the goal of having an *Execution ability* for a *Performance* with the *Instrumental use* of the *Performance description*, where the execution of this plan includes a *Concurrent process Periodically scheduled* during the *Execution* of the *Performance*. During each *Concurrent process*, the planner *Attends* to the set of *Descriptions* that *Describe Components* of the *Performance* that include the *Current moment* in the performance, with the goal that this *Information* is to be *Remembered*.

P11. MEMORIZE BY CHUNKING FAMILIAR PATTERNS

Performance: When trying to memorize a piece, look for familiar patterns.

The planner has an *Execution ability* for a *Performance* with the *Instrumental use* of a *Performance description*. The planner has the goal of an *Execution ability* for a *Performance* without the *Instrumental use* of the *Performance description*. The *Performance* is *Compositional*. The planner executes a plan of *Analyzing* the *Performance description* with the goal of *Recognizing patterns*. During the *Analysis*, the planner *Monitors* for *Pattern recognition*, and these *Patterns* are included in a set. The planner then plans and executes for the goal of having an *Execution ability* for the *Performance* with the *Instrumental use* of the *Performance description*, with the inclusion of *Monitoring* during the *Execution* for the *Moments in a performance execution* that are the *Starts* of *Performance components* that are described by elements of the set of *Patterns*. At these moments, the planner *Suspends* the *Instrumental use* of the *Performance description* for *Executing* the performance, and instead *Executes a performance* which is *Described* by the *Pattern* and the *Performance parameters* of the *Execution* that was *Suspended*. At the *Completion* of this *Execution*, the planner *Resumes Execution of the performance* at a *Moment* in the *Performance execution* that is after the *End* of the *Performance component* that is *Described* by the *Pattern*.

P12.   MEMORIZE WITH YOUR SENSES

Performance: When trying to memorize a piece, use your visual-perceptual abilities.

> The planner has an *Execution ability* for a *Performance* with the *Instrumental use* of a *Performance description*. The planner has the goal of an *Execution ability* for a *Performance* without the *Instrumental use* of the *Performance description*. The *Execution* of the *Performance* is *Perceptible* to the planner during its *Execution*. The planner plans and executes to achieve the goal of *Executing the performance* with the *Instrumental use* of the *Performance description*, that includes *Concurrent processing* that is *Periodically scheduled*. During each *Concurrent processing*, the planner *Attends* to the sets of *Perceptive information content* of each *Perceptive modality* available to the planner, and *Monitoring* for *Perceived actions*, which are *Attended* to with the goal of *Remembering*. After *Repeated executions* of this plan, the planner *Adapts* the plan to include *Monitoring* of *Pattern recognitions* during the *Concurrent processing*, where the planner *Suspends* the *Instrumental use* of the *Performance description*, and *Executes a plan* generated by *Submitting a sensory-motor request* of the *Remaining pattern* of the *Recognition*, followed by a *Resumption of the execution* at the *Moment* in the *Performance execution* that is after the *Component* of the performance that is *Described* by the *Pattern*.

P13.   MEMORIZE WITH SEEMINGLY RANDOM ASSOCIATIONS

Performance: Even non-performance based memory cues are useful in memorizing pieces.

> The planner is executing a plan to achieve the goal of an *Execution ability* for a *Performance* without the *Instrumental use* of a *Performance description*. The planner modifies the plan to include the *Monitoring* for *Remindings* during the *Execution of the performance* or during an *Analysis* of a *Performance description*. The set of *Remindings* are each included in a set of *Memory cues* used for the *Performance component* that was being *Executed* or *Analyzed* when the *Reminding* occurred.

P14. USE MEMORY AIDS TO REMEMBER YOUR MEMORY AIDS

Performance: Write down your memory cues in the sheet music of a performance piece.

> The planner has the *Execution ability* for a *Performance* with the *Instrumental use* of a *Performance description* and is executing a plan to achieve *Execution ability* of the *Performance* without the *Instrumental use* of the *Performance description*. During this execution, the planner has a set of *Memory cues*. The planner executes a plan to *Suspend the execution* of the current plan, *Encode* the *Memory cues* in the location of the *Performance description*, and *Adapt* the *Remaining plan* to include the *Monitoring of Forgetting*, at which time the planner plans and executes for the goal of *Remembering* the *Memory cues* with *Instrumental use* of the *Performance description*.

P15. DEVELOP CONTINUITY AFTER MEMORIZATION

Performance: After a piece has been memorized, practice it as a whole to improve continuity.

> The planner has achieved the goal of an *Execution ability* for a *Performance* without the *Instrumental use* of a *Performance description*, and has the goal that *Possible events* of *Evaluating* the planner's *Execution of the performance* will result in higher *Evaluation results*. The planner plans and executes to achieve this goal, and includes a *Planning constraint* which prohibits the *Execution of a performance* which is a *Component* of the *Performance*.

P16. ISOLATE EXECUTION PROBLEMS

Performance: When learning a musical piece, repeatedly attempt a recognized problem.

> The planner is executing a plan to have an *Execution ability* for a *Performance*. The performance is *Compositional*. The planner has an *Execution failure* during the *Execution of the performance*, and has a *Reminding* of a past *Execution failure* at an equivalent *Performance moment*. The planner executes a plan to *Suspend execution* of the *Performance*, then *Repetitively execute a Subplan* of *Executing a performance* that is a new performance that is equal to the series of *Performance components* of the original *Performance*, where in the first *Repetition* the *Component* is one or more components before the *Performance moment* of the *Execution failure*, and *Ending* one or more components after this moment. The *Repetition termination* occurs after several *Consecutive repetitions* that each are *Executed* without *Execution failures*. Then, the planner *Resumes execution* of the original plan.

P17.   FAVOR MODERATE TEMPOS

Performance: When learning a musical piece, too slow of a tempo can hide problems.

> The planner is *Planning* for the goal to have an *Execution ability* for a *Performance*. The *Components* of the performance have an *Execution duration* that is a multiple of a *Performance tempo*. The planner adds a *Risk* that must be *Avoided*. The risk is a *Partial envisionment* that is one *Branch* of *Envisioned states preceding a planning decision* where the *Planning decision* is the *Selecting a value* for the *Performance tempo*. *Selecting a value* that is lower than a *Specific value Causes Execution failures* in the *Execution of plans* where the *Performance tempo* is *Increased* after *Successful execution* at the *Performance tempo* that is the *Selected value*.

P18.   LOOK FOR AWKWARDNESS

Performance: When learning a musical piece, weird or awkward feeling is a sign of a problem.

> The planner is *Executing* a plan to have an *Execution ability* for a *Performance*, where the performance is *Compositional*. The plan includes the *Execution of the performance*. The planner includes in the plan a *Concurrent processing* during the *Execution of the performance*. During this processing the planner *Compares* the *Sensation of execution* at any *Moment* in the *Execution* to previous moments, according to the dimension of being *Natural*. The planner *Classifies* each sensation as being a member of the *Majority set* or the *Minority set*, based on the comparisons. The planner then assigns each of the members of the *Minority set* to be *Execution problems* in the *Execution of the performance*, and *Replans* with the goal that there are no *Execution problems* for the *Execution of the performance*.

P19.   OPTIMIZE PERFORMANCE EFFICIENCY

Performance: When learning a musical piece, use the biggest muscle to reduce fatigue.

> The planner has an *Execution ability* for a *Performance* that is *Compositional*, and has the goal that the *Execution Expends energy* to a lesser degree. The planner executes a plan to *Analyze* the *Execution* of each *Performance component* to determine if an *Alternate execution option* exists. For each option, the planner *Judges* whether the *Alternative execution option Expends* more or less *Energy* than the *Execution* of the *Performance component* of the planner. If so, the planner *Replans* with the goal of having an *Execution ability* for the *Performance*, with the additional goal that the *Alternative execution options* are *Selected*.

P20.   CONSULT THE COMPOSER

Performance: When learning a musical piece, look for solutions to problems in the score.

> The planner has the goal of an *Execution ability* for a *Performance*, where the performance includes an *Execution problem* and the *Performance specification* is not a *Work product* of the planner, but rather another agent. The planner executes a plan to achieve a *Knowledge goal* to determine if the agent *Envisioned* that other agents, including the planner, would have *Execution problems* during the *Execution of the performance*, where one of them was equal to the *Performance problem* that the planner has. If this *Knowledge goal* is achieved, and the determination is that the agent had this envisionment, then the planner plans and executes to achieve the *Knowledge goal* to determine if the agent had a *Plan to Avoid* the *Execution problem*, and if so, what this *Plan* was. If this *Knowledge goal* is achieved, the planner *Envisions* the execution of this plan by the planner, *Executes* the plan if the plan is envisioned to be successful, or *Adapts* the plan if it is not.

P21.   ADAPT THE WORK OF INCOMPETENT COMPOSERS

Performance: When learning a piece that has problems due to incompetence, adapt the piece.

> The planner has the goal of an *Execution ability* for a *Performance*, where the performance includes an *Execution problem* and the performance is a *Work product* of another agent. The agent executes a plan to achieve the *Knowledge goal* of whether the agent, at the time that the *Execution of work* was done, had the *Ability* to *Correctly envision* the *Execution* of the *Performance* by other agents, including the *Planner*. If not, the planner executes a plan to *Adapt* the *Specification of the performance* at the *Component* of the performance that corresponds to the *Moment* of the *Execution problem*.

P22.   ADAPT BY REMOVING UNNECESSARY PARTS

Performance: When trying to solve a performance problem, try removing unnecessary notes.

> The planner has the goal of *Adapting* the *Specification of a performance* to remove an *Execution problem*, where the *Performance* is *Compositional*. The planner executes a plan to *Iterate* through the set of *Performance* com-

ponents at the *Moment of execution* when the *Performance problem* occurs. For each *Component*, the planner *Composes* a new *Performance specification* that does not include the *Component*, and plans and executes to achieve the *Knowledge goal* of whether the resulting *Performance specification* causes an *Execution problem* when the planner *Executes the performance*. For the set of *Performance specifications* that do not, the planner *Orders the set* according to a *Value in an envisionment*, where the value is the *Envisioned likelihood* that an *Unspecified agent* will *Perceive* that the planner, during the *Execution* of the new *Performance specification*, is not *Executing* the original *Performance specification*. The planner selects the new *Performance specification* that has the smallest value, and *Adapts* the *Specification of the performance* by *Substituting* the new *Performance specification* for the existing one.

P23. ADAPT BY SUBSTITUTING PROBLEMATIC PARTS

Performance: Change problematic musical notes to similar, easier ones.

The planner has the goal of *Adapting* the *Specification of a performance* to remove an *Execution problem*, where the *Performance* is *Compositional*. The planner executes a plan to *Compose* a new *Specification of a performance component* that satisfies an *Envisionment goal*. This goal is that when the planner *Executes the performance*, any *Unspecified agent* will *Believe* that the planner is *Executing* the original *Specification of the performance*, and not the new specification. On the successful completion of this plan, the planner *Adapts* the *Specification of the performance* by *Substituting* the new *Performance specification* with the existing one.

P24. FAVOR ADAPTING NON-ORIGINAL WORKS

Performance: Favor modifications to transcriptions of music over those to original pieces.

The planner has the goal of *Avoiding* an *Execution problem* for a *Performance*, and is *Planning* to achieve this goal. Multiple *Possible plans* exist, some of which include the *Adaptation* of the *Specification of the performance*. The planner executes a plan to achieve a *Knowledge goal* of whether the *Specification of the performance* is an *Adaptation* of a different *Specification of a performance*. If not, the planner *Favors plans* that do not include the *Adaptation* of the specification.

P25. RECORD YOURSELF

Performance: Record yourself and listen critically to your own practice.

The planner has the goal of an *Execution ability* for a *Performance*. A *Device* exists that causes *Observed signals* that are equal to observed signals during the *Execution of the performance* where the *Start time* of the *Observed signals* is a *Moment* after the *End time* of the execution. The planner executes a goal that includes *Instrumental use* of this device such that the planner *Executes the performance*, and then *Perceives* the performance by *Using* the device. During the *Perception*, the planner *Evaluates the performance* and its *Performance components*, *Monitoring* for *Evaluation results* that are bad. For each *of the Performance components* that has a bad *Evaluation result*, a new *Execution problem* is created. The planner then *Replans* to *Avoid* this set of *Execution problems*.

P26. DIVERSIFY YOUR INSTRUMENTS

Performance: Practice pieces on a diverse set of instruments, of poor and high quality.

The planner has an *Execution ability* for a *Performance*, where the *Execution* includes *Instrumental use* of *Physical objects*. The planner *Envisions* a *Future goal* of *Executing the performance* where the *Physical objects* are *Different instances* of the same *Class category*. The planner executes a plan to *Locate* a set of *Physical objects* that are *Different instances* of the same *Class category* as the ones used in the performance. The planner then *Iteratively Executes the performance* with *Instrumental use* of elements in the set, *Monitoring* for *Execution failures*. *Physical objects* used in executions that include *Execution failures* are included in a set, and the planner *Iterates* over this set, planning and executing with the goal of having an *Execution ability* for the performance with *Instrumental use* of the *Physical object*.

P27. PRACTICE BEING DISTRACTED

Performance: Learn to deal with distractions by practicing with constructed ones.

The planner has an *Execution ability* for a *Performance*, and *Envisions* a future *Evaluation of performance* that includes the *Possible event* that is a *Distraction*, where during the *Execution of the performance* the planner *Attends* to an *Unexpected event*, which causes an *Execution failure*. The planner executes a plan to *Repeatedly Execute the performance*, and *Schedules* the execution of a *Subplan* before the performance that will cause one or more *Events* to occur during the *Execution of the performance* that will be *Unexpected* by the planner, and which the planner *Envisions* will be a *Distraction* causing an *Execution failure*. The planner *Executes the performance*, *Monitoring* for *Execution failures* caused by the event. The *Termination of repetition* occurs when the planner *Consistently* has no *Execution failures* of the performance.

P28.   GIVE YOURSELF PLENTY OF TIME

Performance: Before a performance, avoid stress by allocating plenty of time.

> The planner has *Scheduled* the *Execution of a performance* and *Envisions* a *Possible future* where an *Execution failure* occurs during the performance that is caused by an *Emotional state* of the planner of the type *Anxiety*. The planner executes a plan to create a *Scheduling directive* such that all series of *Plans* and *Subplans* that are scheduled *Immediately preceding* the performance are done so with an *Expected duration* that is closer to the *Maximum duration* rather than to the *Mean duration*.

P29.   USE THINGS THAT REDUCE ANXIETY

Performance: Before a performance, reduce stress by ingesting the right stuff.

> The planner has *Scheduled* the *Execution of a performance* and *Envisions* a *Possible future* where an *Execution failure* occurs during the performance that is caused by an *Emotional state* of the planner of the type *Anxiety*. The planner has the *Expectation* that a set of *Physical objects* or *Physical substances* can be *Instrumental* in preventing an agent from having an *Emotional state* that is of the *Anxiety* type. The planner executes a plan that is *Iterative* over the set of *Physical objects and substances*, and for each, *Envisions* whether the *Instrumental use* of it by the planner would cause *Execution failures* in the *Execution of the performance*, or would reduce the *Execution ability* of the planner. If so, it is removed from the set. If elements remain in the set after the *Iteration*, the planner plans and executes for the goal of *Instrumentally using* the *Physical object* or substance so that at the *Scheduled time* of the performance, the planner is not in an *Emotional state* of the type *Anxiety*.

P30.   WARM UP

Performance: To warm up for a performance, play non-performance pieces or hard passages.

> The planner has *Scheduled* the *Execution of a performance*. The planner envisions a *Possible future* that includes *Execution failures* during the performance caused by a *Readiness state* of the planner to *Execute the ability* that the planner has to *Execute the performance*. Also, the planner envisions a *Possible future* that includes that the planner is not in this *Readiness state* at the scheduled execution time. The planner executes a plan to *Generate a subplan* to achieve the goal that the planner is in the *Readiness state*, with the *Planning constraint* that this *Subplan* does not include the *Execution of the performance*. The planner then *Schedules* the *Subplan* so that the planner is in the *Readiness state* at the scheduled time of the performance execution.

P31.   THINK ABOUT SOMETHING ELSE

Performance: Avoid thinking about your performance piece until you are on stage.

> The planner has *Scheduled* the *Execution of a performance* and *Envisions* a *Possible future* where an *Execution failure* occurs during the performance that is caused by an *Emotional state* of the planner of the type *Anxiety*. The planner executes a plan to *Schedule* the *Monitoring* of the planner's *Attending actions* during *Waiting* for where the subject is the *Envisionment* of the *Execution of the performance*. On the occurrence of this event, the planner executes a plan to *Attend* to something that has the property of being *Unrelated* to the *Execution of the performance*.

P32.   IGNORE YOUR COMPETITORS

Performance: Avoid listening to the performances of people who compete before you.

> The planner has scheduled a *Competition* with other agents, where the *Success ordering* is determined by the *Execution of a performance* by the agents and the planner. The *Execution of the performances* by the agents and the planner are *Sequentially scheduled*, and one or more agents are *Scheduled* to *Execute a performance Before* the planner is *Scheduled*. The planner *Envisions* a *Possible future* where an *Execution failure* occurs during the performance that is caused by an *Emotional state* of the planner of the type *Anxiety*. The planner plans and executes to achieve the goal that the planner does not *Perceive* the *Execution of the performances* that are *Scheduled Before*.

P33.   EXPECT DISTRACTIONS

Performance: Have the expectation that your audience will cause distractions.

The planner has scheduled the *Execution of a performance* and *Envisions* a *Possible future* where an *Execution failure* occurs during the performance that is caused by the planner *Attending* to an *Unexpected event*. The planner executes a plan to have the *Expectation* that an *Event* will occur during the performance that is a *Distracting event*, and plans that when this *Event* occurs, the planner will *Ignore* it.

P34.   CHANGE AS LITTLE AS POSSIBLE

Performance: Perform in familiar clothes and adjust the instrument to be familiar.

The planner has scheduled an *Execution of a performance* and has *Completed* a plan to have the *Execution ability for this performance*, which was *Executed* in an *Environment* with a set of *Environmental properties*. The planner plans to *Monitor* their *Planning* for a period *Ending* at the *Execution of the performance* for *Planning decisions* where one *Branch* causes an *Environmental property* during the scheduled execution that is different from the completed execution, where in another *Branch*, the *Environmental property* is the same. In these events, the planner *Prefers* the branch where it is the same.

P35.   IMAGINE THE BEGINNING BEFORE BEGINNING

Performance: Seconds before starting a performance, imagine the piece's beginning.

The planner has scheduled an *Execution of a performance*. The planner schedules a *Subplan* that *Ends* exactly at the *Start time* of the execution. This subplan is to *Imagine a perception* of the *Execution of the performance* for a small *Duration*. When the duration has past, the planner begins *Execution of the performance*.

P36.   PLAY TO THE STRENGTHS OF AN INSTRUMENT

Performance: Adapt your performance to bring out the best qualities of the instrument.

The planner has scheduled an *Execution of a performance* that makes *Instrumental use* of a *Physical object* that is other than a *Physical object* that the planner had in a *Previously executed plan* to have the *Execution ability for the performance*. The planner executes a plan to achieve the *Knowledge goal* of a set of *Properties* of the *Physical object* that are different from the previous object. The planner then *Iterates* over this set, and *Generates goals* that can be achieved with the *Instrumental use* of an object with the property. The planner then plans to *Monitor* for *Execution decisions* during the *Execution of the performance* where the decision is a choice between *Satisfied execution goals*. When these occur, the planner *Favors* the *Execution decision* where the intersection of *Satisfied execution goals* and the generated goals is the largest number.

P37. ADJUST TO YOUR ENVIRONMENT

Performance: Modify your performance so that it is appropriate for the performance hall.

The planner has scheduled an *Execution of a performance* where the *Environment* of the execution is different from the one that the planner had *During* the *Execution* of a plan to have the *Execution ability* for the performance. The intersection of the set of *Environmental properties* of the new and old *Environments* is not the empty set. The planner executes a plan to *Iterate* over the intersecting set, and *Generates goals* that are *Threatened goals* by these *Environmental properties*. The planner then plans to *Monitor* the *Execution decisions* during the *Execution of the performance* where the decision is a choice between *Satisfied execution goals*. When these occur, the planner *Favors* the *Execution decision* where the intersection of *Satisfied execution goals* and the generated goals is the smallest number.

P38. CORRECT PROBLEMS AS THEY OCCUR

Performance: Look for problems in the instrument or the environment, and adapt accordingly.

The planner has scheduled an *Execution of a performance*. The planner executes a plan to *Monitor* for *Threat detection* during the execution. On the occurrence of this event, the planner executes *Concurrent processing* to *Plan* to *Remove the threat*, with the *Planning constraint* that the plan cannot contain the *Suspension of execution* or *Termination of execution* of the performance. The planner then schedules this plan *Concurrently* with the current *Execution*.

P39. NEVER STOP IN THE MIDDLE

Performance: Avoid the interruption of your performance except in the most extreme cases.

The planner has scheduled an *Execution of a performance*. The planner executes a plan to *Monitor* for *Planning decisions* during the execution that include the *Suspension* or *Termination of execution*. When these events occur, the planner *Begins concurrent processing*, where the processing *Iterates* over the set of goals that are not *Achieved* in the *Branch* that does not include *Suspension* or *Termination of the execution*. If any of these goals have the property of being *Never violated*, the planner *Makes a planning decision* to do the *Suspension* or *Termination Branch*. Otherwise, the planner *Terminates* the *Concurrent processing*.

4.8 RELATIONSHIP (22 STRATEGIES)

All you need is love. Love is the only reason good enough. Love will find a way. Our understanding of the concept of love is inextricably tied with human intentions, as a goal to be forever pursued, an indisputable justification for action, and a force that can always be favorably factored into the imagined success of any plan. In some places in the world, many of these ideals have a strong influence in the cultural ways that couples come together and form relationships. In others, these personal relationships have become a planning domain all its own, where finding, keeping, and disposing of loving partners is pursued in very strategic ways, as seen in the 22 relationship strategies presented here.

For a number of cultural reasons, the pursuit of love in a strategic manner is not generally viewed as an admirable course of action. First, our understanding of the concept of love is often seen as contrary the cold, calculated ways that we pursue other goals in our life. That is, we should *trust our hearts* rather than our minds in the pursuit of love, a preference for decisions of action made on less-conscious intuition rather than reason. It is for this value that we can simultaneously be delighted for a person who met their spouse by chance while traveling on an airplane, and disgusted at a person who flew on airplanes in order to meet a spouse. Intentions make all the difference.

A second reason for our distaste for the strategic pursuit of love is that the culturally shared strategies of relationships are often deceptive, even manipulative, in nature. A cautious or skeptical person may instruct a friend to interrupt them halfway through a first date with a stranger, giving them the opportunity to fabricate an excuse to leave if the date is going badly. A person worried about getting a second date with someone they like may secretly leave something valuable to them in the possession of the other person, later to report to them that it was left by mistake, giving them an excuse to meet a second time to make the exchange. A manipulative partner may try to coax a person into making a commitment by surrounding them with other people that have made similar commitments, in hopes that they will serve as role models. Neither deception nor manipulation are seen as viable approaches in the pursuit of love, but perfectly reasonable if your intentions are otherwise, as is the case in each of the strategies presented here.

Relationship strategies 1 through 5 serve the goal of finding a potential mate. Strategies 6 through 10 are used during the activity of dating, and serve to cut dates short when they are going badly, or ensure that a future date will occur. Strategies 11 through 14 are those used to avoid future dates with someone you don't like, while strategies 15 through 21 serve to increase the level of commitment in your dating partner, as when eliciting a marriage proposal. On a somber note, this set ends with strategy 22, designed to wreck a relationship when it is no longer wanted by facilitating the problems and weakness of your partner.

R1. GO WHERE THE MATCHES ARE

Relationship: Look for dates in the places where good candidates hang out.

The planner has the goal of *Locating an agent* that has some *Agent qualities*. The planner executes a plan to *Imagine a new agent* that has the same *Agent qualities*. For this agent, the planner *Guesses agent goals* based on the *Agent qualities*. For each goal, the planner does *Other agent planning* to achieve the goal. Each *Possible plan* may include *Activities* which have *Location classes*. The planner adds to their set of *Persistent goals* the goal of *Being at a location* where the location is the set of instances for the *Location class*.

R2. MATCH WITH FRIENDS OF FRIENDS

Relationship: Look for dates among the friends of your friends.

The planner has the goal of *Locating an agent* that is a *Potential candidate for a role* where the role is in a *Symmetric relationship* where the planner will have the other role. This *Symmetric relationship* is based on *Compatibility of features* where the features are a set of *Agent qualities*. The planner currently has a role in one or more *Symmetric relationships* with other agents also based on *Compatibility of features* where the features are a different set of *Agent qualities* where some of the set members are the same. The planner executes a plan to *Iterate* over this set of other agents. For each agent, the planner plans to achieve a *Knowledge goal* where the thing to be known is the set agents who are in *Symmetric relationships* with the agent that are based on *Compatibility of features* with the same features that the planner has with the agent. The union of all of these sets is a set of *Potential candidates*.

R3. JOIN A DISPLACED GROUP

Relationship: Join a group of people whose ties to other people have all been broken.

The planner has the goal that an agent *Accept a role* where the role is in a *Symmetric relationship* where the planner will have the other role. The *Symmetric relationship* includes activities that have *Activity preconditions* that include *Agent collocation* of the agents in the relationship. The planner has an *Agent model* which includes the *Belief* that an agent that does not have a role in any instances of this *Symmetric relationship* will have the goal of *Accepting a role* in this *Symmetric relationship*. The planner executes a plan to achieve the goal of *Accepting a role* in an activity. In this activity, the role is as a *Member of a group*. This activity has *Sub-activities* that include a

Relocation activity for each of the *Members of the group*, the destination being the *Location* of one or more latter sub- activities.

R4.   HIRE A MATCHMAKER

Relationship: Use the services of a professional matchmaker to find a suitable partner.

The planner has the goal of *Locating an agent* where the agent is a *Potential candidate for a role* where the role is a *Symmetric relationship* where the planner will have the other role. The *Symmetric relationship* is one that will be a *Persistent relationship* if there is *Compatibility of features* where the features are a set of *Agent qualities*. The planner believes that *Making a judgment* about this *Compatibility of features* is an *Agent skill*, and that the planner is a *Novice* in this *Agent skill*. The planner executes a plan to *Locate an agent* that is an *Expert* in this *Agent skill*. The planner acts to cause the *Expert* to have the goal and to act so that the planner achieves the goal of *Locating an agent* for the *Symmetric relationship*.

R5.   DO THINGS THAT REQUIRE PARTNERS

Relationship: Use an event that requires partners as an excuse to approach a prospect.

The planner has the goal that a specific agent *Accept a role* in a *Symmetric relationship* where the planner has the other role. The planner *Envisions the possibility* that the agent would *Accept this role* if the planner the planner *Made a request* to do so, but the *Alternate envisionment* is *Highly undesirable*. The planner envisions that the agent would *Accept a request* if the planner *Requests assistance*. The planner executes a plan to *Request assistance* from the other agent by *Accepting a role* in an *Activity* that is done by *Pairs of agents* that have the *Symmetric relationship*. The planner *Informs* the agent that their goal is to *Complete the activity* and the *Acceptance of the role* satisfies a precondition to this goal.

R6.   HAVE A REMOVABLE TIME PRESSURE

Relationship: On a first date, a time constraint can be used to end a bad experience.

The planner is *Scheduled* to *Execute an activity* that will also include another agent, where the activity is of *Variable duration*. The planner believes that during *the Activity execution*, the planner's *Assessment of the activity* will be based on *Qualities of the agent*. The planner does not know the *Qualities of the agent* to envision what the assessment will be, and envisions a possible state where the *Assessment of the activity* is very bad. The planner executes a plan to inform the agent that the planner has *Scheduled* a different *Execution of an activity* where the other agent is not included, and that the *Start of this activity* is after the start of the scheduled activity with the agent, and that the *End of the activity* with the agent must therefore be before that. The *Scheduled duration* of the activity is near the *Minimum duration* of the *Variable duration activity*. The planner schedules an *Assessment of the activity* during the *Execution of the activity*, and if it is bad, then the planner *Ends the activity* at the scheduled *End time*. If the assessment is good, then the planner *Reschedules* to extend the *Duration of the activity*.

R7. PLAN TO BE INTERRUPTED

Relationship: On a first date, plan an interruption to give you the option of leaving.

The planner is *Scheduled* to *Execute an activity* that will also include another agent. The planner envisions that during *Activity execution*, the planner's *Assessment of the activity* may be either good or bad. The planner executes a plan to cause a third agent to *Schedule* the *Execution of a plan* during the *Execution of the activity* that the planner will do. The plan of the third agent will cause the second agent to believe that the planner is the recipient of an *Inform action*, but the second agent will not know the *Information* which is included in this action. At this time, the planner will make an *Assessment of the activity*, and if it is very bad, then the planner will *Inform* the second agent that the *Information* requires that the planner *Terminate the activity* in order to achieve a new goal. If the assessment is good, then the planner informs the agent that the *Information* can be *Disregarded*, and that the *Execution of the activity* can *Continue*.

R8. BORROW SOMETHING VALUABLE

Relationship: When you want to see them again, borrow something they value.

The planner is *Executing the process* of *Doing something* with another agent and has the goal that the agent *Schedule* to *Do something* with the planner in the future. The planner does not know if the agent has this goal. At the *Location of the execution*, there is a *Thing* which is *Owned* by the agent and is *Instrumental* to the agent's *Future goal pursuit*. The planner executes a plan to *Inform* the agent that the *Thing* is *Instrumental* to a *Cur-*

rently pursued *goal* of the planner's, and *Makes a request* that the agent *Transfer possession* of the *Thing* to the planner, and *Informs* the agent that the planner will *Pursue the goal* to which the thing is instrumental, and then *Transfer possession* of the thing to the agent. After the *Execution is finished* the planner makes a plan to *Schedule* a new activity of *Doing something* with the agent, which will include the *Transfer of possession* of the thing to the agent.

R9.   LEAVE SOMETHING VALUABLE BEHIND

Relationship: When you want to see someone again, leave something behind that you value.

The planner is *Executing the process* of *Doing something* with another agent and has the goal that the agent *Schedule* to *Do something* with the planner in the future. The planner *Possesses* a thing that is *Instrumental* to the planner's *Future goal pursuit*. The planner executes a plan such that after *Termination of execution* and when the planner is no longer in the *Location* of the agent, the thing will be in the *Possession* of the agent, and the agent will *Believe* that this state was not a *Goal state* of the planner, but rather caused by a *Planning failure* of the planner not to *Secure possessions* before *Changing locations*. At some later time, the planner *Informs* the agent that a *Planning failure* has been made, and that the planner has the goal of *Possessing* the thing that is *Instrumental* to the planner's *Future goal pursuit*, with the goal that the agent will have the goal to *Schedule* to *Do something* with the planner where during the *Execution*, the *Transfer of possession* can be scheduled.

R10.   LEAVE ONE FAVOR UNPAID

Relationship: When you want to see someone again, leave one favor unpaid.

The planner has the goal that another agent *Schedule* an *Activity* with the planner in the future, at a time after all *Scheduled activities* with the agent have been *Executed*. During these activities, one or more *Acts* are done by the planner or the agent, where the *Acts* involve the *Expenditure of energy* or the *Expenditure of resources* by the acting agent, and are *Steps in plans* that achieve goals of the other agent. Both the planner and the agent have the *Expectation* that the *Value of the resources* or the *Quantity of energy* expended by both agents in these *Acts* will be equal at some future time. The planner executes a plan to cause the agent to believe that at the *Termination of execution* of the last *Scheduled activity*, the *Value of the resources* or the *Quantity of energy* expended is unequal, which will cause the agent to have the goal of *Scheduling a new activity* during which an additional *Act* can be *Executed*.

R11.   CAUSE DISSATISFACTION FOR AN UNWANTED PARTNER

Relationship: When you want out of a relationship, purposefully be a jerk.

The planner *Has a role* in a *Relationship* with an agent, such that the agent has an *Expectation* that the planner will *Execute* a set of *Activities* with the agent, and that the agent will be included in the planner's *Future goal pursuit*. The planner has the goals that the agent *Remove this expectation* and that the planner's *Future goal pursuit* does not include the agent. The planner envisions that *Executing* a plan of *Informing* the agent of the planner's goals would be bad. The planner executes a plan to cause the agent to *Evoke an emotional response* where the emotion is an *Anger emotion* directed at the planner, causing the agent to have the goal of not being included in the *Future goal pursuit* of the planner.

R12.   GO INTO SECLUSION

Relationship: When you want out of a relationship, make yourself unavailable.

The planner *Has a role* in a *Relationship* with an agent, such that the agent has an *Expectation* that the planner will *Execute* a set of *Activities* with the agent, and that the agent will be included in the planner's *Future goal pursuit*. The planner has the goals that the agent *Remove this expectation* and that the planner's *Future goal pursuit* does not include the agent. The planner envisions that *Executing* a plan of *Informing* the agent of the planner's goals would be bad. The planner executes a plan to *Prevent* the agent from *Locating* the planner or from *Communicating* with the planner in the future. After some time, the planner will believe that the agent no longer has the *Expectation* that they will be included in the planner's *Future goal pursuit*, at which time the planner will *Stop actively pursuing* the *Prevention* goal, and will *Modify their expected activities* in a manner so that the *Envisioned likelihood* of being in the *Location of the agent* is small.

R13.   STRESS AN IDEOLOGICAL DIVIDE

Relationship: When you want out of a relationship, take an opposing ideological position.

The planner *Has a role* in a *Relationship* with an agent based on *Compatibility of agents*, such that the agent has an *Expectation* that the planner will *Execute* a set of *Activities* with the agent, and that the agent will be included in the planner's *Future goal pursuit*. The planner has the goals that the agent *Remove this expectation* and that the planner's *Future goal pursuit* does not include the agent. The planner envisions that *Executing* a plan of *Informing* the agent of the planner's goals would be bad. The planner executes a plan to *Inform* the agent that an *Activity* that the agent has *Executed* or *Plans to execute*, or an *Ideological belief* that the agent has, is a *Quality of an agent* that it in opposition to an *Ideological belief* that the planner has, and this *Violates the requirement* of *Compatibility of agents*, the basis for the *Relationship*.

R14. CLAIM PREVENTION FROM A THIRD PARTY

Relationship: When you want out of a relationship, feign parental dissatisfaction.

The planner is *Scheduled* to do an *Activity* with another agent or the agent has an *Expectation* that they will be included in the planner's *Future goal pursuit*. The planner has the goal of *Avoiding the execution*, or *Removing the expectation*. The planner has a *Power relationship* with a third agent, where the third agent is the more powerful of the two. The planner envisions that *Executing* a plan of *Informing* the second agent of the planner's goals would be bad. The planner executes a plan to *Inform* the second agent that the third agent is *Preventing* the planner from *Executing* the *Scheduled activity*, or that the planner envisions that the third agent will *Prevent* the planner from including the second agent in *Future goal pursuit*.

R15. INCREASE COMMITMENT THROUGH ACCOMMODATION

Relationship: When you want a more committed partner, make a big move for them.

The planner *Has a role* in an *Intentional relationship* with another agent where the agent has an *Expectation* about the *Duration of the relationship*. The planner has the goal that this duration be longer, or an *Indefinite duration*. The *Intentional relationship* involves a set of *Expected activities* which are *Planned* and *Executed* by the planner by *Adapting plans* which are the *Continual plans* of the planner. This adaptation requires an *Expenditure of resources* or an *Expenditure of energy* of some quantity. The planner executes a plan to *Terminate* the planner's *Continual plans* and *Plan* new *Continual plans* that reduce the quantity of *Resources* or *Energy Expended* for the *Adaptation of these plans*. During the planner's *Planning*, a set of *Potential plans* may be generated as *Continual plans* that also have reduced *Execution costs*. If this is the case, the planner *Selects the potential plan* that minimizes the *Adaptation costs*, rather than one that minimizes *Execution costs*. The planner then *Informs* the agent that the agent is the *Cause* of the *Planning decision*.

R16. INCREASE FAMILIARITY BY FOLLOWING A LENGTHY PLAN

Relationship: When you want to step up your relationship, take a vacation together.

The planner *Has a role* in an *Intentional relationship* with another agent, and both are *Executing continual plans* that include or are *Adapted* to include *Activities* that include both agents. The planner has the goal that the *Intentional relationship* include an additional set of *Activities* and *Expectations* of a *Persistent relationship*. The planner believes that a precondition of this goal is that the agent has a better *Agent model* of the planner, but envisions that *Continued execution of continual plans* and *Adapted continual plans* will not cause this state, or that this state will occur later than the planner's *Deadline*. The planner believes that *Learning* the *Agent model* requires *Continual* and *Cooperative execution* of *Activities* for a *Duration of time*. The planner executes a plan to cause the planner and the agent to *Suspend the execution* of *Continual plans* for a *Duration* equal to or less than the *Resumption deadline of the suspension*, which must be greater than the duration required for learning. The planner and the agent *Cooperatively plan* to achieve some *Mutual goal*, such that the *Duration of the plan* is equal to the *Duration of the suspended execution*.

R17. DO ACTIVITIES WITH EXPECTED ROLES

Relationship: Bring a date to weddings and funerals where a significant role is expected.

The planner has the goal that an agent *Adopt a role* in an *Intentional relationship* with the planner. The planner executes a plan to cause the agent to do an *Activity* with the planner and one or more agents, where the other agents have the *Expectation* that the agent has *Adopted the role* in the *Intentional relationship*. These other agents must be *Acquainted* with the planner but be *Unacquainted* with the agent, and the planner must envision that during the *Execution of the activity*, the other agents will be *Acquainted* with the agent.

R18. DOWNPLAY THE SIGNIFICANCE OF A DESIRED ACTION

Relationship: Encourage a marriage proposal by taking marriage very lightly.

The planner has the goal that an agent *Make a planning decision* that the planner envisions will change many of the agent's *Goals*, *Plans*, and *Expectations*. The planner believes that *Making this planning decision* is *Invoking an emotion* in the agent which is a *Fear emotion* based on the agent's

Envisionment of the results of the *Planning decision*. The planner executes a plan to cause the agent to *Have the belief* that the *Planning decision* is *Insignificant*, or that changes in the agent's *Goals*, *Plans*, or *Expectations* are the result of a different *Planning decision* that can be *Indefinitely postponed*.

R19.   STRESS WHAT A DECISION FACILITATES

Relationship: Encourage a marriage proposal by stressing financial benefits.

The planner has the goal that an agent *Make a planning decision* that the planner envisions will result in a state that *Achieves* one of the planner's own *Goals*. The planner believes that *Making the planning decision* requires the agent to *Make a judgment* of whether or not an *Envisioned result of the decision* does *Satisfy a goal* that the agent has. The planner executes a plan to cause the agent to have the *Belief* that *Making the planning decision* will result in a *Precondition* for *Achieving* a different *Goal* that the agent has.

R20.   ENCOURAGE A DECISION WITH ROLE MODELS

Relationship: Encourage a marriage proposal by hanging around your married friends.

The planner has the goal that an agent *Make a planning decision* that is *Invoking emotions* which are *Fear emotions* caused by the agent's *Envisionment* of *Possible outcomes* which are bad. The agent *Has a role* in one or more *Symmetrical* and *Intentional relationships* with agents that have *Made a planning decision* in the past that is equal to the goal decision, and the planner believes that these agents believe their *Planning decisions* were good. The planner executes a plan to cause the planner and the agent to change the *Continual adaptation* of *Continual plans* so as to increase the number of *Scheduled activities* that are *Cooperatively executed* by the agent and those in *Symmetrical* and *Intentional relationships* with the agent.

R21.   CLAIM PRESSURE FROM A THIRD PARTY

Relationship: Encourage a marriage proposal by relaying the desires of your parents.

The planner *Has a role* in an *Exclusive intentional relationship* with the another agent. The planner has the goal that this other agent *Make a planning decision*. The *Planning decision* is one where the agent does not *Envision* an *Obvious best decision*, or is one that the agent wants to *Postpone indef-*

initely. The planner is in a *Relationship* with a third agent, where the planner *Plans* and *Executes plans* to achieve the goals of this third agent. The planner executes a plan to *Inform* the agent that this third agent has the goal that some agent *Make this planning decision*, and that agent is the other agent in the *Exclusive intentional relationship* with the planner. The planner causes the agent to envision that if the agent does not *Make the planning decision*, then the planner will *Terminate the relationship* in order to *Locate an agent* to *Accept a role* in a new *Exclusive intentional relationship* with the planner, and *Make the planning decision*, all to *Achieve the goal* of the third agent.

R22.   FACILITATE THE PROBLEMS OF AN UNWANTED PARTNER

Relationship: Create grounds for divorce by facilitating your partner's weakness and vices.

The planner *Has a role* in an *Intentional relationship* with another agent. The planner has the goal to not *Have this role*. The planner envisions that *Executing a plan* of *Terminating the relationship* would fail due to *Inadequate justification*. The planner executes a plan to *Imagine possible executions* of the agent that would cause the *Execution of the plan* to *Terminate the relationship* to succeed in the planner's envisionment of their own actions. The planner then adds the *Preconditions of these executions* to their set of *Persistent goals*, along with the *Persistent goal* that the agent not *Believe* that the planner has these goals. During the planner's *Continual planning*, *Possible plans* which meet these *Preconditions* are *Selected* over *Possible plans* that *Most effectively* achieve other goals. When the planner believes that the agent has *Executed* one of the possible executions, the planner *Executes the plan* of *Terminating the relationship*.

4.9 **SCIENCE** (34 STRATEGIES)

The ninth set of strategies presented here are those employed in the pursuit of scientific knowledge among members of the scientific research community, broadly defined. The 34 strategies presented here are those that have struck me as interesting over the past several years of my own life, as I've made the transition from graduate student to professional scientist. The first 14 strategies focus on the array of methods that researchers use in the pursuit of knowledge goals, from classical scientific experiments and field studies to contemporary techniques such as simulations and exhaustive search. The second set of strategies, 15 through 19, describe the ways that scientists ensure that the best theories move forward in the face of competing theories, in parallel with the advancement of the best minds to develop these theories. These strategies all involve the use of competition at different scales, correlating the success of researchers with the success of science.

Regardless of whether one is a research professor in a university or a research scientist in a public or private institution, the contemporary pursuit of scientific knowledge begins with funding. In the United States, government foundations have traditionally served as the primary sources of research funds, although private foundations and private corporations also play a significant role. While every scientist would like it to be the case that there were more funds available to pursue research, the system succeeds partly because there is not enough funding available to pursue everyone's research interests. The effect is to create a competitive environment, where ideas compete in a marketplace of funding. All other things being equal, the best ideas generally find their way to available funds, while marginal or unpromising ideas starve for lack of interest. Of course, all things are not equal, and researchers have developed a wide variety of ways to tip the funding balance in their favor. Strategies 20 through 30 explore the ways that researchers advance their ideas by increasing their own prestige and fame, assessing the funding environment, and influencing the research community at large.

The last handful of strategies presented in this section, 31 through 34, focus on the strategic ways that scientists engage in collaboration and discussion. While most scientific fields support very formal means of collaboration, from the presentation of work at conferences and in published journals, these strategies are those used to push scientific goals in ways that more directly support the work of the community as a whole.

S1.   SIMULATION-BASED MODEL TESTING

Science: A theory is supported by comparing its predictions with reality.

> The planner has the goal of *Ordering a set* of *Causal explanations* for a set of *World states* that includes *Future world states* and that include *Unobserv-*

able world states. The planner *Iterates* through the set of *Causal explanations*, and for each, executes a plan to *Design a thing* with a *Designed use* that is *Instrumental use* of the thing to *Achieve the knowledge goal* of a *Subsequent world state* when an agent has an *Encoding* of a *World state*, with a *Design constraint* that the planner envisions that *If it were the case* that the planner *Selects from the set* of *World states* in the *Causal explanation*, the *Instrumental use* of the thing with an *Encoding* of the *World state* would *Achieve the knowledge goal* of a *Subsequent world* state that is equal to the *Subsequent world state* in the *Causal explanation*. The planner then *Encodes* the *Current world state*, and *Iterates* through the set of things, and for each, executes a plan that includes the *Instrumental use* of the thing to *Achieve the knowledge goal* of a *Subsequent world state*. The planner then adds an *Ordering principle* to *Order the set* of *Causal explanations* that advances those where the *Instrumental use* of the thing designed for the explanation caused a *Subsequent world* state that was equal to *Subsequent world state* of the *Current state*.

S2. ENGINEERING PROOF

Science: A theory is supported by creating a working artifact based on its principles.

The planner has the *Knowledge goal* of a *Causal explanation* for a set of *World states* and has a *Candidate explanation* that includes *Causes* that include *Unobservable world states*. The planner executes a plan to *Design a thing* with a *Design goal* that the *Designed use* of the thing is *Instrumental use*, with a *Design constraint* that the planner has an *Envisionment* where the *Instrumental use* will cause the *Goal achievement* with a *Causal chain* that includes the *Causes* in the goal. The planner then executes a plan to *Make the thing*, followed by a plan to cause the planner to *Observe* the *Instrumental use* of the thing that is the *Designed use*. *If it is the case* that there is an *Execution failure* with a cause of *Instrument failure*, then the planner *Rejects the candidate explanation*, and *If otherwise Accepts the candidate explanation*.

S3. PROOF OF CORRECTNESS

Science: A function is supported by proving that it is correct in a system of logic.

An agent has executed a plan to *Design a Function* to *Satisfy goals* that are *Design goals*. The planner has the *Knowledge goal* of the *Envisioned likelihood* that the *Function output* of a *Function Satisfies goals* that are the *Design goals* of this agent. A set of agents has an *Execution ability* for a *Skill* that includes *Encoding information* that includes *Characteristics* of *Functions*, and the planner envisions that *If it were the case* that this *Skill* was *Successfully executed* with the *Function* in the goal, then the *Envisioned likelihood* would be a *Definite likelihood*. The planner executes a plan to cause an agent in this set to *Execute the skill* with the *Function* in the goal and *Inform* the planner *If it is the case* that the *Execution of the skill* is a *Successful execution*.

S4.   INCREMENTAL THEORY TESTING

Science: A theory is developed by adding additional assertions through experimentation.

The planner has the *Knowledge goal* of the set of *Causes* for a set of *Observable world states*, where a subset of the *Causes* are known, and where there is a set of *Candidate explanations* that include a disjoint set of *Causes*. The planner has a *Partial plan* for *Achieving the knowledge* goal of whether there is a *Causal relationship* between two *World states* that includes *Assumptions* that include other *Causes*. The planner *Iteratively executes* a plan that includes the *Partial plan* where the *Assumptions* include the *Causes* that are known, and the *Cause* in the *Causal relationship* is a member of the set of *Causes* in the *Candidate explanations*. In each *Iteration*, *If it is the case* that there exists a *Causal relationship* that includes the *Cause*, then the *Cause* is added to the set of *Causes* that are known. At the *Completion of iteration*, the planner *Achieves the knowledge goal* with the set of *Causes* that are the known causes.

S5.   CONTROLLED EXPERIMENT

Science: A hypothesis is tested by comparing data from experimental and control groups.

The planner has the goal of *Achieving the knowledge goal* of whether there is a *Causal relationship* between *Characteristics* of *Instances of a class* of things and the execution of a *Partial plan*. The planner has a partial plan for *Achieving the knowledge goal* of these *Characteristics*, and a *Partial plan* for *Achieving the knowledge goal* of whether the *Similarity* of two sets of *Characteristics* is *Significantly different*. The planner executes a plan to *Imagine a set* that is the set of *Instances of the class* of things, and then executes a plan to *Imagine sets* that are two sets of equal *Quantity* where members of the sets are added by *Selecting from the set* of class instances using a *Selection criteria* of *Random choice*. The planner then *Adds the threat* that *Characteristics* of the things in the sets are *Changed characteristics* with a cause that is not the execution of plans by the planner. The planner then *It-*

erates over one of the sets, and for each member, executes the *Partial plan* in the goal on the thing in the set. The planner then *Imagines sets* that are two sets of *Characteristics* that are caused by *Iterating* over the two sets, and for each member the planner executes the partial plan for *Achieving the knowledge goal* of the *Characteristics* of the thing. The planner then executes the plan to *Achieve the knowledge goal* of the *Similarity* of the sets, and *If it is the case* that the sets are *Significantly different*, the planner *Achieves the knowledge goal* that was the original goal that there is a *Causal relationship*, and *If otherwise*, that there is not a *Causal relationship*.

S6. CLINICAL TRIAL

Science: A promising treatment is tested for safety and effectiveness in a small population.

The planner has a plan that is the result of *Other agent planning* for a set of agents to *Achieve their goal* to *Modify characteristics* of a second set of agents, and has an *Envisioned likelihood of successful execution* that is a *High envisioned likelihood*. A *Threat* exists that there will be an *Execution failure* with a *Cause of failure* being an *Envisionment failure* by the planner, and that this failure will cause the *Violation of goals* that are goals of members of the two sets of agents. The planner has the *Knowledge goal* of whether there has been an *Envisionment failure*. The planner executes a plan to *Locate a set of agents* that is a subset of the second set of agents of a particular *Quantity*, and plans and executes a plan to *Achieve the knowledge goal* of whether the plan in the original goal *Achieves the goal* of *Modifying characteristics* of this set. *If it is the case* that the plan achieves the goal, the planner executes a plan to cause the first set of agents to execute the plan on the *Remaining set* that is not the subset in the second set of agents, and *If otherwise*, adds a *Planning failure* where the failure occurred with a cause of *Envisionment failure*.

S7. DOUBLE-BLIND STUDY

Science: Observer biases are counteracted by concealing membership in experimental groups.

The planner has a plan to *Achieve the knowledge goal* of the *Causal relationship* between a *Modification of characteristics* of a thing and the execution of a *Partial plan*, that includes a *Subplan* to *Achieve the knowledge goal* of the *Similarity* of *Characteristics* between two sets of things. The planner *Envisions a possible threat* that the *Subplan* will have an *Execution failure* with a *Failure cause* that includes *Expectations* of the agent executing the *Subplan* of the *Characteristics* of the things in the set. The planner *Replans the subplan* with the *Planning constraint* that *During the execution* of the *Subplan* the agent that executes the *Subplan* does not know that a thing is a member of one of the sets.

S8.   DESIGN BY TESTING ALL POSSIBILITIES

Science: New drugs are found by testing every possibility on identical cell cultures.

The planner is planning a *Reusable plan* to achieve the goal of *Modifying characteristics* of a thing, and has a *Partial plan* that includes the *Instrumental use* of a thing that is an *Instance of unknown class*. The planner has the *Assumption* that the that the *Unknown class* is a member of a set of classes, and has the *Planning problem* of *Selecting from the set* the member of the class where the inclusion of *Instances of the class* in the plan cause the plan to be a *Successful plan*. The planner executes a plan to *Iterate* over the set of *Classes*, and for each achieve the goal of having an *Instance of the class*, then *Attempting the execution* of the *Partial plan* with the instance as the thing. The planner then *Monitors* for the *Successful execution of the plan*, *In which case* the planner *Selects from the set* the *Class* for which the thing is an *Instance of the class*.

S9.   RATIONAL DESIGN

Science: New drugs are designed by modeling to our theories of molecular shapes.

The planner is doing *Design* of a thing and has a *Design constraint* that the *Designed use* of the thing will *Achieve a goal* in a *Cause–effect environment*. The planner has a *Design failure* with a cause that a subset of *Characteristics* of the *Things* in the *Cause–effect environment* are *Unknown characteristics* that are *Unobservable characteristics*. The planner executes a plan to *Create a new envisionment* that includes the *Things*, the *Known characteristics* of the thing, and *Causes* that are *Causal influences* on the *Unknown characteristics*. The planner then *Monitors the envisionment* for *Consistent envisionments* where the *Unknown characteristics* are *Deduced characteristics*, and *Adds to a set* of *Candidate characteristics* these *Deduced characteristics*. The planner then *Orders the set* of *Deduced characteristics* with an *Ordering principle* that advances characteristics with a greater *Envisioned likelihood* in the *Envisionment*. The planner then *Makes an assumption* that the *Characteristics* of the *Things* are equal to the *First in the ordered set* of *Deduced characteristics*, and *Resumes the execution* of doing *Design*. The planner then *Monitors* for *Execution failures* that include the *Designed use* of the thing in the goal, and

Prefers explanations of the *Execution failure* that include *Lack of understanding* of the *Causal influences*.

S10. USE TECHNIQUES FROM OTHER FIELDS

Science: Fields with stagnant progress benefit from applying tools developed in other fields.

The planner is a member of a set of agents that each have *Knowledge goals* in a *Knowledge domain*. Agents in the set have a set of *Shared partial plans* for *Achieving knowledge goals* that are the result of *Planning* by agents of the set. Different sets of agents have different sets of *Knowledge goals* in a different *Knowledge domain*. The planner executes a plan to achieve the *Knowledge goal* of the set of *Shared partial plans* for *Achieving knowledge goals* of agents in these different sets. The planner then *Iterates* through the set of *Shared partial plans*, and for each, does *Plan adaptation* of the plan with the *Adaptation goal* of *Achieving knowledge goals* that are goals of the planner, with the *Planning expectation* that there will be an *Adaptation failure* with a cause of *Inappropriate base plan*. The planner *Monitors the planning* for *Successful adaptation*, and *In this occurrence*, the planner *Attempts the execution* of the *Adapted plan* to *Achieve knowledge goals*, and *If it is the case* that the plan is *Successfully executed*, the planner executes a plan to cause the *Adapted plan* to be a *Shared partial plan* in the original set of agents.

S11. SCALE-UP TO REVEAL NEW PROBLEMS

Science: New problems are revealed by broadening the scope of solutions to small problems.

The planner is a member of a set of agents that each have *Achieved knowledge goals* in a *Knowledge domain*, where the *Knowledge goals* include *Causes* in a *Cause–effect environment*. These goals have been achieved by the *Execution of plans* that include different *Cause–effect environments* with a *Quantity* of *Causal influences* that is smaller than the original environment. The agents that executed these plans have the *Assumption* that the *Causes* in the different *Cause–effect environment* are equal to those in the *Knowledge goals*. The planner *Envisions the possibility* that the *Knowledge* in these goals is *False knowledge* with a cause that the *Assumption* is a *False assumption*, and has the *Knowledge goal* of *Verifying a world possibility*. The planner executes a plan to *Adapt the plans* that have been executed with the different *Cause–effect environment* with the *Replacement adaptation* of this environment with a third *Cause–effect environment* where the *Quantity* of *Causal influences* is *Similar* to that of the original environment. The planner then executes these plans to *Achieve the knowledge goals*, and *Monitors* for the *Achievement of knowledge goals* where the knowledge is *Contradictory knowledge* to that in the original *Achieved knowledge goals*.

S12. GENERAL PURPOSE SCIENCE LAB

Science: Investment in broad range of tools allows researchers to quickly explore new ideas.

The planner has a set of *Knowledge goals* in a *Knowledge domain*. The planner has a plan to *Achieve knowledge goals* that are a subset of these goals that includes the *Acquisition of things* that are these things through the *Expenditure of resources* that are *Resources* of the planner. The planner envisions *Future goal pursuit* that will include different plans to *Achieve knowledge goals* that are a disjoint subset of the original goals, and has a *High envisioned likelihood* that this *Future goal pursuit* will include the *Expenditure of resources* to cause the *Acquisition of things* that are *Unknown things* for *Instrumental use*. A *Threat* to this *Future goal pursuit* exists that there will be a *Planning failure* with a cause of *Lack of resources*. The planner does planning of *Partial plans* for achieving the disjoint subset of the original goals, and *Monitors planning* for the *Instrumental use* of *Specified things*, *In which case* the planner *Adds to an imagined set* the thing. The planner then *Replans* the original plan to *Achieve the knowledge goals* with the *Planning preference* for plans that include the *Instrumental use* of *Things* in this new imagined set.

S13. STANDARDS RESEARCH

Science: Working to make other research data comparable improves cooperation in a field.

The planner has a *Leadership role* over a set of agents that are executing plans to achieve a set of *Shared goals* that are *Knowledge goals* in a *Knowledge domain*. The execution of plans by the agents include *Subplans* to *Achieve the goal* of *Encoding information*, where each subplan is different, where the *Information Satisfies knowledge preconditions* of the plans and where the *Decoding of information Requires Expending resources*. The planner does *Other agent planning* for the set of agents of *Shared subplans* to achieve the goals of *Encoding information* and *Decoding information* with the *Planning goal* of *Minimizing an amount* that is the *Amount of resources* that are *Expended resources* in the *Shared subplan*. The planner then executes a plan to cause the agents in the set to *Adapt the plans* to achieve the *Shared goals* with the *Adaptation* that is the *Replacement of subplans* that are the old subplans for the new *Shared subplans*.

S14. FIELD STUDY

Science: Observing phenomenon outside of a lab helps to avoid reductionism in theories.

The planner has a set of *Knowledge goals* of the *Causes* in a *Cause–effect environment* and has a set of *Reusable plans* to achieve a subset of these goals that include the *Assumption* that *Causes* in a different *Cause–effect environment* are equal to those in the original one, where the *Quantity* of *Causal influences* in the original one is greater than those in the different one. The planner executes a plan of a *Plan duration* to *Observe world states* that are a set of *Continuous world states* where *State change* is caused by *Causes* in the *Cause–effect environment*. The planner then *Schedules the execution* of the *Reusable plans* after the *End time* of the *Duration*, and *Monitors* for *Assumptions* that *Causes* are equal, *In which case* the planner *Makes a judgment* of whether the *Cause* in the *Assumption* is equal to a member of the set of *Causes* in the *State changes*. In the case that it is not, the planner *Rejects the assumption*, *Terminates the execution* of the *Reusable plan*, and *Replans*.

S15. ENGINEERING COMPETITIONS

Science: Competitions of artifacts help determine the most promising theoretical approaches.

The planner has the goal of *Ordering* a set of *Causal explanations* with an *Ordering principle* that advances *Explanations* that include *Causes* in a *Knowledge domain* that are *True causes*. The planner has a *Planning failure* in *Ordering the set* with a *Failure cause* that the set of *True causes* is are *Unknown causes*. A set of agents have an *Execution ability* for a skill that includes *Envisionment* with a set of *Causes* in the *Knowledge domain*, and where there exists a member of the set where the *Causes* include the *Causes* in each of the *Explanations*. The planner executes a plan to cause the agents to have a *Competitive relationship* with each other where the *Achievement of the goal* that is the *Competitive goal Requires* the *Execution of the skill*. The planner *Monitors* for the *Successful execution* of the ability by the agents, and *In this event* advances the *Causal explanation* where the *Causes* are in the *Envisionment*.

S16.   PEER REVIEW

Science: Review of research by other researchers improves quality and significance of work.

> The planner has a *Leadership role* over a set of agents that are executing different plans to achieve *Shared goals* that are *Knowledge goals* in a *Knowledge domain*. The planner has the goal of *Ordering the set* of plans with an *Ordering principle* that advances plans that have a greater *Envisioned likelihood of success*. The planner has a *Planning failure* in the *Ordering of the set* with a *Failure cause* of an *Envisionment failure* with a cause of *Lack of understanding* of the *Knowledge domain*. The planner executes a plan to cause the agents in the set to do *Collaborative planning* to achieve the goal of *Ordering the set* of plans.

S17.   QUALIFYING EXAMS

Science: Difficult requisite examinations ensure that the research community is well populated.

> The planner has a *Leadership role* in an *Organization* of agents that have *Shared goals* that are *Knowledge goals* in a *Knowledge domain*. Agents in the organization are *Executing plans* that include the *Execution of skills*, and agents in the set have the *Expectation* that the *Execution ability* of other agents in the set of these *Skills* is a *High execution ability*. A different set of agents have the goal of being a member of the *Organization* and are *Executing plans* to *Achieve this goal*. The planner *Envisions the possibility* that a subset of these agents have less than a *High execution ability* for these skills and that after the *Successfully executed* of these plans these agents will cause *Execution failures* in the *Future plans* of different agents in the *Organization* to achieve the *Shared goals*. The planner executes a plan to *Block* the *Achievement of the goal* to be a member in the *Organization* for all of the set of agents that have this goal, with the *Planning constraint* that there will be a *Failure to block* the plans of agents that have a *High execution ability* for the *Skills*.

S18.   COMPETITIVE FUNDING

Science: Competition for grant money validates research programs as valuable to the field.

> The planner has a *Leadership role* over a set of agents that have *Shared goals* that are *Knowledge goals* in a *Knowledge domain*. These agents have different plans for *Achieving these goals* that include the *Expenditure of resources* that are *Resources* of the planner, and where the *Amount of resources* of the

set of resources in these plans is greater than the *Amount of resources* that are *Possessed resources* of the planner. The planner has the goal of *Maximizing a value* that is the *Quantity* of plans that are *Successfully executed* by the agents. The planner executes a plan to cause the agents in the set to have a *Competitive relationship* with the other agents in the set, where the *Competitive goal* is to cause the planner to have a greater *Envisioned likelihood of success* of the plans of the agent *If it were the case* that the *Resource preconditions* were *Satisfied preconditions*. The planner then *Schedules a plan* to *Order the set* of agents with an *Ordering principle* that advances agents for which the planner has a greater *Envisioned likelihood of success*, and then executes a plan to *Iterate* through the ordered set of agents, and for each agent, *Satisfy the preconditions* of the plans that are *Resource preconditions* with a plan that includes the *Transfer of possession of Resources* of the planner. The planner *Adds the expectation* that the plan will have an *Execution failure* with a cause of *Lack of resources*.

S19. TENURED PROFESSOR

Science: The tenure process encourages theories that may be unpopular but correct.

The planner has a *Leadership role* in an *Organization* of agents that have *Shared goals* that are *Knowledge goals*. Agents in the organization are each *Executing plans* with a *Precondition* that the agent is a member of the organization. The planner has a *Reusable plan* to *Achieve the goal* of *Removing from the set* of agents in the *Organization* an agent, and envisions that this will *Violate the precondition* and cause an *Execution failure* for the agent. The planner *Envisions* that the *Planning* of the agents in the organization includes the *Threat* that the planner will *Execute the plan* that is the *Reusable plan*, and that this *Threat* is the cause of *Planning failures*. The planner *Iterates* over the set of agents, and for each, *Schedules the execution* of a plan that includes *Making a decision*, where the *Deciding factors* include the *Previously executed* plans of the agent, and where the *Decision outcomes* include either the execution of the *Reusable plan* on the agent or the *Adding of a planning constraint* against the execution of the *Reusable plan* on the agent in *Future goal pursuit*.

S20. PARTNER WITH A POPULAR INSTITUTION

Science: Gain support for research by linking it with an institution that is widely valued.

The planner is a member of a set of agents that have *Shared goals* that are *Knowledge goals*, and has a plan that includes *Achieving goals* that are a subset of these *Knowledge goals* and that *Requires* the *Agency* of agents in the set. The planner envisions an *Execution failure* with a cause of *Unmet requirement* that is this *Agency*. There is an *Organization* of agents that are not agents in the set, where the agents in the set have the *Planning preference* that the agents in the *Organization Achieve goals* that are *Organizational goals*. The planner executes a plan to cause a *Cooperative relationship* with the planner and the agents in the *Organization*. The planner then *Informs* the agents in the set of the *Cooperative relationship*, and then executes the original plan.

S21. BE THE ONLY RESEARCHER IN YOUR AREA

Science: Differentiate yourself as a researcher by working in an unpopular research area.

The planner is a member of set of agents that have *Shared goals* that are *Knowledge goals* in a *Knowledge domain* and who are executing plans to achieve subsets of these goals. Agents in the set have a *Competitive relationship* with each other, where the *Achievement of goals* that are *Knowledge goals Enables* the *Achievement of the goals* that are the *Competitive goals*. The planner executes a plan to *Order the set* of *Knowledge goals* with an *Ordering principle* that advances goals where the *Quantity* of plans executed by agents in the set to achieve the goal is fewer. The planner then does *Goal assessment* with the *Goal preference* for goals in the *First few in the set* of ordered goals.

S22. BE THE BEST OF THE PACK

Science: Gain credibility by aiming to be the best researcher in popular research areas.

The planner is a member of the set of agents that have *Shared goals* that are *Knowledge goals* in a *Knowledge domain* and who are executing plans to achieve subsets of these goals. Agents in the set have a *Competitive relationship* with each other, where the *Achievement of goals* that are *Knowledge goals Enables* the *Achievement of the goals* that are the *Competitive goals*. The planner has an *Envisioned likelihood of success* for *Achieving a goal* that is an *Arbitrary member of the set* of *Shared goals* that is greater than the *Envisioned likelihood of success* of plans executed by other agents for the same goal. The planner executes a plan to *Order the set* of *Knowledge goals* with an *Ordering principle* that advances goals where the *Quantity* of plans executed by agents in the set to achieve the goal is greater. The planner then does *Goal assessment* with the *Goal preference* for goals in the *First few in the set* of ordered goals.

S23.   BE ECCENTRIC IN THE FAME GAME

Science: Gain support for your research by striving to be famous for something else.

The planner is a member of a set of agents that have *Shared goals* that are *Knowledge goals*, where agents in the set have a *Competitive relationship* with each other and where plans to achieve the *Competitive goal* are *Enabled* by the *Agency* of *Unknown agents* that are members of a different set of agents. The planner envisions that *If it were the case* that the *Unknown agents* had *Agent acquaintance* of the planner, then the *Envisioned likelihood of successful execution* of the *Shared plan* by the planner would be greater. The planner executes a plan to cause an *Expectation violation* for members of this different set, where the *Expectation* includes the *Normally executed plans* of members of the original set, and the *Expectation violation* includes the *Normally executed plans* of the planner.

S24.   TARGET THE POPULAR PRESS

Science: Gain support for your research by creating a buzz in the nonscientific community.

The planner is a member of a set of agents that have *Shared goals* that are *Knowledge goals*, and where each agent has different plans to achieve these goals. The plans of the planner *each Require* that they are a member of the *First few in an ordered set*, where the *Agency* of the *Ordering of the set* is a different set of agents. The planner envisions that the *Ordering principle* of this different set of agents will include an *Ordering consideration* that advances plans that are *Knowledge* of a third set of agents. A fourth set of agents are executing *Continually plans* to *Inform* the third set of *Information* that includes plans of agents in the first set. The planner executes a plan to cause the *Information* to include the plan of the planner.

S25.   USE GRADUATE STUDENTS AS DISCIPLES

Science: Gain support for your research by graduating students that work with your theories.

The planner is a member of a set of agents that have *Shared goals* that are *Knowledge goals*, each of whom is *Executing plans* to achieve subsets of these goals. The planner has the goal that other agents in the set have an *Envisioned likelihood of success* for the plans of the planner that is greater than the *Envisioned likelihood of success* for the plans of other agents in the set. The planner envisions that *If it were the case* that a subset of some *Quantity* of the other agents were executing the plan that of the planner, then the *Remaining subset* of agents would have *Envisioned likelihoods of success* for this plan that was greater. The planner executes a plan to *Locate agents* that are not members of the set that have subsets of the *Shared goals*, and cause them to have a *Cooperative relationship* with the planner, where the *Cooperative goal* is that the agents are members of the set, and that they are *Executing a plan* to achieve the *Shared goals* that is the plan of the planner.

S26.   JOIN A CORPORATE RESEARCH LAB

Science: Fund your research by joining a corporation that can capitalize on your work.

The planner has a set of *Knowledge goals* in a *Knowledge domain*, and has a *Planning failure* of a plan to achieve these goals with a cause of *Lack of resources*. An *Organization* exists that has a *Competitive relationship* with other *Organizations*, and is executing a *Competitive plan* that has *Knowledge preconditions* that are an intersecting set of the *Knowledge goals* of the planner. The *Organization Possesses resources* of an *Amount of resources* that is greater than the *Resource requirements* in the *Partial plan* of the planner. The planner executes a plan to cause the planner to be a member of the *Organization*, and to have a *Cooperative relationship* with other members of the organization, where the *Cooperative goal* is the *Achievement of the knowledge goals* that are the intersection of the two sets of goals, and which include the execution of the *Partial plan* of the planner.

S27.   RESEARCH IN WEALTHY AREAS

Science: Do research that is applicable to medicine or the military to ensure long-term funding.

The planner has a set of *Knowledge goals* in a *Knowledge domain*, and has a *Planning failure* of a *Partial plan* to achieve these goals with a cause of *Lack of resources*. There exists a set of *Organizations* that have *Competitive relationships* with other *Organizations* that are *Executing continual plans* that are different and that include the *Expenditure of resources* of an *Amount of resources* to achieve the *Competitive goals*. These plans have *Unsatisfied preconditions* that are *Knowledge preconditions* where the *Knowledge* are different subsets of the *Knowledge goals* of the planner. The planner executes a plan to *Imagine a set* that is the set of *Knowledge goals* in all of the plans that are equal to *Knowledge goals* of the planner, and then *Orders the set* with the *Ordering principle* that advances goals with a greater *Amount of resources* that are *Expended resources* of the agents that are *Executing plans* with *Knowledge preconditions* that are *Satisfied preconditions* by the *Achieve the knowledge goal*. The planner then executes a plan to cause *Organizations* in the set to have a *Cooperative relationship* with the planner, where the *Cooperative plan* includes the *Transfer of resources* from the *Organization* to the planner, and where the planner *Achieves the preconditions* that are the *Knowledge preconditions* in the plans of the *Organization*, with *Planning preferences* for *Cooperative relationships* with *Organizations* with *Knowledge preconditions* that are *More advanced in the set* of goals.

S28.   BE A BIG FISH IN A LITTLE POND

Science: Join local scientific communities where your stature is greater.

The planner is a member of a set of agents that have *Shared goals* that are *Knowledge goals* in a *Knowledge domain*, and where the set is a *Compositional set*, for which the planner is a member of a subset of members. The planner has a *Reusable plan* that includes a *Precondition of Agency* of members of the subset of the planner, and envisions an *Execution failure* with a *Failure cause* of *Lack of agency* of other agents in the set. The planner envisions that *If it were the case* that agents in the subset had an *Envisioned likelihood of success* of the plan of the planner that was a *Greater likelihood of success* than the *Envisioned likelihood of success* of their own plans, then they would execute plans that would *Satisfy the precondition* of *Agency*. The planner executes a plan to *Order the set of subsets* of agents with an *Ordering principle* that advances subsets where the *Envisioned likelihood* of success for agents in the subsets of their own plans is a *Lower envisioned likelihood*, and where the current subset for which the planner is a member has a *Rank in the ordered set*. The planner then *Imagines a set* that is the set of subsets with a *Rank in the ordered set* that is a *Better rank in the ordered set*. The planner then executes a plan to cause the planner to be a member of a different subset, with a *Planning constraint* that the subset is a member of the *Imagined set* and where the planner envisions that agents in the set will have an *Envisioned likelihood of success* of the plan of the planner that is greater than the *Envisioned likelihood of success* of the plans of the agents in the set, and a *Planning preference* for subsets that are *Later in the ordered set*. The planner then *Adapts the partial plan* with an *Adaptation* that is the *Substitution of agency* of the other agents in the original subset with agents in the new subset.

S29. TEACH AT A FEEDER SCHOOL

Science: Push a theoretical perspective by teaching students at influential schools.

> The planner has a set of *Knowledge goals* in a *Knowledge domain* and has a *Partial plan* for achieving these goals with *Preconditions* of the *Agency* of members of an *Organization*. The planner envisions a *Plan failure* with a cause of *Lack of agency* of these members. The *Organization* is executing a *Continual plan* to cause agents that are not members of the *Organization* to be members, that includes *Locating an agent* and a *Planning preference* for agents that are members of sets of agents that are executing *Cooperative plans* with a different set of *Organizations* to achieve the goal that the agents have an *Execution ability* for a set of *Skills*. The planner executes a plan to cause the planner to be a member of one of these other *Organizations* and to *Have a role* in the *Cooperative plans*. The planner *Concurrently executes* a plan to cause agents to have the *Planning preference* that *If it were the case* that in *Future states* the agents were members of the *Organization* in the goal, then they would execute plans to achieve the *Preconditions* of the original *Partial plan*. The planner then *Monitors future states* for these agents to be members of the *Organization*, and *In this* occurrence executes the *Partial plan*.

S30. BE THE HUB OF RESEARCH IN YOUR AREA

Science: Push a theoretical perspective by working to be the hub of research in your area.

> The planner is a member of set of agents with *Shared goals* that are *Knowledge goals* in a *Knowledge domain*, where agents each have different plans for different subsets of these goals. The planner envisions that *If it were the case* that the *Quantity of agents* in the set that had *Knowledge* of the plan of the planner were greater, then the planner would have an *Envisioned likelihood of success* of the plan that would be greater. The planner executes a *Continual plan* to *Monitor for the execution* of plans by agents in the set that have the goal of *Achieving knowledge goals* that are goals of the planner, and *In this occurrence Adds to an imagined set* the agent. The planner schedules the *Periodic execution* of *Informing* agents in the *Imagined set* of other agents in the set and of the *Execution of the plan* of the planner.

S31. SHARE DATA WITH OTHERS

Science: Encourage fast advancement in a scientific area by widely distributing data.

The planner is a member of a set of agents that have a *Knowledge goal* and that have different plans to achieve this goal that include the *Encoding of information* that is *Evidence for knowledge* that is the *Knowledge goal*. The planner envisions that *If it were the case* that the planner had *Knowledge* of the *Information* that is the *Evidence for knowledge*, then the *Envisioned likelihood of success* of the plan of the planner would be greater. The planner executes a plan to cause the agents in the set to have a *Shared subplan* of *Informing agents* in the set of *Information*, and to *Modify the plan* that they have to *Schedule the subplan* after *Each execution of the subplan* of *Encoding of information*, where the *Information* in the two subplans is the same.

S32. MAKE YOUR PREPRINTS IMMEDIATELY AVAILABLE

Science: Encourage fast advancement in a scientific area by making in-press papers available.

The planner is a member of a set of agents that have a set of *Shared goals* that are *Knowledge goals* in a *Knowledge domain*. The agents are executing different plans that include *Encoding information* that is a *Description of events* where the events include the *Execution of plans* to *Achieve a knowledge goal*, with a *Start time* after the *Achievement of the knowledge goal*, followed by the *Transfer of possession* of the *Encoding of information* to a second set of agents. The second set of agents are executing continual plans that include the *Transfer of possession* of the *Encoding of information* from the first set, followed by *Making a decision* where the *Positive outcome* of the decision is the *Execution of a plan* to *Inform* agents in the set of the *Encoded information*, with a *Duration of execution* between the *Transfer of possession* and the *Informing*. The planner envisions that *If it were the case* that a subset of agents had the *Information* at a *Moment* that was earlier, then the *Envisioned likelihood of success* of their plans would be greater. The planner *Modifies the plan* that is the *Shared plan* of the agents in the first set to *Enable the execution* of a plan to *Transfer the possession* of the *Encoding of information* to *Any arbitrary member* of the set *Immediately after* the *Encoding of information* by the planner for a *Duration* that has an *End time* that a *Conditional end time*, where *If it is the case* that the *Making of a decision* is the *Negative outcome*, then the *End time* is the *Moment* of the *Negative outcome*, and *In the other case*, the *End time* is the *Informing* of the set of agents of the *Information*.

S33. BUILD A COOPERATIVE LAB

Science: Combine resources to build labs that are time-shared between multiple research efforts.

The planner has a *Leadership role* over a of set of agents that have a set of *Shared goals* that are *Knowledge goals* in a *Knowledge domain*, and each of whom has different plans to achieve subsets of these goals that include the *Expenditure of resources* to cause the *Transfer of possession* of *Designed things* and the later *Instrumental use* of these things. The planner envisions that the plans of these agents will be *Failed plans* with a *Cause of failure* of *Lack of resources*. The planner executes a plan to *Imagine a set* of *Designed things* that are the things in the plans, and *Order the set* of things with an *Ordering principle* that advances things where the *Quantity* of plans that include *Instrumental use* of the thing is greater. The planner does *Other agent planning* for the agents in the set of a *Shared plan* that includes the *Transfer of resources* of the agents to the planner, the *Expenditure of resources* by the planner to *Transfer the possession* of the *Imagined set* of things to the planner, and the *Scheduling* of subplans of the agents that include the *Instrumental use* of these things. The planner adds a *Planning preference* for the *Expenditure of resources* that causes the *Transfer of possession* of things that are *More advanced in the set*. The planner then causes the agents in the set to execute this *Shared plan*.

S34. HOLD A WORKSHOP IN YOUR AREA

Science: Build collaboration and interest in an area by hosting workshops and conferences.

The planner has a *Leadership role* in a set of agents with *Shared goals* that are *Knowledge goals* in a *Knowledge domain*. Agents in the set are executing different plans to achieve these goals that include *Replanning* after the *Achievement of subgoals* that are *Knowledge goals*. The planner has *Partial knowledge* of the plans of these agents, and *Envisions the possibility* that the *Knowledge goals* that are the subgoals in these plans are subgoals in a *Quantity* of plans that is greater than 1. The planner executes a plan to *Periodically schedule* the execution of a plan to cause the agents to execute a plan that includes *Informing* other agents in the set of *Knowledge goals* that are *Achieved goals* and of *Partial executed plans* to achieve the *Shared goals*, and also includes the execution of *Collaborative planning* with other agents in the group to achieve these *Shared goals*.

4.10 WARFARE (45 STRATEGIES)

The final section of strategies in this collection contains those used in classical warfare between armies. There is perhaps no greater catalog of culturally shared warfare strategies than the classic Chinese text, *The Art of War*, written by military strategist Sun Tzu around the 5th century BC (Project Gutenberg, 1994). This text was chosen as representative of the domain, and combed to identify the warfare strategies to serve as the subject of analysis. Remarkably, this text outlines the principles of military strategy with little reference to the specific nature of Chinese warfare technology of the period. Indeed, the contemporary popularity of this book may be partly due to the ease with which the reader can adapt its advice to modern conflicts, in warfare or otherwise. Still, the contemporary reader will find little in it that is surprising or innovative, as the strategies that it describes have largely been integrated into our common culture, and are now merely common sense.

While the domain warfare may be much broader than what Sun Tzu described, *The Art of War* is commendable for its strategic breadth. Among the strategies are those for supply logistics, psychological operations, specification of mission goals, attack scheduling, troop maneuvers, retreat, the execution of a siege, the relationships between armies and civilians, soldier morale, information warfare, and espionage. In addition to the 43 strategies that were identified, two strategies presented here are not from Sun Tzu's work. Strategy 2 (Practice a scorched earth policy) is presented as a modern counterplan to strategy 1 (Forage in enemy territories). Strategy 9 (Demonstrate a surgical strike) is offered as a contemporary interpretation of strategy 8 (Attack vital targets first) where the damage is more psychological than material.

Even with the addition of these two strategies, there seems to be little in this collection that reflects the realities of strategic warfare at the start of the 21st century. With the outbreak of every new conflict between the people of the world, the creativity of mankind is demonstrated in the most violent manner. Contemporary conflicts challenge our fundamental assumptions about what constitutes a war, the types of people that are involved, the purpose of an attack, where battles are fought, and how we determine who are the winners and losers. After an amazingly long run, *The Art of War* may have to be retired for lack of relevance.

It is perhaps these warfare strategies above all others presented in this collection that question the cultural origins of strategies, and the assumptions about human reasoning that they entail. While it is very popular in contemporary Western culture to imagine that different people in distant cultures have worldviews (and self-views) that are completely orthogonal to our own, at some level this belief must be false. The strategies authored by Sun Tsu nearly two and a half millennium ago (albeit through the lens of a modern translation) seem no more difficult to describe using an intentional (or planning-based) vocabulary than those of any other planning domain. If one takes the position that our commonsense psychological models are acquired through enculturation (rather than innate to our biology), then we are immediately faced with challenging questions concerning the cultural evolution of these models throughout human history—where explaining the similarities across cultures is as important as highlighting the differences.

W1. FORAGE IN ENEMY TERRITORIES

Warfare: Support armies with supplies obtained through conquest.

The planner is in an *Adversarial relationship* with another agent and has the goal of executing a *Partial plan* where the *Location of execution* is in a *Region* that is a *Defended region* of the adversary and that includes a set of *Attacks* of the other agent and the *Changing of locations* to this *Region*. The planner has a *Planning problem* that the *Amount of resources* that are *Expended resources* in the partial plan is greater than the *Carrying capacity* of the planner during the *Changing of locations*. The planner executes a plan to *Determine if it is the case* that the successful execution of an *Attack Enables the execution* of a plan to *Acquire resources* that are at the *Location of execution*. *If it is the case*, then the planner *Modifies the partial plan* to include the *Acquisition of resources* after each *Attack*.

W2. PRACTICE A SCORCHED EARTH POLICY

Warfare: Destroy supplies that may be useful to an advancing army.

The planner has an *Adversarial relationship* with another agent and envisions a *Possible future state* with a *High envisioned likelihood* that the other agent will *Acquire resources* that are currently *Possessed resources* of the planner, and that they will be *Instrumental* to the *Adversarial plans* of the other agent. The planner executes a plan to *Schedule* before the *Moment* of the *Possible future state* a plan to *Permanently block* the *Instrumental use* of the *Resources*.

W3. USE DECEPTION TO CONTROL ENEMY ACTIONS

Warfare: Feign inaction, preparation, disorder, etc. to inhibit counterplanning.

The planner has an *Adversarial relationship* with another agent and envisions that the agent is *Counterplanning* against the planner, which includes *Other agent plan deduction* of the planner based on *Actions* of the planner that are *Observed* by the agent. The planner has an *Adversarial plan* that includes *Actions* that are *Observed* by the agent, and envisions that the *Other agent plan deduction* of the agent will be *Successfully executed* and that this will lead to the *Successful execution of a counterplan*. The planner *Imagines a set* of *Actions* that can be *Concurrently executed* with the *Adversarial plan* that would be *Observed* by the agent. The planner then *Iterates* through this set, and for each does *Other agent planning* for the agent that includes *Other agent plan deduction* and *Counterplanning*. For each counterplan, the planner *Envisions the likelihood of success* of the *Adversarial plan In the case that* the agent executes the *Counterplan*. The planner then *Modifies the plan* that is the *Adversarial plan* to include the *Concurrent execution* of the *Actions* that result in the *Greatest envisioned likelihood of success* of the *Adversarial plan*.

W4. BAIT YOUR ENEMY

Warfare: Cause an enemy army to advance by offering a false opportunity.

The planner has an *Adversarial relationship* with another agent and has the goal that the agent *Schedule* to *Execute an attack* on the planner at a specific *Moment*. The planner envisions that *If it were the case* that the agent *Envisioned a high likelihood* that an *Attack* would be *Successfully executed* at the *Moment*, then the agent would *Schedule* an *Attack* at the moment. The planner has a set of plans to cause the *Agent* to believe *Information* about the planner that is not *True information*, or to cause the *Agent* to not know *Information* about the planner. The planner *Iterates* through the set of plans, and for each, *Envisions the likelihood* that the agent will *Attack* for each plan. The planner then *Selects a plan* from the set of plans that result in a *High envisioned likelihood*, and then executes this plan.

W5. IRRITATE YOUR ENEMY

Warfare: Cause an enemy to attack at an inopportune time by irritating them.

The planner has an *Adversarial relationship* with another agent and has the goal that the agent *Schedule* to *Execute an attack* on the planner at a specific *Moment*. The planner has a plan to *Invoke an emotion* in the agent that is an *Anger emotion*. The planner envisions that *If it were the case* that the planner *Executed this plan*, the agent would execute an *Attack*, with a *Duration* between the *Start time* of the execution and the execution of the attack. The planner schedules the execution of the plan at a *Moment* that is before the specific *Moment* in the goal by the *Duration*.

W6.   OCCUPY THE TIME OF YOUR ENEMY

Warfare: Reduce readiness of your enemy by providing them with distractions.

The planner has an *Adversarial relationship* with another agent and has the goal that the *Adversarial plans* of this agent have *Execution failures*. The planner envisions that *If it were the case* that the *Duration* between the *Moment* that a *Subgoal is added* by the agent and the *Deadline* that a plan to *Achieve the subgoal* were less, then the executed plans of the agent would be *Failed executions* due to *Lack of time*. The planner plans and executes to achieve the goal that new *Goals are added* by the agent that require *Planning* and the *Execution of plans* to achieve that is *Consecutive*.

W7.   CONDUCT BRIEF CAMPAIGNS

Warfare: Reduce the risk of draining the wealth of the state by launching short campaigns.

The planner has an *Adversarial relationship* with another agent, and is planning to *Execute a set of attacks* on the agent. The planner envisions that the *Duration* of the plan is within a *Range of quantities*, where plans with a greater *Duration* include the *Expenditure of resources* at a greater *Amount of resources* than plans with a lesser *Duration*. The planner *Adds a planning preference* for plans with a lesser *Duration*, and *Adds a threat* to the *Selected plan* that the *Duration* of the plan will cause *Plan failure* with the reason of *Lack of resources*.

W8.   ATTACK VITAL TARGETS FIRST

Warfare: Reduce the costs of war by striking targets that are broadly used.

The planner has an *Adversarial relationship* with another agent and has the *Planning preference* that *Adversarial plans* executed by the planner *Expend resources* of an *Amount of resources* that is the *Minimal amount*. The planner does *Other agent planning* for the agent with the goal of *Identifying a set* of *Partial plans*. The planner then *Identifies the set* of *Things* that have *Instrumental use* in this set of plans, and *Orders the set* with the *Ordering principle* that advances *Things* that are included in a greater number of plans. The planner then plans and executes to achieve the goal that the *Instrumental use* of the *First few in the order* is *Permanently blocked*.

W9.   DEMONSTRATE A SURGICAL STRIKE

Warfare: Instill fear in enemy's command by demonstrating a surgical strike.

The planner has an *Adversarial relationship* with another agent and has the goal that the other agent *Abandon plans* that are *Adversarial plans* to the planner. The planner has a *Partial plan* for *Informing* the agent of an *Execution ability* of the planner that includes *Describing a past event*. The planner then *Monitors the execution* of their own *Adversarial plans* for *Events* that include the *Destruction of a thing*, where *Adjacent things* were not *Destroyed*, and where it is *Surprising* that adjacent things were not destroyed. The planner then *Executes* the *Informing plan* where the event in *Describing a past event* is the *Destruction event*, and that this event *Achieved a goal* of the planner through *Successful execution of a plan*.

W10.   CONQUER YOUR ENEMY IN WHOLE

Warfare: Avoid problems of partial victories by taking your enemy as a whole.

The planner has an *Adversarial relationship* with an *Organization of agents* and is planning to *Permanently block* the organization from executing *Adversarial plans* against the planner. The planner has plans with a *High envisioned likelihood of success* to achieve the *Subgoal* that a subset of the *Organization* is *Permanently blocked* from executing *Adversarial plans*, and a lower *Envisioned likelihood of success* for plans that include the whole *Organization*. The planner adds a *Planning preference* against plans that achieve the subgoal and not the goal.

W11.   SURROUND YOUR ENEMY

Warfare: Surround your enemy when your forces greatly outnumber them.

The planner has a *Leadership role* over an *Organization of agents* that has an *Adversarial relationship* with a different *Organization of agents* and has the goal to *Destroy* the other organization. Agents in the other organization are *Spatially clustered* at a single *Location*. The *Quantity of agents* in the organization of the planner is *Many times greater* than the *Quantity of agents* in the other organization. The planner executes a plan that includes *Coordinated movement* of agents in the organization to a set of *Locations* that *Surround* the *Location* of the other organization followed by an *Attack* by the organization of the planner.

W12. ATTACK WHEN THEY ARE DEFENSELESS OR WEAK

Warfare: Schedule attacks when the defenses of your enemy are down or reduced.

> The planner has an *Adversarial relationship* with another agent and has the goal to *Permanently block* the execution of *Adversarial plans* by the agent against the planner. The agent has an *Execution ability* to execute a *Defense*. The planner envisions the *Likelihood of successful execution* of the *Defense* to be in a *Range of likelihoods* with a set of *Likelihood dependencies* that include *Characteristics of the agent* and *Characteristics of the environment* of the agent. The planner *Imagines a set* that is the set of *Characteristics* that result in a *Likelihood of success* that is the *Low values in the range*. The planner plans a plan that includes an *Attack* of the agent where the *Start time* of the attack is a *Triggered start time*, and then executes a plan to *Monitor the environment* and *Monitor the agent* for *Characteristics* in this set. In the event that the *Characteristics* exist, the planner *Triggers* the attack plan.

W13. DIVIDE AND CONQUER

Warfare: Divide your army when you are several times stronger.

> The planner is in a *Leadership role* over an *Organization of agents* that has an *Adversarial relationship* with another *Organization of agents*. The planner has the goal to *Destroy* the other organization. The *Quantity of agents* in the organization of the planner is *Several times greater* than the *Quantity of agents* in the other organization. The planner envisions that a subset of the organization of the planner has an *Execution ability* to execute an *Attack*. The planner plans a *Partial plan* that includes an *Attack* on the other organization, where the *Agency* is a subset of the organization that is *Unspecified in the partial plan*. The planner executes a plan to *Imagine a set* of *Possible subsets* of the organization of the planner, then *Orders the set*. The *Ordering principle* advances subsets that have *Lesser quantity* of agents in the subset. The planner then *Iterates through the ordered set*, and for each envisions the *Likelihood of successful execution* of the *Partial plan* by the current subset of the organization. The planner *Terminates the iteration* on the *Iteration termination condition* that the *Envisioned likelihood* is a *High envisioned likelihood*. In the case that the *Iteration was terminated*, the planner executes a plan to *Divide the organization* into the subset in the termination and the *Remaining subset*. The planner then executes the *Partial plan* with the first of these two organizations.

W14.   ENGAGE IN BATTLE WITH AN EQUAL ENEMY

Warfare: Attack when you believe that your force is equal in strength to the enemy force.

> The planner is in an *Adversarial relationship* with another agent and has the goal to *Destroy* the other agent. The planner has an *Execution ability* to execute an *Attack* and a *Defense* that is equal to the *Execution ability* of the agent to execute an *Attack* and a *Defense*. The planner adds a *Planning preference* for *Adversarial plans* that include an *Attack* on the other agent.

W15.   AVOID AN ENEMY THAT IS MORE POWERFUL

Warfare: Avoid attacking an enemy that overpowers your forces.

> The planner has an *Adversarial relationship* with another agent and has the goal to *Destroy* the other agent. The planner has an *Execution ability* to execute an *Attack* and *Defense* that is a *Lesser ability* than the *Execution ability* of the agent to execute an *Attack* and *Defense*. The planner executes a plan to *Prevent* the agent from executing an *Attack* on the planner, and adds a *Planning constraint* against executing plans that include an *Attack* on the agent. The planner then *Monitors* for the case that the *Execution ability* of the planner to execute an *Attack* and *Defense* equals the *Execution ability* of the agent to execute an *Attack* and *Defense*, *In which case* the planner *Removes the planning constraint*.

W16.   FLEE AN ENEMY THAT IS MUCH MORE POWERFUL

Warfare: Flee when your forces are greatly overpowered by those of an enemy.

> The planner has an *Adversarial relationship* with another agent and has the goal to *Destroy* the other agent. The planner envisions that the *Envisioned likelihood* that the agent will *Execute an attack* is a *High envisioned likelihood*, and that the *Likelihood of successful execution* of this attack is also a *High envisioned likelihood*. The planner *Terminates the execution* of plans that include an *Attack* on the agent, adds a *Threat* to the *Preservation goals* of the planner, and executes a plan to *Prevent the execution* of an *Attack* on the planner by the agent.

W17. DEFEND AND WAIT FOR OPPORTUNITY

Warfare: Have a strong defense in place and wait for an opportunity to attack.

The planner has an *Adversarial relationship* with another agent and has the goal to *Destroy* the other agent. The planner envisions that the *Execution of an attack* by the planner on the agent will have a *Low likelihood of successful execution*. The planner has a *Reusable plan* that includes executing a *Defense In the case that* the agent executes an *Attack*, and the planner envisions that this plan will be *Successfully executed* for a *Duration*. The planner executes this plan and *Schedules* the *Termination of this plan* at the *End time* of the *Duration*. The planner then *Concurrently executes a Periodic plan* to envision the *Likelihood of a successful execution* of an attack on the agent, with a *Period duration*. In the case that the *Likelihood* is a *High likelihood*, the planner *Terminates the defense plan*, and executes a plan that includes an *Attack* on the agent.

W18. FOSTER ALLEGIANCE AMONG THE CIVILIANS

Warfare: Gain the support of the nearby civilians when fighting an enemy.

The planner has an *Adversarial relationship* with another agent and has the goal to *Destroy* this agent. The planner envisions that *Future events* will include *Attacks* executed by the planner or the agent at a specific *Location of execution*. This *Location of execution* is the *Location of execution* of plans of a set of other agents that do not have an *Adversarial* or *Cooperative relationship* with the planner. The planner executes a plan to cause this set of agents to have a role in a *Cooperative relationship* with the planner, where the *Cooperative expectation* is that the agents will plan and execute plans that *Assist* the planner in the execution of *Adversarial plans* and *Hinder* the execution of *Adversarial plans* by the other agent.

W19. SIEGE THE STRONGHOLD OF AN ENEMY

Warfare: Overcome the defenses of an enemy by launching a siege of an enemy stronghold.

The planner has an *Adversarial relationship* with another agent and is executing an *Attack* on the agent. The agent is *Executing a reusable plan* that includes a *Defense* that is *Blocking the execution* of the *Attack*. The planner envisions that *If it were the case* that the planner *Repetitively executed* the *Attack*, the *Defense* would be *Successfully executed* for a *Duration*. The planner executes a plan to achieve the goal that the *Attack* is *Repetitively executed* over a second *Duration*, where the *End time* of the second *Duration* is later than the *End time* of the first.

W20.   COORDINATE LARGE ARMIES BY SIGNALING

Warfare: Use long distance communication means to coordinate attacks and defenses.

The planner has a *Leadership role* in an a *Organization* that has an *Adversarial relationship* with another organization. The planner has a *Partial plan* that includes the *Coordinated execution* of plans by *Exclusive subsets* of the *Organization* with different *Locations of execution*. The planner *Adds a threat* to the *Partial plan* of a *Execution failure* with a cause of *Lack of coordination*. The planner then does *Other agent planning* for the set of agents with *Leadership roles* in the *Organization* with the goal of having an *Execution ability* of a *Subplan* that includes *Informing* the *Rest of the set*, with a *Planning preference* for plans that *Minimize the quantity* that is the *Execution duration*. The planner then *Monitors* for *Planning* that includes *Coordinated execution* of plans by *Exclusive subsets* of the *Organization* with different *Locations of execution*, *In which case* the planner adds the *Planning preference* to include the *Subplan* to *Achieve the subgoal* of scheduling the *Coordinated execution*.

W21.   REACH THE BATTLEFIELD FIRST

Warfare: Be more prepared than your enemy by reaching the battlefield first.

The planner is in an *Adversarial relationship* with another agent and is planning a plan that includes an *Attack* on the agent at a *Location*. The agent and the planner have a *Location* that is not equal to the *Location*. The planner envisions that both the planner and the agent will *Move locations* from their *Current location* to the *Location*, and that the agent will *Arrive at a location* at a specific *Moment*. The planner envisions that the *Execution ability* of the planner and the agent to execute an *Attack* has an *Envisionment dependency* on the *Preparedness* of the agent. The planner also envisions that the *Preparedness* of an agent to execute an *Attack* at an *Execution location* will *Increase proportionally* with the *Duration* between the *Start time* of the execution and the *Moment* that the agent *Arrives at the location*. The planner plans and executes to achieve the goal that the *Moment* that the planner *Arrives at the location* is before the moment that the agent arrives.

W22.   MOVE IN UNCONTESTED TERRITORY

Warfare: Move troops through neutral or uncontested territory.

The planner is a member of set of agents with *Adversarial relationships* with other agents in the set, where each agent in the set has the goal of *Possession* of a set of *Regions*. The planner envisions that *Future plans* will include

Transferring locations where the *Origination location* is in one *Region*, the *Destination location* is in a second region, and the *Path of travel* includes *Locations* that are in a third region. The planner adds a *Planning preference* against plans where the third *Region* is a member of the set of *Regions* in the goal.

W23.   HOLD UNASSAILABLE POSITIONS

Warfare: Position troops in locations that cannot be attacked.

The planner has an *Adversarial relationship* with another agent, and believes that the agent has a plan that includes *Executing an attack* on the planner in the future. The planner has the goal of *Blocking the execution* of this attack for a *Duration* that *Immediately follows* and *Immediately precedes Partial plans* of the planner that include *Transferring locations*, and where the *Location* of the planner for the *Duration* is unknown. The planner executes a plan to *Imagine a set* of *Regions*, with the *Boundary definition* between different regions is a different *Envisioned likelihood* of *Successful execution* of an *Attack* on the planner *If it were the case* that the *Location* of the planner was a location in the region. The planner then adds a *Planning preference* for *Selection of plans* where the *Location* of the planner for the *Duration* is in a *Region* with a *Greater envisioned likelihood*.

W24.   ENABLE RETREAT THROUGH SWIFTNESS

Warfare: Maintain the opportunity of retreating by being faster than your enemy.

The planner has an *Adversarial relationship* with another agent, and envisions that *Future plans* of the planner will include a *Defense* of an *Attack* by other agent. The planner has the goal of *Blocking a threat* to *Preservation goals* caused by a *Possible execution failure* of the *Defense*. The planner and the agent have an *Execution ability* to execute a *Transfer of location* with a *Duration* that is *Directly proportional* to the *Distance* between the *Origination location* and the *Destination location* on the *Path of travel*. The planner plans and executes to achieve the goal that the *Duration* of the *Transfer of location* by the planner is a *Shorter duration* for an *Arbitrary path of travel* than the *Duration* for the agent for the same path. The planner then *Blocks the threat* to *Future plans*. The planner then *Monitors future planning* for the plans that include a *Defense* in a *Location* where there exists no *Path of travel* with an *Origination location* of the *Location* that does not include the *Location* of the agent. *In this event*, the planner *Adds the threat* in the original envisionment to the plan.

W25. ATTACK ELSEWHERE TO FORCE ENEMY MOVEMENT

Warfare: Force out an entrenched enemy away from defenses by attacking somewhere else.

> The planner has an *Adversarial relationship* with two agents that have a *Cooperative relationship*, where each has a different *Location*. One of these agents is executing a *Defense* plan that has a *Satisfied precondition* that the agent is in their *Location*. The planner has the goal that this agent is not at this *Location*. The plans of this agent *Require* the *Cooperative execution* of the other agent. The planner has a plan to execute an *Attack* on the other agent, and a *Threat* to this plan exists if the agent in the goal executes a *Defense* at the *Location* of the agent of the *Attack*. The planner envisions that the *Duration* of this attack is greater than the *Duration* of the execution of a *Transfer of location* by the agent in the goal from their current *Location* to the *Location* of the attack. The planner *Schedules* the plan that includes the *Attack*, an *Adds the expectation* that the plan will have an *Execution failure* caused by the execution of *Defense* by the agent in the goal, which will cause the *Goal satisfaction* of the original goal.

W26. PREVENT ATTACKS BY PRESENTING SOMETHING
UNEXPLAINABLE

Warfare: Act unexplainably to force threatening troops to question their plans.

> The planner envisions that another agent will *Successfully execute* an *Attack* on the planner at a future time. The planner envisions that *If it were the case* that *Characteristics of the world* or *Characteristics of the planner* were different, then the agent would *Replan* between the *Current time* and the *Start time* of the attack. The planner executes a plan to *Generate subplans* where the goal is unknown and with the *Planning constraint* that the *Duration* of the subplans is less than the *Duration* between the *Current time* and the *Start time* of the attack and that the execution of the subplan would be an *Observed execution* by the agent. The planner then *Iterates through the set*, and does *Other agent reasoning* with the goal of *Explaining the cause* of the event of the execution of the subplan by the planner. If the *Explaining the cause* results in an *Unexplained cause*, the planner *Terminates the iteration*, executes the *Subplan*, and *Replans*.

W27.   SPREAD ENEMY DEFENSES OVER LARGE AREAS

Warfare: Cause an enemy to spread their defenses by enabling many points of attack.

The planner has an *Adversarial relationship* with another agent that is *Located* in a *Region*. The planner has a location that is not in the *Region*, and has the goal of *Transferring locations* to a *Location* that is in the *Region*. The planner has a plan to achieve this goal that includes an *Attack* on the agent at a *Location* on the *Border of the region*, and envisions that this plan will have an *Execution failure* caused by an *Effective counterplan* which is a *Defense* that includes the *Instrumental use* of *Resources* or of other agents. The planner envisions that *If it were the case* that the agent had a *Quantity of resources* or *Quantity of agents* that was a *Lesser quantity*, then the execution of the *Attack* would be *Successful execution* with specific *Execution duration*. The planner executes a plan to *Imagine a set* of other *Locations* at the *Border of the region* where the planner envisions that the execution of a *Moving of resources* or *Transfer of location* of the agents would have an *Execution duration* that is greater than the attack duration. The planner then *Iterates* over the set of *Locations*, and for each, plans and executes to achieve the goal of *Enabling a plan* of *Transfer location* with a *Destination location* of the *Location* on the *Border of the region*. The planner plans to achieve the goal that the agent has *Knowledge* of these plans, and then *Adds the expectation* that the a subset of the *Resources* and agents of the agent will be *Located* at each of these *Locations* at some future state. The planner then *Waits for the occurrence* of this event. The planner then *Selects from the set* a *Location*, and executes the plan of *Transferring locations*.

W28.   ROUSE AN ENEMY TO LEARN THEIR PLANS

Warfare: Partially execute a maneuver in order to initiate and reveal an enemy counterplan.

The planner has an *Adversarial relationship* with another agent and is planning an *Adversarial plan*. The planner envisions that after the *Start time* of the execution of the *Adversarial plan* the other agent will execute a *Counterplan* that was the result of *Counterplanning* by the agent that occurred before the *Start time*. The planner has the *Knowledge goal* of the *Counterplan*. The planner *Delays the expected start time* and *Suspends planning* of the *Adversarial plan*, then plans a *Partial plan* at the previous *Start time* with the *Planning constraints* that *If it were the case* that the *Partial plan* was *Terminated* at *Any point in the execution*, then the planner has an *Execution ability* to execute *Adversarial plans* that is equal to the *Execution ability* to execute *Adversarial plans* before the execution of the *Partial plan*. The planner then *Begins the execution* of the *Partial plan*, and *Monitors* the agent for the execution of a *Counterplan. In this case*, the planner begins the *Concurrent execution* of a *Repetitive plan* of *Plan deduction* on the execution of the agent, with a *Termination of repetition condition* that the *Knowledge goal* is an *Achieved goal*. Then the planner *Terminates the execution* of the *Partial plan*, and *Replans* the *Adversarial plan*.

W29.   SEND LIGHT TROOPS WHEN SPEED IS CRITICAL

Warfare: Send a light division of troops when speed is more important than force.

The planner has a *Leadership role* in an *Organization* of agents. The planner has a *Planning failure* in planning a plan that includes the *Agency* of the *Organization* with a cause of *Missing a deadline*. The plan includes the *Cooperative execution* by agents in the *Organization*, where the *Cooperative plan* includes *Waiting* by agents for the *Completion of execution* of *Subplans* of other agents in the set. The planner executes a plan to *Order the set* of agents in the organization with an *Ordering principle* that advances agents that have an *Execution ability* to execute the subplans where the *Duration of execution* is a *Lesser quantity*. The planner *Adapts the plan* that is the *Cooperative plan* so that the agents in the plan are a subset that is a *Front subset in the ordered set*.

W30.   USE LOCAL GUIDES

Warfare: Get advice from local residents when traveling through foreign territory.

The planner has a *Leadership role* in an *Organization* of agents. The organization is executing a plan where the *Location of execution* is in a *Region* that is not the *Location of execution* of *Previously executed plans* of agents in the organization. A set of other agents are executing *Normal plans* where the *Location of execution* is in the *Region*. The planner plans and executes to achieve the goal of having a role in a *Cooperative relationship* with a subset of these other agents. Then the planner *Suspends the execution* of the original plan, and *Replans* the original plan by *Cooperative planning* with the subset of agents, with the *Threat* to the *Cooperative planning* that the *Cooperative relationship* is a *Deceptive relationship*.

W31. LEAVE THE ENEMY A MEANS OF RETREAT

Warfare: Allow enemies a means of retreat to prevent desperate defenses.

The planner has an *Adversarial relationship* with another agent, and is planning a plan that includes an *Attack* on the other agent. The agent has an *Execution ability* to execute a *Defense* and an *Attack*, and the planner envisions that *If it were the case* that the agent envisioned that an *Execution failure* of a *Defense* would cause the *Violation of goals* that are *Preservation goals* of the agent, then this *Execution ability* would be greater. The planner adds the *Planning constraint* that *Preserves preconditions* that *Enable the execution* by the agent of a plan that does not include an *Attack* or a *Defense* that *Maintains preservation goals* during the execution of the *Attack*.

W32. ATTACK WHEN ENEMY IS HALF MIRED

Warfare: Schedule an attack when the enemy is halfway over bad terrain.

The planner has a *Leadership role* in an *Organization* that has an *Adversarial relationship* with another organization, and is *Scheduling* a plan that includes an *Attack* on the other organization by the organization of the planner at some time in a *Duration*. Agents in the other organization have a *Cooperative plan* to execute a *Defense* that includes *Coordinated execution* of *Subplans*. The *Execution duration* of these subplans is *Causally dependent* on *Characteristics* of the *Execution environment*. The planner envisions that a *Characteristic* in this set will have the same *State change* in the *Execution environment* of all members of the set of other agents, and envisions that these *State changes* will not be *Simultaneous*. The planner plans and executes a plan to achieve the *Knowledge goal* of the *Moment* that the *Quantity* of *Execution environments* that have the old *Characteristic* is equal to the *Quantity* of *Execution environments* that has the new *Characteristic*. The planner then *Schedules* the *Start time* of the *Attack* to be equal to this *Moment*.

W33. WAIT FOR TERRAIN TO IMPROVE

Warfare: Delay movement of troops across terrain that will improve.

The planner has an *Adversarial relationship* with another agent. The planner is *Scheduling* a plan where a *Variable characteristic* of the *Execution environment* is *Directly proportional* to the *Execution ability* of the planner to execute a *Defense*. A *Threat* to the plan exists *In the case that* the other agent executes an *Attack During the execution* of the plan. The planner executes a plan to *Imagine a set* of *Characteristic states* of the *Variable characteristic*, and then *Orders the set* with the *Ordering principle* that advances *Characteristic states* that the planner envisions to have a *Higher likelihood of occurrence* and that *Maximizes the value* that is the *Execution ability*. The planner *Schedules* the plan to have a *Triggered start time* where the *Triggered start time condition* is that the *Variable characteristic* is a member of the *First few in the order* of *Characteristic states*.

W34. POSITION THE ENEMY BETWEEN YOU AND BAD TERRAIN

Warfare: Position your enemy between your troops and terrain that is difficult to cross.

The planner has an *Adversarial relationship* with another agent, and has the goal of executing an *Attack* on the other agent, who has an *Execution ability* to execute a *Defense*. The agent is *Located* at a *Location* that is *Adjacent* to a *Region*. The planner envisions that *If it were the case* that the agent executed a *Defense* where the *Location of execution* was in the *Region*, then this *Execution ability* of the agent would be a *Lesser amount*. The planner adds a *Planning preference* for plans where the *Location of execution* of the *Attack* is a *Location* where the *Direction* from the *Location* to the *Location* of the agent is equal to the *Direction* from the *Location* of the *Agent* to *Locations* in the *Region*.

W35. GUARD SUPPLY LINES

Warfare: Protect the territory by which resources travel to your forces.

The planner has a *Leadership role* in an *Organization* that has an *Adversarial relationship* with another organization, and has *Scheduled* the execution of an *Adversarial plan*. The planner has the *Expectation* that an *Unmet precondition* of the plan will be a *Satisfied precondition* at the *Start time* of the plan with a cause of the *Successful execution* of a *Movement of resources* between a different location and the *Location of execution*. The planner *Adds a threat* that the other organization will execute an *Attack* on the agent that has *Agency* in the *Movement of resources*. The planner executes a plan to achieve the goal of *Blocking the execution* of a *Transfer of location* of agents in the other organization with a *Destination location* that is on the *Path of movement* of the *Movement of resources*.

W36.   CAPTURE SOMETHING VALUABLE

Warfare: Overtake a greater enemy by capturing something that they highly value.

The planner has an *Adversarial relationship* with another agent, and has a *Planning failure* to achieve the goal of executing an *Attack* on the other agent, with a cause being an *Execution ability* of the other agent to execute a *Defense*. The other agent has a *Preservation goal* that includes a *Thing* that is not the agent. The planner executes a plan that includes the *Taking possession* of the *Thing*, planning to achieve the goal to *Destroy* the *Thing*, and then *Informing* the other agent of the execution and the plan. The planner then *Threatens* the agent, with a *Demand* that the agent *Execute plans* that *Achieve goals* of the planner that are *Adversarial goals* against the agent, and the *Threatened action* is the execution of the destroy plan.

W37.   STRENGTHEN DETERMINATION THROUGH RISK

Warfare: Put soldiers at risk to strengthen their determination to succeed.

The planner has a *Leadership role* in an *Organization* that has an *Adversarial relationship* with an agent. The planner is planning a *Cooperative plan* to be executed by agents in the *Organization* and has *Identified a threat* that *During the execution* of the plan agents in the organization will *Abandon the execution* of the plan with a cause being a *Threat* to *Preservation goals* of the agents. The planner adds a *Planning preference* for plans where *Abandoning the execution* of the *Cooperative plans* by the agents will cause a the *Violation of goals* of the agents that are *Preservation goals*.

W38.   KEEP YOUR FORCES IGNORANT

Warfare: Mystify troops with false reports and appearances to maintain secrecy of plans.

The planner has a *Leadership role* in an *Organization* that has an *Adversarial relationship* with a different organization and is planning *Adversarial plans* against this organization. The planner *Envisions the possibility* that agents in the organization have the *Opportunity* to execute plans that include *Informing* agents in the other organization of plans. The planner adds a *Planning constraint* that the *Adversarial plans* are not *Knowledge* of the agents in the *Organization*. The planner then *Schedules* the *Periodic execution* at *Moments* between the *Current time* and the *Start time* of the *Adversarial plans* to execute a plan that includes *Informing agents* in the *Organization* of *Information* of *World* states that is *False information*. The planner then *Schedules* the *Periodic execution* of the planning an execution of *Partial plans* where the goal is an *Unspecified goal* with the *Planning constraint* that the plans do not *Violate preconditions* of the *Adversarial plans*.

W39. PERSISTENTLY ATTACK TO DEFEAT AN ENEMY

Warfare: Multiple attacks will eventually weaken the defenses of an enemy.

The planner has an *Adversarial relationship* with another agent, and has an *Execution failure* of a plan that includes an *Attack* on the agent with a cause of a *Successful execution* of a *Defense* by the agent. The plan of the agent includes the *Expenditure of resources* or the *Coordinated execution* of *Co-operative plans*. The *Preconditions* of the *Failed plan* of the planner are *Satisfied preconditions*. The planner executes a plan to *Repetitively execute* the plan that includes the attack, and *Adds the expectation* that the execution of the attack will be a *Failed execution Until it is the case* that the *Repetition number* is some *Unknown quantity*, with a *Threat* to the new plan of *Lack of resources* or *Lack of time*.

W40. DESTROY RECORDS

Warfare: Destroy information that would allow an enemy to learn your plans.

The planner has an *Adversarial relationship* with another agent, and is planning *Adversarial plans* against the agent. There are *Encodings of information* where the *Information* is of the *Characteristics* of the planner or where the encodings were *Instrumental* to the planning of *Adversarial plans*. The planner *Envisions the possibility* of a *Future state* where the *Encodings* are *Possessed* by the agent. The planner executes a plan to *Destroy* the things, and adds a *Planning constraint* to plans that include the *Instrumental use* of *Encodings of information* for planning that the *Instrumental use* is followed by a subplan to *Destroy* the encodings.

W41. BLOCK THE FLOW OF INFORMATION

Warfare: Close frontier passes and stop the passage of emissaries to block information flow.

The planner has an *Adversarial relationship* with another agent, and is planning *Adversarial plans* against this agent. The *Locations* of the planner and the agent are different and in different *Regions*. There is a set of agents with a *Location* in the *Region* of the planner that have *Information* about the

Characteristics of the planner. The planner executes a plan to *Block* the execution of plans by agents in this set that include the *Transfer of location* with a *Destination location* that is not in the *Region* of the planner.

W42. USE ENEMY OFFICIALS AS SPIES

Warfare: Have spies high in the chain of command of the forces of the enemy.

The planner has an *Adversarial relationship* with an *Organization*, and envisions a *Future state* where the planner is planning *Adversarial plans* against the organization or is *Counterplanning* against the *Adversarial plans* of the organization. The organization has an *Organizational structure*, where a set of agents have *Leadership roles*. The planner plans and executes to achieve the goal that a *Member of the set* has a *Cooperative relationship* with the planner, and that other agents in the organization have the *False belief* that the agent has an *Adversarial relationship* with the planner. The planner then does *Cooperative planning* with this agent to achieve the goal that the planner has *Information* about the *Characteristics* and *Planning* of agents in the *Organization*.

W43. USE DOUBLE AGENTS

Warfare: Use the spies of the enemy as your own.

The planner has a *Leadership role* in an *Organization* that has an *Adversarial relationship* with another *Organization*. The planner has a *Revealed false belief*, where the *False belief* is that an agent in the organization of the planner has an *Adversarial relationship* with the other organization, and the *True belief* is that the agent has a *Cooperative relationship* with the other organization and has *Attempted the execution* of *Cooperative plans* that include *Informing* agents in the other organization of *Characteristics* and *Planning* of the organization of the planner. The planner executes a plan to *Block the execution* of plans by this agent. The planner then plans and executes to achieve the goal that the agent has a *Cooperative relationship* with the planner where agents in the other organization have the *False belief* that the agent has an *Adversarial relationship* with the planner. *If it is the case* that this is an *Achieved goal*, the planner does *Cooperative planning* with the agent to achieve the *Knowledge goal* of the *Characteristics* and *Planning* of agents in the other organization.

W44.   GIVE FALSE INFORMATION TO ENEMY SPIES

Warfare: Secretly use enemy spies to send deceptive information to your enemy.

> The planner has an *Adversarial relationship* with another agent. A third agent has a *Cooperative relationship* with the other agent to execute *Cooperative plans* that include *Informing* the agent of *Information* that involves the planner. The third agent has the *False belief* that the planner has a *False belief* that the planner has a *Cooperative relationship* with the third agent. The planner *Monitors* their planning for *Adversarial plans* that have a *Threat* that the adversary agent will *Successfully execute* a *Counterplan*. In this case, the planner executes a plan to cause the third agent to have a *False belief* about the *Adversarial plan*, and then *Enables* the *Cooperative plan* of this agent that includes *Informing*.

W45.   GATHER SURVIVOR STORIES

Warfare: Gather information about enemy tactics from soldiers that survive losing battles.

> The planner has a *Leadership role* in an *Organization* that has an *Adversarial relationship* with another *Organization*. A subset of the organization of the planner has had an *Execution failure* of an *Attack* or a *Defense* with the other organization with a cause of *Successful execution of a counterplan* by agents in the other organization. The planner executes a plan to *Cooperatively plan* for agents in this set a plan that includes *Informing* the planner of the *Event history* of the execution of the *Failed plan*. The planner then *Imagines an agent* that *In the past* did planning that resulted in the *Collaborative plan* executed by the other organization. The planner then does *Plan deduction* of the *Collaborative plan*. The planner *Unschedules* and *Replans* plans that include an *Attack* or a *Defense* on the agent.

CHAPTER 5

Conceptual Index to Strategies

The following list contains every lexical form that was tagged as a significant concept in the 372 strategy representations authored in this study. To create this list, each capitalized and italicized word or phrase in the representations was algorithmically extracted. The resulting instances were reduced to the following list of lexical forms by removing duplicate instances. In order to produce a controlled vocabulary from these forms, groups of synonymous forms were identified, and a single controlled form was chosen from among each group. In the list that follows, controlled terms are accompanied by a reference (in parentheses) to which of the 48 representational areas of chapter 6 the controlled term has been assigned. In the line after each controlled term entry is a list of each strategy where the term or its synonym was used, indicated as a letter (the first letter of the strategic domain) and a number. Uncontrolled terms are listed with a pointer to their controlled forms.

A = Animal strategies
B = Business strategies
C = Counting strategies
E = Education strategies
I = Immunology strategies

M = Machiavelli strategies
P = Performance strategies
R = Relationship strategies
S = Science strategies
W = Warfare strategies

Constraining execution rules (30. Causes of failure) A37, B49

Constraint duration (37. Plan construction) B54

Contained in an area, *see* Location in region

Contained thing (5. Physical entities) C8

Contained within a region, *see* Location in region

Contained within the other region, *see* Location in region

Contained within the region, *see* Location in region

Contents, *see* Contained thing

Continual, *see* Continuous execution

Continual adaptation, *see* Continuous adaptation

Continual execution, *see* Continuous execution

Continual plan, *see* Continuous plan

Continual planning, *see* Continuous planning

Continual plans, *see* Continuous plan

Continually plans, *see* Continuous planning

Continue, *see* Continue execution

Continue execution (44. Execution control) R7

Continue indefinitely (3. Events) B1

Continue repetition (45. Repetitive execution) P5

Continued execution of continual plans, *see* Continuous execution

Continuous adaptation (38. Plan adaptation) R20

Continuous execution (43. Execution modalities) B47, R16, S27

Continuous goal, *see* Persistent goal

Continuous plan (14. Plans) A3, A4, A5, A6, A31, B1, B2, B3, B4, B5, B6, B7, B8, B9, B10, B11, B12, B13, B14, B15, B16, B17, B18, B25, B26, B27, B28, B29, B32, B33, B34, B35, B37, B38, B39, B40, B42, B43, B44, B45, B46, M5, R15, R16, R20, S29, S30

Continuous plan start precondition (15. Plan elements) B5, B6

Continuous planning (35. Planning modalities) R22, S24

Continuous plans, *see* Continuous plan

Continuous world states, *see* Consecutive state

Contradiction (23. Managing knowledge) S11

Contradictory knowledge, *see* Contradiction

Control failure (30. Causes of failure) A26

Control relationship (10. Agent relationships) A25, A26, A27, I6, I9, I10, I17, I19, I20, I21, M23

Cooperating agent, *see* Collaborating agent

Cooperating agents, *see* Collaborating agent

Cooperative execution, *see* Collaborative execution

Cooperative expectation, *see* Collaborative plan

Cooperative goal, *see* Collaborative goal

Cooperative plan, *see* Collaborative plan

Cooperative planning, *see* Collaborative planning

Cooperative plans, *see* Collaborative plan

Cooperative relationship, *see* Collaborative relationship

Cooperative relationships, *see* Collaborative relationship

Cooperative specification, *see* Specify characteristic

Cooperatively executed, *see* Collaborative execution

Cooperatively plan, *see* Collaborative plan

Coordinated execution (43. Execution modalities) W11, W20, W32, W39

Coordinated movement, *see* Coordinated execution

Copy thing (22. Physical interaction) E4

Correct envisionment (28. World envisionment) P21

Correctly envision, *see* Correct envisionment

Cost, *see* Negative decision outcome

Cost-benefit analysis (40. Decisions) M21

Costs, *see* Negative decision outcome

Counterplan (14. Plans) A1, A12, A13, A14, A15, A16, A18, A20, A21, A32, A34, A37, B40, I5, I11, I12, I13, I14, I15, I17, I18, I20, I21, M4, W3, W28, W44

Counterplanning (35. Planning modalities) A14, A16, W3, W18, W28, W42

Counterplans, *see* Counterplan

Create a new envisionment, *see* New envisionment

Create a thing, *see* Create thing

Create a threat, *see* Add threat

Create agent (21. Agent interaction) A33, I6, I9, I10, I17, I19, I20, I21

A36, B32, B38, B39, B40, B44, B45, C16,
C20, E20, E25, E28, E29, E30, I11, I17,
I19, I20, M40, S31, S32, W3
Modify rule (47. Observation of execution)
B53, B56
Modify rules, *see* Modify rule
Modify state (22. Physical interaction) C16,
E17, E19
Modify subplan (38. Plan adaptation) C13
Modify the goal, *see* Modify goal
Modify the plan, *see* Modify plan
Modify the plans, *see* Modify plan
Modify the world state, *see* Modify state
Modify their expected activities, *see* Modify
normal activity
Modify thing (22. Physical interaction) B27,
E29, I15, S6, S7, S8
Modifying characteristics, *see* Modify thing
Moment (1. Time) A3, A8, A10, A13, A15,
B27, B41, E28, I8, M49, M54, P11, P12,
P18, P21, P25, S32, W2, W4, W5, W6,
W21, W32, W38
Moment in duration (1. Time) P37
Moment in execution (29. Execution
envisionment) A6, A21, A37, E18, E26,
P11, P16, S7, W33, W37
Moment in period (29. Execution
envisionment) M54
Moment of execution, *see* Execution start time
Moments, *see* Moment
Moments in a performance execution, *see*
Moment in execution
Moments in a period, *see* Moment in period
Monitor (42. Monitoring) A1, A10, A11,
A18, A19, A23, A27, A33, A35, A36,
A37, B1, B3, B4, B8, B13, B14, B42, B44,
B46, B57, C3, C4, C9, C13, C14, E18,
E19, I3, I4, M48, M51, M57, M59, P1,
P2, P3, P4, P9, P11, P12, P13, P14, P25,
P26, P27, P31, P34, P36, P37, P38, P39,
S8, S9, S11, S14, S15, W15, W20, W28,
W44
Monitor agent (42. Monitoring) W12
Monitor environment (42. Monitoring)
C15, S29, W12
Monitor envisionment (42. Monitoring)
A28, A37, S9
Monitor events (42. Monitoring) B13
Monitor execution (42. Monitoring) A2, A3,
A5, A24, A30, A36, I20, S30, W9
Monitor for self-execution, *see* Monitor
self-execution

Monitor for the execution, *see* Monitor exe-
cution
Monitor planning (42. Monitoring) A34,
E19, M43, M58, S10, S12, W24
Monitor self-execution (42. Monitoring)
A11
Monitor the agent, *see* Monitor agent
Monitor the environment, *see* Monitor en-
vironment
Monitor the envisionment, *see* Monitor
envisionment
Monitor the execution, *see* Monitor execu-
tion
Monitor thing (42. Monitoring) A22
Monitoring, *see* Monitor
Monitoring a thing, *see* Monitor thing
Monitoring duration (42. Monitoring) I4
Monitoring occurrences, *see* Monitor
events
Monitoring of execution, *see* Monitor exe-
cution
Monitoring of the execution, *see* Monitor
execution
Monitoring the execution, *see* Monitor exe-
cution
Monitors, *see* Monitor
Monitors for planning, *see* Monitor planning
Monitors for the state, *see* Monitor envi-
ronment
Monitors future planning, *see* Monitor
planning
Monitors future states, *see* Monitor envi-
ronment
Monitors planning, *see* Monitor planning
Monitors the envisionment, *see* Monitor
envisionment
Monitors the execution, *see* Monitor execu-
tion
Monitors the planning, *see* Monitor planning
Monitors the plans, *see* Monitor planning
More advanced in the set, *see* Later in order
More near, *see* Closer distance
Most effectively, *see* Greatest envisioned
likelihood of success
Move locations, *see* Transfer location
Movement of resources, *see* Transfer re-
source
Moves past a point, *see* Pass location
Moving of resources, *see* Transfer resource
Mutual goal, *see* Shared goal
Narrated, *see* Inform
Natural, *see* Natural movement

Transfers resources, *see* Transfer resource
Transfers the location, *see* Transfer location
Trigger condition, *see* Conditional plan trigger condition
Triggered monitor (42. Monitoring) A18
Triggered monitoring, *see* Triggered monitor
Triggered start time (15. Plan elements) W12, W33
Triggered start time condition (15. Plan elements) W33
Triggers, *see* Satisfy monitor condition
True belief (23. Managing knowledge) W43
True cause (27. Explanations) S15
True causes, *see* True cause
True information (20. Information acts) M22, M23, M26, W4
Type class, *see* Class
Unacquaintance (9. Agents) R17
Unacquainted, *see* Unacquaintance
Unblockable plan (14. Plans) A14
Uncertain planning decision (40. Decisions) M58
Uncertainty, *see* Uncertain planning decision
Unchanged state (2. States) A7
Uncoordinated execution, *see* Lack of coordination
Unexpected (31. Managing expectations) P27
Unexpected event (31. Managing expectations) P27, P33
Unexplained cause, *see* Unknown cause
Unfound condition, *see* Unsatisfied condition failure
Unfound object in start location, *see* Unsatisfied condition failure
Unintentional plan (14. Plans) A9, A11
Unknown (23. Managing knowledge) B41, I7
Unknown ability (17. Abilities) A29
Unknown agent (9. Agents) S23
Unknown agents, *see* Unknown agent
Unknown cause (27. Explanations) S15, W26
Unknown causes, *see* Unknown cause
Unknown characteristic (7. Classes and instances) S9
Unknown characteristics, *see* Unknown characteristic
Unknown class (7. Classes and instances) S8
Unknown class instance (7. Classes and instances) S8

Unknown execution ability, *see* Unknown ability
Unknown execution environment (29. Execution envisionment) E24
Unknown goal (12. Goals) A17, A25
Unknown goals, *see* Unknown goal
Unknown location (4. Space) A34
Unknown quantity (6. Values and quantities) A33, W39
Unknown things (5. Physical entities) S12
Unlikely, *see* Low envisioned likelihood
Unmet precondition, *see* Unsatisfied precondition
Unmet requirement, *see* Unsatisfied precondition
Unobservable characteristic (7. Classes and instances) S9
Unobservable characteristics, *see* Unobservable characteristic
Unobservable state (2. States) S1, S2
Unobservable world states, *see* Unobservable state
Unobserved execution (47. Observation of execution) A11
Unobserved executions, *see* Unobserved execution
Unpredictable, *see* Envisionment failure
Unrelated (2. States) P31
Unsatisfiable precondition, *see* Unsatisfiable precondition failure
Unsatisfiable precondition failure (30. Causes of failure) A2
Unsatisfied condition (46. Plan following) I1
Unsatisfied condition failure (30. Causes of failure) C7, C8, I15, R13
Unsatisfied goal (12. Goals) E9
Unsatisfied knowledge goal (12. Goals) A30
Unsatisfied precondition (46. Plan following) B24, B52, S20, S27, W35
Unsatisfied preconditions, *see* Unsatisfied precondition
Unschedule plan (41. Scheduling) E22, W45
Unscheduled duration (41. Scheduling) M30
Unschedules, *see* Unschedule plan
Unselected candidate plan (37. Plan construction) A5
Unspecified agent (9. Agents) A26, B20, B33, B34, B38, B42, B59, P22, P23
Unspecified agents, *see* Unspecified agent
Unspecified goal (12. Goals) E23, M7, M8, M9, W38

Uncontrolled terms: 1,751
Controlled Terms: 988
Indexes: 5,965

CHAPTER

6

Representational Areas

6.1 TIME (23 TERMS)

Twenty three terms were used to reference concepts concerning time. Time concepts included moments (points in time), durations (intervals of time), and sets of moments or durations with certain properties. Relational concepts included many of the ways in which moments and durations can be ordered, although several other possibilities do not appear. Research on commonsense temporal reasoning has been strong for nearly two decades, and has succeeded in authoring axiomatic theories that can express the majority of concepts presented in the following list, often using notation imbedded in specialized temporal logics.

RELATED READINGS

Allen, J. (1983). Maintaining knowledge about temporal intervals. *Communications of the ACM, 26,* 832–843.

Hobbs, J. (2002). Toward an ontology of time for the semantic web. In Proceedings of the Workshop on Annotation Standards for Temporal Information in Natural Language, Third International Conference on Language Resources and Evaluation, Las Palmas, Spain.

DEFINITIONS

Arbitrary duration: Any duration in a set of unspecified durations.

Average duration: A duration with a length that is the average length of a set of other durations.

Before: A moment with a lesser position in an ordered set of moments.

Current moment: The moment that is now in the real world or in envisioned worlds.

Disjunctive duration set: A set of durations with no equivalent moments.

Duration: The ordered set of all moments between two non-equivalent moments.

Duration end: The last moment in a duration.

Envisioned duration: A duration that is envisioned by an agent.

Envisioned end time: The duration end of an envisioned duration.

Envisioned start time: The duration start of an envisioned duration.

Every moment: Any moment in a set of moments.

Greater duration: A duration with a larger set of moments than another duration.

Immediately after: A moment with a later position in an ordering with none in between.

Immediately before: A moment with a lesser position in an ordering with none in between.

Indefinite duration: A duration that does not have a duration end.

Lesser duration: A duration with a smaller set of moments than another duration.

Maximum duration: The duration in a set that has the greatest length.

Minimum duration: The duration in a set that has the smallest length.

Moment: A single point in time.

Moment in duration: A moment that is a member of the set of moments in a duration.

Start time: The first moment in a duration.

Total duration: The additive lengths of a set of durations.

Variable duration: The length of an arbitrary duration in a set with different lengths.

6.2 STATES (18 TERMS)

Several terms were used to make reference to world states, meant to encapsulate everything that might be described about a world, real or imagined, as it exists at some moment in time. A handful of representational notations for states and their relations are widely employed in axiomatic theories of time and change, particularly the Situation Calculus of McCarthy and Hayes (1969), which may be adequate to express many of the concepts listed below. Some other state concepts, particularly those that qualify the epistemic features of a state (e.g., Unobservable state) and those that rely on the notion of a context or environment (e.g., Outside current context), may benefit from approaches in epistemic logic and formal treatments of context.

RELATED READINGS

McCarthy, J., & Hayes, P. J. (1969). Some philosophical problems from the standpoint of artificial intelligence. In D. Michie (Ed.), *Machine Intelligence, 4*. New York: American Elsevier.

DEFINITIONS

Consecutive state: A state after another with none in between.

Current state: The state at the current moment in time.

Environment: A subset of state characteristics that have relationships to an instance.

Environment characteristic: A member of the set of state characteristics of an environment.

Future state: A state at a single moment that is after the current moment.

Next state: The state after another in an ordered set of states with none in between.

Observable: A property of an instance or state that can be observed by an agent.

Observable state: The subset of state characteristics that are observable.

Observed state: The subset of state characteristics that have been observed by an agent.

Outside current context: Instances that are not in the environment of the current state.

Persistent state: A state that remains the same for a subsequent duration.

Previous state: The state before another in an ordered set of states with none in between.

State: A configuration of class instances at a single moment in real or imagined time.

State change: A description of the inequalities between two consecutive states.

State characteristic: A property that describes an instance or relation in a state.

Unchanged state: A state that is equivalent to the previous state.

Unobservable state: The subset of state characteristics that cannot be observed.

Unrelated: A property of an instance that is outside the environment of another.

6.3 EVENTS (11 TERMS)

Several terms were used to reference events and the relationships that hold between events. Classes of events are distinguished by the truth of the their occurrence (e.g., Possible event) or by their temporal characteristics. The proper representation of events has long been a difficult problem in axiomatic theories, but an enormous amount of research attention has been directed to this area in the pursuit of satisfactory solutions to a handful of high-profile issues (e.g., the frame problem). Current representational approaches adequately express the relationships between two different events (e.g., concurrent and consecutive events), but less attention has been directed toward capturing our commonsense understanding of events that recur over time with some frequency.

RELATED READINGS

Kolwaski, R., & Sergot, M. (1986). A logic-based calculus of events. *New Generation Computing, 4*, 67–95.
Shanahan, M. (1995). A circumscriptive calculus of events. *Artificial Intelligence, 77*(2), 249–284.

DEFINITIONS

Concurrent event: An event that overlaps in time with another event.
Consecutive event: An event that has a start time that is the moment immediately after another event.
Continue indefinitely: A property of an event whose duration is an indefinite and includes the current moment.
Event: A moment or duration of change in a causal chain.
Frequency: A property of periodic events describing the duration between their start times.
Observed event: An event that has been observed by an agent.
Past event: An event whose duration is entirely before the current moment.
Periodic event: One of a set of events where the durations between start times are equivalent.
Possible event: An event that is envisioned by an agent to be possible.
Similar events: Two or more events that have been judged to be similar by an agent.
Simultaneous event: An event that has a start time equal to another event.

6.4 SPACE (40 TERMS)

Among the largest set of related terms that were used is that which concerns space. Concepts in this area include locations, regions, paths, directions, and distances, each of which may have a variety of possible relationships to the others. An increasing amount of work is being conducted in the area of qualitative spatial reasoning, resulting in representations that are expressive enough to account for many of the terms listed below. Much of the past work has focused on understanding the possible relationships that locations and regions can have with each other, with less attention on the concepts of paths and directions. Among the more complex concepts that do not seem to appear in previous work are boundary definitions, which are descriptive and arbitrary rules that determine the separation between locations inside an outside a region, and the compositional concept of passing a location, which may be best expressed in conjunction with a theory of events.

RELATED READINGS

Cohn, A. G., & Hazarika, S. M. (2001). Qualitative spatial representation and reasoning: An overview. *Fundamental Informaticae, 43*, 2–32.

Casati, R., & Varzi, A. C. (1999). Parts and places: The structures of spatial representation. Cambridge, MA: MIT Press.

DEFINITIONS

Adjacent location: A location where there is no closer location to another location.

Arbitrary location: Any location in a set of unspecified locations.

Arbitrary transfer path: Any path in a set of unspecified paths.

Arrival location: A location that is the endpoint of a transfer.

Blockade: A partial state that is configured such that transfer on a path is impossible.

Boundary definition: A rule that specifies the separation between two regions.

Closed loop: A path where the endpoint and starting point are equivalent.

Closer distance: A distance that is smaller in value than another distance.

Closer location: A location where the distance to another location is a closer distance.

Current location: The location of an instance at the current moment.

Destination location: An arrival location that is envisioned by an agent.

Direction: The non-reflexive spatial relationship between one location and another.

Disjunctive region: A region with subregions that are not adjacent.

Distance: A value of the space between two locations.

Linear path: A path where the directions between locations are equal or opposite directions.

Location: A description of the spatial relationships held by an instance.

Location class: A location defined by a subset of the spatial relationships of an instance.

Location in region: A location that is contained within a region.

Location on path: A location that is in the set of locations that are in a path.

Nearest location: The location from a set where the distance is closer than all others.

Opposite direction: The direction that is the inverse of another direction.

Origin location: The endpoint path that is the location of an object before a transfer.

Parallel path: A path that has the same directions as a different path.

Pass location: The event in which a moving thing has a specific location.

Path: The set of locations that exist between two endpoints.

Path direction: A direction of transfer along a path toward one of the endpoints.

Path endpoint: A location on a path that has only one adjacent location in the set.

Populated region: A region that contains members of a set of agents.

Possible location: Any of the set of locations that can describe the location of a thing.

Possible path: A path for a thing where every location on the path is a possible location.

Region: A set of locations inside a boundary.

Region boundary: One or more closed loops that separate the inside from the outside of a region.

Region capacity: The envisioned maximum quantity of things that can simultaneously have a location in the region.

Relative boundary: A boundary that is defined by the location of a thing.

Serial path: A path where locations between endpoints have exactly two adjacent locations.

Spatial organization: A pattern that describes the location relationships among a set of things.

Spatial relationship: A relationship between the locations of two things.

Spatially clustered: A spatial organization where the distribution of locations are near a center.

Subregion: A subset of adjacent locations in a region.

Unknown location: A location of a thing that is not known by a specific agent.

6.5 PHYSICAL ENTITIES (24 TERMS)

Objects in the world and other substances that take up space are the classes of physical entities. Closely associated with the representation of space, previous representation research has worked to formalize many of the basic concepts that surround physical objects, particularly part–whole relationships, containment and attachment, and shapes. Less explored in representation work are the aspects of physical objects as people use them. That is, few physical object theories capture inferential differences between things that are natural as opposed to those that are designed and manufactured by people, or make reference to the configurations of configurable things, or the functions of things that serve as instruments of some sort. Of particular philosophical interest is the object concept of a physical body of an agent, where this is seen as something lesser than the whole of a person.

RELATED READINGS

Davis, E. (1993). The kinematics of cutting solid objects. *Annals of Mathematics and Artificial Intelligence, 9*(3,4), 253–305.

Hayes, P. (1985). Naïve Physics I: Ontology for liquids. In J. Hobbs & R. Moore (Eds.), *Formal theories of the commonsense world* (pp. 71–108). Norwood, NJ: Ablex.

DEFINITIONS

Adjacent thing: A thing that has an adjacent location to that of another thing.

Attachment: Two things that are configured such that transfer of one transfers the other as well.

Closest thing: The thing that has the nearest location to a specific location.

Component: A member of the set of parts of a composed thing.

Composed thing: A thing that has a set of parts that are its components.

Compositional level: The level in which a component is recursively part of things that are themselves components of other things.

Configurable state: The states of all characteristics of a thing that can be changed.

Contained thing: A thing that has a location that is a subregion of that of a different thing.

Designed thing: A thing that is the result of a design plan of an agent.

Detached component: A component of a composed thing that is not attached.

Instrument variance: The characteristics of an instrumental thing that may change.

Observable shape: The boundary of the region that is the location of an observed thing.

Physical body: The thing that is the body of an agent.

Physical characteristic: A characteristic of a physical thing.

Physical constraint: A constraint on transfer caused by physical characteristics of a thing.

Physical contact: A relationship between two things whose volumes have a point in common.

Physical container: A thing where a different thing can occupy a subregion of its volume.

Physical entities: The superclass of both substances and things.

Physical entity volume: The space that is the location of an object.

Subcomponent: A component of a thing that is itself a component.

Substances: Collections of stuff that cannot be individuated as distinct things.

Things: Collections of stuff that are individuated as distinct things.

Unknown things: A thing that exists but that is unknown to an agent.

Work product: A thing that is caused to exist through the execution of a work plan.

6.6 VALUES AND QUANTITIES (21 TERMS)

The area of representation of Values and Quantities includes all of the terms used in strategies related to magnitudes in some way, either in a quantitative or in a qualitative manner. Types in this area include quantities (numbers), amounts (stuff), and values (variables), each with its own set of qualifiers and relationships. Expressive representational notations and axiomatic theories for many of these concepts have been well explored in the area of qualitative reasoning, where process simulations (typically in the domain of physics) are computed without using numerical information. An important concept explored in this work is the notion of a confluence, a solution to an equation that involves qualitative rather than quantitative values. Additional work in this area has begun to explore the additional predictive power that is gained when something is known about the order of magnitude of simulation values, and may serve to represent concepts such as *Several times greater*, as seen in the list below. Also included in this list are terms that reference specific mental actions of a quantitative nature, namely those of calculating a value using some function and incrementing a mental counter.

RELATED READINGS

De Kleer, J., & Brown, J. (1984). A qualitative physics based on confluences. *Artificial Intelligence, 24,* 7–83.

Forbus, K. (1984). Qualitative process theory. *Artificial Intelligence, 24,* 85–168.

DEFINITIONS

Amount: A value of the quantity of things or the concentration of a substance.

Calculate: The event that a calculation function obtains a calculation result.

Calculation element: A value that is a component in a calculation function.

Calculation function: The method of computation of a value.

Calculation result: The value that is the result of the application of a calculation function.

Decrease: The movement of a value on a scale in the direction of zero.

Directly proportional: A direct relationship between two scales of values.

Greater rate: A rate where the change in value for a duration is greater than another rate.

Lesser amount: An amount with a value that is lower than another amount.

Minimal amount: The lowest possible value for an amount.

Minimum value: The lowest possibility for a value on a given scale.

Possible data value: A value that is in the value range for a measured thing.

Proportional increase: The value that a directly proportional relationship increases over a duration.

Quantity: A value that is quantitative rather than qualitative.

Several times greater value: A value that is larger than several multiples of another value.

Unknown quantity: A reference to a quantitative value of that is not known.

Upper bound of possible value: A reference to the value that is the greatest in its possible range.

Value: A qualitative or quantitative indicator of position on a scale.

Value range: The set of values between two non-equal values on the same scale.

Variable amount: An amount whose value has variance over time.

Variance over time: A value that is different at different moments in a duration.

6.7 CLASSES AND INSTANCES (21 TERMS)

The representational area of Classes and Instances contains terms that refer to concepts themselves, and the relationships that concepts have with each other. Here a class is a semantic type that can be more or less specific than other semantic types, and for which some instances of the class may be known. Characteristics of a class may be known at different levels of specification, where the characteristics of an instance could be described as compatible or not compatible. Also included in this list are terms meant to refer to mental processes involving the management of taxonomic knowledge, including the act of specifying a class or a characteristic of a class. Knowledge representation in the area of classes and instances has received a great deal of attention throughout the history of AI as well as in classical philosophical literature. Among the work most relevant to the representational requirements presented in this list is that related to reasoning about inheritance hierarchies, where the core concepts of classes and instances are often paired with notations for class characteristics in axiomatic theories, as well as work on semantic networks in general, where specifying class inheritance relationships has been a primary application.

RELATED READINGS

Horty, J., Thomason, R., & Touretzky, D. (1990). A skeptical theory of inheritance in nonmonotonic semantic networks. *Artificial Intelligence, 42*, 311–349.

Stein, L. (1992). Resolving ambiguity in nonmonotonic inheritance hierarchies. *Artificial Intelligence, 55*, 259–310.

DEFINITIONS

Categorize information: The event in which information is classified into a class.

Characteristic: A property of a class instance.

Characteristic change: The event in which a characteristic changes.

Characteristic state: The value of a characteristic at a particular moment.

Class: A set with a criteria that determines inclusion as a member of the set.

Class instance: An entity that meets the criteria for inclusion in a class.

Classify: The event that a class is assigned to an unclassified entity.

Compatible characteristic: A characteristic whose value meets a given criteria.

Different instances: Instances of the same class that have different characteristics.

Guess characteristic: The event in which a characteristic of an instance is inductively assigned.

Known characteristics: The set of characteristics of an instance that are known.

Observable characteristic: A characteristic that can be known through observation by an agent.

Specified class instances: The instances of a specified class.

Specified classes: A class in which the criteria for inclusion is membership in a specified set.

Specify characteristic: The event in which a characteristic of a class instance is assigned.

Specify class: The event where a more specific class is assigned to an instance.

Unknown characteristic: A value of a characteristic that is unknown to an agent.

Unknown class: The class that is unknown to an agent for a given instance.

Unknown class instance: An unspecified instance that is a member of a class.

Unobservable characteristic: A characteristic that cannot be observed by an agent.

Variable characteristic: A characteristic of an instance whose value changes over time.

6.8 SETS (31 TERMS)

A surprising variety of concepts used in strategy representations relate directly to the concept of a set, an ordered or unordered collection of elements. Many of the concepts listed below have direct correlates to algebraic set theory, including the operations of conjunction, disjunction, and intersection, but other concepts are outside the traditional scope of set theory, including the concepts of majorities and minorities, arbitrary set members, common member characteristics, and unspecified sets. Many of these terms concern ordered sets, such as referents to the first, next, and last element in an order, which were often used in strategy representations to describe the iterative execution of plans involving the elements of a set of arbitrary size. Several terms refer to specific mental operations that involve sets, from imagining a set in the first place, adding and removing members to the set, and ordering the members using some ordering principle. A relevant reexamination of set theory from a commonsense reasoning perspective is provided by Pakkan and Akman (1995).

RELATED READINGS

Pakkan, M., & Akman, V. (1995). Issues in commonsense set theory. *Artificial Intelligence Review, 8*, 279–308.

DEFINITIONS

Add to set: The event in which a entity is made a member of a set.

Arbitrary member: Any single member of a set.

Arbitrary subset: Any subset of the members of a set.

Common member characteristic: A characteristic that is held by all members of a set.

Composed set: A set that has subsets.

Disjunctive set: The subsets of set members that are not in the intersection of two sets.

Divide set: The event in which a set is divided into two sets.

First in order: The member of an ordered set that has the first position.

First subset in order: The subset in an ordered composed set that has the first position.

Intersecting set: The subset of set members that are in the intersection of two sets.

Last subset in order: The subset in an ordered composed set that has the last position.

Later in order: The ordered set member with later order than another member.

Lesser in order: The ordered set member with a earlier order than another member.

Majority portion: A subset with over half of the members of a composed set.

Member condition: The criteria for inclusion in a set.

Minority portion: A subset with less than half of the members of a composed set.

Next in order: The set member with a set order that is one greater than another member.

Order set: The event in which members of a set are ordered by some ordering criteria.

Ordering principle: A transitive rule that determines the ordering between two set members.

Ordering principle component: A contributing factor in an ordering principle.

Previous in order: The set member with a set order that is one less than another member.

Remaining subset: The subset of set members that has not participated in an iteration.

Remove member: The event in which a set member is removed from the set.

Reorder ordered set: The event in which an ordering principle is applied to an ordered set.

Set conjunction: The set that is the conjunction of two sets.

Set member: An entity that is a member of a set.

Set order: The quantity that is the order of a member in an ordered set.

Set portion: The ratio of the quantity of members in a subset to the total number of members.

Specific member: A reference to a single member of a set.

Subset: A set where all of the members are members of another set.

Unspecified set: An set where the full set of members is unknown.

6.9 AGENTS (22 TERMS)

The vast majority of the terms used in strategy representations refer to aspects of agents, where this word is used to refer primarily to individual people. However, when whole organizations of people or non-people are viewed in an anthropomorphic manner within a strategy representation, the term *agent* is used as well. With so many terms related to agents in these representations, it may be surprising to find that the majority of the 22 terms in this representational area do not appear to be primitive—instead they largely classify agents based on other representational concerns. Many agent classes are distinguished by the goals that agents have (e.g., adversarial agent, competing agent), the plans that they are executing (e.g., informer agent, employing agent), and the roles that they hold (e.g., successional role agent). The few exceptions that may be seen as more primitive to this area of representation are the base concept of an agent, the general concepts of agent characteristics and roles, and epistemic qualifiers of being unknown, unspecified, or unacquainted. The notion that agents can be discriminated into different types based on their roles has become an issue of practical concern in computational models of teams of heterogeneous agents (e.g., Stone & Veloso, 1999), however the roles that are typically identified within the context of this line of research share little in common with the ones listed below.

RELATED READINGS

Stone, P., & Veloso, M. (1999). Task decomposition, dynamic role assignment, and low-bandwidth communication for real-time strategic teamwork. *Artificial Intelligence, 110*(2), 241–273.

DEFINITIONS

Acquaintance: An agent that is known by another agent through experience.

Advancing competitor: A competing agent that has achieved the competitive goal.

Adversarial agent: An agent that has a goal that the goal of a different agent is not achieved.

Agent: A thing that pursues the goals that it holds.

Agent characteristic: A property of an agent.

Agent couple: Two agents that have roles in an agent relationship.

Agent role: A role in a knowledge structure that is filled by an agent.

Collaborating agent: An agent that is collaboratively pursuing a goal shared with another agent.

Collocated agent: An agent that has the same or an adjacent location to another agent.

Compatible agent: An agent that can possibly fill an agent role.

Competing agent: An agent pursuing a goal shared by another agent that can only be achieved by one.

Employed agent: An agent filling an employee role in an employment plan.

Employing agent: An agent filling an employer role in an employment plan.

Expert agent: An agent with a large amount of knowledge in a knowledge domain.

Informer agent: An agent providing information in an information transfer action.

Novice agent: An agent with a small amount of knowledge in a knowledge domain.

Populated region agents: The set of agents that have locations in a populated region.

Successional role agent: An agent having a role that will be filled by a second agent when the first agent no longer has the role.

Target agent: The agent whose goals are the target of an adversarial agent.

Unacquaintance: An agent that is not known by another agent through experience.

Unknown agent: An agent that is unknown to another agent.

Unspecified agent: An unspecified member of a set of agents.

6.10 AGENT RELATIONSHIPS (18 TERMS)

When describing sets of two or more agents, a useful conceptual construct is the relationship that holds between these agents within the context of a situation or a period of time. Theoretically, the possible sorts of relationships that exist between agents are not well constrained, and may include spatial relationships, temporal relationships, and any comparative relationship that holds between any pair of entities in the world. In strategy representations, however, the sorts of agent relationships are largely determined by agent goals, planning behavior, and execution. Distinguishing features for many of the relationship types evident in terms in this area are sometimes quite subtle. For example, an adversarial relationship can be distinguished from a competitive relationship in that a competitor has a goal that is incompatible with the goal of another agent, whereas an adversary has the goal that the other agent fails to achieve their goal. An assistive relationship differs from a collaborative relationship in that the former holds when the goals to be achieved are held only by one of the agents involved. A power relationship can be distinguished from a control relationship in that the former involves the transfer of plans from one agent to another, while the latter also forces their execution regardless of the will of the recipient. While the definitive work on agent relationships does not yet exist in the field of knowledge representation, recent work in authoring heterogeneous autonomous agent systems has succeeded in making operational some of the ideas that parallel our commonsense understanding of relationships, particularly concerning cooperation.

RELATED READINGS

d'Inverno, M., & Luck, M. (2001). *Understanding agent systems*. Heidelberg, Germany: Springer-Verlag.

DEFINITIONS

Adversarial relationship: A relationship where an agent has the goal that the goals of another agent fail.

Assistive relationship: A relationship where an agent executes plans so that the goals of another are achieved.

Collaborative relationship: A relationship where agents share the same goal and both execute to achieve it.

Competitive relationship: A relationship where agents have the same goal that can only be achieved by one.

Control relationship: A relationship where an agent causes another to execute plans to achieve their own goals.

Deceptive relationship: A relationship where one agent falsely believes they have a different relationship with another agent.

Exclusive intentional relationship: A relationship that holds between exactly two agents that have the goal of having the relationship.

Intentional relationship: A relationship among a set of agents that have the goal of having the relationship.

Leadership role: A role held by an agent that does planning in a power relationship.

Paid work relationship: A relationship where the goals of one agent are achieved by another who is paid.

Persistent relationship: A property of a relationship that holds for an indefinite duration.

Power relationship: A relationship where the planning of an agent generates plans for other agents.

Protective relationship: A relationship where the goal of an agent is to block the adversarial plans of a second agent aimed at the goals of a third agent.

Relationship: A definition of an inclusion criteria for sets of two or more agents.

Relationship class: The relationship class for a specific instance of a relationship.

Relationship duration: The duration for which a relationship holds.

Successional role: A role in a relationship that is held successively among multiple agents.

Symmetric relationship: A relationship between two agents where the roles are the same.

6.11 COMMUNITIES AND ORGANIZATIONS (10 TERMS)

A small number of representational terms were used in strategy representations to refer specifically to entire groups of interrelated agents. Although the distinction between a community and an organization is subtle, the former term is used here to indicate sets of interrelated agents that share some common characteristics, whereas the latter term connotes groups where some structure of roles exists independent of the particular agents that may fill those roles at any given moment, and where this structure facilitates organizational processes that achieve organizational goals. Along with these constructs, the list of terms below also includes references to processes of organizational change (division, union, and structural change). While the study of organizations (especially corporations) is now a science in its own right, few formal representational notations are widely used to refer to these entities in the abstract. However, within the context of research on heterogeneous autonomous agent systems, formal notations have been proposed that capture most of the concepts presented in this list.

RELATED READINGS

Ferber, J., & Gutknecht, O. (1998). A meta-model for the analysis and design of organizations in multi-agent systems. In Y. Demazeau (Ed.), *Proceedings of the third international conference on multi-agent systems* (ICMAS98) (pp. 128–135). Washington, DC: IEEE Computer Society.
Glaser, N., & Morignot, P. (1997). The reorganization of societies of autonomous agents. In M. Boman & W. VanDeVelde (Eds.), *Proceedings of the 8th modelling autonomous agents in a multi-agent world workshop* (pp. 98–111). Heidelberg, Germany: Springer-Verlag.

DEFINITIONS

Community: A set of agents that have a set of characteristics that are the same.
Divide organization: The event in which an organization becomes multiple organizations.
Joined community: The conjunctive set of agents in two communities.
Organization: A set of agents that has a structure, goals, and processes.
Organizational agency: Execution where the agents of execution are agents in the organization.
Organizational goal: A goal that is held by an organization.
Organizational process: A plan that is executed by agents in an organization.
Organizational structure: A set of relationships with roles that are filled by agents in an organization.

Reorganize organization: The event in which the organizational structure of an organization is changed.

Top organizational role: The role in an organization that holds a power relationship over other agents in the organization.

6.12   GOALS   (27 TERMS)

The concept of a goal is one that is of central importance to understanding strategies. Every strategy that is represented in the collection includes a reference to a goal of the planner that is employing the strategy—typically the goal that is achieved through its execution—in much the same way that every instantiated plan achieves a goal. Just as strategies are, in some respects, abstractions over specific plans, the goals in strategy representations are abstractions over specific goals. Rather than using a single abstract term (i.e., "goal"), many distinctions between goals were used in these strategy representations, both to distinguish the applicability of a strategy to a particular situation and to restrict the ways that a strategy is implemented. The philosophical understanding of goals (along with desires and intentions) has been rigorously pursued in the last two decades, and some of this theoretical work has led to the development of formal notations that distinguish between some types of goals listed here in support of deductive inference (notably Cohen & Levesque, 1990). However, the breadth of goal classes that are presented in the following list suggests that a large amount of additional formalization work could be done. Of particular interest among the goals presented below are the few that refer to desires for the successful completion of some cognitive process, which include envisionment, knowledge, and planning goals.

RELATED READINGS

Cohen, P. R., & Levesque, H. J. (1990). Intention is choice with commitment. *Artificial Intelligence, 42*(3), 213–261.

DEFINITIONS

Adaptation goal: A planning goal to successfully adapt a plan for a new situation.

Adversarial goal: A goal achieved by the failure of the goal of another agent.

Auxiliary goal: A goal that is pursued insofar as it does not interfere with other goals.

Collaborative goal: A goal held by two agents in a collaborative relationship.

Compatibility goal: A goal that the characteristics of one thing are compatible with another.

Competing subgoal: A subgoal whose achievement would violate a different subgoal.

Competitive goal: A goal held by multiple agents that can be achieved only by one.

Conflicting goal: A goal whose achievement would violate a different goal.

Design goal: A reasoning goal to specify a designed thing that is instrumental toward another goal.

Envisioned future goal: A goal that is not held now, but is envisioned to be held in the future.

Envisionment goal: A reasoning goal to generate a correct envisionment.

Future goal: A goal that is not held now, but will be held in the future.

Goal: A partial description of a state at moments in a duration intended by an agent.

Knowledge goal: A reasoning goal to have knowledge about something.

Never violated goal: A preservation goal that has not been violated in the past.

Normal goal: An expectation of a goal of an agent by another agent.

Persistent goal: A goal that can never be fully achieved.

Planning goal: A reasoning goal for success in some stage of the planning process.

Possible envisioned goal: An envisioned goal in a possible envisioned branch.

Preservation goal: An achieved goal where the agent wants it to continue to be achieved.

Satisfied execution goal: A reasoning goal for successful execution that has been satisfied.

Shared goal: A goal that is held simultaneously by a set of agents.

Subgoal: A goal that is to be achieved only to achieve a different goal.

Unknown goal: A reference to a goal that is unknown to an agent.

Unsatisfied goal: A goal that has not been satisfied.

Unsatisfied knowledge goal: A knowledge goal that has not been satisfied.

Unspecified goal: A goal whose achievement conditions are not specified.

6.13 GOAL THEMES (6 TERMS)

The notion of a goal theme was introduced by Schank and Abelson (1977) in an effort to explain how the roles that people play in their lives give rise to specific goals that they would pursue. In their original conception, a goal theme was provided as the justification for a goal, and a mechanism by which people would preference and order multiple conflicting goals. In commonsense terms, the notion of a goal theme seems to be closely aligned with the life values that people hold, from the desire to live an honest and productive life, to being a good parent or successful professional. Although Domeshek (1992) greatly expanded the notion of what goal themes are and demonstrated their utility for case indexing, no computational planning systems were ever developed that employed themes for goal generation or ordering, and it is still unclear whether or not these functions are subsumed by other goal-management mechanisms. Still, some utility for the inclusion of goal theme concepts in strategy representations was found, specifically in the handful of goal theme-related terms listed below.

RELATED READINGS

Domeshek, E. A. (1992). *Do the right thing: A Component theory for indexing stories as social advice.* Doctoral Dissertation, Computer Science, Yale University.
Schank, R., & Abelson, R. (1977). *Scripts, plans, goals, and understanding.* Hillsdale, NJ: Lawrence Erlbaum Associates.

DEFINITIONS

Evil theme agent: An agent whose goals arise from a desire to be an evil agent.

Follow beliefs theme: The desire to be an agent that acts on unjustified or partially justified beliefs.

Generous theme: The desire to be an agent that pursues assistive goals for the benefit of other agents.

Good person theme: The desire to be an agent that pursues goals believed to be inherently good.

Retaliation theme: The desire to be an agent that pursues goals against adversarial agents that have successfully achieved their goals.

Theme: A justification for goals based on the type of agent the planner would like to be.

6.14   PLANS   (30 TERMS)

References to plans are, along with goals, among the most central concepts that participate in strategy representations. Characteristics of existing plans discriminate between situations to determine the applicability of a strategy, while the generation and use of a plan of a certain class may be required in a strategy's execution. After decades of research on plan generation algorithms in artificial intelligence, the last decade has seen an increased interest in the representation of plans as mental constructs. Much of this work has been motivated by problems in task-oriented dialogue processing, where multiple agents are engaged in conversations about the selection and execution of plans. Despite these advances, many distinctions between types of plans were made in strategy representations that have not been addressed in current formal representation work. Several of these distinctions, however, are made not by the content of the plans, but rather by the type of goal that it achieves. For example, the exact same plan could be considered adversarial, competitive, or assistive depending on the context in which it is applied. Yet other distinctions are more structural, such as a continuous plan (e.g., the operating plan of a corporation) or a collaborative plan (as explored by Grosz & Kraus, 1996). Additional representational distinctions are made to refer to how the plan has been processed by the agent that holds it, including concepts of an envisioned future plan, an executed plan, a failed plan, and an unintentional plan.

RELATED READINGS

Grosz, B. J., & Kraus, S. (1996). Collaborative plans for complex group action. *Artificial Intelligence, 86*(2), 269–357.
Pollack, M. E. (1990). Plans as complex mental attitudes. In P. N. Cohen, J. L. Morgan, & M. E. Pollack (Eds.). *Intentions in communication*, (pp. 77–103). Cambridge, MA: Bradford Books, MIT Press.

DEFINITIONS

Adversarial plan: A plan that achieves the goal of violating a goal of another agent.

Assistive plan: A plan that achieves a goal of another agent.

Collaborative plan: A plan that includes the agency of multiple agents that achieves a shared goal held by all of them.

Competitive plan: A plan to achieve a goal that is held by multiple agents where the goal can only be achieved by one.

Concurrent continuous plan: A property of a continuous plan that is being executed concurrently with other plans.

Conditional plan: A plan that will be executed only if certain specified conditions are met.

Continuous plan: A plan with an indefinite execution duration.

Counterplan: A plan that will cause an execution failure of the plan of another agent.

Envisioned future plan: A envisioned plan of an agent in the future.

Envisioned plans: A plan that is envisioned to be held by an agent.

Envisioned possible plan: A envisioned plan in a possible envisionment branch.

Executed plan: A property of plan that has been executed by an agent.

Failed plan: An executed plan that has not achieved its intended goal.

Modified plan: A plan that has been the subject of plan modification by an agent.

Normal plan: A plan that an agent expects would be selected and executed given a goal.

Occasionally executed plan: A reusable plan that has been executed multiple times in the past.

Opposing adversarial plan: The adversarial plan of the agent that is the target of another agent's adversarial plan.

Opposing competitive plan: The competitive plan of an agent that has the same competitive goal as another agent.

Partial continuous plan: A continuous plan where there exists periodic durations with behavior that remains to be planned.

Partial plan: A plan for which there exists durations with behaviors that remain to be planned.

Periodic plan: A reusable plan that is executed again a duration after the previous start time.

Plan: A description of behavior over a duration that an agent believes will achieve a goal.

Repetitive plan: A reusable plan with a conditional start of its own previous successful execution.

Reusable plan: A plan where the behaviors in the plan achieve a goal across a range of initial states.

Shared partial plan: A partial plan that is known to multiple agents.

Shared plan: A plan that is known to multiple agents.

Strategy: An abstract description of behavior that achieves goals across multiple planning domains.

Strategy instance: A strategy where all the abstractions have been instantiated into a plan.

Unblockable plan: A plan for which there exists no counterplan.

Unintentional plan: Behaviors that are executed by an agent without the intention to do so.

6.15 PLAN ELEMENTS (30 TERMS)

When describing the contents of plans in strategy representations, a wide variety of concepts pertaining to structural elements are employed, particularly those that allow for the specification of plans to be executed in uncertain environments. Representational notations (and algorithms) for plans in uncertain environments have received a great deal of attention over the last decade among the artificial intelligence planning researchers, prompted in part by Pednault's influential work (1989) to expand the classical view of a plan operator to include conditional, context-dependent effects. Uncertainty about the context of an action before its execution necessitates the planning for contingencies, which in turn are encoded as branches in a nonlinear plan that separate at some decision point. Some plan construction algorithms have included explicit notations for both the decisions and the knowledge preconditions that influence these decisions (Pryor & Collins, 1996). The parallels between these decision points and the sorts of conditional statements that appear in programming languages have created new interest in using procedural logic notations in plan representations (Levesque et al., 1997), an approach that may also accommodate many of the other flow-of-control concepts listed here concerning repetition and iteration.

RELATED READINGS

Levesque, H., Reiter, R., Lespérance, Y., Lin, F., & Scherl, R. B. (1997). GOLOG: A Logic Programming Language for Dynamic Domains. *Journal of Logic Programming, 31,* 59–83.

Pednault, E. P. D. (1989). ADL: Exploring the middle ground between strips and the situation calculus. In *Proceedings of the First International Conference on Principles of Knowledge Representation and Reasoning* (KR'89) (pp. 324–332). San Francisco, CA: Morgan Kaufmann.

Pryor, L., & Collins, G. (1996). Planning for contingencies: A decision-based approach. *Journal of Artificial Intelligence Research, 4,* 287–339.

DEFINITIONS

Analogous subplan: A subplan that has corresponding relational structure to another subplan.

Condition: A branching point in a plan determined by the current state during execution.

Conditional agency: A behavior description for an agent in a subplan in a conditional branch.

Conditional end time: An end time of a plan that is determined by conditions during execution.

Conditional plan trigger condition: A partial state description that would cause an agent to begin the execution of a plan.

Continuous plan start precondition: A precondition that must be achieved before the execution of a continuous plan.

Duration preceding condition: The duration between the start time of a plan and a condition.

Else then: The branch following a condition that is executed if the condition is not met.

Exception condition: A condition in a plan where the expectation is that the condition will be met at the time of execution, but where a contingency branch is also described.

First repetition: The subplan of a repetitive plan beginning from its start and ending at the moment of repetition.

If then: The branch following a condition that is executed if the condition is met.

Iterate: To execute a plan or subplan a specific number of times.

Iteration termination condition: A condition in an iteration that stops the execution before completion.

Knowledge precondition: A precondition for a subplan that an agent has specific knowledge.

Partial subplan: A subplan for which there exists durations with behaviors that remain to be planned.

Period duration: The duration between the start times of executions of a periodic plan or subplan.

Periodic subplan: A subplan that is executed multiple times in a plan with a period duration.

Plan duration: A reference to the duration in which a plan is to be executed.

Precondition: A partial state description that must exist before a subplan can be executed.

Repetition: The quantity that is the times that a repetitive plan or subplan has been started.

Repetition termination condition: A condition that causes an agent to terminate the execution of a repetitive plan or subplan.

Repetitive subplan: A subplan that is repetitively executed until some condition is met.

Require: A precondition in a plan where no conditional branch exists that does not include the precondition.

Required subplan: A subplan in a plan where no conditional branch exists that does not include the subplan.

Resource precondition: A precondition that an agent has a certain amount of a resource.

Shared subplan: A subplan that is known to multiple agents.

Subplan: A partial plan that achieves only subgoals required to achieve a goal.

Triggered start time: A start time for a plan or subplan that begins when a condition is met.

Triggered start time condition: The condition in a triggered start time.

Unspecified partial plan element: A reference to a plan element in the unspecified part of a partial plan.

6.16   RESOURCES   (16 TERMS)

The concept of a resource is a useful abstraction over things that are preconditions for many types of plans and actions and whose use is governed by some constraints (e.g., food, energy, and money). Among the terms related to resources in strategy representations, two special classes of resources, wealth and energy, could not be easily abstracted to the more general term in the representations in which they appear. Resource constraints have recently become the subject of interest within research on Artificial Intelligence planning systems, where the availability of resources may constrain the space of possible plans. The majority of the work that is done in this area treats resources as quantified values that may change as planning operators in a plan are executed, and encode them either as operator effects (Koehler, 1998) or as a rate of consumption (or generation) over an operator's execution duration (Haslum & Geffner, 2001). One problem with these representation approaches is that many of the concepts in the list below correspond only to non-reified events that occur during the execution of the planning system (e.g., expend resource, generate resource), prohibiting their reference and participation in representations in support of reasoning outside of plan construction.

RELATED READINGS

Haslum, P., & Geffner, H. (2001). Heuristic planning with time and resources. *Proceedings of the Sixth European Conference on Planning* (ECP-01). Heidelberg, Germany: Springer-Verlag.

Koehler, J. (1998). Planning under resource constraints. In *Proceedings of the Thirteenth European Conference on Artificial Intelligence* (ECAI-98) (pp. 489–493). Hoboken, NJ: Wiley.

DEFINITIONS

Acquire resource: The event in which an agent assumes ownership of a resource.

Acquire wealth: The event in which an agent assumes ownership of an amount of wealth.

Amount of resource: The amount that characterizes the quantity of a resource.

Envisioned resource desirability: An agent's belief about the value of a resource for a different agent.

Expend energy: An event where an amount of energy resources are expended by an agent.

Expend resource: An event where an amount of a resource is expended by an agent.

Expend wealth: An event where an amount of wealth resources are expended by an agent.

Expended resource: A reference to the resource that has been expended by an agent.

Generate resource: An event where an amount of a resource is increased by an agent.

Limited resource: A resource that can be completely expended.

Maintain resources: An event where a preservation goal of an amount of a resource is achieved.

Possess resource: A property of an agent that possesses an amount of a resource.

Resource: A class of entities that are instrumental in a broad range of plans.

Resource class: The subclass of which a resource is an instance.

Transfer resource: The event of a change in the location of a resource.

Wealth: A resource that is instrumental in plans because of an agreement among a set of agents.

6.17 ABILITIES (13 TERMS)

Several terms used in strategy representations pertain to the notion of ability, meant to refer to the potential that an agent has for executing a given action or plan. Suppose that someone has just stolen your wallet and is running away, and you imagine a new plan to get your wallet back that involves picking up a nearby rock and throwing it such that it lands on the thief's head and knocks him unconscious. We might assess the plan to be feasible, but the expected success of the plan will depend on your ability to land a rock on his head from a distance. Different agents may have different ability levels for the skill of throwing rocks, and there may be some ability level that distinguishes those who are competent rock-throwers from those who are not. Planning algorithms have not yet been constructed that explicitly reason about competency or ability levels, favoring instead to make the assumption that actions have either fully predictable outcomes or conditional effects determined by the context of execution rather than by the performance of the execution system. However, some foundational work in representing the basic notions of ability has been done (e.g., van der Hoek, van Linder, & Meyer, 1994) which could serve as a basis for defining the full set of concepts listed below.

RELATED READINGS

van der Hoek, W., van Linder, B., & Meyer, J. C. (1994). A logic of capabilities. In *Lecture Notes in Computer Science, 813,* 366–378. Heidelberg, Germany: Springer-Verlag.

DEFINITIONS

Ability: A property of an agent that is predictive of the successful execution of a plan.

Ability level: The value of the ability property for an agent.

Ability prediction: The ability level that an agent expects of another agent for a plan.

Competent ability: An ability level where the expectation is success.

Greater ability: An ordering of the expected success of an agent's execution over another.

High ability: An ability level where the expectation is that there will rarely be failure.

Learn ability: An event where an agent executes to increase an ability level.

Learn skill: An event where an agent executes to increase an ability level for a skill.

Learning activity: An activity that causes an agent to learn an ability.

Lesser ability: An ordering of the expected success of an agent's execution under another.

Practice skill: A reference to the execution of a skill in an execution environment different from the execution environment that is expected in the execution of a skill.

Skill: A reference to a shared plan for which there are degrees of ability.

Unknown ability: An ability level for an agent that is unknown to another agent.

6.18 ACTIVITIES (16 TERMS)

The concept of an activity is meant to refer to the set of culturally shared expectations about behaviors and events that will occur in situations. Examples of activities include taking a coffee break at work and taking the commuter train to work in the morning. In each of these examples, people have expectations about the roles, events, things, places, and topics that relate to these activities, even if they've never taken a coffee break or they've never been on a commuter train. Early representation work on activities referred to them as *scripts*, and some psychological evidence was collected to support their existence as *mental representations* (Abelson, 1981). More recently, theorists working in the area of situated cognition have revisited the question of whether activities should be viewed as a sort of mental representation (Clancey, 1997). While there has not been a great deal of interest in developing systems that reason about activities as mental representations, some encyclopedic taxonomies of commonsense activities have been authored (Gordon, 2001).

RELATED READINGS

Abelson, R. (1981). The psychological status of script. *American Psychologist, 36,* 715–729.

Clancey, W. J. (1997). The conceptual nature of knowledge, situations, and activity. In P. Feltovich, R. Hoffman, & K. Ford (Eds.), *Human and machine expertise in context* (pp. 247–291). Menlo Park, CA: AAAI Press.

Gordon, A. S. (2001). Browsing image collections with representations of commonsense activities. *Journal of the American Society for Information Science and Technology, 52*(11), 925–929.

DEFINITIONS

Activity: Set of shared expectations about behaviors and events in which agents play a role.

Activity actor: An agent that has a role in an activity.

Activity completion: The event of the ending of the execution of an activity.

Activity component: The expectations of behaviors and events within the duration of an activity.

Activity duration: The duration between the start and end times of an activity.

Activity duration end: The end time of the duration of the activity.

Activity precondition: A partial state description that must be true before agents can execute an activity.

Activity role: One of the set of roles that are adopted by agents in an activity.

Adopt role: The event that an agent begins a role in a relationship or activity.

Agent with role: The agent that has adopted a specific role in an activity.

Composed activity: An activity that is divisible into multiple components.

Normal activities: Expectations of the set of activities that an agent will execute over a duration.

Role: A reference to the identifier for an agent that plays in a relationship or activity.

Role theme: The goal themes that provide the expected intentions of the agent in role.

Terminate role: The event that an agent ends a role in a relationship or activity.

Variable duration activity: An activity where the expected duration is a variable duration.

6.19 COMMUNICATION ACTS (23 TERMS)

The representational area of Communication Acts, which abstracts over partial plans, is among those that have received a significant amount of formal attention. Existing representational theories are generally more expressive than the terms revealed through the representation of strategies as listed below. Following early theoretical work on speech acts, many researchers have developed taxonomies to support reasoning about and recognition of speech acts. One of the theoretical distinctions that is made is between illocutionary and perlocutionary speech acts, the two main categories in which the terms listed here would fall. Illocutionary acts would be those that are performed in saying something, such as making a request or answering a question, while perlocutionary acts would be those that are performed by saying something, such as persuading and threatening. The relationship between speech acts and formal semantics has been explored (Vanderveken, 1990), although few axiomatic theories to support inference about these acts are widely used (although see Singh, 1993). However, representations of speech acts are increasingly being employed in computational systems, particularly in the areas of human–computer dialogue systems (Stolcke, et al., 2000) and in autonomous agent communication (Traum, 1999).

RELATED READINGS

Singh, M. P. (1993). A semantics for speech acts. *Annals of Mathematics and Artificial Intelligence, 8*(1–2) 47–71.

Stolcke, A., Ries, K., Coccaro, N., Shriberg, E., Bates, R., Jurafsky, D., Taylor, P., Martin, R., Van Ess-Dykema, C., & Meteer, M. (2000). Dialogue act modeling for automatic tagging and recognition of conversational speech. *Computational Linguistics, 26*(3), 339–373.

Traum, D. R. (1999). Speech acts for dialogue agents. In M. Wooldride & A. Rao (Eds.), *Foundations of Rational Agency* (pp. 169–201). Dordrecht, The Netherlands: Kluwer, 1999.

Vanderveken, D. (1990). On the unification of speech act theory and formal semantics. In P. R. Cohen, J. Morgan, & M. E. Pollack (Eds.), *Intentions in communication* (pp. 195–220). Cambridge, MA: MIT Press.

DEFINITIONS

Accept offer: An event where an agent informs another that they will execute an offer condition.

Accept permission request: An event where an agent informs another that they will permit an execution.

Accept request: An event where an agent informs another that they will execute a request.

Activity request: An event where an agent informs another that they want them to adopt a role in an activity.

Ask question: An event where an agent informs another that they want them to satisfy a knowledge goal.

Broadcast inform: An event where an agent informs a set of agents of something simultaneously.

Broadcast teach: An event where an agent informs a set of agents of a set of explanations.

Inform: An event where an agent informs another of knowledge.

Make offer: An even where an agent informs another that they will execute on some condition that includes the agency of the other agent.

Make request: The event of an agent informing another of a goal that they execute a plan.

Negotiate: A set of inform events between two agents where one has made an offer and the second will accept the offer if the offer condition is different.

Offer condition: The condition that will cause an execution by an agent accepting an offer.

Offer option: A branch of either the offer condition or offered action that is determined by some condition.

Offered action: The plan that will be executed by the person making the offer if accepted.

Offered thing: A physical entity in an offered action that includes the transfer of possession of the entity.

Persuade: A set of inform events made by an agent with the goal that the other agent have a goal or a belief.

Possible question answer: A set of inform events that are expected by an agent that asks a question.

Reject offer: The event where an agent informs another that they will not execute an offer condition.

Request permission: The event where an agent informs another in a power relationship over the agent that they have the goal that the agent permit an execution by the agent.

Teach: The event where an agent informs another of a set of explanations.

Threat demand: A condition of agency by an agent that will prevent the execution of an adversarial plan.

Threaten: An event where an agent informs another that they will execute an adversarial plan unless a threat demand is met.

Threatened action: An adversarial plan that is threatened by an agent.

6.20 INFORMATION ACTS (12 TERMS)

A few terms used in strategy representations are meant to refer to the acts of communicating information, and the information content of communication itself. These concepts are meant to abstract over a wide range of possible means of encoding and decoding information streams, from the simple use of written messages to the complex encrypted messaging that may be required in secure electronic transactions. Most of the terms listed here can be directly related to concepts described in the introduction to Claude Shannon's seminal work in Information Theory (1948), which included an Information source, Message, Transmitter, Signal, Noise source, Received signal, Receiver, and Destination. While there is no widely known axiomatic theory that captures our commonsense understanding of the relationships between these entities and events, Shannon's terms (used to provide as a commonsense context for his mathematical descriptions) would serve as a more appropriate basis for future formalization work than the terms listed below, with the possible inclusion of notation for the truth values of communicated messages that may be known (referred to below as *False information* and *True information*).

RELATED READINGS

Shannon, C. E. (1948). A mathematical theory of communication. *The Bell System Technical Journal, 27*, 379–423.

DEFINITIONS

Acquire information: The event in which information begins to be managed by an agent.

Decode information: The event of acquiring information that is encoded information.

Encode characteristic information: The event of encoding information about characteristics.

Encode event information: The event of encoding information about an event.

Encode information: The event of creating encoded information that is the same as information being managed by an agent.

Encoded information: A non-agent entity that is the product of the event of encoding. information, and which can be the subject of a decode information event.

False information: Information that includes assertions that are false.

Information: Assertions that can be made explicit and shared among multiple agents.

Observed signal: A signal that is being received by an informed agent.

Signal: The event of where information is being transferred by an informing agent.

Signal production: The set of causes that result in a signal event.

True information: Information that includes assertions that are true.

6.21   AGENT INTERACTION   (21 TERMS)

The representational area of Agent Interaction consists of a varied collection of abstractions over agent actions, with little reason to group them except that each involves the interaction between multiple agents that is not primarily communicative in nature. None of the concepts listed below should be viewed as primitive actions. Instead, each concept participates in our larger understanding of complex social interactions, particularly concerning ownership, obligation, instruction, confrontation, and collaboration. Some representational work has been completed in each of these areas from widely different research traditions. Particularly strong is the work on the representation of the concept of ownership (McCarty, 2002), the use of Deontic logic notations to describe obligation (Horty, 2001), and work on causation and rational action to define confrontation and collaboration (Ortiz, 1999).

RELATED READINGS

Horty, J. F. (2001). *Agency and deontic logic*. Oxford University Press.
McCarty, L. T. (2002). Ownership: A Case Study in the Representation of Legal Concepts. *Journal of Artificial Intelligence and Law, 10*(1–3), 135–161.
Ortiz, C. L. (1999). A commonsense language for reasoning about causation and rational action. *Artificial Intelligence, 111*(2), 73–130.

DEFINITIONS

Accept candidate: The event in which an agent is selected from a set where each member had this goal.

Acquire ownership: The event of changing the property of ownership of a thing to a new agent.

Assist: An event where an agent executes to achieve the goal of another agent.

Attack: An event where an agent executes to violate a preservation goal of another agent.

Begin relationship: The event in which all of the agents in a relationship have adopted their role.

Competition: An event where multiple agents are planning and executing to achieve an exclusive goal.

Create agent: An event where an agent executes to cause another agent to exist.

Defend: An event where an agent executes to block an attack.

Defended region: A region for which an agent is executing in order to defend it.

Destroy agent: An event where an agent executes to cause another agent to not exist.

Do service: To execute a subplan as intended in the plan of another agent.

Evoke emotion: An event where an agent causes another agent to change their emotional state.

Execute offer: To execute the offered action in an offer.

Manage: An event where an agent plans for multiple other agents that are under the agent in a power relationship.

Own: A relationship between a thing and an agent that holds after a transfer of ownership.

Paid work: The event that an agent does a service on the condition that the planning agent transfers resources to the servicing agent.

Portion of ownership: A relationship between multiple agents and a thing where the set of agents is viewed as a single agent in the ownership relation.

Switch relationship roles: The event that the roles held by two agents are exchanged.

Terminate ownership: The event of changing the property of ownership of a thing from an agent.

Terminate relationship: The event where each of the agents that held roles in a relationship no longer do so.

Trade: The event where multiple agents interact by making complimentary offers for multiple things.

6.22 PHYSICAL INTERACTION (13 TERMS)

The last of the plan/action representational areas concerns the interaction that agents have with their physical environment. These terms include concepts surrounding the movement, creation, destruction, and modification of physical objects by an agent, each of which has the flavor of an interpretation of action, rather than that of primitive planning operators. Representational work related to this area has been done in research on integrating actions into qualitative physics simulations (e.g., Forbus, 1989), however the level of conceptual abstraction has been much lower than is apparent in the list below. A more recent theoretical trend is to view agent–environment interaction as emergent behavior that is encouraged by the affordances of things in the world and cultural factors (e.g., Agre & Horswill, 1997), a framework particularly useful for understanding the notion of Instrumental use, included below.

RELATED READINGS

Agre, P., & Horswill, I. (1997). Lifeworld analysis. *Journal of Artificial Intelligence Research, 6*, 111–145.

Forbus, K. D. (1989). Introducing actions into qualitative simulation. In N. S. Sridharan (Ed.), *Proceedings of the Eleventh International Joint Conference on Artificial Intelligence* (IJCAI '89) (pp. 1279–1284). San Mateo, CA: Morgan Kaufmann.

DEFINITIONS

Acquire thing: An event where the property of possession of a thing is changed to an agent.

Configure thing: An event where the configurable state of a thing is changed by an agent.

Copy thing: An event where an agent causes a new thing to exist that has the properties of the original.

Create thing: An event where an agent causes a new thing to exist.

Destroy thing: An event where an agent causes a thing to not exist.

Instrumental use: The execution of a plan of an agent involving a thing where the thing causes the achievement of a goal or subgoal.

Make work product: Creating a thing when executed as part of a plan of work.

Measure: An event where an agent quantifies a characteristic of a thing through observation.

Modify state: An event where an agent changes any property of the current state.

Modify thing: An event where an agent changes a property of a thing.

Possess: A spatial relationship between an agent and a thing that has a location in a region with a boundary condition relative to the agent.

Transfer location: An event where an agent changes the location of a thing.

Transfer possession: An event where an agent changes the location of a thing to be possessed by a different agent.

6.23 MANAGING KNOWLEDGE   (30 TERMS)

The representational area of Managing Knowledge begins the list of areas that concern the mental processes that are referenced in strategy representations. Research in this area, like nearly all of the ones that follow, can be characterized as strong with respect to computational process models, but weak on representational models of process. That is, the list of terms presented below contains many that refer to aspects of knowledge-based computational systems, particularly to assumption-based and justification-based truth-maintenance systems (Forbus & de Kleer, 1993). In truth-maintenance systems of these sorts, many of the concepts below exist as either functional calls (e.g., Add assumption), as arguments to these function calls (e.g., Justification), or as function return values (e.g., Contradiction). Their participation in strategy representations argues that these concepts should be reified as part of a representational theory of knowledge management, where both the processes and structures listed below can be expressed using a representational notation. The reification of these concepts, in particular, offers some intellectually challenging possibilities, such as the authoring of cognitive processes models for managing knowledge that make assumptions about contradictions, affirm the certainty of revealed false beliefs, and disregarding information about ignoring information. While representational models of the processes of managing knowledge are not available, strong work in the areas of epistemic logic and reasoning about knowledge (Halpern, Fagin, Moses, & Vardi, 1995) provides a strong basis for future work by providing notation used to reference the subjects of these processes (e.g., Assumptions, Justifications, Beliefs).

RELATED READINGS

Forbus, K., & de Kleer, J. (1993). *Building problem solvers*. Cambridge, MA: MIT Press.
Halpern, J., Fagin, R., Moses, Y., & Vardi, M. (1995). *Reasoning about knowledge*. Cambridge, MA: MIT Press.

DEFINITIONS

Add assumption: A mental event of introducing a proposition as an assumption.

Affirm certainty: A mental event of adding an additional justification for a justified belief.

Assumption: A proposition with a truth value assigned without a justification.

Belief: A proposition with a truth value based on some justification.

Common belief: A belief that is held by a set of multiple agents.

Contradiction: A characteristic of a set of propositions with inconsistent truth values.

Disregard information: The mental event prohibiting the consideration of inferences justified by a proposition.

Event knowledge: A set of beliefs about a single event.

Evidence information: A belief that participates in a justification.

False assumption: An assumption of a truth value different from that which is believed.

False belief: A belief of an agent that is believed to be incorrect by another agent.

False induction: An inference of an agent that is believed to be incorrect by another agent.

Forget information: The mental event of removing a proposition.

Ignore information: The mental event of inhibiting the participation of a proposition for inference.

Information processing: The set of mental processes in managing knowledge.

Information processing failure: A failure in any process of managing knowledge.

Instructed belief: A belief that is justified in that it was informed by another agent.

Justification: The set of propositions that determine the truth value of another proposition.

Knowledge: The entire set of beliefs for an agent.

Knowledge domain: Subsets of knowledge with membership conditions that are shared among a set of agents.

Learn: Any set of mental events that result in a change in the truth value of a proposition.

Learn knowledge domain: Any set of learning events where the propositions are within a knowledge domain.

Partial knowledge: A set of propositions about some entity where some propositions are unknown.

Poor justification: A justification for a belief that is not judged to be sound.

Predictive knowledge: Any set of beliefs that can be used for prediction of future states.

Remove assumption: The mental event of removing any truth value assigned to an assumption.

Revealed false belief: A false belief that previously was thought to be correct by an agent.

Shared knowledge: Any set of beliefs that are held by multiple agents.

True belief: A belief of an agent that another agent believes to be correct.

Unknown: A proposition that does not have an assigned truth value.

6.24 SIMILARITY COMPARISONS   (16 TERMS)

Many terms used in strategy representations concerned the mental processes involved in drawing comparisons between two or more things. This group of terms brings together three types of comparisons that have been closely associated with each other in the cognitive sciences: similarity comparisons, analogical comparisons, and classification. Several computational models of these sorts of comparisons have been proposed, including the theory of Structure Mapping (Gentner & Markman, 1997) that served as a basis for the work presented in this book. Future representation research in the area of Similarity Comparisons will need to take a somewhat broader view than has been concretized in any existing computational models to provide coverage over the terms listed below, where terms like Recognize pattern and Similarity metric stretch the scope of what is tackled in any single theory (although see Forbus, Mostek, & Feruson, 2002).

RELATED READINGS

Forbus, K., Mostek, T., & Ferguson, R. (2002). An analogy ontology for integrating analogical processing and first-principles reasoning. In *Proceedings of the Fourteenth Innovative Applications of Artificial Intelligence Conference* (IAAI-02) (pp. 878–885). Menlo Park, CA: AAAI Press.

Gentner, D., & Markman, A. (1997). Structure mapping in analogy and similarity. *American Psychologist, 52*, 45–56.

DEFINITIONS

Analogous set: An analogy between sets of represented things.

Analogy: The relational correspondence between two structured, compositional concepts.

Analogy mapping: The one-to-one correspondence between concepts in an analogy.

Class similarity: A metric of the degree of similarity between two conceptual classes.

Compare: The mental event of aligning two concepts to judge their differences.

Compare characteristic: The mental event of aligning two characteristics to judge their differences.

Dissimilar member set: A set where all members are dissimilar to other members.

Dissimilarity: A metric of the degree of difference between two concepts.

Make analogy: The mental event of aligning the relational structures of two concepts.

Pattern: A set of relationships that can be held between multiple pairs of concepts.

Recognize pattern: The mental event of classifying a set of relations as a pattern.

Significantly different similarity: A value of dissimilarity that is very high.

Similar: A metric for the degree of sameness between two concepts.

Similar characteristics metric: A similarity metric based on characteristics of concepts.

Similar member set: A set where all members are similar to other members.

Similarity metric: A metric for use in determining the similarity between concepts.

6.25 MEMORY RETRIEVAL (3 TERMS)

Somewhat surprisingly, there were only a handful of concepts used in strategy representations that referred to mental abilities surrounding memory. Aside from the purposeful attempt to remember something in the future (Memorize) and the event of remembering something (Memory retrieval), the only additional concept that was employed was the notion of a memory cue—something that causes a person to remember something else when they focus their attention on it. While occasionally the issue of memory participates in complex theories of knowledge and action (e.g., Davis, 1994), the terms listed below are not generally reified as representational elements, and unrealistic assumptions regarding memory are generally made (e.g., people have perfect recall of anything they once knew). Computational models of memory retrieval have not generally addressed issues of purposeful memorization or memory cues, although compelling theories of retrieval based on representational structure have been proposed (Forbus, Gentner, & Law, 1995).

RELATED READINGS

Davis, E. (1994). Knowledge preconditions for plans. *Journal of Logic and Computation, 4*(5), 253–305.
Forbus, K., Gentner, D., & Law, K. (1995). MAC/FAC: A model of similarity-based retrieval. *Cognitive Science, 19,* 141–205.

DEFINITIONS

Memorize: The mental event of storing information in memory so that it can be retrieved later.
Memory cue: A concept that causes a memory retrieval of information when it becomes the focus of attention.
Memory retrieval: The mental event of retrieving information from memory.

6.26 EMOTIONS (8 TERMS)

The representational area of emotions has received a significant amount of formal attention, but interestingly not in support of deductive inference. Instead, most of the work to date has been in support of computational models of emotional appraisal. Researchers in this area have noted that the emotional responses of a person are highly dependent on how they understand their current situation. By describing the all of the relevant situational features for each type of emotion, computational models of emotional appraisal can be authored. The most influential work in this area continues to be that of Ortony, Clore, and Collins (1988), which attempts to specify the appraisal conditions for a wide assortment of emotions in an informal manner. Since the publication of that book, a number of researchers worked to formalize the appraisal conditions for use in computational systems (Elliot, 1992), especially to improve the believability of synthetic characters in virtual reality environments (Gratch, 2000). As the appraisal conditions of emotions typically involve the mental states of agents, goal-based relationships, and the execution of plans, the greatest inhibitor of progress in this area has been the lack of expressive representational vocabularies for describing the situation that is being appraised.

RELATED READINGS

Elliott, C. (1992). *The affective reasoner: A process model of emotions in a multi-agent system*. Doctoral Dissertation, Northwestern University.

Gratch, J. (2000). Emile: Marshalling passions in training and education. In C. Sierra (Ed.), *Proceedings of the 4th International Conference on Autonomous Agents* (pp. 325–332). Barcelona, Spain; New York: ACM Press.

Ortony, A., Clore, G. L., & Collins, A. (1988). *The cognitive structure of emotions*. Cambridge University Press.

Sanders, K. E. (1989). A logic for emotions: A basis for reasoning about common-sense psychological knowledge. In G. Olson & E. Smith (Eds.), *Proceedings of the Eleventh Annual Conference of the Cognitive Science Society*, Ann Arbor, Michigan. Hillsdale, NJ: Lawrence Erlbaum Associates.

DEFINITIONS

Anger emotion: An emotion of displeasure concerning the actions of another agent.

Anxiety emotion: An emotion of displeasure concerning a possible future state, particularly an execution failure by the agent.

Emotion state: A characteristic of an agent describing the emotion they are experiencing.

Fear emotion: An emotion of displeasure concerning a possible future state, particularly where preservation goals are violated.

Liking emotion: An emotion of pleasure concerning the existence or relationship of an entity to the agent.

Love emotion: A liking emotion where the degree of pleasure is the highest possible degree for the agent.

Pride emotion: An emotion of pleasure concerning the actions of a different agent with a relationship to the agent.

Sympathetic emotions: An emotion of displeasure concerning the violation of goals of a different agent with a relationship to the agent.

6.27   EXPLANATIONS   (17 TERMS)

The concept of causality holds a privileged role in our intellectual lives, serving as the basis for our abilities for prediction and planning (Pearl, 2000), but our everyday lives are filled with states and events that occur with causes that are only partially known, at best. Explanations are guesses about the nature of selected unknown causes, and the process of explanation is to generate these guesses based on existing knowledge. Traditionally, computational models of the explanation process have focused on logical abduction, where premises (or abductive assumptions) are inferred that entail the truth of a state or event that is being explained. Algorithms for generating these premises typically include either a form of backward chaining (reverse deduction) or case-based retrieval and adaptation; see Leake (1995) for a comparison of these two approaches. Terms related to the mental processes of explanation encompass the sorts of explanations themselves, the components of structured explanations, and the mental events that surround their generation. Although neither of the two dominant computational approaches to explanation generation employs explicit representations of these terms, most of these concepts could be grounded as functions, results, or run-time states of either approach.

RELATED READINGS

Leake, D. B. (1995). Abduction, experience, and goals: A model of everyday abductive explanation. *Journal of Experimental and Theoretical Artificial Intelligence, 7,* 407–428.
Pearl, J. (2000). *Causality: Models, reasoning and inference.* Cambridge, UK: Cambridge University Press.

DEFINITIONS

Add candidate explanation: The mental event of adding a candidate to the list of possible explanations for a mystery.

Add explanation preference: The mental event of adding a general preference for classes of explanations.

Additive effect: A cause that is composed of multiple factors.

Candidate cause: One of a set of causes that an agent believes is possibly true for a mystery.

Candidate explanation: One of a set of explanations that an agent believes is possibly true for a mystery.

Causal explanation: An explanation where all of the causal influences are specified.

Execution failure explanation: An explanation where the mystery is the cause of an explanation failure.

Explain: The mental process of replacing a mystery in an envisionment with an explanation.

Explain expectation failure: The mental process of identifying the cause of an expectation failure.

Explanation: A set of causal relationships that would account for an effect in an envisionment.

Explanation belief: A proposition that must be correct if a candidate explanation is a true cause.

Explanation failure: A mental event where no explanation can be generated by an agent for a mystery.

Explanation preference: A preference used by an agent to order the acceptability of candidate explanations.

Failure explanation: An explanation for a mystery that causes a failure of a process.

Remove candidate explanation: The mental event of removing a candidate explanation for consideration as a true cause.

True cause: A reference to the correct causes for an effect in the world.

Unknown cause: The mysterious cause of an effect in an envisionment that has not been explained by an agent.

6.28 WORLD ENVISIONMENT   (48 TERMS)

Perhaps the single most prevalent mental faculty referenced in strategy is that of envisionment, the imagination of states of the world that have not been experienced. Used as a verb, the term *envisionment* includes prediction (the possible states that could occur in the future), counterfactual reasoning (how things would be different if some current or previous fact were changed), and historical reasoning (the way things could have been in the past that would lead to the current state). As a noun, the meaning of an envisionment is borrowed here from work in the area of qualitative reasoning (Kuipers, 1994), where it has a more precise definition as the set of all possible qualitatively different states in a system and all legal causal transitions between them (Forbus, 1987). It is within the qualitative reasoning community that the most work has been done on building computational models of envisionment, with designs motivated by applications rather than by cognitive plausibility (see Roese & Olson, 1995, for psychological concerns). Most of the terms listed below can be grounded in the functionality of these computational models, perhaps with increased emphasis on likelihood reasoning (probability and possibility).

RELATED READINGS

Kuipers, B. (1994). *Qualitative reasoning: Modeling and simulation with incomplete knowledge.* Cambridge, MA: MIT Press.

Forbus, K. (1987). The logic of occurrence. In J. McDermott (Ed.), *Proceedings of the Tenth International Joint Conference on Artificial Intelligence* (IJCAI-87) (pp. 409–415). San Francisco: Morgan Kaufmann.

Roese, N. J., & Olson, J. M. (Eds.). (1995). *What might have been: The social psychology of counterfactual thinking.* Mahwah, NJ: Lawrence Erlbaum Associates.

DEFINITIONS

Alternate envisionment: A reference to an envisionment that is qualitatively different from another.

Causal agent: A cause in an envisionment that is the behavior of an agent.

Causal chain: A set of envisioned states and events ordered by time where each is linked to the one that follows by a causal relationship.

Causal influence: A member of a set of causes that have a causal relationship to an effect.

Causal relationship: A relationship between two envisioned states or events ordered by time where the first is the cause of the second.

Causal system: A network of envisioned states and events linked by causal relationships.

Combined envisioned likelihood: The envisioned likelihood that one or all of a set of envisioned states or events are correct.

Consistent envisionment: An envisionment comprised of beliefs that are not contradictory.

Correct envisionment: A reference to an envisionment where the envisioned states and events. correspond to events or states that have or will actually occur.

Definite likelihood: An envisioned branch that is believed to be one hundred percent likely to occur.

Envisioned amount: An amount in an envisionment.

Envisioned event: An event in an envisionment.

Envisioned likelihood: The degree of belief that an envisionment branch is correct.

Envisioned likelihood dependency: A cause in an envisionment that determines the envisioned likelihood of a later envisionment branch.

Envisioned likelihood range: A value range of the set of envisioned likelihoods for a single envisioned branch.

Envisioned moment: A moment in an envisionment.

Envisioned past events: Events in an envisionment that occur at moments that are before the current moment.

Envisioned state: A state in an envisionment.

Envisioned state characteristic: A state characteristic of a state in an envisionment.

Envisionment: A causal network of states and events at moments on a time line.

Envisionment branch: A portion of an envisionment that is believed correct on the condition of the correctness of preceding states or events that are uncertain.

Envisionment branch preference: A single causal chain within an envisionment that an agent believes best satisfies their goals.

Envisionment constraint: A constraint that an agent places on their own envisionment process in order to control how their envisionments are constructed.

Envisionment dependency: A condition that is a precondition for an agent to begin an envisionment process.

Envisionment failure: A mental event where an agent has a reasoning failure in the process of envisionment.

Envisionment state: A description of the mental state of an agent engaged in the envisionment process.

Greater envisioned likelihood: An envisioned likelihood that is greater than another.

High envisioned likelihood: An envisioned likelihood of an envisionment branch believed to be correct.

Imagine agent: The mental event of adding a new agent into an envisioned state.

Imagine duration: The mental event of adding a new duration into an envisionment.

Imagine perception: The mental event of adding a perception for an agent into an envisionment.

Imagine region: The mental event of adding a new region into an envisioned state.

Imagine set: The mental event of adding a new set into an envisioned state.

Imagine value: The mental event of adding a new value into an envisioned state.

Imagine world: The mental event of beginning an envisionment that is not causally related to states and events in existing envisionments.

Lesser envisioned likelihood: An envisioned likelihood that is lesser than another.

Low envisioned likelihood: An envisioned likelihood of an envisionment branch not believed to be correct.

New envisionment: An envisionment with states and events not causally related to a previous envisionment.

Partial envisionment: An envisionment where the effects of causes have not all been imagined.

Possible envisioned maximum value: An envisioned value that is the largest possible value for an envisioned state characteristic.

Possible envisioned state: A state where all preceding causal relationships are linked states or events with non-zero envisioned likelihoods.

Possible motion: An envisioned event that is the transfer of location of an object over a duration.

Quantitative envisionment: The mental process of attempting to assign quantities to envisioned values in an envisionment.

Random chance: A cause that is an envisionment branching condition that an agent believes to be unknowable.

Value quantification: The mental event of change an envisioned qualitative value into a quantity.

Verify possible envisioned state: The mental event of marking an envisioned state or event as correct.

World model: The state characteristics that define states in an envisionment.

Wrong envisionment: A reference to an envisionment where the envisioned states and events do not correspond to events or states that have or will actually occur.

6.29   EXECUTION ENVISIONMENT   (23 TERMS)

One type of envisioning process specifically concerns prediction, counterfactual, and historical reasoning that involves the actions of people, especially those of the agent itself. It is this type of reasoning that allows us to predict whether a particular plan will achieve a goal in a specific context. Most of the terms listed below are in relation to this execution envisionment function. Success and failure of actions are represented explicitly (as in Giunchiglia, Spalazzi, & Traverso, 1994), but in an indeterminate manner that allows for the specification of high and low envisioned likelihoods of success. Current research in reasoning about actions is directed at many of the remaining representational requirements below, particularly work on action and time (as in Allen & Ferguson, 1994). Among those that have not yet received formal treatment are terms related specifically to the process itself (e.g., Imagine possible execution), the environment in which plans are executed, and the conditions that are at the Limit of failure between successful and unsuccessful execution.

RELATED READINGS

Allen, J. F., & Ferguson, G. (1994). Actions and events in interval temporal logic. *Journal of Logic and Computation, 4*(5) 531–579.
Giunchiglia, F., Spalazzi, L., & Traverso, P. (1994). Planning with failure. In K. Hammond (Ed.), *Proceedings of AIPS-94, Second International Conference on AI Planning Systems* (pp. 74–79). Chicago, IL; Menlo Park, CA: AAAI Press.

DEFINITIONS

Agency: A set of changes in world states that are caused by the behavior of an agent.

Arbitrary execution moment: A reference to any moment in an execution duration.

Envisioned activity: An envisioned execution of an activity by a set of agents.

Envisioned activity duration: The envisioned duration of an envisioned activity.

Envisioned execution: An envisionment that includes the execution of a plan by one or more agents.

Envisioned failure: An envisioned event that is an execution failure for an agent.

Envisioned likelihood of success: The envisioned likelihood that the execution of a plan will achieve its goal.

Envisioned possible failure: An envisioned failure in an envisionment branch with a non-zero envisioned likelihood.

Greater envisioned likelihood of success: An envisioned likelihood of success that is greater than another.

Greatest envisioned likelihood of success: An envisioned likelihood of success that is greater than all others in a set of envisionment branches.

High envisioned likelihood of success: An envisioned likelihood of success where an agent expects the achievement of the goal.

Imagine possible execution: The mental event of creating an envisionment that includes the execution of agents in envisioned branches with non-zero envisioned likelihoods.

Indefinite repetition duration: The envisioned duration of the execution of a repetitive plan.

Limit of failure: A value in an envisionment branching condition that determines between a branch containing an envisioned failure and one containing success.

Low envisioned likelihood of success: An envisioned likelihood of success where an agent expects a failure to achieve the goal.

Moment in execution: A moment in an execution envisionment.

Moment in period: A moment in an execution envisionment of a periodic plan.

Opportunity: An execution envisionment that achieves a goal where the agency is different from the current plans of an agent.

Planner: A self-reference to the agent engaged in envisioning the execution of their own plans.

Possible action duration: An envisioned range for the duration for the execution of an action.

Possible execution failure: An envisioned branch that contains an execution failure that has a non-zero envisioned likelihood.

Side effect: Envisioned states and events that have as their cause the execution of a plan, where the states and events are not goals or subgoals of the plan.

Unknown execution environment: A reference to states in an envisioned execution with unknown state characteristics.

6.30 CAUSES OF FAILURE (31 TERMS)

Whereas the previous section, Execution Envisionment, described our faculties for judging whether a plan would fail, this section focuses on the sorts of reasons that would cause these failures to occur. The list of terms should be viewed as a collection of patterns that are applicable when explaining the failure of a plan, and each may have a rich conceptual structure of its own. This set of 31 patterns is just over half the size of a similar list provided by Owens (1990). In a project that parallels the present work on strategy representation, Owens analyzed 1,000 proverbs in an attempt to identify an indexing vocabulary for organizing plan failure explanation patterns, resulting in 59 indexing labels. With only partial overlap between these two lists, future work in this area would benefit from combining these lists into a single, functional taxonomy.

RELATED READINGS

Owens, C. (1990). *Indexing and retrieving abstract planning knowledge.* Doctoral dissertation, Yale University.

Owens, C. (1991). A functional taxonomy of abstract plan failures. In K. Hammond & D. Gentner (Eds.), *Proceedings of the Thirteenth Annual Conference of the Cognitive Science Society* (pp. 167–172). Hillsdale, NJ: Lawrence Erlbaum Associates.

DEFINITIONS

Attachment failure: An execution failure caused when attached things become unattached.

Conflicting plan: A plan whose execution causes an execution failure of a different plan by the same agent.

Constraining execution rules: An execution failure due to over-constraining execution rules.

Control failure: An execution failure caused by a reasoning failure.

Failed block: An event that is the execution failure of a counterplan.

Failed search: An event that is the execution failure of a plan to locate an object.

Failure cause: A reference to the class of a failure.

False knowledge goal achievement: An execution failure caused by the achievement of a knowledge goal with information that is incorrect.

False triggered monitor: A monitoring failure caused when the triggering condition is satisfied by beliefs about a state that are incorrect.

Full schedule failure: A scheduling failure caused when there is no remaining free time in which to schedule a plan.

Inappropriate base plan: A plan adaptation caused by a base plan that is too different from the target plan.

Incompatibility failure: An execution failure caused when the characteristics of things are incompatible.

Instrument failure: An execution failure caused by the characteristics of a thing where the plan includes the instrumental use of the thing.

Insufficient quantity failure: An execution failure caused when a quantity in a plan is insufficient.

Insufficient resource failure: An execution failure caused by an insufficient quantity of a resource.

Lack of ability: An execution failure caused by an agent that has insufficient ability to execute the plan.

Lack of agency: An execution failure caused when the agency of an agent in a plan does not occur.

Lack of certainty: An envisionment failure caused when an agent cannot generate envisioned likelihoods.

Lack of coordination: An execution failure caused when the executed behaviors of an agent are not coordinated.

Lack of opportunity: A planning failure caused by future world states where no executions of the agent are envisioned to achieve goals.

Lack of preparedness: An execution failure caused by execution preconditions that are not met.

Lack of resource: A planning failure caused by a resource that is not available.

Lack of time: A scheduling failure caused when the duration of the plan to be scheduled is longer than the duration before the deadline of its end time.

Lack of understanding: An envisionment caused by world models that are incorrect or incomplete.

Nonconscious execution conflicting with conscious execution: An execution failure caused by behavior of the body of an agent that disrupts the execution of the plan of the agent.

None remaining failure: An execution failure of an iterative plan caused by an insufficient quantity of members in a set.

Search space too large: An execution failure of a plan to locate a thing caused by a set of possible locations that is too large.

Subplan clobbers subgoal: A planning failure caused by a subplan that undoes an achieved subgoal.

Successful execution of opposing competitive plan: An execution failure of a competitive plan caused by the successful execution of the plan of a competitor.

Unsatisfiable precondition failure: A planning failure caused by a precondition that cannot be satisfied.

Unsatisfied condition failure: An execution failure caused by an execution condition that is not satisfied.

6.31 MANAGING EXPECTATIONS (8 TERMS)

A handful of terms appear in strategy representations that concern expectations, which presumably have a strong relationship with predictive envisionments with high envisioned likelihoods. Although strongly related to envisionment, a few of the terms listed below suggest that expectations might be managed separately, e.g., one may be able to add an expectation of a future state that isn't envisioned with a high likelihood. Although some treatments of expectations have been explored in relationship to deductive reasoning (Gardenfors & Makinson, 1994), no formal representations for managing expectations are widely used. The concept of an Expectation violation has received a great deal of attention among researchers interested in case-based reasoning and explanation-based learning, particularly in work based on Schank's (1982) cognitive model of a dynamic memory, which is itself a model related to expectation-dependent classical conditioning (Rescorla & Wagner, 1972).

RELATED READINGS

Gardenfors, P., & Makinson, D. (1994). Nonmonotonic inference based on expectations. *Artificial Intelligence, 65,* 197–245.

Rescorla, R. A., & Wagner, A. R. (1972). A theory of Pavlovian conditioning: Variations in the effectiveness of reinforcement and nonreinforcement. In A. H. Black & W. F. Prokasy (Eds.), *Classical conditioning II: Current research and theory* (pp. 64–99). New York: Appleton-Century-Crofts.

Schank, R. C. (1982). *Dynamic memory: A theory of reminding and learning in computers and people.* Cambridge: Cambridge University Press.

DEFINITIONS

Add expectation: The mental event of adding an expectation of the occurrence of an envisioned state or event.

Expectation: A partial description of an envisioned future state or event.

Expectation violation: A mental event where there is a mismatch between an expectation of the current state and the current state.

Planning expectation: An expectation about the success of a planning process.

Remaining temporal pattern: The subset of expectations from a set containing events over time that occur at moments after the current moment.

Remove expectation: The mental event of removing an expectation of an upcoming state or event.

Unexpected: A property of a state or event that is in an expectation violation.

Unexpected event: An event that is in an expectation violation.

6.32   OTHER AGENT REASONING   (8 TERMS)

A small number of terms used in strategy representations refer to the mental processes involved in reasoning about the thoughts of other people, or envisioning what it would be like to be in someone else's place. Strong experimental work on the psychology of this sort of reasoning is currently being done across a wide range of fields (Baron-Cohen, Tager-Flusberg, & Cohen, 2000) under the banner of Theory of Mind, and two competing cognitive theories of other agent reasoning have been proposed. First, the Theory Theory hypothesizes that Theory of Mind abilities are computed using representational theories (axiomatic theories of folk psychology; e.g., Gopnik & Meltzoff, 1997; Nichols & Stich, 2000). Second, the Simulation Theory argues that Theory of Mind abilities are computed by using your own cognitive abilities to simulate the reasoning of another person—inferring the cognitive state of another person through perception of your own (Goldman, 2000). Both theories require rich representations of a person's cognitive state (including all of the representational areas presented here), but the Theory Theory argues that it is their accompanying axiomatic formulas that will enable prediction, whereas Simulation Theory argues that is the accompanying cognitive functions (or models of these functions in computational systems) that allow for prediction. The handful of terms related to other agent reasoning listed below suggest that these abilities are, themselves, part of our representational theory of mind. Of those listed here, deducing another agent's plans has received the most attention as the subject of computational modeling efforts (e.g., Kautz, 1991).

RELATED READINGS

Baron-Cohen, S., Tager-Flusberg, H., & Cohen, D. (Eds.). (2000). *Understanding other minds: Perspectives from developmental cognitive neuroscience*, (2nd ed.). Oxford: Oxford University Press.

Goldman, A. (2000). Folk psychology and mental concepts. *Protosociology, 14*, 4–25.

Gopnik, A., & Meltzoff, A. (1997). *Words, thoughts, and theories*. Cambridge, MA: MIT Press (Bradford).

Kautz, H. (1991). A formal theory of plan recognition and its implementation. In J. F. Allen, H. A. Kautz, R. N. Pelavin, & J. D. Tennenberg (Eds.), *Reasoning about plans* (pp. 69–126). San Francisco, CA: Morgan Kaufmann Publishers.

Nichols, S., & Stich, S. (2000). A cognitive theory of pretense. *Cognition, 74*, 115–147.

DEFINITIONS

Agent model: World model knowledge of an agent concerning other agents.

Deduce other agent plan: The mental event of envisioning the plan that is being followed by another agent.

Envisioned desirability: An envisioned branch preference that is envisioned to be held by another agent.

Guess expectation: An expectation that is envisioned to be held by another agent.

Guess goal: The mental event of envisioning the goal of another agent.

Other agent envisioned value: A value that is envisioned to be envisioned by another agent.

Other agent reasoning: The mental event of envisioning the reasoning processes of another agent.

Recognize plan: The mental event of classifying the execution of another agent as the execution of a shared plan.

6.33   THREAT DETECTION   (15 TERMS)

Several terms used in strategy representations concerned the detection and tracking of threats in the environment as envisioned by a planner. Two primary epistemic forms of threats were identified, first where a goal of an agent is violated in a possible future state, and second where this agent envisions the existence of this threat. The meaning of the term *Threat* here should not be directly equated with its use in research on partial-order planning systems, where it specifically refers to a plan step that would violate a causal link in a plan under construction. The commonsense use of the term refers to changes in the world that are not the actions of the planner, a possibility that planning research is just beginning to address. A number of researchers have had the insight that threat detection may be the corollary to opportunity recognition (Pryor, 1996), for which some efficient computational models have been proposed. Representational theories of threat detection are not available, and seem to first require a satisfactory treatment of envisioned possibilities.

RELATED READINGS

Pryor, L. (1996). Opportunity recognition in complex environments. In W. Clancey & D. Weld (Eds.), *Proceedings of the 13th AAAI*, Portland, OR (pp. 1147–1152). Menlo Park, CA: AAAI Press.

DEFINITIONS

Add threat: The mental event of adding a threat to a list of known threats.

Cause threat: The set of causes that lead from the current state to a threat in an envisionment.

Envisioned future threat: An envisioned threat to a goal that will be held in the future.

Envisioned possible threat: An envisioned threat in an envisionment branch with a non-zero envisioned likelihood.

Envisioned threat: An envisioned possible state or event that has a causal relationship with a subsequent envisioned state or event that violates a goal held by an agent.

Envisioned undesired state: The envisioned state or event that violates a goal following an envisioned threat.

Future threat: A future event or state that causes the violation of a goal that will be held by an agent at a future state.

Goal in threat: The goal held by an agent that is violated by a threat.

Realized threat: A threat where the state or event causing a goal violation has occurred.

Remove threat: The mental event of removing a threat from a list of known threats.

Threat: An event or state that causes the violation of a goal held by an agent.

Threat benefit analysis: The mental event of ordering envisioned branch preferences in an envisionment that contains envisioned threats.

Threat condition: A branching condition in an envisioned state that determines the occurrence of a threat.

Threat detection: The mental event of recognizing threats in an envisionment to goals held by an agent.

Threat to preservation goal: A threat where the goal violation is of a preservation goal.

6.34   GOAL MANAGEMENT   (27 TERMS)

The representation area of Goal management begins a series of areas that center on the processes of human planning. Goal management refers to the suite of concepts that involve the adoption, ordering, and removal of goals from the set of those that are held by a planner. Among these terms are several that refer to complex interrelated mental functions, including the resolution of conflicting goals, goal prioritization, goal modification and specification, and goal assessment. The processes of goal management have received some attention in relationship to autonomous agent technology (within the Belief-Desire-Intention framework), where it has been formalized as "deliberation" functions that compute a new set of intentions based on an agent's internal state (Wooldridge & Parsons, 1999). Beaudoin's (1994) theoretical work on goal processing more closely overlaps with the set of terms listed below, but adequately expressive representational theories (and process models) of goal management remain to be authored.

RELATED READINGS

Beaudoin, L. P. (1994). *Goal processing in autonomous agents.* Doctoral thesis, School of Computer Science, The University of Birmingham.

Wooldridge, M., & Parsons, S. (1999). Intention Reconsideration Reconsidered. In J. P. Muller, M. Singh, & A. Rao, (Eds.), *Proceedings of intelligent agents V: Agent theories, architectures, and languages* (pp. 63–79). Heidelberg, Germany: Springer-Verlag.

DEFINITIONS

Abandon goal: The mental event of removing an unachieved goal from the list of those to be pursued.

Abandon knowledge goal: The mental event of removing an unachieved knowledge goal from the list of those to be pursued.

Achieve goal: The mental event of removing a goal whose achievement conditions have been met.

Achieve greater goal: The mental event of removing a goal whose achievement conditions are subsumed by those of another goal that has been achieved.

Achieve knowledge goal: The mental event of removing a knowledge goal whose achievement conditions have been met.

Achieve preservation goal: The mental event of removing the goal to maintain a preservation goal in threat.

Achieve subgoal: The mental event of removing a subgoal whose achievement conditions have been met.

Add auxiliary goal: The mental event of adding a goal to a list of those that are to be pursued as auxiliary goals.

Add goal: The mental event of adding a goal to the list of those that are to be pursued by an agent.

Add persistent goal: The mental event of adding a persistent goal to the list of those that are to be pursued.

Add subgoal: The mental event of adding a subgoal to the list of those that are to be pursued.

Conflicting goal resolution: The mental event of modifying or removing goals that are conflicting goals.

Currently pursued goal: The goal for which an agent is currently planning or executing plans to achieve.

Goal assessment: The mental event of analyzing a goal to determine if it should be modified.

Goal failure: The mental event of removing a goal whose achievement conditions cannot be satisfied.

Goal justification: A set of beliefs that an agent assigns to a goal as its justification for pursuit.

Goal preference: A ordering principle used to prioritize goals that are to be pursued.

Goal prioritization: The mental event of ordering the list of goals that are to be pursued.

Goal satisfaction: A duration in which a goal of an agent is achieved.

Goal violation: A world state where a preservation goal of an agent is violated.

Greater priority: A relationship between goals where one has been assigned a higher priority.

Modify goal: The mental event of changing the achievement conditions of a goal that is to be pursued.

Remove auxiliary goal: The mental event of removing a goal from a list of those that are pursued as auxiliary goals.

Satisfy execution goal: The mental event of removing an execution goal whose achievement conditions have been met.

Specify goal: The mental event of changing the achievement conditions of a goal to be more specific.

Suspend goal: The mental event of inhibiting an unachieved goal that is held by an agent from being the subject of pursuit.

Violate preservation goal: The mental event of removing a preservation goal whose conditions are no longer met.

6.35   PLANNING MODALITIES   (17 TERMS)

The process of planning can be broadly construed as the problem of deciding what to do in advance of doing it, and has been a fundamental area of research in Artificial Intelligence since its inception as a field. Over several decades, many types of planning algorithms have been proposed, each with its own merits. Modern approaches included partial order planners, hierarchical task network planning, and case-based planning, among others, where a wide variety of algorithms exist—each of which may be used in a variety of different ways. The representational area of planning modalities catalogs the qualitatively different ways of planning that appear in strategy representations. Several of these terms make distinctions that are based more on the sorts of goals that are pursued than on the style of reasoning that is employed (e.g., Assistive planning). Others seem to make a stronger commitment to the use of particular reasoning abilities (e.g., Analogical planning). Distinctions among planning processes of this sort have not been made in representational theories of agent reasoning, although some basic references to classes of planning algorithms has appeared in planning systems that incorporate multiple techniques (Traverso, Cimatti, & Spalazzi, 1992). In contrast, an enormous amount of work has been done in developing planning algorithms tailored for most of the styles of reasoning that appear in this list, with strong current research in adversarial planning and continuous planning, in particular.

RELATED READINGS

Traverso, P., Cimatti, A., & Spalazzi, L. (1992). Beyond the single planning paradigm: Introspective planning. In B. Neumann (Ed.), *Proceedings of the Tenth European Conference on Artificial Intelligence* (ECAI-92), Vienna, (pp. 643–647). Hoboken, NJ: Wiley.

DEFINITIONS

Adversarial planning: The mental process of constructing a plan to violate the goals of others.

Analogical planning: The mental process of constructing a plan by adapting a plan for a different situation.

Assistive planning: The mental process of constructing a plan to achieve the goals of others.

Attempt opportunity: The mental process of constructing a plan to achieve the goal in an opportunity.

Auxiliary goal pursuit: The mental process of modifying existing plans to achieve auxiliary goals as well.

Collaborative planning: The mental process of constructing a plan through discourse with a collaborating agent.

Competitive planning: The mental process of constructing a plan to achieve a competitive goal.

Continuous planning: The mental process of modifying a continuous plan.

Counterplanning: The mental process of constructing a plan to cause a plan of another agent to fail.

Future goal pursuit: A reference to planning and execution done by an agent in future states.

Goal pursuit: A reference to planning and execution done by an agent.

Imagined world planning: The mental process of constructing plans to be executed in envisioned worlds.

Normal goal pursuit: A set of expectations of the goal pursuit of an agent over a duration.

Other agent planning: The mental process of constructing a plan to be followed by another agent to achieve their goal.

Past planning: A reference to planning that was done before the current moment.

Path planning: The mental process of identifying a possible transfer path for a physical object.

Planning: The mental process of constructing a description of agent behavior that will cause the achievement of a goal.

6.36 PLANNING GOALS (28 TERMS)

The representational area of Planning Goals concerns the intended causal relationships between the planned actions of an agent and states in the world, and includes the commonsense causal notions of avoiding, blocking, enabling, delaying, and preserving world states through action (or deliberate inaction). This representational area is aligned here with the processes of constructing plans, with the intuition that the adoption of these goals will significantly impact the process by which an agent constructs and adapts plans. However, these terms could alternatively be viewed as part of a fundamental representational area of causality in general, or as a corollary area to Goals. There has recently been a renewed interest in formal representations of causality, yielding theories that include many of the terms listed below. Among the efforts that overlap significantly with this term list is the work of Ortiz (1999), who employs counterfactual semantics to define causal relationships including enablement, helping, hindering, coercion, and prevention, among others. Hobbs (2001) streamlines this work by introducing the notion of a causal complex, and by allowing the use of negative events in causal definitions.

RELATED READINGS

Hobbs, J. (2001). Causality. In E. Davis, J. McCarthy, L. Morgenstern, & R. Reiter (Eds.), *Working Notes of the Fifth International Symposium on Logical Formalizations of Commonsense Reasoning.* New York: New York University.

Ortiz, C. L. (1999). A common sense language for reasoning about causation and rational action. *Artificial Intelligence, 111*(2), 73–130.

DEFINITIONS

Avoid: A planning goal that an event does not occur.

Avoid action: A planning goal that a type of action is not performed by an agent.

Avoid execution: A planning goal that a plan of an agent is not executed.

Block: A planning goal that it is not possible for an event to occur.

Block agency: A planning goal that behavior of an agent does not occur.

Block cause: A planning goal that the cause in a causal relationship does not occur.

Block execution: A planning goal that it is not possible for an agent to execute a plan.

Block goal: A planning goal that it is not possible for an agent to achieve a goal.

Block goal violation: A planning goal that it is not possible for a goal to be violated.

Block threat: A planning goal that a recognized threat is not a realized threat.

Block transfer: A planning goal that the location of a thing is not changed to another location.

Block transfer path: A planning goal to block transfer by eliminating the transfer path.

Delay duration end: A planning goal that the end time of a duration is later than expected.

Enable: A planning goal to change the world state so that an event is possible in future states.

Enable action: A planning goal to change the world so that it is possible for an agent to execute an action.

Enable envisionment: A planning goal to cause it to be possible that an agent generates a true envisionment.

Enable execution: A planning goal to satisfy the execution preconditions of a plan.

Enable threat: A planning goal to make it possible that an envisioned threat is a realized threat.

Locate: A planning goal to identify an entity that satisfies a set of criteria.

Locate agent: A planning goal to identify an agent that satisfies a set of criteria.

Locate location: A planning goal to identify a location in the world that satisfies a set of criteria.

Locate thing: A planning goal to identify a physical object in the world that satisfies a set of features.

Maintain preservation goal: A planning goal that a preservation goal is not violated in future states.

Maximize value: A planning goal that a value is its maximum possible value for a characteristic.

Minimize value: A planning goal that a value is its minimum possible value for a characteristic.

Other agent goal satisfaction: A planning goal to satisfy the goals of another agent.

Permanently block: A planning goal that it is not possible for an event to occur at any future moment.

Preserve precondition: A planning goal that a satisfied precondition is always satisfied at future moments.

6.37   PLAN CONSTRUCTION   (30 TERMS)

Plan Construction refers to the process of generating a new plan to achieve a goal, and should be distinguished from Plan Adaptation only in that the main tasks in plan construction involve the selection and ordering of actions rather than the modification of some existing plan. Plan construction continues to be a central problem in Artificial Intelligence with an active community of researchers proposing new algorithms and approaches. A distinction that is commonly made among approaches is between algorithms that know only the primitive actions (operators) in a planning domain and those that include additional domain knowledge to guide the plan construction process (Bacchus, 2001). Progress on the former of these two approaches has centered on the translation of traditional planning problems into propositional satisfiability problems, then employing various systemic or stochastic methods (Weld, 1999). The latter of the two approaches is best exemplified by hierarchical task network (HTN) planners, which incorporate domain-specific methods as intermediaries between goals and primitive operators (Wilkins & desJardins, 2001). Several researchers have proposed that representations of the planning process itself could be used to improve planning algorithms, an approach that is associated with the term meta-planning, although no representational theories have been proposed that approach the breadth of concepts contained in the terms below. These terms can roughly be divided into those that refer to the inputs and outputs of the planning process (e.g., planning preference, candidate plan), events that occur during the process (e.g., planning failure, successful planning), and the controls that a reasoning system has over this process (e.g., add planning constraint, replan).

RELATED READINGS

Bacchus, F. (2001). AIPS '00 Planning Competition: The Fifth International Conference on Artificial Intelligence Planning and Scheduling Systems. *AI Magazine, 22*(3), 47–56.
Weld, D. S. (1999). Recent advances in AI planning. *AI Magazine, 20*(2), 93–123.
Wilkins, D., & desJardins, M. (2001). A call for knowledge-based planning. *AI Magazine 22*(1), 99–115.

DEFINITIONS

Add planning constraint: The mental event of adding to the current list of planning constraints.
Add planning preference: The mental event of adding to the current list of planning preferences.
Add precondition: The mental event of adding a precondition to a plan or subplan.

Add subplan: The mental event of adding a subplan to a plan.

Add to partial plan: The mental event of adding a subplan to a partial plan.

Assess plan: The mental event of evaluating the quality of a plan.

Candidate plan: A plan in a set of plans where each is intended to achieve the same goal.

Complete planning: The mental event of terminating the planning process.

Constraint duration: A specification of the duration that a planning constraint is to be applied.

Locate subplan: The mental event of identifying among a set of known subplans one that meets a subgoal.

Obstacle: A reference to an entity that is the cause of a planning problem.

Order subtasks: The mental event of ordering a set of unordered subplans.

Planning constraint: A partial description of plans that are not allowable products of the planning process.

Planning decision: A decision in the planning process where the choice set are different partial plans that are being considered.

Planning failure: The mental event that the process of planning ends without producing a plan to achieve a goal.

Planning option: A member of the set of partial plans in a planning decision.

Planning preference: A partial description of plans that are to be preferred by an agent when making a planning decision.

Planning problem: A planning decision where none of the known planning options are satisfactory.

Remove planning constraint: The mental event of removing a planning constraint.

Remove planning preference: The mental event of removing planning preference.

Replan: The mental event of planning for a goal that has already been the subject of previous planning.

Replan subplan: The mental event of planning for a subgoal where there is already a known subplan.

Resolved problem: A reference to a planning problem where a satisfactory planning option has been identified.

Select candidate plan: The mental event of selecting a single plan from a set of candidate plans that each achieve the same goal.

Selected plan: A reference to a candidate plan that has been selected from a set.

Specify partial plan: The mental event of describing unspecified components of a partial plan.

Specify subplan: The mental event of describing unspecified components of a partial subplan.

Successful planning: The mental event of completing the planning process and having identified a plan that achieves the goal.

Suspend planning: The mental event of stopping the planning process with the intention of resuming the process in the future with the current partial plan.

Unselected candidate plan: A reference to a candidate plan that was not selected.

6.38 PLAN ADAPTATION   (18 TERMS)

The corollary to the mental process of Plan Construction is that of Plan Adaptation, where new plans are identified not by selecting and ordering operators, but rather by retrieving an existing plan from memory and adapting it to achieve the current goals. Plan adaptation should be viewed as a component process of case-based planning (Hammond, 1990; Spalazzi, 2001), which also includes plan retrieval and plan retention—necessary processes that are not well indicated by the terms identified in strategy representations. Instead, the terms that are listed below focus on qualifying the process itself (e.g., Adapt continual plan, Adapt subplan) and the various ways in which a plan can be adapted (e.g., Increase amount, Add subplan modification). Although plan adaptation has not previously been the focus of representational theories, existing case-based planning algorithms collectively have many of the functionalities described by these concepts. Among the few that have received little attention are the (possibly continuous) processes of adapting a continual plan, and algorithmic consideration of adaptation costs.

RELATED READINGS

Hammond, K. J. (1990) .Case-based planning: A framework for planning from experience. *Cognitive Science, 14*(3), 385–443.
Spalazzi, L. (2001). A survey on case-cased planning. *Artificial Intelligence Review, 16*(1), 3–36.

DEFINITIONS

Adapt continual plan: The mental event of modifying an existing continuous plan to achieve a new goal.
Adapt partial plan: The mental event of modifying an existing partial plan to achieve a new goal.
Adapt plan: The mental event of modifying an existing plan to achieve a new goal.
Adapt subplan: The mental event of modifying an existing subplan to achieve a new subgoal.
Adaptation cost: A value for the amount of modification necessary to adapt an existing plan for a new goal.
Adaptation failure: The mental event where an agent is unsuccessful in adapting an existing plan for a new goal.
Add subplan modification: The mental event of adapting a plan through the addition of a subplan.

Continuous adaptation: A set of mental events in which a continuous plan is adapted over an indefinite duration.

Increase amount: The mental event of adapting a plan through the increment of a value in the plan.

Modifies partial plan: The mental event of changing a description of a partial plan.

Modify normal activity: The mental event of changing the set of activities that an agent expects that they will execute over a duration.

Modify plan: The mental event of changing a description of a plan.

Modify subplan: The mental event of changing a description of a subplan.

Remove subplan: The mental event of modifying a plan by removing a subplan.

Substitute value adaptation: The mental event of adapting a plan by replacing a value in the plan with another value.

Substitution adaptation: The mental event of adapting a plan by replacing part of the description of the plan with another description.

Substitution of agency adaptation: The mental event of adapting a plan by replacing an agent in a plan with another agent.

Successful adaptation: The mental event in which the plan adaptation process is completed and has produced a new plan that achieves a goal.

6.39 DESIGN (8 TERMS)

Some of the terms used in strategy representations refer to concepts that participate in design, a variation of plan construction. In planning terms, design is the construction of a plan for the creation or configuration of an artifact, process, or information. Accordingly, these things may have some designed use, which is a plan itself, and real-world instances of these things may have some degree of adherence to the original design. Features of the process of design are referenced in these terms as well, including the actions of adapting a design, composition as a type of design, and the event in which the design process has failed. Theoretical and empirical investigations of the design process have generally focused either on understanding the relationship between structure and function in devices (Chandrasekaran & Josephson, 2000) or the sorts of concurrent reasoning processes in which designers must engage (Kavakli & Gero, 2002). Although there has been little work done to formalize the commonsense meanings of the terms listed below to support reasoning about the design process, several of them have been operationalized in cognitive process models (see Sgouros, 1993).

RELATED READINGS

Chandrasekaran, B., & Josephson, J. R. (2000). Function in device representation. *Engineering with Computers, 16*, 162–177.

Kavakli, M., & Gero, J. S. (2002). The structure of concurrent cognitive actions: A case study of novice and expert designers, *Design Studies, 23*(1), 25–40.

Sgouros, N. (1993). *Representing physical and design knowledge in innovative engineering design*. Doctoral thesis, Northwestern University, Evanston, IL.

DEFINITIONS

Adapt design: The mental process of adapting a plan where the plan is a design.

Compose: The mental process of generating a design where the design goal is for a compositional entity and where the components are not the subject of the design process.

Design adherence: A value for the correspondence between the product of a design process and a physical object in the world that was created using the design.

Design constraint: A planning constraint that describes designs that are not allowable products of the design process.

Design failure: The mental event in which the design process ends without producing a design that achieves a design goal.

Design information: The mental process of design where the design goal is for information that will be communicated to another agent.

Design thing: The mental process of design where the design goal is for a physical entity.

Designed use: An envisioned successful execution that includes the instrumental use of a designed entity by an agent.

6.40 DECISIONS   (38 TERMS)

Closely related to the area of Plan Construction is that of Decisions, where an agent is faced with making a selection among candidate options. Many theorists view planning as a specialization of decision-making, where the choice is a plan of action. In strategy representations, decisions are more often treated as events within a plan, with the notion of a planning decision being a special case. Much of the recent work in computational models for decision-making has explored stochastic, or probabilistic, approaches. Borrowing from techniques in operations research, Markov decision processes (MDPs) take as input a state of the world and produce as output actions that maximize some utility value. More recently explored partially observable Markov decision processes (POMDPs) have generalized this approach for situations where the current state is uncertain (see Kaelbling, Littman, & Cassandra, 1998). Although these approaches are extremely general, many of the terms used to describe the decision-making process in strategy representations can be operationalized within these stochastic approaches. Others, including the notion of a preference, have received substantial formal attention in work on qualitative decision theory (e.g., Tan & Pearl, 1994).

RELATED READINGS

Kaelbling, L., Littman, M., & Cassandra, A. (1998). Planning and acting in partially observable stochastic domains. *Artificial Intelligence, 101*, 99–134.

Tan, S.-W., & Pearl, J. (1994). Qualitative decision theory. In B. Hayes-Roth & R. E. Korf (Eds.), *Proceedings of the 12th National Conference on Artificial Intelligence* (pp. 928–933). Menlo Park, CA: AAAI Press.

DEFINITIONS

Alternate execution option: A reference to an execution option that is not selected.

Analysis: The mental event of ordering the desirability of the consequences of each member of a choice set.

Best candidate: A reference to the member of the choice set with a consequence that an agent has ordered as the most desirable.

Candidate agent: A member of a choice set of agents.

Candidate agent characteristics: Characteristics of agents in a choice set that are used in preferences or selection criteria.

Candidate role agent: An agent role that will be adopted by the selected agent from a choice set.

Choice set: A set of entities, where the selection of a member of the set by an agent would result in different consequences.

Cost benefit analysis: The mental event of analysis where there is a preference for selections whose consequences involve a lower expenditure of a resource.

Decision: A mental event where an agent selects from a choice set during a reasoning process.

Decision consequences: States and events that are caused by the selection of a candidate.

Decision factor: A member of the set of preferences or analyses that an agent considers to be justification for a decision.

Decision justification: A set of preferences or analyses that promote one candidate over others in a decision.

Decision series: A set of mental events that are decisions made over a duration.

Enumerate possible decisions: The mental event of composing a choice set.

Envisioned decision consequence: Envisioned states and events that would be caused if an agent selects a candidate.

Envisionment preceding decision: A reference to the envisionment process that generates envisioned decision consequences.

Execution decision: A decision that occurs during the execution of a plan that contains the decision.

Insignificant decision: A decision where there are no differences in the favorability of consequences.

Negative decision outcome: Consequences that violate goals of the agent.

Obvious best decision: A reference to a member of a choice set where preferences or analyses reveal that the choice is far better than all others.

Other choice: A reference to a candidate that is not selected in a decision.

Positive decision outcome: Consequences that achieve goals of the agent.

Possible selection: A member of a choice set.

Preference: A partial description of decision options that are to be favored over others.

Previous selection: A reference to a selection that was made when a previous decision was made over the same choice set.

Random choice: A selection criteria where the selection is made without preference or analysis.

Resume planning decision: The mental event of resuming a suspended planning decision.

Select: The mental event that a member of a choice set is identified as the selected choice.

Select agent: The mental event that a member of a choice set of agents is identified as the selected choice.

Select thing: The mental event that a member of a choice set of physical objects is identified as the selected choice.

Select value: The mental event that a member of a choice set of values is identified as the selected choice.

Selected agent: A reference to the member that is selected by an agent from a choice set of agents.

Selected choice: A reference to the member of the choice set that is selected by an agent.

Selected thing: A reference to the member that is selected by an agent from a choice set of physical objects.

Selected value: A reference to the member that is selected by an agent from a choice set of values.

Selection criteria: An ordering principle composed of choice characteristics used by an agent in a decision.

Suspend planning decision: The mental event of stopping a planning decision without selecting a choice with the intention of resuming the decision at a future moment.

Uncertain planning decision: A planning decision where preferences or analyses do not identify a most favorable choice.

6.41 SCHEDULING (22 TERMS)

The representational area of Scheduling concerns the selection of execution times for plans of an agent. Although closely related to the process of plan construction, scheduling elaborates on a set of concerns other than selecting operators, including the notions of a scheduling constraint, a deadline, and a pending plan (one that is not yet scheduled). Although representational theories of scheduling have not been a research concern, the ubiquity of real-world scheduling problems has led to the creation of innumerable automated scheduling algorithms, particularly in the operations research community. While Artificial Intelligence researchers have traditionally viewed the problem of scheduling as a variant of automated planning, a recent trend has been to explore general planning and scheduling approaches with various degrees of integration (Garrido & Barber, 2001; Smith, Frank, & Jónsson, 2000). Within these frameworks, the strengths of planning algorithms for searching an operator space are paired with generalized scheduling algorithms that are optimized for time and resource considerations. Contemporary algorithms for integrative planning and scheduling instantiate many of the terms listed below, with a notable weakness in the area of periodically scheduled plans.

RELATED READINGS

Garrido, A., & Barber, F. (2001). Integrating planning and scheduling. *Applied Artificial Intelligence: An International Journal, 15*(5), 471–491.
Smith, D., Frank, J., & Jónsson, A. (2000). Bridging the gap between planning and scheduling. *Knowledge Engineering Review, 15*(1), 61–94.

DEFINITIONS

Add scheduling constraint: The mental event of adding to a list of scheduling constraints.

Collaborative scheduling: A duration where a set of agents schedule the execution of a collaborative plan.

Completion deadline: A deadline for the end time of the execution of a plan.

Deadline: A scheduling constraint of the latest possible moment for the execution of a plan.

Execution deadline: A deadline for the start time of the execution of a plan.

Immediately after scheduled plan: The first moment after end time of a scheduled plan.

Indefinitely postponed: A characteristic of a plan that is removed from a schedule and is not a pending plan.

Next scheduled period plan: The start time of the next scheduled execution of a periodic plan .

Pending plan: A plan that an agent intends to schedule but is not yet scheduled.

Reschedule: The mental event of removing a plan from a schedule and scheduling it for a different duration.

Schedule: The mental event of selecting future moments as the intended execution duration for a pending plan.

Schedule periodically: The mental event of assigning multiple start times for a reusable plan where the duration between start times is a period.

Schedule subplan: The mental event of assigning an intended execution duration for a subplan in a scheduled plan.

Scheduled plan: A plan that has been scheduled by an agent.

Scheduled plan duration: The intended execution duration for a scheduled plan.

Scheduled previous subplan: The subplan in a scheduled plan with an end time closest to a latter moment.

Scheduled start time: The intended start time of a scheduled plan.

Scheduling constraint: A description of scheduling options that an agent does not allow as products of the successful scheduling of a plan.

Scheduling failure: The mental event where an agent ends the process of scheduling without identifying an intended execution duration for a plan.

Suspension resumption deadline: A deadline for the resumption of a suspended plan.

Unschedule plan: The mental event of removing a plan from a schedule and adding it to a list of pending plans.

Unscheduled duration: A duration in the future that does not overlap with the intended execution durations of the plans of an agent.

6.42 MONITORING (18 TERMS)

The cognitive process of monitoring serves to delay some action or execution until some conditions are met, if ever. By specifying a set of trigger conditions and an action to take when these conditions are met, an agent can be reactive in a dynamic, unpredictable environment. Although a common set of terms is listed below, the research community has generally drawn a distinction between the monitoring of the external environment and monitoring an agent's internal reasoning processes. Empirical studies and theoretical work have suggested that for monitoring the external environment, both *periodic* and *interval reduction* strategies are used to enable people to divide attention between the subject of interest and other tasks (Atkin & Cohen, 1996). These strategies may be instrumental in operationalizing several of the terms listed below (e.g., Monitor thing, Monitor environment). Monitoring an agent's own internal reasoning processes (traditionally called *cognitive monitoring*) has received substantial amounts of attention in the field of cognitive psychology since the publication of Flavell's influential theory (1979). Computational models of cognitive monitoring have proved difficult to construct outside of the scope of very specific tasks, although generalized monitoring of the planning process has often been proposed as the basis for meta-planning heuristics and critics.

RELATED READINGS

Atkin, M., & Cohen, P. R. (1996). Monitoring strategies for embedded agents: Experiments and analysis. *Journal of Adaptive Behavior, 4*(2), 125–172.

Flavell, J. H. (1979). Metacognition and cognitive monitoring: A new area of cognitive-developmental inquiry. *American Psychologist, 34,* 906–911.

DEFINITIONS

First monitor triggering: A reference to the first occurrence of the triggering of a monitor.

Future monitor triggering: A reference to occurrences of the triggering of a monitor at future moments.

Last triggering of monitor: A reference to the most recent occurrence of the triggering of a monitor.

Monitor: The mental process of intending to execute a behavior when certain criteria are met by the current state.

Monitor agent: A monitoring process where the trigger condition describes the behavior of a different agent.

Monitor environment: A monitoring process where the trigger condition describes characteristics of the environment.

Monitor envisionment: A monitoring process where the trigger condition describes characteristics of an envisionment that has been generated by the agent.

Monitor events: A monitoring process where the trigger condition describes the occurrence of an event.

Monitor execution: A monitoring process where the trigger condition describes the execution of a plan by a different agent.

Monitor planning: A monitoring process where the trigger condition describes characteristics of the planning process of the agent.

Monitor self-execution: A monitoring process where the trigger condition describes the execution of a plan by the agent engaged in monitoring.

Monitor thing: A monitoring process where the trigger condition describes properties of a physical entity.

Monitoring duration: The duration of a monitoring process for an agent.

No monitor trigger: A characteristic of a monitoring process that has not been triggered.

Previous monitor triggering: A reference to a member of the set of previous occurrences of the triggering of a monitor.

Satisfy monitor condition: The mental event in which the conditions described in the trigger condition of a monitoring process are met.

Terminate monitoring: The mental event of terminating a monitoring process.

Triggered monitor: A characteristic of a monitoring process that has been triggered.

6.43   EXECUTION MODALITIES   (11 TERMS)

The representational area of Execution Modalities begins a series related to plan execution, the transition from planning what the best course of action would be to actually performing these actions in the world. This first set of terms used in strategy representations include those that draw some distinctions among the different manners that plans can be executed–the different modalities of the plan execution process. The assumption that underlies this list is that different types of plans or execution environments will warrant qualitatively different types of execution processes on the part of the agent. Collaborative, coordinated, and simultaneous executions are modalities that relate an agent's execution of a plan to those of other agents in the environment. Concurrent, continuous, consecutive, repetitive, and periodic executions are distinctions based on temporal relationships between plans executed by a single agent. To follow execution rules is a modality of purposefully constrained execution, where the execution rules serve some other goals of the agent. These sorts of execution distinctions are not generally made within the context of any single computational model of plan execution, although many of these distinctions are evident in the approaches of existing plan execution systems that address specific types of problems. For example, coordinated execution is increasingly studied in the context of research on multi-agent systems (e.g., Durfee, 2001), while very different approaches are used to support the execution (and modification) of continuous plans (desJardins et al., 1999).

RELATED READINGS

Durfee, E. H. (2001). Scaling up agent coordination strategies. *IEEE Computer, 34*(7), 39–46.
desJardins, M., Durfee, E., Ortiz, C., & Wolverton, M. (1999). A survey of research in distributed, continual planning. *AI Magazine, 20*(4), 13–22.

DEFINITIONS

Collaborative execution: A duration where multiple agents execute portions of a collaborative plan.
Concurrent execution: An execution where a single agent simultaneously executes multiple plans.
Concurrent process: A mental process of an agent that is simultaneously engaged in other mental processes.
Concurrent processing: A duration where an agent is simultaneously engaged in multiple mental processes.
Consecutive execution: An execution of a set of plans where the start time of the next plan is the end time of the previous plan.
Continuous execution: An execution of a continuous plan.
Coordinated execution: A collaborative execution of a collaborative plan by multiple agents where scheduled execution deadlines of subplans are met.

Follow execution rules: An execution where the agent intends to adhere to a set of execution rules.

Periodic execution: An execution of a periodic plan.

Repetitive execution: An execution of a repetitive plan.

Simultaneous execution: A set of executions by multiple agents with overlapping execution durations.

6.44   EXECUTION CONTROL   (29 TERMS)

Regardless of the modality of execution that is employed, there is an assumption that execution control processes are employed that translate the instructions of a plan into actions of the agent. During these processes, plans of partially or fully ordered operators are serially or concurrently executed. Interruptions may occur due to distracting events, which may require the suspension or even the abandonment of an executing plan. Delays may occur between scheduled start times and actual start times, and the execution of a plan may or may not continue through to its completion. As a topic of knowledge representation research, execution control has received significant attention over the last decade beginning with Davis (1992), with continued interest within the context of research on rational action and change (Ismail & Shapiro, 2000; De Giacomo, Lespérance, & Levesque, 1997). These theories include notation that is expressive enough to capture the majority of concepts listed below, and could be expanded to include those that have not been adequately addressed (e.g., Distracting event). Distinctions made in strategy representations concerning the type of plan that is executed are also included in the list below (e.g., actions, activities, explicit plans, partial plans, skills, subplans), although it is unclear whether these distinctions are intuitively or even operationally distinct.

RELATED READINGS

Ismail, H. O., & Shapiro, S. C. (2000). Conscious error recovery and interrupt handling. In H. R. Arabnia (Ed.), *Proceedings of the International Conference on Artificial Intelligence* (IC-AI'2000) (pp. 633–639). Las Vegas, NV: CSREA Press.

De Giacomo, G., Lespérance, Y., & Levesque, H. (1997). Reasoning about concurrent execution, prioritized interrupts, and exogenous actions in the situation calculus. In M. Pollack (Ed.), *Proceedings of the Fifteenth International Joint Conference on AI* (IJCAI'97) (pp. 1221–1226). San Francisco, CA: Morgan Kaufmann.

Davis, E. (1992). Semantics for tasks that can be interrupted or abandoned. In J. Hendler (Ed.), *The First International Conference on Artificial Intelligence Planning Systems* (AIPS '92) (pp. 37–44). San Francisco, CA: Morgan Kaufmann.

DEFINITIONS

Abandon execution: To actively remove a pending behavior.

Begin concurrent processing: To begin an additional process concurrently with current executions.

Continue execution: To actively move to the next behavior in an execution.

Distracting event: An event whose perception and attention by the executing agent involuntarily suspends plan following.

Execute: To turn the intention of behavior into behavior.

Execute action: To execute a single behavior that hasn't been further deconstructed by the executing agent.

Execute activity: To execute according to the expectations that the agent has of execution of an agent with their role in an activity.

Execute counterplan: To execute a counterplan.

Execute explicit plan: To execute according to a plan that has been explicated as a set of instructions.

Execute partial plan: To attempt the execution of a partial plan where unspecified plan elements are improvised.

Execute performance: To execute a performance to be observed by another agent.

Execute plan: To execute a plan.

Execute reusable plan: To execute a reusable plan by adapting to the current execution environment.

Execute skill: To execute a skill that is not further deconstructed by the executing agent.

Execute subplan: To execute a subplan in a plan.

Execution completion: The event in which a plan has ended the execution process.

Execution constraint: A partial description of an execution that is not to be satisfied by the executing agent.

Execution delay: A duration with a start time of the scheduled execution time of a plan and the actual start time of execution.

Indefinite execution delay: An execution delay that is an indefinite duration.

Remove execution constraint: To actively remove an execution constraint from the active list.

Resume execution: To start the execution of a suspended execution at the point in the execution in which it was suspended.

Resumption moment: A reference to the moment in which a suspended plan is resumed.

Suspend activity: To stop the execution of an activity in a manner such that it could be resumed.

Suspend continuous subplan: To stop the execution of a continuous subplan in a manner such that it could be resumed.

Suspend execution: To stop an execution in a manner such that it could be resumed.

Suspend plan until: To suspend execution and to schedule a resumption moment.

Suspended execution duration: A duration with a start time of the suspension of a plan and an end time of the resumption moment.

Terminate activity: To stop the execution of activity without the intention of resumption.

Terminate execution: To stop an execution without the intention of resumption.

6.45 REPETITIVE EXECUTION (16 TERMS)

A significant number of terms used in strategy representations concerned execution control concepts specifically dealing with repetitive execution and iterative loops, warranting its inclusion as a separate representational area in its own right. While closely related to iteration and repetition concepts in the area of Plan Elements, the meaning of the terms listed here are grounded only when an agent is in the process of executing a repetitive plan, rather than during planning. For example, the previous, current, next, and last repetition may all describe the execution of the same repetitive plan or subplan, but the executions themselves are distinguished by their realization in time. Although many of the same formalizations used to describe repetition and iteration in plans may be useful in developing representational notations for the terms below, their semantics are perhaps best defined with reference to execution scenarios (Beetz & McDermott, 1997) for reactive plan execution.

RELATED READINGS

Beetz, M., & McDermott, D. (1997). Expressing transformations of structured reactive plans. In S. Steel & R. Alami (Eds.), *Fourth European Conference on Planning* (ECP '97) (pp. 66–78). Heidelberg, Germany: Springer-Verlag.

DEFINITIONS

Consecutive repetition: A characteristic of the execution of a repetitive plan where the start time of the repetition is the end time of a previous repetition.

Continue repetition: The mental event of executing the next repetition in a repetitive plan.

Current iteration: A reference to the execution duration of a repetitive plan that is being executed at the current moment.

Execution repetition: A member of the set durations in which a repetitive plan has been executed.

Increment counter: The mental event of incrementing a quantity indicating repetition executions by one.

Iteration completion: The mental event in which the execution of an iterative plan has completed and where the quantity of iterations is equal to that which was specified in the plan.

Iterations quantity: The quantity of times that an iterative plan has been executed.

Last repetition: The execution of a repetition in a repetitive plan completed before the current repetition.

Next repetition: The future execution of a repetition in a currently executing repetitive plan that will immediately follow the current repetition.

Previous iteration: A reference to a member of the set of executed iterations of a currently executing iterative plan.

Previous repetition: A reference to a member of the set of executed repetitions of a currently executing repetitive plan.

Remaining repetition: A reference to a member of the set of repetitions of a currently executing repetitive plan that will be executed in future moments.

Repetition quantity: The quantity of times that a currently executing repetitive plan has been executed.

Suspends repetitive execution: The mental event of ending the execution of a repetitive plan with the intention of resuming the execution at a future moment.

Terminate iteration: The mental event of ending the execution of an iterative plan before completion.

Terminate repetition: The mental event of ending the execution of a repetitive plan.

6.46   PLAN FOLLOWING   (30 TERMS)

The representational area of Plan Following is premised on the assumption that the execution of plans is not an infallible process. In order to deal with the uncertainty of real-world execution environments, an agent needs to monitor the execution process itself, noticing when operators complete successfully or fail, when preconditions are met, and when deadlines are missed or met. Often referred to as *execution monitoring* in the artificial intelligence planning literature, issues related to plan following have arisen in the context of real-world plan execution systems where robust autonomy is critical, e.g., controlling unmanned spacecraft (Pell, Gat, Keesing, Muscettola, & Smith, 1997). Much of current work on these computational systems follow from earlier work on validating operator post conditions during execution (Ambros-Ingerson & Steel, 1988; Doyle, Atkinson, & Doshi, 1986), but within these frameworks, many of the terms listed below could be operationalized in a manner that informs the development of representational theories of the human plan-following process.

RELATED READINGS

Ambros-Ingerson, J., & Steel, S. (1988). Integrating planning execution and monitoring. *Proceedings of the seventh national conference on artificial intelligence* (AAAI 88) (pp. 83–88).

Doyle, R. J., Atkinson, D. J., & Doshi, R. S. (1986). Generating perception requests and expectations to verify the execution of plans. *Proceedings of the 5th National Conference on Artificial Intelligence*, 81–88.

Pell, B., Gat, E., Keesing, R., Muscettola, N., & Smith, B. (1997). Robust periodic planning and execution for autonomous spacecraft. In M. Pollack (Ed.), *Proceedings of the Fifteenth International Joint Conference on Artificial Intelligence* (IJCAI-97) (pp. 1234–1239). San Francisco, CA: Morgan Kaufmann Publishers.

DEFINITIONS

Achieve precondition: The mental event in which a precondition for a plan or subplan is believed to have been successfully achieved by the executing agent.

Consistent execution: A characteristic of a set of executions of a reusable plan that has been executed without execution errors.

Constant across continuous execution: A state characteristic that has not changed in the duration of a continuous execution.

Currently executing plan: A plan that is currently being executed by an agent.

Execution costs: A quantity that indicates the total amount of resources expended over an execution duration.

Execution duration: A duration between the moment an agent begins the execution of a plan and the moment in which the execution of the plan is terminated.

Execution environment: A reference to the set of world states that occur during an execution environment.

Execution failure: The mental event in which an execution ends without the completion of a plan.

Execution location: A member of the set of locations of agents that have agency in a plan during its execution.

Execution precondition: A condition of state characteristics that must be met before the start time of the execution of a plan.

Execution start time: The moment of the start time of the execution of a plan.

Miss deadline: An event in which a deadline for the execution of a plan is a past moment and where the plan has not been executed.

Partially executed plan: A reference to the portion of the currently executing plan that has been executed.

Preceding subplan: A reference to the executed subplan that is most recent for a plan that is being executed.

Previously executed plan: A reference to the plan that was most recently executed by an agent.

Remaining plan: A reference to the portion of the currently executing plan that has not been executed.

Satisfied characteristic precondition: A satisfied condition that is a state characteristic of an execution environment.

Satisfied condition: A condition in a currently executing plan that is satisfied by the world state.

Satisfied execution precondition: An execution precondition for the currently executing plan that was satisfied by the state at the start time of the execution.

Satisfied precondition: A precondition for a subplan in the currently executing plan that is satisfied by the world state.

Satisfy knowledge precondition: The mental event of marking a knowledge precondition in the currently executing plan as being satisfied by knowledge of the agent.

Satisfy precondition: The mental event of marking a precondition in the currently executing plan as being satisfied by the world state.

Successful execution: The mental event in which a goal has been achieved by the completion of the execution of a plan.

Successful skill execution: The mental event of successful execution where the plan is a skill.

Successfully blocked: The mental event of successful execution where the plan includes a block

Successfully executed counterplan: The mental event of successful execution where the plan is a counterplan to another plan that has failed.

Successfully executed plan: A reference to the plan in a successful execution.

Unsatisfied condition: A condition in a currently executing plan that is not satisfied by the world state.

Unsatisfied precondition: A precondition for a subplan in the currently executing plan that is not satisfied by the world state.

Violate precondition: The event in which the state of the world changes and a satisfied precondition in the currently executing plan becomes unsatisfied.

6.47   OBSERVATION OF EXECUTION   (28 TERMS)

As with the representational area of Plan Following, Observation of Execution concerns the monitoring of an executing plan, but where a different person is conducting the execution. Within this framework, the plan (which is known to both the observer and the executing agent) is referred to as a *performance*. Most of the terms listed below are related to the notion of an *assessment*, where the observation of an execution is being conducted in order to make a judgment as to the correspondence between the execution and the performance. Within an assessment, judgments are made based on adherence to assessment criteria (rules), which may be implicit or explicit. While several of the terms below appear closer to particular activities within specific domains (e.g., encode performance information), monitoring the execution of other people (through perception of any sort) could reasonably be postulated as an innate cognitive ability of significant importance (see Rizzolatti, Fadiga, Gallese, & Fogassi, 1996). From a functional perspective, the interesting question is whether such abilities are based primarily on our capacity to monitor our own execution of plans, or if they employ entirely separate processes.

RELATED READINGS

Rizzolatti, G., Fadiga L., Gallese, V., & Fogassi, L. (1996) Promotor cortex and the recognition of motor actions. *Cognitive Brain Research, 3,* 131–141.

DEFINITIONS

Add rule: The mental event of adding to the list of rules in a performance specification.

Assessment: The mental process of observing an execution to determine the correspondence between the execution and a performance specification.

Assessment coverage: A subset of a knowledge domain that participates in rules of a performance specification.

Assessment criteria: A rule in a performance specification.

Assessment of activity: An assessment process where the execution is of an activity.

Assessment of knowledge: An assessment process where the execution includes knowledge preconditions.

Assessment of skill: An assessment process where the execution is of a skill.

Assessment of work product: An assessment process where the execution is of a plan that includes creating a work product.

Assessment question: An assessment criteria with a knowledge precondition.

Assessment result: A correspondence between an execution and a performance specification.

Encode performance information: The mental event of encoding information where the information is a description of a performance.

Execution rule: An execution constraint held by an agent for executions of another agent.

Explicit rule: An assessment criteria that is informed to the agent that is the subject of the assessment.

Modify rule: The mental event of modifying an assessment criteria in a performance specification.

Observable execution: The portion of the execution of a plan that may be perceived by another agent.

Observe execution: The mental event of directing the focus of attention to the execution of another agent.

Observed execution: An execution of a behavior by an agent that is perceived by another agent.

Perfect assessment result: An assessment result where there is a complete correspondence between an executed performance and the performance specification.

Performance: A partial collaborative plan that includes an observation of execution by another agent.

Performance characteristic: A characteristic of the execution of a performance.

Performance component: A portion of the execution of a performance.

Performance encoding: Encoded information where the information is a performance specification.

Performance tempo characteristic: A value that determines the execution duration of a performance.

Poor assessment result: A performance assessment where there is a low correspondence between the execution and the performance specification.

Specify performance: The mental event of specifying partial plans in a performance specification.

Submit after deadline: The event that a transfer of possession in a performance specification occurs after a deadline.

Submit before deadline: The event that a transfer of possession in a performance specification occurs before a deadline.

Unobserved execution: A reference to any portion of an execution that is not observed by another agent.

6.48   BODY INTERACTION   (15 TERMS)

The representational area of Body Interaction is premised on the assumption that reasoning in people is layered, or that a useful distinction can be made between the mind and the body. Body interaction terms include those that refer to behaviors of the body that are only partially controllable by the mind (e.g., physical body request, perceptive control) and the information that the mind receives as a consequence of executing these behaviors (e.g., sensation of execution, observe). Within the scope of this representational area are notions of non-conscious behavior, i.e., actions taken by the body that are not the known intentions of the mind. While these terms have not yet been the subject of knowledge representation research, many of these ideas have been realized in the control mechanisms of real-world robot systems. Particularly relevant is the ongoing debate concerning three-layer architectures, where deliberation, sequencing, and sensory-motor control are partitioned as different processes that enable flexible and reliable robot control (Gat, 1998; Stein, 1997).

RELATED READINGS

Gat, E. (1998). On three-layer architectures. In D. Kortenkamp, R. P. Bonnasso, & R. Murphy (Eds.), *Artificial intelligence and mobile robots* (pp. 195–210). Cambridge, MA: MIT.

Stein, L. A. (1997). Postmodular systems: Architectural principles for cognitive robotics. *Cybernetics and Systems, 28*(6), 471–487.

DEFINITIONS

Attend: The mental event of changing the focus of attention to be a concept or a perception coming from the physical body of an agent.

Energy amount: An amount that characterizes the capacity for the physical body of an agent to execute behaviors.

Expended energy: An energy amount that is removed from the physical body of an agent during an execution duration.

Greater effort: An amount of expended energy for an execution duration that is greater than another.

Impaired agency: Execution of an agent where the physical body of the agent does not operate as expected.

Low effort: An amount of expended energy for an execution duration that is low in the range of previous expended energy amounts.

Natural movement: A behavior of the physical body of an agent that does not generate a negative sensation of execution.

Nonconscious execution: A behavior of the physical body of an agent that is not caused by a physical body request by the agent.

Nonconscious perceptual execution: A behavior of a perceptual modality of an agent that is not caused by a physical body request by the agent.

Observe: The mental process of updating beliefs about the current state based on perceptual signals.

Perception modality: A member of a set of components of the physical body of an agent that generate perceptual signals.

Perception signal: A signal that is generated by a perceptual modality that provides information about the current world state.

Perceptual control: The mental event of executing a physical body request to a perceptual modality.

Physical body request: The mental event of informing the physical body of an agent of the intention that it executes some behavior.

Sensation of execution: A signal that is generated by the physical body of an agent that provides information about its operation during an execution duration.

References

Baron-Cohen, S. (2000). Theory of mind and autism: A fifteen year review. In S. Baron-Cohen, H. Tager-Flusberg, & D. Cohen (Eds.), *Understanding other minds: Perspectives from developmental cognitive neuroscience*, (2nd ed.). Oxford, UK: Oxford University Press.

Benyus, J. M. (1998). *The secret language and remarkable behavior of animals*. New York: Black Dog and Leventhal Publishers.

Cohen, P., & Levesque, H. (1990). Intention is choice with commitment. *Artificial Intelligence, 42*(3), 213–261.

Collins, G. (1987). *Plan creation: Using strategies as blueprints*. Doctoral dissertation, Yale University, New Haven, CT.

Corcoran, R. (2001). Theory of mind in schizophrenia. In D. Penn & P. Corrigan (Eds.), *Social cognition in schizophrenia*. Washington, DC: American Psychological Association.

Davis, E. (1998). The naïve physics perplex. *AI Magazine, Winter,* 51–79.

de Kleer, J., & Brown, J. S. (1984). A qualitative physics based on confluences. *Artificial Intelligence, 24,* 7–83.

Dyer, J., Shatz, M., & Wellman, H. (2000). Young children's storybooks as a source of mental state information. *Cognitive Development, 15,* 17–37.

Einstein, A., & Infeld, L. (1976). *The evolution of physics from early concepts to relativity and quanta*. New York: Simon & Schuster. (Original work published 1938)

Falkenhainer, B., Forbus, K., & Gentner, D. (1989). The structure-mapping engine: Algorithm and examples. *Artificial Intelligence, 41,* 1–63.

Ferguson, G. (1995). Knowledge representation and reasoning for mixed-initiative planning. Doctoral Dissertation, Computer Science Department, University of Rochester, Rochester, NY.

Fikes, R., & Nilsson, N. (1971). STRIPS: A new approach to the application of theorem proving to problem solving. *Artificial Intelligence, 2*, 189–208.

Forbus, K. (1984). Qualitative process theory. *Artificial Intelligence, 24*, 85–168.

Forbus, K. D. (2001). Exploring analogy in the large. In D. Gentner, K. Holyoak, & B. Nokinov (Eds.), *The analogical mind: Perspectives from cognitive science* (pp. 23–58). Cambridge, MA: MIT Press.

Frith, C., & Frith, U. (2000). The physiological basis of theory of mind: Functional neuroimaging studies. In S. Baron-Cohen, H. Tager-Flusberg, & D. Cohen (Eds.), *Understanding other minds: Perspectives from developmental cognitive neuroscience*, (2nd ed.). Oxford, UK: Oxford University Press.

Gelman, R., & Gallistel, C. R. (1978). *The child's understanding of number.* Cambridge, MA: Harvard University Press.

Gelman, R., & Meck, E. (1983). Preschoolers' counting: Principles before skill. *Cognition, 13*, 343–359.

Gentner, D. (1983). Structure-mapping: A theoretical framework for analogy. *Cognitive Science, 7*, 155–170.

Gil, Y., & Blythe, J. (2000). PLANET: A sharable and reusable ontology for representing plans. *Proceedings of the AAAI 2000 Workshop on Representational Issues for Real-World Planning System* (pp. 28–33). Menlo Park, CA: AAAI Press.

Goldman, A. (2000). Folk psychology and mental concepts. *Protosociology, 14*, 4–25.

Gopnik, A., & Meltzoff, A. (1997). *Words, thoughts, and theories.* Cambridge, MA: MIT Press.

Greeno, J., Riley, M., & Gelman, R. (1984). Conceptual competence and children's counting. *Cognitive Psychology, 16*, 94–143.

Halford, G. S., Wilson, W. H., Guo, J., Gayler, R. W., Wiles, J., & Stewart, J. E. M. (1994). Connectionist implications for processing capacity limitations in analogies. In K. Holyoak & J. Barnden (Eds.), *Advances in connectionist and neural computation theory: Vol. 2. Analogical connections* (pp. 363–415). Norwood, NJ: Ablex.

Hammond, C. (1989). *Case-based planning: Viewing planning as a memory task.* London: Academic Press.

Happé, F., Brownell, H., & Winner, E. (1998). The getting of wisdom: Theory of mind in old age. *Developmental Psychology, 34*(2), 358–362.

Happé, F., Brownell, H., & Winner, E. (1999). Acquired "theory of mind" impairments following stroke. *Cognition, 70*, 211–240.

Harris, P. (1996). Desires, beliefs and language: the role of the conversation. In P. Carruthers & P. K. Smith (Eds.), *Theories of theories of mind* (pp. 200–220). Cambridge: Cambridge University.

Hayes, P. (1985). The second naïve physics manifesto. In J. Hobbs & B. Moore (Eds.), *Formal theories of the commonsense world* (pp. 1–36). Norwood, NJ: Ablex.

Holyoak, K., & Thagard, P. (1989). Analogical mapping by constraint satisfaction. *Cognitive Science, 13,* 295–355.

Hummel, J. E., & Holyoak, K. J. (1997). Distributed representations of structure: A theory of analogical access and mapping. *Psychological Review, 104,* 427–466.

Kokinov, B. N. (1994). A hybrid model of reasoning by analogy. In K. J. Holyoak & J. A. Barnden (Eds.), *Advances in connectionist and neural computation theory: Vol. 2. Analogical connections* (pp. 247–318). Norwood, NJ: Ablex.

Lepper, M., Woolverton, M., Mumme, D., & Gurtner, J. (1993). Motivational techniques of expert human tutors: Lessons for the design of computer-based tutors. In S. P. Lajoie & S. J. Derry (Eds.), *Computers as cognitive tools* (pp. 75–105). Hillsdale, NJ: Lawrence Erlbaum Associates.

Machiavelli, N. (1995). *Il Principe: Nuova edizione a cura di Giorgio Inglese.* Torino, Italy: Einaudi Tascabili.

McDermott, D. (2000). The 1998 AI Planning Systems Competition. *AI Magazine, 21*(2), 35–55.

Newell, A., & Simon, H. (1963). GPS: A program that simulates human thought. In E. A. Feigenbaum & J. Feldman (Eds.), *Computers and Thought* (pp. 279–293). New York: McGraw-Hill.

Nichols, S., & Stich, S. (2000). A cognitive theory of pretense. *Cognition, 74,* 115–147.

Nichols, S., & Stich, S. (2002). How to read your own mind: A cognitive theory of self-consciousness. In Q. Smith & A. Jokic (Eds.), *Consciousness: New philosophical essays.* Oxford University Press.

Ortiz, C. L. (1999a). A commonsense language for reasoning about causation and rational action, *Artificial Intelligence, 111*(2), 73–130.

Ortiz, C. L. (1999b). Introspective and elaborative processes in rational agents. *Annals of Mathematics and Artificial Intelligence, 25*(1–2), 1–34.

Pednault, E. (1989). ADL: Exploiting the middle ground between STRIPS and the situation calculus. In R. Brachman & H. Levesque (Eds.), *Proceedings of the First International Conference on Principles of Knowledge Representation and Reasoning* (Vol. 1, pp. 324–332). San Francisco: Morgan Kaufmann.

Project Gutenberg. (1994). The Art of War, by Sun Tzu. (L. Giles, Trans.). Available at http://www.gutenberg.org

Project Gutenberg. (1998). *The Prince,* by Niccolo Machiavelli. (W. K. Marriott, Trans.). Available at http://www.gutenberg.org

Rao, A., & Georgeff, M. (1995). BDI agents: From theory to practice. *Proceedings of the First International Conference on Multiagent Systems* (pp. 312–319). Menlo Park, CA: AAAI Press.

Shipley, E., & Shepperson, B. (1990). Countable entities: Developmental changes. *Cognition, 34,* 109–136.

Spellman, B., & Holyoak, K. (1992). If Saddam is Hitler then who is George Bush? Analogical mapping between systems of social roles. *Journal of Personality and Social Psychology, 62,* 913–933.

Wellman, H. M., & Lagattuta, K. H. (2000). Developing understandings of mind. In S. Baron-Cohen, H. Tager-Flusberg, & D. Cohen (Eds.), *Understanding other minds: Perspectives from developmental cognitive neuroscience*, (2nd ed.). Oxford, UK: Oxford University Press.

Wilkins, D. (1988). *Practical planning: Extending the classical AI planning paradigm*. San Francisco: Morgan Kaufmann.

Author Index

Subject Index

Printed and bound by CPI Group (UK) Ltd, Croydon, CR0 4YY

23/10/2024

01777872-0001